UNDER SUBMISSION

THE COLUMNS OF ARTHUR GILBERT

THE FIRST 20 YEARS (1988-2008)

CONTINUING LEGAL EDUCATION **TRG**™ PROGRAMS AND PUBLICATIONS

THE RUTTER GROUP™
A DIVISION OF THOMSON WEST

Cover Art by Barbara Embree

Not all judges are piano players, but certainly all piano players are judges. They sit on a bench and hand down decisions to fingers directing them on which key to strike in what order and when. The sound heard is the soundness of the judgment rendered. If the music is select, you must elect! Based on this argument you will be receiving my vote in the upcoming contest.

Charles Embree, writer, artist, musician.

ABOUT THE AUTHOR

Justice Arthur Gilbert is currently a Presiding Justice on the California Court of Appeal, Second District. He has been a judge for over 33 years, serving on the Los Angeles Municipal and Superior Courts. His written opinions are known for their scholarship and clarity. He has been dubbed "The Court of Appeal's Poet Laureate." His articles and columns have appeared in a variety of publications throughout the United States. He has taught judges in California and abroad on the philosophy of judging and the art of crafting opinions. When asked by a reporter, "What is it like being an appellate justice?" Gilbert replied, "It is just the two of us in a room, me and my brain - only often I'm alone."

Not many people know that Justice Gilbert is also a jazz pianist and plays occasional gigs in venues in the Los Angeles area. To keep a clear separation between music and judging, the modest Gilbert bills himself under the alias, Art Gilbert.

PREFACE

The Daily Journal is a legal periodical published in California. One ordinary day in 1988, an editor from the paper called me and asked if I would write an article about "depublication." That was a practice then widely used by the California Supreme court to make published cases "disappear" without the burden of writing an opinion.

My article was published in June of 1988. That is how it all started. Now 165 columns later, neither I nor my readers are the same. The columns may be read in any order. Those who read Hebrew can start at the end of the book and work backward.

Also included in this collection are a few short stories in which human and legal themes converge.

INTRODUCTION

"Justice Gilbert's collection of brief essays provides a comedic and intellectual romp. Mozartian brio and wit combine with a wonderfully Swiftian skewering of the many follies perpetuated upon the legal landscape. Readers will need to be attentive to the risk that their breaking out in laughter may lead to their missing some profound truths. Within these pages is a persistently delightful match of entertainment and illumination." - **Herbert Morris**, *Professor of Philosophy and Professor of Law Emeritus; former Dean of Humanities UCLA*

FOREWARD

For many years, Justice Arthur Gilbert of the California Court of Appeal has delighted the bench and bar, and even the general public, with his scintillating essays and stories. What a pleasure it is to see them finally collected into a single volume, so that Gilbert fans will have ready access to them. And he will doubtless win scores of new fans.

Justice Gilbert expresses a wide range of provocative opinions in these pages. He even devotes an entire essay to a disagreement that he has with me – one that we've fought to a good-humored stalemate. But whatever the subject to which Gilbert turns his attention – whether it's the optimal placement of citations on a page; the law of kitten ownership; the role of shame in law; the lure of *Who's Who* books; the fallibility of memory; Shaquille O'Neal's word games; the influence of U.S. Senator S.I. Hayakawa, the legendary semanticist; Madonna as a book author; or any of the other myriad subjects he deals with – readers are sure to be enchanted with his light touch, his urbane wit, and his acute insight.

Bryan A. Garner
President, LawProse, Inc.
Editor in Chief, *Black's Law Dictionary*
Dallas, Texas

ACKNOWLEDGEMENTS

I dedicate this book to my mother and father who thought I told good stories. I think it was a compliment.

This book also honors the memory of my friend Tony Trattner. He insisted I publish a collection of my columns. Tony, here they are.

Thanks to my wife, Barbara, a superlative editor and grammarian, who often helped me replace ambiguity with clarity. Also, she had an unerring sense of what to strike from column drafts thus saving my judicial career.

Thanks to my judicial assistant and friend, Valerie Bereman, who spent many a lunch hour putting these columns in order and offering sound editorial advice. I am indebted to friend and poet, Marcia Katz Wolf, whose critical eye and editorial suggestions greatly improved the final product. And thanks to my mentor, and special friend, with whom I practiced law over 40 years ago, Robert Bertholdo. He has consistently shown me the way. His revisions will help readers find their way. I would like to also thank Bonnie Edwards and Rose Whipple for some last minute proof reading and Marc Thompson for invaluable technical advice.

Particular thanks to my friends William A. Rutter and Kalman S. Zempleny, II, for publishing this book, the proceeds of which go to charitable legal service organizations.

TABLE OF CONTENTS

THE FIRST COLUMN

1988

IT NEVER HAPPENED

Back in the 1980's the California Supreme Court was depublishing a large number of Court of Appeal opinions. It prompted an article, which became my first column for the Daily Journal on June 9, 1988. Rumor has it that the Supreme Court tried to depublish the column, but it had no jurisdiction. You can cite the column without the threat of sanctions.

Most people don't know what Court of Appeal justices do, and that includes many trial judges. Generally a Court of Appeal justice writes opinions; "grinds them out" would be a better way of saying it. Henry Ford would approve. The opinions bump along the assembly line and then chug down the road to oblivion. Along the way they are used or misused by attorneys or judges, who sometimes read them.

But deep within the heart of every appellate justice there lies the seed of an occasional masterpiece, a gem that would make Benjamin Cardozo turn green with envy. It starts with a case that fortuitously comes your way. Something special occurs during this random encounter. You begin to feel ideas growing and developing in your brain.

The Unseemly and Grotesque Stage

During an appropriate period of gestation, the ideas coalesce into a concept. When the concept fights and claws its way out of your brain and plops in a heap on the page, you know you are ready to write the first draft of the opinion. When you're done, that draft is wiggling with life but not ready for public consumption. It is unseemly and grotesque, like the mutant baby in the cult film classic "Eraserhead."

But it's your baby, and you nurture it and shape it, draft after painstaking draft. And then you know, as if by instinct, that the opinion is ready. It shimmers with clarity and reason. Magnanimously, you acknowledge that the brief on the winning side was persuasive, but the opinion has your signature- figuratively and literally. The opinion reflects your style, your panache, your essence.

Shortly after the publication of your chef d'oeuvre, you happen to attend a cocktail party given by the local bar association. You try to avoid an attorney known for his unctuous fawning, but when he starts praising your new opinion, you find his conversation engaging and stimulating. You tell him in a modest, self-effacing tone that you hope the opinion will be useful. You think it might be unseemly to tell him that you know the opinion illuminates the law, gives it meaning and purpose, that it persuades and sparkles with reason and insight.

I have experienced this. But it's hard to talk about because it never happened. No, I don't mean I imagined it. I don't mean I'm crazy and hallucinating. It's much more than that. I mean the state Supreme Court depublished it. Someone up there simply pulled the switch on an opinion that had just begun to bask in the light of recognition.

The ostensible reason for this ignominious termination is that the opinion reached the right result, but for the wrong reason. Maybe so, but the recent use of depublication on such a wide, unprecedented scale means that there is a large group of justices writing poorly reasoned opinions. I suppose the depublication rule helps stem the flood of cases inundating the California Reports, but it also keeps ideas locked in the closet.

No Useful Purpose

Whatever the reason for the rule, it serves no useful purpose. Why hide the reasoning of an opinion, whether good or bad, from the rest of the world? If the Supreme Court does not care for an opinion, it can decertify it. The opinion may lack precedential value, but at least it exists as an object of either enlightenment or of ridicule. Another interpretation of the law is at least accessible to scholars, lawyers or collectors of the bizarre and occult.

Decertifying instead of depublishing opinions will not increase the Supreme Court's caseload. It will, however, permit the expression of all ideas and will serve an important educational function for the bar and the public. And, who knows, the spurned opinion just might become the law in the next millennium.

I'm not holding my breath that the rule will be changed in the near future. If it does not change soon, one of my colleagues suggested that we publish all the depublished cases. That's a brilliant idea. I just may start an underground publishing firm that will publish only depublished cases. I'll call the company East's Oxymoron Publishing Co.- "Cases That Can Get You in Lots of Trouble if You Cite Them."

Better yet, maybe we can change the rule so that justices on the Court of Appeal rather than the Supreme Court will have the last word on the whether a case is published or depublished. I can just imagine what would happen with such a rule. Assume I have decided not to publish a case, but the Supreme Court wants it published.

"Oh please, publish this case," the Supreme Court asks me.

"No," I answer. "I don't think it really merits publication."

"But it's so good, you have crystallized your ideas into a succinct, readable treatise on this complex issue of law. There is a desperate need for your opinion. Its publication will be a significant contribution to the people of this state, and the legal profession."

"Well…I'll think about it."

THE MOST RECENT COLUMN

2008

EXTRA CREDIT

Credit. I'm no different from anyone else. I take it whenever I can. But it makes me anxious. Credit, no matter what type, has its downside. Just ask those struggling to make mortgage payments.

Politicians take credit for their speeches—particularly the ones that go over well. Never mind that seldom do they write their own. In fact, everyone knows they have "speech writers." Nevertheless, if the speech bombs, the politician, not the speech writer gets the "credit." Think "nattering nabobs of negativism" was the product of Vice-President Spiro Agnew's creative mind? (Does anyone remember Spiro Agnew? He was convicted of tax evasion and money laundering.) The credit for the alliteration belongs to William Safire. But Agnew got the "credit" for the remark. Had he gone to prison he may have also gotten credits for good time.

Historians usually write their own books, but not every word on the page always comes from their pen. Some of the few who have become "popular" are so busy cranking out books that they rely on research assistants to draft a paragraph or two, or maybe even a chapter. A brilliant or incisive paragraph earns credit for the historian and continuing employment for the research assistant. But when the assistant gets it wrong, or plagiarizes from another work, the historian is discredited.

This takes me to the "Hollywood writers" strike in the news these days. Can you believe it? The late night comedians rely on writers to pen their witty lines. Imagine, they get laughs for jokes created by faceless writers. Where are they without their writers?

Without a good writer, a comedian can fall on his or her face. Assume a late night host starts out with a joke. "A dog, a parrot and a moose go into a bar." Then what? How would he finish the joke without a writer? The bartender says, "So what's the joke?" That is the joke. Get it? If you are asking the same question as the bartender, that means you did not get the joke. But someone has to write the joke, the whole joke, not just half the joke. No writer, no joke. But the "joke" about the dog, parrot and moose that not everyone got had to be written. We would not be having this discussion had the joke not been written. No matter that it would have been better if the joke had not been written in the first place.

What is a joke is the way judges are treated. We judges often get the blame for society's ills. We are accused of coddling criminals or denying justice, overprotecting or underprotecting the environment, favoring or being hostile to business or workers.

I suppose that is why it is important for us to take credit now and then. We will gladly take credit for a decision that earns praise. But like the late night comedians, we do not always write every word of a decision or opinion for which we take credit. There you have it. The secret is out of the bag.

Trial judges do not always draft statements of decision. The winning side is glad to accept that chore. A busy trial judge sitting in a law and motion department may rely on a research assistant to draft a few sentences or a paragraph or two in a minute order

Appellate court justices have full time research attorneys. And this is where my anxiety comes in. What if the research attorneys joined forces with the Hollywood writers and went on strike? Why would they want to do that? The residuals our opinions generate are emotions, not revenue. And that I share in abundance with my staff. Retired Justice Robert Thompson who co-authored with John Bilyeu, "Law Clerks and the Judicial Process" California University Press (1980) cautions that an over-reliance on law clerks can lead to the "bureaucratization of justice" at the expense of a fresh intellectual development of the law. I do not agree with that assessment. But Thompson may have a point when he suggested that if research attorneys have a hand in drafting opinions, their names should be listed in the California Reports. They could then at least take some of the blame.

But what if the research attorneys out of boredom or perversity, did go on strike? The thought of having to draft every word of every opinion makes me willing to negotiate at the first hint of a strike. But on second thought, perhaps my fears are unfounded. Writers are not always held in high esteem. Was it Samuel Goldwyn who referred to his screenwriters as "the mice"? Some producers have suggested that television can survive without writers.

Crisis fosters innovation. Maybe the Court of Appeal too, can survive without written opinions. The screenwriter's strike could be a sign that it's time for the bugle to play silent taps for written opinions. In its place will be unwritten opinions. To those who say a silent bugle and an unwritten opinion are impossibilities I say, "Not." (In view of the delicate nature of this subject, no research attorney has had a hand in drafting any part of this column.)

My idea just could work. There is a well-known concert hall composition, John Cage's work, "4'33" (Four Minutes, Thirty-Three Seconds). It is a silent piece of music in which a pianist sits at the Steinway on a concert stage and does not play the three movements of the composition. All one hears is the nervous titters and coughs of the audience. Some think the piece is designed to make listeners truly aware of sound. His second composition in this genre, "5'07" I hear is a real showstopper.

My unwritten opinions would follow John Cage's model. The opinion, like Cage's composition, would have a title, e.g. *People v. Lamont Cranston.* In this respect, the unwritten opinion, does not abjure the written word. In civil cases I would state whether the judgment was "affirmed" or "reversed." In criminal cases, the name of the case would suffice in most instances. After all, most are affirmed.

Some might argue that this approach erodes predictability in the law. Perhaps: but is it so predictable now? Retired judges who have entered the lucrative world of private judging argue forcefully to their clients that going to trial is a "real crap shoot." Lawyers would still file briefs, requiring an appellate judge to cut through forests of invective and scorn. She or he will get to the same result that was reached in the past. But now no need to explain it all in a dense convoluted opinion.

It just occurred to me now that I have written most of this column, that I will not get away with filing unwritten opinions. The California Constitution, Article 6, section 14, requires that our "decisions be in writing with reasons stated." I know how picky the Supreme Court can be. It will probably decide that a case name and the word "affirmed" or "reversed" is insufficient to constitute a written opinion. Darn! Jay Leno is writing his own jokes, so if there is a research attorney's strike, I suppose I will have to write my own opinions in their entirety. Believe me, you will know the difference. You won't see a bunch of citations and stilted legal language. Here's one I wrote as an example.

"Defendant broke into a house and took lots of things. The jury decided he is a burglar. He is. People saw him do it and he admitted to the police he did it. He whines that he is not guilty, the judge hated him, and his sentence to state prison is too harsh. Only an ass would believe that and the law is not an ass."

It's short, punchy, and gets right to the point. That is the kind of opinion I might write. Only, I wouldn't take credit for it.

ALL THOSE IN BETWEEN

MOTIONS WITH LITERARY STYLE

The motions lawyers draft are often staid, unimaginative and boring. It is not all their fault. The subject matter can be deadly. Take a motion to be relieved from default for example.

A typical paragraph starts out as follows: My secretary inadvertently mislaid the file and another client with a similar name had a case that was settled, and so when the partnership broke up and the associates stole all the files, I assumed this matter had been taken care of. Then when the fire destroyed all the furniture and remaining files, there was no way for me to know that blah, blah, blah, blah, blah, etc.

If motions were written in a literary style, they would be more interesting, and the discerning judge would be more responsive. I have offered a few examples of how a motion to be relieved from default might be written in the style of the following people:

Ernest Hemingway

It was busy and there was commotion. I looked out the window where the wind touched the top of the trees and far below, the street, white from the sunlight, and the cars inching forward, but I could feel up here that I would not be good, but there was nothing one could do. Pilar, my secretary looked at me and her eyes told me that this was as bad as when the bulls are running toward you and there is nowhere to climb and you know you will be trampled, but you know that until they do you can live a good life, a short, happy life. And when I asked her for the file and said, "What file Ingles?," I knew that the bulls were loose and there was nowhere to go; there was no yesterday, no tomorrow, but that was then and now is here, your Honor. There was a time when it was good, but now it is a time when it is bad and you can make it good again, and if you can't, it's a rotten shame.

T.S. Eliot

Thirty days to answer
It's the cruelest month.
Dead, dying decay, an apt description
For my brain, withered, not resplendent now,
A supplicant, having been etherized upon a table
During the time to answer
I ask for relief,
Not with a bang, but a whimper.

James Joyce

HelpmeohGod Time is cretupandIsaidyesohheyesyesyesyesyesyesI need relief nowfromignominious default default fault-d de fault is mine ohhelptheteatiscaughtintheproceduralwringer. Relief.

William Faulkner

Benji had taken the file and went along the fence with it and lost it through the spaces in the fence where the flowers were curling. That's what they said. I started to cry. Caddy, who smelled like trees, and Quentin, who just smelled, came to find the file, but I didn't holler 'til mother shouted at Dilsey for bringing me cheap store cake. Dilsey took me up to bed. Quentin told Caddy he had to answer. He had to find the file. Caddy did not know that Benji had taken the file, and Benji could not know that he had taken the file, because this motion is written from Benji's point of view, and his IQ is 17.

e.e. cummings

the time where
        zip, who knows,
        not i
        it goes. my time
        I hope it has not come for me.
        Nobody, not even i,
        loses all the time.
I need relief
        or I should start a worm farm

Henry Miller (expurgated)

So I saw my ****** secretary throwing files away. I know how to deal this this. I ****** **** and then she **** ***** and we ******** ******* ******. I need ***** ******* *** relief.

Tennessee Williams

Stanley: (In a rage) Stella. Stella I wrote the date in a calendar.
Stella: Date, what date?
Stanley: The date for when, when they fault you.
Stella: You mean default
Stanley: Yeah, that's it, and Blanche - she lost the calendar, she and her highfalutin' ways
Stella: Try to be nice and don't smash anything

Blanche: (Emerging from the bedroom with the air of royalty) Why I declare. Did I hear my name?

Stanley: (Glowering) Where the hell is my calendar?

Blanche: I simply do not respond to profanity or the grunts of an ape. Who cares about a silly old date in a calendar when there's poetry and there's music.

Stanley: (Overturning the breakfast table) Don't forget I'm king around here, and I want the calendar so we can find out the date to stop a fault- a default.

Blanche: (Spraying herself with an atomizer) I don't want dates, I want magic.(Stanley moves menacingly towards her. The stage darkens.)

Albert Einstein

(This is for those who wish to take a scientific approach using sophisticated concepts in mathematics and physics.)

Yes, the time went by your Honor, but only from your point of view. Time- it's all relative. In fact, maybe the accident didn't happen yet.

The Judge

(I cannot render the judge's response in an appropriate literary or scientific style. There is not much you can do with a single word.)

SILENCE OF THE CLAMS

With apologies to Hannibal Lecter, this column was written when I was an Associate Justice on the California Court of Appeal.

Call me AJAR. It is an acronym that stands for Associate Justice, Accommodating Reasonable- though not everyone agrees as to what the last two letters stand for. To some they mean Arcane Research. To others, "A" and "R" stand for less flattering appellations. Toward these people I bear no acrimony or resentment.

Recently, during my leisure reading time in chambers, I was browsing through criminal cases: "Defendant beaten senseless by authorities before he confesses. Conviction affirmed. Harmless error." ... "Police break into wrong house because of mistake in search warrant and find stolen Rembrandts. Conviction affirmed. Harmless error." And so on.

I was about to read the 10th harmless error case when I drew a blank. It took me a moment to discover it was the page and not my mind. As I was reflecting on this puzzling phenomenon, I was interrupted by the angry buzz of the intercom. It was the P.J. who needed to talk to me about an urgent matter. I walked down the hall and entered his chambers.

"Ajar...the door," he said. "You mean the door...ajar," I said. "Whatever...just close the door Ajar." I decided to overlook the oxymoron, and hear what was on the P.J.'s mind.

"We've got a major problem. Someone or something is wasting opinions."

I asked the obvious. "What do you mean?"

"Whoever or whatever is stripping opinions of all their vitality. They are being replaced by blank pages in the reports."

"I just came across one when you buzzed. Who would do something like this?

"We are not sure, but there's one person who we think could help us with this case...the brilliant maniac lawyer...Sutton Lectern."

"You mean Sutton the Glutton?"

"Yes, despite his superior mind, he could never win a case on appeal."

"Because every time he had a case supporting his position it was depublished."

"Correct. One day he went berserk and started eating the California Reports, binders and all."

"The indigestion must have been horrible," I said.

"Frightful."

"I get an upset stomach just reading my own opinions."

"You should be used to it," he said. You've had to eat your words quite a bit."

"But not the whole opinion."

"Only Lectern has the fiendish mind that could help us solve this mystery. We want you to talk to him, to establish rapport with him, and draw him out."

"But why me? Lectern is so bizarre, so odd, so weird, so grotesque."

The P.J. just looked at me.

I decided not to fight the logic, but to accept the assignment and visit Lectern. On the way out the P.J. called to me. "Be careful! Don't let him fill your mind with misleading points and authorities."

I found Lectern at the County Courthouse. He was being confined in an attorney conference room. I was not allowed into the room for fear he might eat my calendar. A glass partition separated us, but we could speak through microphones.

"Hello Ajar," he said through ink stained lips.

I saw shreds of the Daily Journal on the floor. He had just swallowed a municipal court judge's profile. "Not bad," he said licking his lips. "You want my help in finding out who is erasing these opinions?"

"Yes, perhaps you can…."

He interrupted me. "I wanted a deal." I asked him what were his terms.

"I want West's Annotated Codes."

"All of them?"

"Yes, and Corpus Juris Secundum."

"I can't imagine anyone reading all of the codes."

"I find them delectable," he said with a serpent-like smile. I agreed he could have them.

"And the supplements, too," he demanded.

"All right, but I need your help."

"I find you interesting," he said, changing the subject.

I tensed up.

"You're as tight as a clam," he said. I was amazed at his perception. My hands were clammy.

"Tell me about your childhood," he said narrowing his eyes.

"I lived near the beach," I said nervously. "Now give me a clue."

"The drought," he said.

"What about the drought?"

"Then you must have played near the water," he said, going back to my childhood.

"You just said there was a drought."

"So I did, but when you were a child, you played near the water."

"I did."

"What did you do at the seashore?"

"I played with my friends, swam in the ocean, and…"

"And…what?"

"Oh, dug for clams."

"And when you found the clams, you did something to them didn't you?"

"I didn't, but my best friends did," I said quietly.

"What did your friends do to the clams?"

"They forced the clams to open."

"And you tried to stop them, didn't you?"

I didn't have to tell him. He knew he was right.

"Everyone laughed at you because they could not understand how anyone could care for a clam."

"Yes," I said with a lump in my throat.

"And only you could hear the clams crying out… and you still hear them today. They are like the opinions… crying out to be heard. If you can find out who is destroying the opinions, then maybe the clams will cease crying out." There was a pause. "You long for the silence of the clams."

Another pause.

We started at one another for a while. I tried to compose myself. "The clues," I said. "You mentioned the drought."

"There's no justice in water," he said enigmatically.

He was right about that. The water allocation plan was ridiculous.

"Look to the mountains. There you'll find answers… answers to the drought … and other answers."

He put some advance sheets to his mouth. I didn't want to see it. I got up to leave.

"Remember those codes," he said. I hurried away, but I heard him yell, "You're no Hemingway."

I felt like my mind had been blown. I pondered the clues. He said there was the drought, and there were answers in the mountains. What could that mean? Water comes from the mountains… of course, the snow pack. It provides water. But what about snow? Snow is…snow is…it's white. Snow White! Was I on to something? What could Snow White tell me about missing opinions? … And then it hit me and it all came together. Snow White and the … of course, that's it… there's Happy and Grumpy and …by George…I solved it.

I wrote my report and turned it in to the P.J. No one read it. I was depublished.

RUNNING - (FINISHING) THE 2004 LOS ANGELES MARATHON

Last month I performed an unnatural act -- not an easy admission for anyone to make, let alone a judge, I mean a state judge. Federal judges are a different story. Today, persons often perform unnatural acts to receive a judicial appointment, a practice that presumably continues if they pass Senate confirmation. But after that rare occurrence, a federal judge's principled sensitivity to the electorate is commendable but not crucial. With state judges, however, it is crucial, in fact, it's mandatory.

My transgression occurred almost a month ago to the day. I ran the Los Angeles Marathon. O.K. "ran" is a gross exaggeration. On the other hand "crawled" is too self-effacing though closer to the truth. Let's go with the neutral "finished" as in "I finished the L.A. Marathon!"

That 24,000 foolish people decided to subject their bodies to relentless torture for 26.2 miles in 90 degree weather does not make the run any less abnormal, nor give legitimacy to this crime against nature. How far is 26.2 miles? Imagine running to Catalina without the ocean, and then add two tenths of a mile. The 10, 000 people who entered and did not finish the L.A. Marathon, either because they had passed out or dropped out, were perhaps fortunate. The rest of us soon got used to the ambulances racing by with sirens wailing.

The 17th century philosopher Descartes spoke of the mind-body dichotomy. Whatever your religious or philosophical orientation, I will let you in on a little secret about the body: it is not a temple. It is not a cathedral. It is not even a chapel. It's a machine, a mechanism with moving and stationary parts. And as any idiot or consumer lawyer knows, machines break down; they fall apart. Savvy manufacturers put warning labels on their products. Our Maker put one on every human body. It says that under no circumstances should this body run more than 20 miles at any one time. I do not put a 100 watt bulb in a lamp that says do not use more than a 75 watt bulb in this lamp. It is obvious the body's warning label was put there for a reason, yet I am not sure why I ignored it.

While the body is running it burns glycogen and fat for energy, but at around 20 miles most bodies run out of these fuels. That is when you hit what is euphemistically called "the wall." It is an apt metaphor because you feel like Humpty Dumpty after the fall, runny and uncontained. Well what can you expect when the body needs fuel and it is out of gas? I have been told that such a body feeds off its own muscle in desperation. That I did this to my body was unassailable proof that the first part of Descartes' theorem, "I think therefore I am," did not apply to me.

When I hit 13 miles, every rational part of my body said, "there is no way you or any other semi-rational human being can do another 13 miles." My body became obstinate and contentious. All its organs went on strike. The cells that made up these organs formed cells of resistance. Like the strikers at Ralphs, they tried to shut down the store. And like the strike itself, it was all about medical benefits. And like the strikers at Ralphs, they lost. Their cogent point was that medical benefits don't do much good for a dead person. The organs and cells tried to reason with the brain. "What the hell is the matter with you?" they cried. The brain mumbled something stupid about a medal, or was it something about a stupid medal? No matter, but through the auditory canals they heard me talking with my running companion who figured out why we were doing this. "We are doing this for the medal," he said. Then he corrected himself and repeated the sentence with an adjective in front of "medal" that would have made Richard Nixon or even Sandra Tsing Loh proud. We high fived. The unthinking brain won.

So maybe I did it for the medal. You wear it around your neck like a noose or the Nobel prize. I thought wearing it over my robes would add to the solemnity and dignity of oral argument, but the Judicial Performance Commission disagreed. My training group "The LA Leggers" also gave finishers a pin in the shape of the numbers, "26." But I can't say these trinkets were worth the last 6 miles to the finish line, particularly the pin which reminded me of my IQ. The unadulterated torture and suffering I endured for those miles had Mel Gibson bidding on the film rights.

There must have been some other reason I had imposed this agony on myself. Perhaps it had something to do with my age, a laudation commemorating the number of years I have spent on earth. They correspond to the number of an interstate highway that makes its way through the United States. A song written by Bobby Troup pays tribute to this great highway which became famous with the Nat King Cole recording in 1947.

"If you ever plan to motor west, travel my way, take the highway that's the best. Get your kicks on Route 66! It winds from Chicago to L.A. More than 2000 miles all the way. Get your kicks on Route 66! Now you go thru St. Louie, Joplin, Missouri and Oklahoma City is might pretty. You'll see Amarillo . . . Gallup, New Mexico: Flagstaff, Arizona: don't forget Winona, Kingman, Barstow, San Bernardino." Hey, hold on--wait a minute---back up to New Mexico-keep going--just one more word, that's it-- "Gallup," sounds like—is . . . maybe I am the horse who needs one last gallop before heading for the pasture, or the glue factory.

Or maybe I ran because of an article in the last winter issue of "Gavel to Gavel," the Los Angeles Superior Court Judicial Magazine. Why do they call it "Gavel to Gavel"? I have been a judge for nearly 30 years and not once have I, or have any of my colleagues, ever used a gavel. But no matter. When I was on the Los Angeles Superior Court, our magazine was a mimeographed bulletin done by the typing class at Le Conte Jr. High School. Now they have a slick magazine with feature articles and pictures. An article about judicial athletes by Judge Rita Miller may have induced me to enter the race. It's not enough that the Los Angeles Superior Court makes more money than anyone else, or so they claim, but many of its judges run marathons in record times, over and over again. One judge performed a wedding ceremony at mile 6 of the L.A. Marathon and then ran with the wedding party to the finish line. If I had performed the wedding ceremony, by the time I crossed the finish line, I could have presided over the couple's custody battle in their divorce proceedings.

But there are uplifting aspects of the marathon. You see parts of the city you have never been to before and you come to realize there is no "bad" section of town. People from a variety of cultures and ethnic backgrounds become united in a grand celebration that honors the city and the thousands of people who challenge their minds and bodies to complete the race no matter what the time. Vast numbers of people along the way cheer you on, long after the winners have gone home, showered and caught the next flight back to Kenya. The feeling of goodwill buoys you along despite the anchor of painful charley horsed muscles trying to pull you down. Cheering crowds drawn together in goodwill and harmony defeat the adversity of the run, and promote mutual respect and tolerance. Even lawyers speak to one another with civility and affection. At mile 16 two lawyers even stipulated to a continuance, although that was after they discovered they worked in the same firm.

From this experience I have found a solution to the problem of crime which I pass on to Police Chief Bratton. Not to worry about the lack of funding for more officers. Simply have a marathon each day and crime will be eliminated from our city. Of course the people running might die, but that's another story.

I also recommend that running a marathon be a mandatory part of the bar exam, and a requirement for all sitting judges. It mellows you, makes you empathetic and more attune to human suffering. Depositions would be less contentious, trials less stressful and arrogant posturing unnecessary. It would give judges on all courts a healthy sense of humility. Yes, even the United States Supreme Court. But for Justice Scalia. I would recommend a triathlon.

I realize that some of us are getting older than others, and if you are like me with bad knees, this run is no picnic. But to quote the character Crouch in Larry Gelbart's play, "The Sly Fox," I can still run but the scenery goes by slowly." Whether slow or fast, finishing the marathon is like finishing a trial. True, not all trials are won, and not all judgments are affirmed, but once trial begins, whether you are a judge or lawyer, you see it to the end, and that is no mean accomplishment whatever the result,. The analogy would fit perfectly except for one significant difference. There is no way to settle in the middle of the marathon. But if it is 90 degrees on the day I run the 2005 L.A Marathon, I just might find a way.

24

MAKING ORDER OUT OF CHAOS IN THE PALSGRAF CASE

Writing does not come easy. It requires effort and commitment to write something of quality. A good finished product comes from several drafts, whether it be an article, a hate letter or a shopping list. It's even harder to write an opinion that is lucid and concise. Take for example the famous opinion in Palsgraf v. Long Island Railroad Co., 249 N.Y. 339, 162 N.E. 99 (1928). It is a paradigm of simplicity and clarity. Here is the statement of facts:

"Plaintiff was standing on a platform of defendant's railroad after buying a ticket to go to Rockaway beach. A train stopped at the station, bound for another place. Two men ran forward to catch it. One of the men reached the platform of the car without mishap, though the train was already moving. The other man, carrying a package, jumped aboard the car, but seemed unsteady as if about to fall. A guard on the car, who had held the door open, reached forward to help him in, and another guard on the platform pushed him from behind. In this act, the package was dislodged, and fell upon the rails. It was a package of small size, about fifteen inches long, and was covered by a newspaper. In fact, it contained fireworks, but there was nothing in its appearance to give notice of its contents. The fireworks when they fell exploded. The shock of the explosion threw down some scales at the other end of the platform many feet away. The scales struck the plaintiff, causing injuries for which she sues."

Justice Cardozo read a large stack of material from which he distilled the facts. I was fortunate to obtain copies of some of the reports he had to consider. As you read them, you will probably feel, as I do, empathy and admiration for this great jurist.

Report of W. Heisenberg, retired police officer, now insurance investigator for Long Island Railroad, to director of claims, E. Schrodinger

RE: *Injuries suffered by plaintiff Palsgrap Aug. 8, 1925, on premises of Long Island Railroad Co.*

I arrived at the scene at 1500 hours and exited my vehicle. I surveilled the platform and observed an Otis Baggage Scale tipped over on its side with valises scattered about. Underneath it all there appeared to be a little old lady mumbling "Is this Rockaway Beach?"

There is no liability here. Why would anyone stand near a baggage scale? Our employees acted properly and in fact behaved heroically. They saved Mr. Podolsky from grievous and serious injury. They also made it possible for said gentlemen to board this train, although the act did occasion the loss of his package.

All witnesses who work for the company are cooperative except one Mr. N. Bohr, number two guard at the station house. I think he feels sorry for Mrs. Palsgraf. He has refused a statement, although I contacted him at his home Sunday morning Aug. 14 at 6:30 a.m. Company may wish to consider employment termination procedures.

Statement of B. Podolsky

It all happened like this, see. Me and me brudder-in-law, Max Planck, was rushin' to make the train that goes to Patchogue. I had these firecrackers all wrapped up real nice for me nephew. Me and Max, we was runnin' to make the train 'cause the subway was late getting there, ya know. We saw da train starting to leave so we start running. Being as Max took track and all, he can run real fast. Also he used to be a bookie. So he got to the train foist 'cause I ain't as fast as I use to be, and besides I got this here package of firecrackers for me nephew. Max takes a leap foist, still hangin' real tight on his valise, and I take a leap right after him. This here conductor grabs me and this other guy pushes me from behind. He pushed me kinda hard and pushed the firecrackers right out of me arms. Me nephew was real disappointed. I expect you guys to buy me new firecrackers.

Conductor-Guard L. De Broglie.

I seen these two gentlemen running like blazes to match the 2:04 which was pulling out of track 9.

The first gentleman was the nimble one, as fast as Charlie Paddock, but the other one was on the plump side. The first one hit the top step of the car alright, and the fat one hits the top step too, only he was ready to topple back down, and he would have if I hadn't grabbed a good hold of his arm. Wolf Gang (Wolf Gang Pauli) gave me a hand alright, by pushing on the backside of the hefty gentlemen. The two of us saved the fella's life I bet. Then we heard this blast. I thought it was those anarchistic wobblies starting something.

Statement of Mrs. Palsgraf

I bought a ticket to go to Rockaway Beach to visit mine granddaughter. I was minding mine own business, watching a train, and that's all, when suddenly-Boom!- was an explosion you wouldn't believe. Something fell on me. Everything hurts.

"Sounds like!" I said . . . screamed . . . that's what I said, but what I did is . . . scream. Maybe shriek is what I did. Whatever. (Strike "whatever.") So I shrieked, no I think "shouted" is better. I shouted, "parameter is not the same as perimeter!" They pulled my hands off the neck of the research attorney who had written, "Within the parameters of our standard of review." Luckily, she didn't fight back. I hate words that come from disciplines I cannot understand even if my life depends on it.

Dictionaries do not agree on the meaning of "parameter" . . . I think. Webster's Third New International Dictionary offers this illuminating definition: "The relative intercept made by a plane on a crystallographic axis, the ratio of the intercepts determining the position of the plane." If that isn't clear, try the Random House Dictionary of English, 2nd edition that explains that "parameter" is "A constant or variable form in a function that determines the specific form of the function, but not its general nature as in $f(x)=ax$, where a determines only the slope of the line described by $f(x)$."

In a measured voice I told the research attorney, "Parameter" is for mathematicians, (or some related field) not judges . . . or their research attorneys. You used "parameter" because it sounds like "perimeter."

She momentarily stopped massaging her neck with lotion and coolly delivered this riposte. "Current usage allows for a broader use of the word. It is quite acceptable in educated circles to use 'parameter' to mean 'boundary' or 'guideline.'"

Maybe so, but not in my circle. Granted, that language and usage change; it is unseemly for a word to acquire a new meaning because it sounds like another word. The period of transition can wreak havoc. Take for example what happened to the transformation of the word "evacuate" in my neighborhood newspaper. A front page headline told of an "armed old man bandit" who robbed a local bank. Put aside for a moment whether a bank can be robbed, and that I was incensed to read that the suspect's age is somewhere between 50 and 60-- just call me Methuselah. No one whose age falls in the decade between 50 and 60 is old. Got it?

Sorry. I got a little hot, and off track. To get back to my point. The article describes the aged robber as victimizing "multiple tellers" at various local banks over the past several months. Come to think of it, he could have victimized various tellers at multiple banks. But, anyway, just last August the elderly bandit "robbed" Washington Mutual. He entered the bank with a gun and threatened to detonate a device that looked like a pipe bomb. The article then states, and I quote, "The employees were ejaculated" and "the area sealed off." Some employees asked the robber when he would call again. Others lit a cigarette. Jay Leno thought the robbery had occurred at a sperm bank.

Language is indeterminate. Even when the right word is used, meaning suffers if the speaker fails to clarify the context. To be understood, we must be precise. At a neighborhood restaurant I ordered soup and stressed that I wanted my soup "hot." The soup came lukewarm, but so peppery I had to drink four glasses of ice water. I like my soup hot in temperature, not spicy.

A reporter friend of mine once interviewed the winner of a beauty queen pageant. She asked the interviewee how it felt being the new reigning queen of an artichoke festival. The queen gazed at the interviewer and with a beatific smile, her teeth gleaming in harmony with the zirconium crown on her head said, . . . wait, first let's see what the reporter wrote in the paper. The beauty queen said, "I feel odd." The next day the outraged beauty queen called to complain that she had been misquoted. How did the beauty queen feel? She felt "awed," perhaps an odd way to express the overpowering emotion at being crowned queen of anything, especially artichokes.

What we write in opinions, statements of decision, briefs and motions may have a profound effect on the outcome and the direction and shape of the law. "Sol rented the store." Was Sol the lessor or the lessee? The context might explain whether Sol was collecting or paying rent, but the sentence standing alone doesn't tell us.

Many years ago I began an opinion with this sentence. "Sometimes a defendant's rights fall between the cracks. Here they fell in the Grand Canyon." Luckily I caught the error before the opinion was published. My comparison of a crack, as a crack in the floor, and that enormous crack in the earth known as the Grand Canyon was a failed metaphor. If the defendant's rights fell between the cracks in the floor, then his rights were preserved because they did not fall in the cracks, just the opposite message I wished to convey. Through harmless oversight, rights of a defendant that fall in the cracks could well be non-prejudicial. But rights that fall in the Grand Canyon might even get a reversal from Justice Thomas.

But it is easy to be hard on those who make an offhanded remark that on reflection sounds ridiculous. This brings me to a list of quotes my friend Dr. Joyce Weisel Barth recently sent me via e-mail. The quotes seemingly sound foolish. I say "seemingly" because despite my obdurate position on "parameter," I have tried to tease a plausible meaning from the speaker's words. Unlike staffers at the New Yorker Magazine who gleefully expose solecisms, non sequiturs, misplaced modifiers and malapropisms that pop up in various publications throughout the country, I will be more forgiving, unless they misuse "parameter." My willingness to so extend myself stems from the likelihood that sooner or later, my name will be among those who have been held up to ridicule. Samuel Goldwyn, Casey Stengel and Yogi Berra, make room.

Take this quote attributed to Philadelphia Phillies manager, Danny Ozark. "Half this game is ninety percent mental." Maybe the math works. If Ozark is speaking about the first half of the game, then 10 percent is brawn or luck. But what of the second half of the game? The second half could also be 90 percent mental, but after a player has spent so much of his mental energy during the first half, the second half could be 20 percent mental and 80 percent whatever. (Strike "whatever.") In fact, my research attorney Peter Cooney believes that half the game could be ninety percent mental and 100% physical. He is right, and he never uses the word "parameter."

Here's a quote attributed to Marion Barry when he was Mayor of Washington D.C.: "Outside of the killings, Washington has one of the lowest crime rates in the country." Petty theft is down 300 percent.

Dan Quale has taken his share of hits. I think it's unfair that he is mocked for favoring California. He is reputed to have said: "I love California. I practically grew up in Phoenix." No wonder he loves California. And besides, it's a great place to eat a *potatoe.*

Joe Theisman, NFL quarterback and sports news analyst tells us "The word 'genius' is not applicable in football. Genius is a guy like Norman Einstein." I would add Norman to the list that includes Rudolph Newton, Jasper Mozart, Morton Freud, and Jimmie Picasso.

Al Gore once warned: "We are ready for an unforeseen event that may or may not occur." It would take someone like Norman Einstein to discover an event that may not occur.

The Department of Social Services of Greenville, North Carolina sends this cheery notice to the moribund: "Your food stamps will be stopped effective March 1992 because we received notice that you passed away. May God bless you. You may reapply if there is a change in your circumstances." Even this message is not as ridiculous as it sounds. Note this reply: " I wish to reapply for food stamps. Sincerely yours, Lazarus."

When Mark Fowler was FCC chairman, he offered these encouraging words to patients using a heart monitor: "If someone has a bad heart, they can plug this jack in at night as they go to bed and it will monitor their heart throughout the night. And the next morning when they wake up dead there will be a record." The manufacturer is working on a jack that monitors the heart without killing the patient.

It would also be salutary if we do not kill the language. But we must allow it to grow and change within flexible parameters, I mean boundaries. Whatever.

JUDGES MUST STAY IN TUNE

Peter Stumpf the principal cellist of the Los Angeles Philharmonic plays a 17th century Stradivarius cello. Although "valued" at around 3 million dollars, some would consider the cello, made by Antonio Stradivari in Cremona, Italy, in 1684, priceless. Stumpf doesn't own the cello. The Philharmonic owns it. But when you are as good as Stumpf the L.A. Phil lets you use it. In legal talk Stumpf is a grateful bailee. The L.A. Phil is the generous bailor. An incident last year no doubt made the L.A. Phil an agitated bailor. Apparently, musicians, like professors and judges, can be absent minded, an attribute to be expected with so many weighty things on their minds. But brain surgeons for example also have weighty things on their minds, and we do not expect them to be absent minded with their scalpels. After all, they make on the spot life and death choices. But I suppose even brain surgeons might forget where they put the shopping list, or the car keys.

Getting back to Stumpf, you may recall reading about his peccadillo. At the time it was no peccadillo, but in light of the subject matter, "peccadillo" sounds so musical and Italian. Stumpf came home late in the evening to his house in Silver Lake after performing in Santa Barbara. He carried the multi-million dollar "Strad" in its case. He put the case down on the front porch of his house, fiddled (pardon the expression) with his keys, opened the front door and went inside . . . without the cello. He left it on the front porch. I guess he was tired. Early the next morning, a thief came by on a bicycle and left with the cello case inside of which was the priceless Stradivarius. A neighbor's security video camera across the street captured the event and showed the thief wobbling on his bicycle as he precariously peddled away while grasping the ungainly cello case. Oh dear! For the inquisitive, an obvious and compelling question comes to mind. On what instrument would Stumpf play at the next concert, if in fact the directors of the Philharmonic did not throttle him first?

Not to worry. The cello was found in a trashcan with minor damage. The cello had not suffered much damage either. I don't know about the trashcan, but the cello was repaired. So what is the point of all this? It leads to a seemingly simple question, pregnant with profound implications: who is Stumpf without the Strad? Yes, yes, I know he is still a world-class cellist, . . . but . . . . "But what . . . ?," the impatient will inquire. Allow me to elaborate. Stumpf is Stumpf just as we all are who we are, except Stumpf the cellist is not Stumpf the cellist without a cello. Well, OK I grant you that if I were introducing Stumpf to someone, and that assumes I know him and I don't, but if I did, and I wanted to impress the person to whom I was making the introduction, I could very well say, "And this is Peter Stumpf, the principal cellist with the Los Angeles Philharmonic." And if I were malicious and not particularly fond of Stumpf, I might add: "This is the clown who left a 3 million dollar Stradivarius cello outside on the front porch of his house."

In fact, I would not utter these words, simply because I am capable of doing the very thing that Stumpf did. Of course this is strictly conjecture because no person, institution, or organization would ever entrust a Stradivarius cello to me under any circumstances, including the presence of a 24-hour armed guard. I feel unworthy playing "I'm in the Mood for Love" on my Steinway. I am not sure if that's because of the title of the song or the instrument. Suffice it to say, my wife does not trust me with a shopping list.

But getting back to my point. We can indeed say that Stumpf is a cellist, and safely introduce him as such, but to realize the unique attribute that makes Stumpf the cellist he is, it is absolutely indispensable that Stumpf have a cello. A cellist without a cello is like a pilot without a plane.

So what about us in the legal profession? Has it occurred to you that we do not have cellos or any reasonably close counterpart? Take judges, for example. Contrary to what is depicted in courtroom scenes in old movies and television shows, we do not even have gavels. We may have a ceremonial gavel or two that friends or associations give us on which is inscribed the same inane rhyme that assumes the judge is peripatetic. Does not anyone realize that "travel" is not the only word that rhymes with gavel? If there must be a rhyme written on a gavel, I prefer "Don't cavil with the gavel." I don't know of one real life judge who uses a gavel. It is true we do wear robes, but they are a symbol of the office. If we left our robes at home, and ignored Government Code section 68110---which requires us to wear them, we could still sentence some poor devil to 20 years.

And what about you lawyers? Sure you have your briefcases, and silk suits, (well some of you) but you could wear polyester and still practice (maybe not in Century City), but you get my drift. We do not have cellos. Think about it. The brain surgeon must use implements, scalpels and precision knives come to mind, and I am sure there are many more indispensable tools that are required for surgery. Not with us.

We have one thing and one thing only: words. That's it. Judges, for example, utter words and people lose their freedom, their money, or have to do things or stop doing things.

Words are so important to our work that we have to be careful how we use them. They are too important to be left out in the cold. They have to be taken inside and watched over. For example, a person's freedom or life can depend upon how judges or jurors view the instruction on reasonable doubt. To arrive at guilt in the old days we had to have an abiding conviction to a moral certainty. No one quite knew what "to a moral certainty" meant though today many people are quite sure of their beliefs to a moral certainty.

In the hope of achieving clarity, "moral certainty" was jettisoned from the reasonable doubt instruction in California. (See CALJIC 2.90) Yet, uncertainty remains. In *People v. Johnson* 119 Cal.App.4th 976, (2004) the trial court tried to explain reasonable doubt to jurors by referring to decisions we make in our everyday lives. The trial judge explained that when you drive through an intersection on the green light, you might be cautious because it is an intersection, but it would not be reasonable to get out of your car and check to see if the red lights controlling cross traffic were malfunctioning. Damned right, and you would be late for court. The criminal conviction was reversed. The *Johnson* case cited the early case of *People v. Brannon*, 47 Cal. 96 (1873) which teaches that it is error to equate ordinary everyday decisions with reasonable doubt.

Here's another Johnson case, *People v. Johnson* 115 Cal. App.4th 1169 (2004). The trial judge told the jury he would not attempt to paraphrase the reasonable doubt instruction, but then indirectly did so by contrasting it with a ridiculous doubt. For example, we all have a doubt whether we will be here tomorrow. He analogized reasonable doubt to doubts a couple might have about whether a new home is a wise investment. The appellate court pointed out that this is a far different calculus than deciding whether the prosecution has proved the case beyond a reasonable doubt.

And that takes us to Supreme Court nominee, John C. Roberts. His words have earned him an extraordinary number of "wins" in the United States Supreme Court. We will see how effective are his words during the confirmation hearing. No doubt there will be questions about judicial philosophy, *Roe v. Wade*, Robert's dissent as a federal appeals court judge in a case involving the Endangered Species Act, and questions about whether the Constitution is an endangered species. But one thing I know beyond a reasonable doubt: Judge Roberts will carefully use his words as though they were a Stradivarius. His ability to use them effectively to advance a reasonable argument should remind us how precious are our instruments. Like the Stradivarius, they must be cared for and treated with respect. They can so easily be stolen and misused when they are carelessly left on the porch after we have locked the front door for the night.

It is hoped (not hopefully) that the Senators use and tune their Stradivari (or whatever the plural is) at Judge Robert's confirmation hearing. If they use second rate instruments the hearings could well degenerate into chaotic dissonance. Will the Senators be well served by using the reasonable doubt instruction to guide their decision? If they do, let us hope they do not rely on the scuttled phrase that requires a decision based on moral certainty. "Moral certainty" is what is left when the Stradivarius goes missing.

Postscript: The Senate held its hearings. I cannot say whether any of the senators read this column, but John C. Roberts is our Chief Justice.

ARGOT CREEP-THE GIG IS UP

The St. Martin's of the Fields gang was locked in a feud with its rival, the Academy of Ancient Music. Drive by playings were a common occurrence. At various times during the past year the St. Martin's gang would park outside the rehearsal studio of the Ancients and play measures from Bach's Brandenburg Concerto No. 3. One of the gang members displayed the bow of his Stradivarius in an obscene manner.

Retribution came as expected. The Ancients retaliated by singing early morning masses late in the evening, and incorporating inappropriate cadenzas.

Would there be a trial? Concerned about critical reviews, potential witnesses cited performance anxiety as an excuse not to testify. But Officer Bernheimer said he would gladly testify. He had 80 hours of formal chamber music training, and over the past several decades had written scathing reviews of chamber ensembles, which had been widely disseminated to the public. He had witnessed the temperamental flare-ups of soloists, and knew the monikers used by string sections. He had seen their graffiti, treble clefs blatantly painted on buildings, or eighth notes wantonly sprinkled over sidewalks and park benches.

He was prepared to testify that a gang member could enhance his or, her status by assaulting a victim with cacophony or in extreme cases, a cello. He also stated that gang members often showed disrespect for one another by playing Stockhausen.

This is what happens when musicians read judicial opinions. They appropriate the language of another culture and adopt it as their own. The consequences are dreadful.

A messy case like this should not be tried. It cried out for settlement by a skilled private judge. I called on a friend of mine, a newly retired judge, to discuss the matter over lunch.

"Can't have lunch today," he said. "I've got a gig in Beverly Hills."

At first I was puzzled. What would having a two-wheeled, one-horse carriage in a town that was anything but "one-horsed" have to do with passing on lunch? But a gig is also a boat reserved for the captain of a ship when going ashore, or a spear- like device for catching fish. Still no discernible connection to lunch.

Then it occurred to me that maybe he was a musician. A job for a musician is a "gig." In fact, a movie called "The Gig" is about the tribulations endured by a group of jazz musicians playing at a summer resort. Perhaps he was going to play Gershwin on an electric keyboard at the Bistro, which along with the clatter of expensive china, would provide a background of ignored sound for negotiations over a power lunch.

35

But on second thought this was impossible. He had not played the piano in the past and could not, in the few months since he had retired, have learned to play the instrument with even minimal skill. Unlike his previous profession, this would be a hard one to fake.

Being au courant, I turned an exposition into an interrogatory. "You're not a musician?" I said.

"No, but I improvise; I swing."

"You mean . . . ."

It was unnecessary to go further. I got it. He had adopted musician terminology, just as the musicians had adopted judicial terminology.

As a private judge he, like many of his colleagues, referred to their cases as "gigs." This term appropriated from the jazz world was now used by judges who make in one hour what a quintet is lucky to make in five. My friend reasoned that because he "jams," "gig" is the right word.

He explained, "Can't stay for lunch because I've got this gig. I'm trying to settle a landslide case in which four cities, a driving range, and a motorcycle track were buried. So far the parties are only two billion dollars apart."

I was compelled to respond in like fashion. "Hey man, I can dig it. Like that's a groovy gig."

This deplorable phenomenon of jargon creep has infected the judiciary in other respects. For example, even sitting judges often refer to a speaking engagement as a "gig." "Can't make bowling tonight, I've got an Arctic Bar Association gig." Some people have referred to this column as a gig. "How's your gig with the Daily Journal?" "O.K. but the pay isn't great."

It's not just the language of music business that has worked its way into the law. The language of business itself has staked a claim. Take for example the accounting term "the bottom line." The bottom line refers to the cost of a project after adding all the individual items. It is the last line of a financial statement used for showing net profit or loss. It has come to mean the deciding or crucial factor, the ultimate result or outcome. It is now used by everyone including those who are arithmetically challenged. Its use in appellate opinions is as ubiquitous as motions for sanctions. For example, "[t]he bottom line is that it was not proper to unilaterally and without cause remove Commissioner Schulte from the case." (*Guardianship of Simpson* (1998) 67 Cal.App.4th 914, 942.) "The bottom line was that Michael was to pay $3,626 in combined child and spousal support." (*In re Marriage of Schulze* (1997) 60 Cal.App.4th 519, 524.) "The bottom-line issue is whether the product is likely to cause harm." (*Hansen v. Sunnyside Products, Inc.* (1997) 55 Cal.App.4th 1497, 1513.)

We must stop the migration of argot across foreign borders. When restless nomenclature looks to settle into alien territory, language and meaning suffer. As

Judge Holmes said, "The minute a phrase becomes current, it becomes an apology for not thinking accurately to the end of the sentence."

Rest assured that this vigilant columnist is on the alert to uncover the insidious movement of argot creep from one discipline to another.

Incidentally, you may recall that my 100th column (celebrated by the Daily Journal with a tiny photograph of me on the first page) appeared shortly before the Academy Award presentations. The gala ceremony reminded me of what I had neglected to do and would like to do now. And that is to thank the many people who made this "gig," my column, possible.

There is my wife Barbara, who is my editor par excellence, Oge and Boz, my two cats who are my copy editors. And then of course there's Satterford Colby, Meredith Dimsdale, McArthur Sloan, Patrick Spandower, Nanette Massery, Sylvester Plaschette, Naomi Sandiford, Nelson Pick, Gabriella Fustonberg, and not to forget Shelby Spector. Thank you all. (Music.)

FASTER THAN A SPEEDING BULLET

I was a relatively new appellate justice and years before I became presiding justice, I wrote this column to offer insight on "hot" writs.

A hamburger chain announces that it has sold hamburgers, the number of which matches the national debt. There is an understandable pride in having made good use of the parts of dead cows and other animals. This staggering number of burgers is a testimonial from the chain's patrons, but it also reflects an insistent demand for quick service. In fact "quick" may be too slow. "Instantaneous" is what is required in today's frantic world where everyone must pit their wits against that implacable enemy, time.

So much for a gourmet meal. The more mouths to feed, the less time to prepare, so that now we associate a first-class meal with the Court of Louis XVI. If you want "fast" and you want quality, then you're one of those who wants the cake, and wants to eat it, too.

It's not only food that's on the fast track. Trial courts are also on fast forward because of increased filings. Judges assigned to the rigorous fast-track program are looking wistfully back to the leisurely days of private practice. With fastness as the all-consuming goal, trial judges have taken speed-reading courses to get through the law and motion calendar.

One trial judge overwhelmed by the mountain of law and motion papers edging him out of his chambers required attorneys to file no more than three-page briefs on any matter before him. Attorneys in a complex case involving a meltdown of a radioactive nuclear plant that contaminated the air, ground and water of five cities balked at the limitation. The trial judge insisted that if you can say it in 150 pages, you can certainly say it in three. He ultimately decided that the essence of any case could be summed up in one word. His desk is littered with dozens of law and motion papers in which the attorneys eloquently state their position in one word. Some say "deny," others say "grant." The burgeoning caseload and its concomitant requirement for fast resolution has touched the appellate courts, as well. Life in the ivory tower is not as leisurely and contemplative as some might think. I was wondering how we on the appellate court with our increased number of filing could also handle cases with alacrity and speed. The solution came to me one night when I was in bed just drifting off to sleep in the house my wife and I were renting while our new house was being built.

The rented house was located just behind a fire station. When the alarm sounded during the night to summon either fire trucks of paramedics, we would lie awake and count the minutes it would take for the trucks to leave the station. We also counted the months left for completion of our new house where we hoped to get a full night's sleep. Meanwhile, we were amazed at the speed at which the courageous firefighters and paramedics responded to alarms.

As we counted the seconds before the great trucks came rumbling out of the fire house, I realized that we, too, on the Court of Appeal often deal with emergencies. When we are needed to step into a crisis, we could act with more alacrity to get the job done. Of course, I'm talking about that mystical, inscrutable area of the law that lawyers look at with wonder, confusion, bewilderment and, yes, even dread- writs, or to be more precise a "hot" writ. A "hot writ" is the judiciary's fire alarm.

An urgent writ petition for immediate relief is appropriately called a "hot" writ. The land is about to be sold, the widow and her high-strung parakeet will be homeless: incalculable harm and catastrophe are imminent because of a trial court's egregious error. Should we not, like the admirable firefighters and paramedics, respond to hot writs whenever relief is needed?

I can visualize how it will happen. It's 3:00 a.m. The special red phone rings. I answer it. A "hot" writ needs my immediate attention. My wife, half asleep, yet proud, watches me climb out of bed and dress hurriedly, slip into my robe, and jump into the car as I go off to meet my colleagues.

We read the writ petition and then look heroically at each other bleary-eyed across the table. Yes, we are sleepy and tired, but not too tired to do what has to be done. We earnestly discuss the merits of the writ petition. We toss ideas back and forth. We check and recheck the record. One of us may play devil's advocate to clarify a point. Then we finally look at one another. We know that we have reached a consensus. Like the fire fighters, we know we have made a difference. We write out decision across the jacket of the writ petition- DENIED. "It Was Tough."

The table is littered with papers, coffee cups and a cardboard carry-out box filed with snacks. I slip my glasses off and rub my tired eyes. Then I look at my colleague sipping coffee.

"It was tough, but now it's done," I say.

He pushes back in his chair and looks at me across the table. "We gave it out best shot," he said.

I relax. Suddenly I discover I'm hungry. "Pass me a hamburger."

THE TALE OF JUDGE FOOTE AND LAWYER STARK

A recurring character in my columns is the redoubtable Judge Learned Foote. In 1992 he made his debut. It is possible the events related here bear a striking similarity to a case that originated in the Los Angeles Superior Court.

Ethyl and Pixley Foote often joked about their name. Pixley used to say, "What good is a hand without a foot." The puns flew fast and furious in the Foote household, especially whenever the word "stool" came up.

Not surprisingly, the Footes' family physician, Dr. Speck, grew tired of this word play and let his irritation show. The Footes in turn grew tired of Dr. Speck. Perhaps this was the reason that when the Footes had a son, they desperately wanted him to be a lawyer, or better yet, a judge.

With a twinkle in their eyes, the Footes named their son "Learned." The name reflected both their quirky sense of humor and a desire that some day their son be a great judge like Learned Hand. They got half their wish.

Their son grew up and became a judge, the well-known Judge Learned Foote.

Even when he was a youth, it was apparent that Learned was destined to ascend to the bench. In high school he carried a briefcase. In college he used Norcross pens, and in law school refused to read Gilbert's outlines.

His name turned out to be appropriate because no one could deny that Learned was learned. He understood the rule against perpetuities. If someone mentioned a retraxit, he knew what they were talking about. He read dissents and concurring opinions with gusto, and often said "ipse dixit" in ordinary conversation. He was uncommonly smart and efficient.

Understandably, he expected lawyers to meet his high standards. These standards became increasingly important as court congestion grew. The court's time and resources could not be abused if the court was to efficiently manage its burgeoning calendar. A judge who fell behind was not doing his or her job and might never catch up. Therefore, he concluded, the rules had to be followed. Unlike hearts, they were not to be broken.

Motions, for example, were to be on opaque, unglazed white paper, 8 ½ by 11, with type no smaller than 11-point open face and could not exceed 11 pages including the points and authorities. Period.

One day attorney Sylvester Stark filed a motion in Judge Foote's court. The points and authorities totaled 14 pages. The clerk said it was OK, relying on the policy of the judge who had preceded Foote in that particular courtroom.

Foote began reading the motion but stopped at the bottom of page 11. The last two letters on the page read "be-." The remainder of the word on Page 12 was probably "cause." It would never be revealed to the eyes of Judge Foote. The 11-page rule had been broken. Foote was furious. If he read beyond the 11 pages, he would lose the precious time he needed to read all of his other motions, not to mention all the cases cited in the points and authorities, which he invariably shepardized.

If Foote had simply left it there, the strange sequence of events I am about to relate would never have happened. But Judge Foote made a decision, resulting in an inexorable linking of rings in a chain of cause and effect, much like what you would find in a Theodore Dreiser novel, that inevitably led to tragedy.

Foote sanctioned Stark. The sanction order was written in elite type, single-spaced on glossy blue paper, and was 13 pages long. Not only was Stark ordered to pay to the county a substantial sum of money, he was also ordered to show the sanction order to any future judge in whose court he intended to file a motion in excess of 11 pages.

As fate would have it, the very next motion Stark filed was assigned to Judge Foote. It was a complicated motion, and Stark, who thought of his client first and himself second, felt that in order to adequately represent his client's interest, his points and authorities would have to be at least 16 pages long. Along with his motion he dutifully filed a copy of Judge Foote's previous sanction order.

Of course, Judge Foote knew about his own sanction order, but a rule is a rule. Stark also felt compelled to include a declaration explaining in detail his view of the circumstances surrounding the previous sanction order. He also filed a declaration explaining the reasons he had to make his points and authorities 16 pages long.

Upon receiving the motion, Foote flew into a rage. He promptly sanctioned Stark again, and wrote a 17-page, single-spaced sanction order. This order required, among other things, that Stark reveal to any judge in whose court he filed a motion, irrespective of whether the motion exceeded 11 pages, the previous two sanction orders. Fate can be cruel—or perhaps just indifferent.

Stark's very next motion was again before Judge Foote. Along with his motion, Stark filed the two previous sanction orders along with exhaustive declarations explaining his view of the circumstances surrounding the two sanction orders. Foote was apoplectic. The explanatory declarations were wasting ever more time. He again sanctioned Stark and again required him to show his sanction order, which was even more detailed and vituperative than the last two, to any judge Stark should ever meet in court—or even socially.

Mathematics tells us how infinitesimal are the odds against black turning up on twenty-three successive turns of the roulette wheel. I bet once in every 100 million-trillion years black could turn up on as many as 20 or 30 successive turns. I know it strains your credulity, but trust me dear reader; all Stark's subsequent 23 motions were heard before Judge Foote.

The sanction procedure seemed to feed off itself. Foote, consumed by rage and an obsession with a misuse of the court's resources, wrote more and more detailed sanction orders requiring that Stark show them to judges, lawyers, and even his friends. Stark, in turn, wrote voluminous declarations explaining his side of the story concerning each of the separate sanction incidents. Foote and Stark seemed bound together in an eternal struggle.

The conflict could not go on forever.

The Stark sanction orders caused Judge Foot to get so far behind in his work that he was removed from office by the Commission on Judicial performance. Stark lost his law practice because all of his time was spent trying to keep up with the orders. For months Foote and Stark wandered the streets of Los Angeles looking for work. One day, to their amazement, they found themselves standing next to each other in the unemployment line. They began chatting about the weather, then about fate, and then about the future.

They soon went into business and became enormously successful. They sell sanction insurance to lawyers. Besides being business partners, Foote and Stark are good friends, but recently they stopped playing golf together. Stark just couldn't stand it any longer. Foote is such a stickler for rules.

44

FOOTNOTES-KICK THEM OUT

An illness of epidemic proportions is spiraling out of control. Most who are afflicted are ashamed to admit it. I have it. It's hard to acknowledge to a friend, or even a spouse. Painful to see them back away. Far easier to make the admission to you, a cluster of anonymous readers, who after an indifferent glance, most likely will use this page to wrap something, like herring or mackerel.

I have Schubert's Syndrome. It's the feeling of unease caused by unfinished work. The larger the amount of unfinished work, the greater the discomfort. This debilitating malady is endemic to my line of work. To mask its signs, many sufferers pass off as finished, work that is unfinished. An example of such dissembling is a proliferation of footnotes in a judicial opinion or legal brief.

I had long suspected that Judge Learned Foote was afflicted with Schubert's Syndrome. He had finagled a stint on the Court of Appeal to avoid the possibility of presiding over the return of the O.J. Simpson case.

I dropped in to see how he was doing. He proudly displayed a case he had just "finished." It was a long dense opinion that eschewed paragraphs but embraced a surfeit of footnotes. Like the opinion, they too were tedious and lengthy, more like yard-notes. As I scanned the opinion, my head nodded up and down, but not as a sign of approval.

He did not have a chance to misinterpret my bobbing. I blurted out, "Lots of footnotes."

"Footnotes are my signature," he said breezily.

His quip left me cold. "Take note, Foote," I replied coldly, "Your footnotes add nothing. Boot them out."

"Much ado about noting," he replied with a Shakespearean smirk.

The sweat on his brow told me he knew what I meant. Footnotes are directly proportional to large caseloads. They are junk yards which crowd the landscape of hastily written opinions. The dash for so many yards betrays an unseemly race for a fast but fake finish.

In academic circles there is a raging dispute about footnotes. Some argue that footnotes are indispensable to establish a scholar's accountability, and thus, his or her credibility and authority. To dispense with footnotes is to display arrogance and possibly to hide incompetence.

On the other hand, some publishers are excising footnotes in the hope of making scholarly works less formidable and more interesting to readers. To alleviate this concern, I have suggested placing footnotes at the back of the book. Publishers have balked because that would add pages to the book, which increases its cost, which in turn defeats the goal of reaching a wider audience.

The controversy about footnotes, however, should be of no concern to writers of opinions or briefs. Writers of law review articles will have to make up their own minds.[1] An opinion or brief is a reasoned argument supported by legal authority. The authority is in the main body of the opinion. Therefore the opinion rarely needs footnotes. They are a diversion that takes the reader away from the text and the flow of the argument. To make a footnote is like bringing a sandwich to Spago.

Professor David Mellinkoff says of footnotes, "The ease of dropping random thoughts into the footnote basement tightens the hold of the footnote habit. It takes time and care to weave those thoughts into the text, or to decide that they really weren't important after all. The writer's burden is sloughed off, but the reader may or may not be willing to assume it." (Legal Writing: Sense and Nonsense (West Publishing 1982) p. 94.) Mellinkoff provides a good rule of thumb: "Nothing essential to understanding the main text should be put in a footnote." (Ibid.)

Robert Leflar, Professor of Law at Arkansas School of Law, and a former Associate Justice on the Supreme Court of Arkansas, says that a footnote "is a good place to quote a statute, set out legislative history," and where necessary, list multiple citations. (I have yet to encounter the situation where multiple citations are necessary.) Leflar states that it is an abuse to use footnotes as a place to put material that would otherwise be omitted from the opinion. (Leflar, Appellate Judicial Opinions (West Publishing 1974) pp. 175-176.)

Former U.S. Circuit Judge Abner Mikva considered footnotes in judicial opinions "an abomination." (Mikva, *Good-bye to Footnotes* (1985) 56 U.Colo.L.Rev. 647.) Senior Circuit Judge, Ruggero J. Aldisert quotes Burton S. Laub, retired Pennsylvania Common Pleas Judge, "anyone who reads a footnote in a judicial opinion would answer a knock at his hotel door on his wedding night." (Aldisert, Opinion Writing (West Publishing 1990) p. 177.) You have a better chance of finding Jimmy Hoffa than a footnote in any of Witkin's treatises.

Does that mean you should never use footnotes?[2] Of course not. As Mellinkoff points out it's a good place for a sidelight, humorous or otherwise, and an ideal spot for a long statute to repose. In this case the footnote keeps the reader's focus on the main text. The statute is there in the footnote for the reader's use.

---

[1] I resisted the temptation to place this sentence in a footnote. If it is out of place-- disregard it.

[2] A flagrant rhetorical question.

I tried to impress these points on Judge Foote, but he defended the practice as necessary to give an opinion weight and prestige. I tried to get in the last word. I told him that an appendix is as necessary to the human body as a footnote is necessary to the body of an opinion.

"But, in some cases an appendix is appropriate," he added.

Not surprisingly, we never finished our argument. That is one good reason to finish this column, but there are two other reasons as well: A. Major points--I have made them. B. Minor[3] points--There are some I did not make. The deadline gave me too little time to weave them into the column without extensive editing. I cannot simply drop them into footnotes, not after all of the foregoing. I am not quite finished, but, take note, that's Schubert's Syndrome for you.

---

[3] EDITOR'S NOTE-Our research reveals that Schubert's Unfinished Symphony is in B Minor.

GIVE THE BOOT TO FOOTNOTES

I hold footnotes in contempt. My colleague Judge Learned Foote loves footnotes. Resting his heels on a footstool, he remarked that an idea that did not fit here or there in an opinion could always be put at the foot of the page.

The affliction that causes one to toss odds and ends into the repository below the line I call Schubert's Syndrome. (See Preceding column.) This malady infects a writer when his or her opinion is unfinished. Where to put thoughts and ideas the writer wishes to express, but cannot, or will not, devote the time and effort to effectively weave into the body of the opinion? Judge Foote would drop-kick them below the line into a footnote. Bad idea, I told him. Footnotes divert the reader from the flow of the text. From this we may note two points: (A.) Major points do not belong in a footnote. They belong in the opinion. (B.) Minor points do not belong in a footnote. If they belong (a question of judgment for the writer), they belong in the opinion.

Of course there are exceptions to the use of footnotes. They can be welcome compartments to house lengthy statutes. In such cases the footnote accomplishes what footnotes generally thwart: helping the reader focus on the flow of the text. Otherwise forget footnotes.

Feigning fortitude, Foote fought forcefully for footnotes, citing redoubtable legal writing guru Bryan A. Garner's revolutionary proposal to expand the use of footnotes. Garner, editor of Black's Law Dictionary, and a noble crusader for good writing, wants judges to expel from the Eden of their opinions citations to case authority and cast them down into footnote Hell.

At a conference of California appellate justices last September, Garner garnered support from a few of my colleagues, including Learned Foote. This view was even touted in the New York Times July 8, 2001, "Legal Citations on Trial." I agree with Garner in almost every point he makes about writing, except that one. With case citations relegated to Australia, the text may look cleaner, but the written opinion suffers, and so does the reader. A judicial opinion is not a magazine article. It should be a reasoned explication of the law. It derives its legitimacy and persuasiveness from a discussion of legal authority.

When that authority is in a footnote, the attentive reader's head mimics repeated nods of approval. If the head is kept still, the reader's eyes are forced into a REM cycle, a disconcerting phenomenon when intense wakefulness is required. Although citations are bothersome to judges who balk at having to support their position with case authority, citations are essential to an opinion. That's why they belong in the body of the opinion.

A judicial opinion need not look like a New Yorker article to be well-written. When opinions are not readable, it is not because they contain citations in the body of the opinion. Opinions that are not readable are badly written. Clarity will not be improved one iota by placing citations in footnotes.

An apostle of Mr. Garner, appellate lawyer Daniel U. Smith, wrote in the Daily Journal April 19, 2001, "Crystal Clear," "when citations are stripped from the text, the writer can draft clear sentences and paragraphs more easily." While some justices endorse this idea, Smith noted the dissent of now California Supreme court Justice Carol Corrigan and myself.

Citing the works of authorities on good writing in the main body of the text, Smith noted the importance of clarity for the reader. Aristotle, William Safire, William Zinsser, E.B. White and Jacques Barzun all note that the reader is paramount. Good writing omits needless words, strives for clarity and enhances comprehension.

From these truths Smith argues that a "citation-free text allows the writer to develop the paragraph's internal logic and more smoothly connect sentences and paragraphs." He cited *Peatros v. Bank of America NT & SA* (2000) 22 Cal.4th 147, as an example of the strain citations in that text put on the reader. It is true that some paragraphs in *Peatros* suffer from a surfeit of citations that make the text appear cluttered. The first paragraph on page 161 mentions that a statement in an 1896 case about the importance of removing suspect officers from banking institutions remains current today. To support this the author cited 13 cases with a brief statement or quote about each one. I suppose it would do no harm to place this paragraph in a long footnote. But what is the point? It is just as easy to read the paragraph in the opinion, or skip over it if you are not interested.

This cite-laden paragraph in *Peatros* cites and discusses the case in question, *Westervelt v. Mohrenstecher* (8th Cir. 1896) 76 Fed. 118, 122. Whatever deficiencies this column may suffer, I doubt it would be improved if I placed the *Westervelt* cite in a footnote.[1] Nor would the *Peatros* case be improved with the *Westervelt* cite in a footnote. In most instances a single citation will suffice. Generally, string citations on the same point do not belong anywhere in an opinion including footnotes. Note the exception in *Peatros*.

Witkin's treatises on California law are a reader's paradise where citations abound in the text with no sacrifice to clarity. You will sooner find a politician with conviction than a footnote in Witkin.

Bryan Garner published a national survey entitled, "Judges on Briefing." (West Group (2001).) He asked judges throughout the country their views about two versions of appellate brief writing. Did the judges prefer #1, the brief that concisely advances two or three cohesive arguments, or #2, the brief that contains all possible information a curious judge might have about the case. My response applies in large part to judicial opinions as well as briefs: "Curiosity has killed more judges than it has cats." A judge whose insatiable curiosity would drive him or her to view #2 as the preferable view will soon die of fatigue, if not boredom. I predict that no seasoned judge, unless masochistic, will pick #2.

My advice to brief-writers is to be brief. Say what you have to say in reasonably short declarative sentences powered by nouns and verbs. If a sentence has more than 20 words, it usually needs to be redrafted. Adjectives often lead one to characterize, or more often, to mischaracterize. A well-reasoned argument without ornate phrases is more likely to compel a judge to draw a correct conclusion. If you are the appellant, deal only with the error that matters, the one that has a chance to produce a reversal. If you find several such errors, you are either extremely lucky, or in error yourself. If one citation will do, a string of them will detract more than it will help. Do not assume the judge knows anything about your case. Ask yourself what this case is about. Then explain it to the judge, who has dozens of briefs besides yours to read. if you make a judge's life easier, he or she will be grateful."

A well-written judicial opinion will be no less so with its citations set out where they belong, in the body of the opinion.

---

1 Then you would have to look down here to get the cite. If you are an informed reader looking for an exposition on the law, you would not want the unnecessary burden of glancing down here to see *Westervelt v. Mohrenstecher* (8th Cir. 1896) 76 Fed. 118, 112.

It was Monday morning and Judge Learned Foote sang to himself as he trundled down the hall to his chambers, lugging his briefcase crammed full of motions he had taken home that weekend and not read. If you had been there, you would have heard him singing, "Tum te tum te tum te dum and little tum de ivy. A diddle de dum de doo wouldn't you."

He glanced at his watch and to his dismay noticed it was a few minutes past 9:00 a.m. That meant he would be late in taking the bench this morning. Damn! He would lose the chance to chew out lawyers who were minutes late because of the slow elevators. He took the bench at 9:05 a.m. and opened the file for the motion set for 900 a.m.

"Mmmph, good morning," he murmured. "What do we have here, an agronomy case?" Judge Foote had been an agronomy major in a local agricultural college in Nebraska. He thought that perhaps he should disclose this little known facet of his background to the litigants, but for some reason did not do so. In fact, the case involved a claim of adverse possession by plaintiff of a large oat field owned by numerous defendants. Plaintiff's horses had been grazing in the field for over a decade. Plaintiff, however, had neglected to name all the defendant owners, and now, just before trial, they were attempting to name additional plaintiffs in a Does paragraph.

Judge Foote wrinkled his brow. "Mmmm," he muttered to himself. He gave plaintiff's counsel his severe look. "Horses graze out there, don't they?"

"They do," answered plaintiff's counsel.

"Horses eat oats," the judge said.

Not sure if the court's words were meant as a declaration or a question, counsel replied, "I believe they do judge."

"Now as to Does," the judge continued.

"We did properly draft a does paragraph and . . ."

"Does eat oats," said Judge Foote in the same ambiguous tone.

Plaintiff's counsel was not sure how to respond. "We did not know about the unserved Does until now," he answered.

"Do lambs graze on this property?" asked Judge Foote.

Counsel was sure that this was a question. Before he could answer, his client whispered in his ear, "We are in the toilet." Counsel, who had momentarily lost sight of his objective, said to his client in a throaty whisper, "No doubt about it, that was a question. Does eat oats, don't they?" He sensed Foote's impatience and did not wait for his client's reply. In a tone betraying just a hint of hysteria he said, "Right again, your honor."

"What is your field?" asked the judge.

"The legal description of the field is . . . ."

"No, no, what is your field of practice?" asked the judge.

"It's certainly not animal husbandry," he answered with a nervous laugh that now revealed more than a hint of hysteria.

The client grimaced. Judge Foote was not sure what prompted his next question. In fact, he was not sure what had prompted any of his questions.

"Is there ivy in this field?"

"If I may have a moment to confer with my client, your honor," asked counsel. (In whispers to his client), "Is there ivy in the field?"

The client answered in a throaty whisper. "I suppose so, but what does that have to do with the Does paragraph? Will he next ask whether Bambi lives there?"

Counsel, in a panicky whisper. "When a judge asks a question, you have to answer it."

The client then referred to his earlier toilet metaphor and said something about hearing a flushing sound. Counsel told him to relax because they could always appeal. By this time Judge Foote had answered his own question. "I bet there is ivy," he said.

Counsel for the defendants kept quiet. Judge Foote took the matter under submission, and ultimately ruled that it was too late to add known Doe defendants who were necessary parties. For this and other reasons, he dismissed the case. A curious phrase, "Dozy doats," appeared in the minute order dismissing the case.

The case was appealed and assigned to Justice Cleanth Peerless, known to bench and bar as Peerless the Fearless. The moniker may have been ironic because Peerless was overly cautious about everything. But on the other hand, in his 23 years as a jurist he consistently demonstrated ample courage to be wrong. Plaintiff's counsel was sure he would do the right thing after reviewing the briefs and transcript. But his client was understandably concerned about whether the appellate court could discern the proper context in which the written words, "does" pronounced "duz," and "does" pronounced "doze," appeared.

This did not perturb Peerless, but the enigmatic minute order captured his attention. He pondered the meaning of the phrase for only a few minutes before a warm smiled played across his face. He knew exactly what it meant. That was because Peerless loved almost everything from the 1940's, not just its jurisprudence, but also its music. His favorite song from that era was Marizy Doats, which is not surprising given his notorious bad taste. He sang the words over in his mind. "Marizy doats and dozy doats and liddle lanzy divey, a kiddley divey too wouldn't you?"

His affable mood was soon replaced by a discomforting wariness when he considered the remote possibility of an ethical conundrum. Does (duz) his knowledge of the song require him to recuse himself from this case involving a does (doze) paragraph? The answer was obvious-no. The case did not involve baby deer. But should he disclose all this to the attorneys on the case whose overwrought imaginations might lead them to view this as a matter of disqualification? He rejected the idea as preposterous. After all, he was merely deciding an issue of law.

He then considered whether Foote, the trial judge, was remiss for not having revealed his agronomy background? Canon 3E of the Code of Judicial Ethics requires a trial judge to "disclose on the record information that the judge believes the parties or their lawyer might consider relevant to the question of disqualification, even if the judge believes there is no actual basis for disqualification." But the case had nothing to do with agronomy. Yet Foote at first believed that it did. If he believed it did, then he must have believed that the lawyers felt this information relevant for disclosure, even though, in fact, the lawyers could not have harbored such a belief.

Justice Peerless perceived this issue to be somewhat like the question of whether there was a sound of a tree falling in the forest when no one was there to hear it fall. Only here, the tree did not fall, even if someone might think that it did. Peerless concluded there was simply nothing to disclose. He forgot about the matter but told his friend Judge Handy, a trial court judge, about the meaning of "Marizy doats." They had a good laugh.

It just so happened that a week later Judge Handy was ruling on a matter in which counsel happened to be plaintiff's counsel in the matter before Justice Peerless. To add a little humor to his ruling, Judge Handy said, "a kid will eat ivy too, wouldn't you?"

Counsel put two and two together and moved to have Justice Peerless removed from the case. "Why do such a silly thing?" his client asked. "He could rule in our favor." "True," said his counsel, "but he could also rule against us. Then what would you do?" The motion was denied. Counsel then brought a conspiracy action against the Court of Appeal, naming all the justices and their research attorneys as defendants. Because he did not know the names of the research attorneys, he sued them in a Does paragraph. In the meantime the appeal has been on hold. No one knows when it will be resolved. The oat field, however, is doing well.

CALAMITOUS CONFERENCE

"I keep six honest serving men.
They taught me all I knew;
Their names are What and Why and When
And How and Where and Who." - Rudyard Kipling

I briefly met these six men whom Mr. Kipling mentions in his pithy poem several years after they had left his employ. I cannot tell you much about Mr. Kipling, but I can tell you I found offensive his notion of "keeping serving men," although it just might have been his quaint way of expressing the employment relationship. As for me, it is hard enough to keep my wits, let alone six serving men, notwithstanding their purported honesty. When I found out something about the six, I understood why Kipling's enthusiasm for their virtues had waned. They all are quite disagreeable.

I met the six men at a settlement conference. Up until that time, settling cases had been one of the most satisfying aspects of my work. The six serving men put an end to that. The conference ended in disaster. I'm not sure what they taught Mr. Kipling, but they taught me a lesson no judge should ever forget. No matter how familiar you may be with the facts of a case, never proceed with a settlement conference unless you know the names of all the parties and their attorneys. But I'm getting ahead of myself. Unfortunately, it was not until after the ill-fated conference that I learned something about the six serving men.

As best I've been able to determine, What and Where waited on tables at the lodge at Mammoth Lakes. Who took care of an old lady living in the Truesdale Estates. At her afternoon bridge parties, he wore her deceased husband's tuxedo and served her cronies tiny crustless sandwiches and tea. When and Why were singing waiters in a Byelorussian restaurant, and How pinch-hit as a maitre d' and accompanied the singers on the piano.

Despite their mediocre talent, five of the serving men aspired to be professional singers. They appeared on the old television show, Rocket to Stardom with How as the accompanist. Their rendition of "On the Road to Mandalay" won them 12th prize, and the opportunity to sing a few numbers at the Los Angeles Superior Court annual dinner dance. The event was catastrophic. Two of the members began singing "Where or When" but some members objected. Then other members refused to sing "Who Can I Turn To?" They began fighting on the bandstand. How tried to stop the scuffle by shouting "We must unify!" The incensed judges, who were then fighting against court unification, leapt into the melee. It was a brutish and ugly scene which seriously damaged the court's image and ended the singing careers of the six serving men.

To make matters worse, they lost their day jobs. During a warm winter, the lodge at Mammoth let Where and What go. The widow in Truesdale died suddenly without having fulfilled her promise to make Who sole beneficiary in her will. The Byelorussian restaurant was bought out by a hamburger chain.

Luckily, it was at this time that Kipling was looking for six honest serving men. The six patched up their differences, contrived resumes with impressive academic credentials and landed the jobs. The pay wasn't bad, and shortsighted Mr. Kipling praised them for their "wisdom." He was so pleased that he penned the poem that opens this column. But the work was exhausting even with six of them. They were on call day and night.

Whether he was writing, taking a shower, or getting ready for bed, Kipling was always calling Who, Why, What, When, Where, or How. Often he called all of them at once. Kipling hung onto them with a desperation that was stifling. Things ultimately came to a head. Who, What and Where, wishing to improve their station in life, attended night law school. It was difficult for How, Why and When to cover for them. They fabricated reasons to an irritated Kipling to account for their colleagues' absences. Why's response to questions Kipling had for What often proved unsatisfactory. Kipling became abusive and insulting.

Kipling demanded that they all be there at his beck and call 24 hours a day. They refused and sued him for wrongful termination. Who and What passed the bar, but an irate Where flunked it the first time. The wrongful termination suit settled with an agreement in which Kipling agreed not to publish his new poem about six deceitful serving men who served him ill.

Wouldn't you know it, no sooner was the case over, then they began squabbling among themselves, each blaming the others for the loss of their jobs. How brought an action against Why and hired Who to represent him. Why hired What to represent him and cross-complained against When. Where, just having passed the bar, represented When.

The case was a mess. No one wanted to try it. I was given the thankless task of holding the settlement conference. If I had not skipped over the names of the parties and their attorneys when I read through the file, the Judicial Performance Commission would never have become involved. But there I go again getting ahead of myself. The following is a transcript of the calamitous conference. For lack of a better name, I'm called judge.

JUDGE: "Who represents the plaintiff?"

WHO: "That's correct, your honor."

JUDGE: "What?"

WHAT: "Yes, your honor."

JUDGE: "I beg your pardon."

WHAT: "I represent the defendant."

JUDGE: "What's your name?"

WHAT: "That's correct your honor."

HOW: (Sarcastically under his breath) "He's got the names right, only he doesn't know it."

JUDGE: "How's that?"

HOW: "I'm the client. Can we talk about the case?"

JUDGE: (To How) "Who are you?"

WHO: (Responding) "That's me."

JUDGE: "What?"

WHAT: "Yes?"

JUDGE: "What?"

WHAT: "You just said my name."

JUDGE: "When?"

WHERE: "He's a cross-defendant and should be dismissed from the case."

JUDGE: "Why?"

WHY: (Turning to his lawyer What) "Should I answer?"

WHAT: "I'll answer for you." (To the judge) "We would just like to settle your honor."

JUDGE: (Sarcastically) "When?"

WHEN: (To Where) "He keeps calling me."

JUDGE: "What?"

WHAT: "Yes?"

JUDGE: "What is your name?"

WHAT: What.

JUDGE: (LOUDER) "I said, what is your name?"

WHAT: (Meekly) "What."

JUDGE: (Exasperated, turning to Who) "What is his name?" (pointing to What)

WHO: "It is."

JUDGE: (Turning to What) "O.K., what's his name?" (pointing to Who)

WHAT: "Who."

JUDGE: "Him," (no answer). "Can anybody help me here?"

WHY: "Judge, I thought you were supposed to help us."

JUDGE: "I can't help you if I don't know your names."

WHY: "We gave you our names."

JUDGE: (Sarcastically) "Oh, I must have missed something. Tell me your name."

WHY: "Why."

JUDGE: "Because I'd like to know. Each of you please give me your names so I can properly address the parties and counsel."

WHERE: "Where."

JUDGE: "Here."

WHEN: "When."

JUDGE: "Now." (Out of control) "This is worse than an Abbott and Costello routine.

       There was a stunned silence. They all stared at me in horror.

WHO: "That remark was uncalled for."

JUDGE: "You're probably right. Maybe the Marx Brothers would have been better."

WHO: "You can't help us settle this case, your honor."

JUDGE: "Why?"

WHY: "Don't ask me."

WHAT: "I agree with my client."

JUDGE: "What?"

WHAT: "Yes?"

JUDGE: "You're right."

They all left my chambers and promptly settled the case themselves. Then they lodged a complaint with the Judicial Performance Commission. The Commission called a special session. The presiding judge asked the prosecuting attorney the order in which the witnesses would testify.

She answered, "Who's on first."

The presiding judge said, "I'm asking you."

A barely detectable sigh of relief passed through my lips.

I HEAR VOICES

I attended a retirement dinner for a prominent Court of Appeal justice. He was leaving the bench after 25 years of distinguished service to become a judge, a rent-a-judge, that is. Now, he would be seeking tax shelters as well as justice.

During the obligatory accolades and affectionate jokes, one of the speakers, a retired justice, suggested that they open a Rent-an-Appellate-Justice office. There were a few laughs and more nervous coughs. A friend next to me said in a frantic whisper, "They will be writing opinions. And you know what that means?" We looked at each other and mouthed the words: "a whole new reporter system."

It was hard to eat another bite. But then, a seductive voice in my head extolled the virtues of a rental appellate system.

"It will open up innumerable employment opportunities. Justices write opinions, but someone has to do the research. Enter the research attorneys with their visors, word processors and vision-care insurance." As I listened, I knew I would make it through dessert.

Someone Has to Write the Headnotes

"Opinions should not just lie on a shelf gather dust. Yes, everything is on line these days. But the law first appeared in hardbound reports. Where else can the dust settle? Once published, someone has to write the headnotes. Enter the cadre of headnote writers, with their red pencils, copies of Strunk and White and psychiatric insurance. Their employer, the new publishing company, will also need a reporter of decisions, whose name will be well-known but whose actual existence will always be in doubt.

"The new publishing concern will improve career opportunities for sales representatives and law librarians. Printers, bookbinders, lumberjacks, paper-mill operators will also find steady employment. Let's not forget the carpenters. Someone has to build the additional cabinet space in law offices and libraries to house the new reports. The rise in employment brings with it wages and a broader tax base. Barring possible inflationary consequences, this additional revenue may improve the economy and even help reduce the budget deficit."

"What happens if the losing side is unhappy with the opinion?" I wondered. "Don't worry," the voice assured me. "The phrase 'We'll take it to a higher court' need not wither on the vine. What use is a Rent-an-Appellate Court without a Rent-a-Supreme Court?"

Present indications are there will be enough bodies to fill the positions. The Rent-a-Supreme Court will be a welcome relief to the present Supreme Court. It will help reduce its caseload of civil cases, and give the justices more opportunity to sink their teeth into the challenging backlog of death penalty cases.

"Exciting consequences will flow from the development of a new body of case law. Reports in the two systems will compete. This will generate more work for lawyers and will give law schools the chance to write even more law review articles criticizing even more poorly reasoned opinions. Politicians will have more targets to strike at when they wish to deflect attention away from more prosaic issues such as pollution, poverty and disease."

Then another familiar voice tried to break in. I remember hearing it in the third grade. Glenda Johnson sat in front of me. I was about to dip her pigtails into my ink well. The voice said, "Don't." Now it was asking questions. "What about the potential problems? The two Supreme Courts will compete for prestige. The authority of one system may ultimately have as little influence as a citation from Madagascar or Texas. Conflicts between the two systems will introduce even more chaos and confusion in the law than already exists."

"Not to worry," said the other voice. "The solution is simple. Conflicts between the two systems can be resolved by an authority whose wisdom is universally recognized and whose judgment is accepted by everyone- Judge Wapner." No votes for Judge Judy.

Intoxicated as I was by the eloquence of the first voice with its unrestrained praise for an expanded rent-a-judge system, the second voice became louder and more forceful. "Shouldn't we drastically overhaul our courts so that all citizens, rich and poor, may have their cases decided quickly and expeditiously?" it asked with indignation. "Maybe everyone should have swift justice, not just those who can afford it. Maybe litigants should freely exchange information, and maybe endless pretrial court appearances over discovery and law and motion matter should be rare. Maybe…"

Then a third voice interrupted. "You are forgetting it is a law of human nature that we leave the hard questions for last. First, the budget deficit."

A NIGHTMARE

You know the story about the patient relating a terrible nightmare he had had the previous night. "Doctor, it was horrendous. I dreamed you were my mother." The doctor replied that indeed it was a disturbing dream. "What did you do after you awoke from the dream?" she asked. "I woke up in a cold sweat, took a shower and had breakfast." "What did you have for breakfast?" asked the psychiatrist. "Coffee and a piece of toast." "You call that a breakfast?"

A similar incident occurred in my home recently. At breakfast my wife told me about her frightful nightmare the night before. "I dreamed that I, not you, am the judge. There I was in my robes, and . . . " What did you feel? I asked. "Don't interrupt when I'm speaking." "But I'm your husband, I always interrupt." She then did something quite unexpected. She waved a finger in front of me. "One more outburst and you'll be in contempt." I let her go on. Finally she let me speak. "I read somewhere that . . . " She interrupted . . . "that's hearsay, inadmissible." "But we are just having a discussion," I said. "Overruled." I said something else. The cat objected and she sustained the objection. I kept speaking and she repeated in a louder voice, "Sustained!" Was that her? I looked around to see if the cat had said anything.

Those readers who have not donned judicial robes might question whether my wife's dream was, in fact, a nightmare. They might believe that the authority she exercised reflects the awesome power and respect real life judges command.

Let me set you straight through an example. I had this idea for a new law related reality show. Yes, I know that the recent reality show, "*The Firm*" went down in flames. Well what do you expect? The emphasis was on trial lawyers and their pathetic efforts to rout their opponents. Yawn. The show would have been a rousing success if the focus had been on the judges instead of the lawyers. My idea for a reality show is based on an old radio show, popular about 60 years ago, called *Queen for a Day* emceed by Jack Bailey.

It's hard to believe, but in those days the contestants were only women. The winning contestant was the one with the most sympathy inducing hard luck story. "My job interview at the telephone company was a disaster. They were about to test my voice but as I sat down to speak into the microphone my nylons tore and I shrieked 'operator.'! I didn't get the job and now the bank is threatening to foreclose on my bungalow."

The winner was crowned queen for the entire day. Jack Bailey would recite the itinerary for the magical day of the queen's reign. "Your majesty will be chauffeured to lunch at the Brown Derby on Vine Street, after which you will be whisked off to Bullock's Wilshire (now a law school), for an afternoon of shopping. A mid-afternoon snack at Pig N' Whistle and later dinner and a show at the

Mocambo where you will be escorted by Cesar Romero or George Raft, if you are not too tall. "

So here's my idea. A reality show that gives deserving lawyers who have lost a disproportionate share of cases because of bad judicial rulings the opportunity to become "Judge for a Day." The emcee will announce to the winner what is in store for her or him, and then we will witness the judge's activities throughout the day. "Before sunup your Honor will be whisked off to the court house in early morning heavy traffic. Once at the courthouse you will wait for the judge's private elevator, and wait and wait until you realize it doesn't work and then climb ten flights of stairs to get to your chambers, where it is freezing cold and piles of motions sit on your desk waiting for your review.

"But first you have a morning settlement conference. You patiently craft a settlement proposal that does justice for all parties. After you have gently cajoled and tried amiably to persuade the parties to settle, the recalcitrant lawyers and their obstinate clients mock your efforts, refuse to settle, or even talk to one another, threaten to file additional causes of action against each other and storm out of your chambers.

"You will then take the bench for the morning law and motion calendar and hear dozens of motions, few of which are written in English. These include a multitude of summary judgment motions, one of which contains six thousand issues of disputed fact. The lawyers vilify one another in their briefs and oral argument.

"Then you will continue with the trial you have been trying to conduct. You promised the jury it will end this day, but a key witness under subpoena has not appeared. The witness, a single working mother with three minor children is vital to the case, and the attorneys are pressing you to issue a bench warrant. A member of the press sitting in the courtroom is busily taking notes.

"You will take a recess and peruse in chambers the charges brought against you before the Judicial Performance Commission by the pro per against whom you sustained the demurrer to his complaint which alleged on information and belief that the mayor is trying to kill him.

It's now time for lunch. You are due to install the officers of the Left Handed Lawyers Bar Association. You will arrive at the local hotel where the gala event is taking place just as they serve you the delectable entrée of chicken fried steak. That evening you attend a cocktail party sponsored by Citizens Against Judicial Abuse where guests cross-examine you about the Rodney King case and Judge Alito, I could go on, but my show idea was rejected in favor of another show called "Test Pilot for a Day."

This proves that being a judge is not all it's cracked up to be. Our power is limited. Some people have real power. Take, for example, the baby naming official in the Czech Republic. Friends of mine who are citizens of that country recently had a baby. A Czech baby must have a name that is listed in the book of names. If the parents wish to name their baby some other name they must get approval from the official "Naming Person." She decides whether or not the name is legitimate, not the baby mind you, but the baby's name. Sure, you can name your baby whatever you wish despite the naming person's disapproval, but try and get a birth certificate. My friends named their baby a name that does not appear in the book of names. Luckily, the Naming Person went along. My respect for the baby's privacy does not permit me to reveal the name. Her gurgles and cooing could be monitored by governmental officials.

American judges do not have the power of the baby naming official. Sure, people stand up for us when we enter the courtroom, but that is only because a bailiff orders them to. Standing up for us literally is far different from doing so metaphorically. Getting up when you are sitting down is annoying, but today people do it for everyone. Every performer, however mediocre, gets a standing ovation. Rock performers, opera singers, mimes, organ grinders, jugglers, weather forecasters--they all get standing ovations.

I think it impolite to leave as the curtain comes down at the opera. We can at least stay and express our appreciation for the performers, but is everyone deserving of a standing ovation? The person in front stands up and you have to stand up to see the singers bow. And soon the entire audience is on its feet. Elderly people have to be awakened and helped up by their caretakers. It's as bad as attending a football game. A good play and everyone is on their feet screaming. I see most of the game by way of instant replays on the giant screens above the end-zones.

But, on the other hand, it sure makes the performers feel good. I therefore thought about instituting standing ovations during oral argument at the Court of Appeal. Not for the lawyer's arguments mind you. Who is going to applaud? Clients seldom attend sessions of the Court of Appeal, and certainly not other lawyers in the courtroom who are far more concerned about their own cases. No, I wanted a standing ovation for the justices. In my division we are known for asking snappy, quirky questions. It might be a bit time consuming for the ovation to occur after each argument. But waiting until the end of the calendar leaves an empty courtroom except for the lawyers arguing the last case.

I guess this is just another forgettable idea. I then thought about encouraging sustained applauds when we take the bench at the opening of the court session. The "APPLAUSE" sign used on Jack Bailey's *Queen for a Day* show might be available on E-Bay. I decided to sleep on this last idea before acting on it but had a terrible nightmare which convinced me to reject that idea as well.

I dreamed I was a lawyer appearing on a law and motion matter. The judge I appeared in front of was me, rudely asking pointed questions. I awoke in a cold sweat. What could be more horrific than me appearing before me? I shuddered and realized neither of us deserved a standing ovation. I suppose this all proves that power, absolute or limited, has little to do with respect. Respect, like anything else worthwhile, must be earned. Doing our work as best we can without thinking about respect is probably the best way to get it. If you think otherwise, you're just dreaming.

WE ALL NEED A MISS LONELY HEARTS

Miss Anne Thrope makes her first appearance in 1992.

Persons of every race, creed, profession and neurosis need to talk about their problems and get advice on how to deal with them. That's why there are advice columns in most major newspapers.

The many suffering people associated with the law profession in particular need such a column. Other channels of expression have proved to be less satisfactory. Psychiatrists are too expensive; fortunetellers too mysterious; talk-radio hosts too insulting; and with the busy signals, it takes forever to get through. Colleagues? Forget it. It is so hard to keep a secret.

There is, however, someone to turn to for advice. It's the same person from whom I sought guidance when I was growing up in the Nathanael West country neat Ivar Street in Hollywood. Her name is Anne Thrope.

She still lives in the old vine-covered bungalow near the Vedanta Temple where Aldous Huxley and Christopher Isherwood attended Sunday services.

When I first sought her counsel, I had limited funds and didn't quite know what to do with them. She advised me to put my money into a law school education and the purchase of Xerox stock. Unfortunately, I didn't have sufficient funds to do both and had to choose. I made the wrong choice. The point is, most of the time she gave me sound practical advice.

Over the years faithful readers of this column have confided in me, revealing their problems, hopes and aspirations. They want answers. Anne Thrope has agreed to help out. Of course, she is quite elderly these days, but when her strength is up, she has promised to answer your letters. I think you'll find Anne's advice is still as useful and sensible as it was when I was a youngster.

Through this column she will periodically offer advice concerning the myriad problems facing people who have any connection with the legal profession. Please send all inquiries to Miss Anne Thrope care of me. What follows is the most recent batch of letters to Miss Anne and her responses.

DEAR MISS THROPE: I'm a deputy D.A. My boss insists that I always ask for the maximum sentence in every case. I don't believe that every case deserves the maximum sentence. The judge says that if I always ask for the most severe sentence in every case I will be in violation of the canons of professional conduct and he will turn me in to the state bar. I'm torn between conscience and job security. If I go before the state bar, should I just tell them I was following orders?

Very truly yours, Perplexed.

DEAR PERPLEXED: IF you opt for the job security, you'll find transcripts of the Nuremberg trials interesting reading.

DEAR MISS ANNE: I'm a judge known to be a tough sentencer. I frankly think everyone needs a taste of prison, and I routinely mete out long prison sentences. I've been taking a lot of flak for this. At first it didn't bother me, but the constant barrage of criticism from lawyers is getting to me. Is this criticism justified or am I just being thin-skinned?

Yours, Thin-Skinned

DEAR THIN-SKINNED: Judges have to do what they think is proper and not be influenced by whiney lawyers. In your case however, some of the criticism may be justified. Those harsh prison sentences are a bit unusual. After all, you're assigned to civil. If you transfer to criminal, there is little chance you will be singled out for criticism.

DEAR MISS ANNE THROPE: I'm a paralegal. I do everything for my boss, like draft volumes of interrogatories and prepare detailed summary-judgment motions that I carefully and accurately research. I do all his trial briefs and jury instructions and buy his jockey shorts. Without me he's rancid horse meat, yet he gets all the credit. Who in the world has it worse than I?

--Yours truly, Unappreciated.

DEAR UNAPPRECIATED: Apparently you haven't heard of the research attorneys who work for the various appellate courts in the state. Their bosses get the credit for their work, but that's not all. They are expected to cure the state budget deficit by taking time off work without pay, and we still expected them to turn out the same amount of work. On top of all this, they still may have their pay reduced even if they take the time off without pay. Many of them are sending resumes to your boss. In the event you lose your job, there may be some openings with the State.

DEAR MS. THROPE: I'm a senior partner in an impressive downtown law firm. This may sound sexist, but I'm enamored of one of the firm's associates. I can't get her tush off my mind. She's learned never to turn her back on me and has threatened to go public if I continue to pester her. What with the Thomas hearings and all, I'm not sure what to do. I feel I've hit rock bottom.

--Sitting it out till I hear from you.

DEAR SITTING IT OUT: Keep on sitting. It's about time you learned that harass is not two words.

DEAR MISS ANNE THROPE: I'm a trial lawyer and in the middle of every night I wake up screaming in my pillow. It's because of all the time limits I have to keep track of. Everywhere I turn there's a statute with a time limit. There are so many days to do this, and so many days to beg for relief. There are so many days in which to move, so many days in which to respond, so many days in which to file, so many days in which to answer, so many days in which to serve, and so many days in which to just think about how many days there are.

When you consider all the files I have, keeping track of these time limits is driving me crazy. I have nightmares in which sanctions take on the form of hideous monsters and tear out my entrails because I missed a time limit. I can't take it anymore. I'd like to do something else, but I'm trained in law, so what else can I do? I'd love to have some cushy job where I could just sit back nonchalantly and let everybody else worry, or better yet, be in a position where I can stir things up so that everyone else worries, but not me. Is there such a job?

--Yours, Ready to go over the edge

DEAR READY TO GO: Apply, or run for a judgeship.

JUDGE NEEDS A LAWYER

Ask lawyers and their clients this question: Judges know the law-true or false? Their answer depends upon whether they won or lost their last case. I'm not even sure what it means to "know the law." In fact, judges often rely on lawyers to educate them about the application of law to the facts of a particular case and hope to discern when they are mis-educated.

But many people think that judges are presumed "to know the law." If judges know the law so well, why do they ask so many questions? "Counsel, would not collateral estoppel apply here?" More often than not this isn't a mere rhetorical device to stimulate discussion. But have you ever heard a judge outside of the courtroom admitting he doesn't know the answer to a question, legal or otherwise? Has anyone ever heard a judge ask a lawyer at a bar function to explain what is a retraxit?

By now dear reader you may have guessed that I am leading up to something. I have a legal problem and I don't know my rights. It is easier to make this admission to you, anonymous reader, than to a person standing before me whose stifled laughter I would notice.

My legal problem can be summed up in one word-CAT, not a tractor or Computerized Axial Tomography, mind you. They at least do some good and they don't scratch furniture. O.K., I am a little upset. So just pretend I am a client sitting across the desk from you. If you are not a lawyer, pretend anyway. If I include facts that are not pertinent, please bear with me. Remember, I am a client.

So here is what happened. We had this cat, Boz. He showed up at the Court of Appeal, a mere kitten, about 16 years ago. So I took him home and he has been with my wife Barbara and me ever since, that is, until he died about a year ago. He was ill, but we made the last several months of his life comfortable. For example, we held off remodeling our house until he passed on. I don't have to tell you how much construction costs had increased when we finally began the project.

After the passage of an appropriate time, we had planned to get another cat to fill the void in our lives left by Boz. If a spouse dies, you don't just go out and get married the next month. But cats are animals, selfish ones at that, and the appropriate grieving period is much shorter than it is for humans. Twenty-four hours is a little tight. So we thought we would wait a week or so.

There must be something in our karma, or maybe it has to do with our astrological signs, or maybe the word goes out in the feline community when there is a vacancy at the Gilbert residence. It never fails: cats always show up on our doorstep just at the time we are contemplating getting one. I don't even know what it means to buy a cat. Do people actually buy cats? I wouldn't be caught dead with an expensive Persian wearing an emerald collar around his neck.

Anyway, as ironic as it seems, a lovely elderly lady who lived up the street died around the same time as Boz. She didn't exactly have a cat, but one lived on her roof for about a year. Her caretaker fed the cat, not on the roof of course. The cat came down to get her meals. During the week they wouldn't let the cat in the house because the caretaker was allergic to cats. But on the weekend the lady's daughter drove up from San Diego to relieve the caretaker who was off Saturday and Sunday. The daughter would let the cat in. I bet that caused havoc with the caretaker when she came back on Monday. But that is neither here nor there.

So when the mother died, the daughter was panicked about what to do with the cat. She wanted to take the cat with her to San Diego, but thought it would be too traumatic, either for her or the cat, I'm not sure which. The daughter begged us to take the cat. She told us that when the cat first showed up it had a collar and a tag with a phone number. When she called, the kid at the other end of the line said they didn't have a cat and hung up. So doesn't that mean it was O.K. for us to take the cat?

I brought the cat over to our house. She, yes, this was a she. We always had males. I can tell you without hesitation male cats are much better tempered than females. I carried her and she actually growled. I bet she thought she was a dog. So I held her tight and brought her into the house. She checked the place out and knew immediately she had a good deal, food, lodging, toys and a medical plan. She purred and meowed and decided right then and there to stay. Simple as that. Barbara even gave her a name. Opus or Oh Puss. Get it?

Opus was temperamental as all get out. But she took to Barbara right away. You would think they were sisters or something. They hung out together all the time, carrying on with their private conversations, snuggling in bed. Most of the time Opus didn't have much use for me, except when she was hungry. I get up earlier than Barbara, and Opus would follow me downstairs for breakfast. That made no sense because we had dry food in her dish at all times. She would look at me and meow for food that was already in her dish. I don't know if this cat was a moron or just liked seeing me do things for her. I didn't even have to put new food in her dish. I just stirred the food around a little and then she would chow down. Go figure.

We bought her a collar and dozens of toys that she drenched in cat spit and left all over the house. She was selfish and egocentric but on occasion thought to redeem herself by reciprocating for our generosity. On various occasions she brought us disemboweled rats, lizards and birds, some still clinging to the last threads of life. That was sweet I suppose, but depositing them on our bed in the middle of the night did not allow for a restful night's sleep.

After close to a year of doting attention, we took her to the vet for a checkup. Yes, she had been "fixed" (a term I find particularly offensive), and the vet tech gave her shots for a cost of $176. I have been told we got off cheap. A few days later Opus went out for an afternoon prowl and simply disappeared. Barbara was heartbroken. We searched the neighborhood, inquired of residents within a two block radius of our home, searched garages and sheds where she might have been trapped. Nothing.

I blamed this loss on coyotes who I was certain had dined on her. But as it turns out, the coyotes did not eat her. Six weeks after her disappearance she shows up, her fur straggly and matted. Although she was grossly overweight, she still begged for a handout. She wore a new collar on which was attached a tag and a phone number. Barbara called the number to inform whoever answered that she or he had our cat and thanks for taking care of her.

The lady at the other end of the line lives on an adjacent street and claims that "Snookie" (her name for Opus), is and always has been her cat who has been missing for (are you ready for this?) two years and she would like to come over and get her. Rather than argue over the telephone, Barbara gave the lady directions to our house and she said she was coming over. An hour later (that's how long it took to find our house which is half a block away), she came in her SUV with her 9 year old daughter who had allegedly been heartbroken over the loss of "Snookie." For two years? Give me a break.

I was ready for some serious negotiations when she whipped out a photo album showing Opus or "Snookie" as a kitten, and then as a mother nursing her young. One of her kittens who is now a grown male, Rex, and still living at his place of birth, was purported to have amorous inclinations towards his mother before she was "fixed." That's cats for you. But to be perfectly honest the photos were convincing. Opus and Snookie are one and the same. No doubt about it. Add to that the presence of a pouting 9 year old daughter and I knew a successful negotiation was as likely as President Bush admitting to a mistake.

In utter defeat I led the mother and daughter upstairs where they scooped up the sleeping Opus, who I think growled. They left with a curt good bye and no offer to pay the recently incurred vet bill. It was obvious that the overweight Opus was not eating proper food. And she had not been brushed since she lived with us. That seemed a good basis for getting her back. I did some research, violating the rule about having an ass for a client, and it was not helpful.

In re Marriage of Isbell, Willoughby (2005) authored last year by my colleague, the now retired Justice Nott, the appellate court concluded that there is no authority in a marital dissolution action, to support who should get custody of Emmit the cat based on the best interest of Emmit. Instead, the court opined the only consideration is whether Emmit is the separate property of the wife. Luckily the opinion is unpublished and therefore not citable.

In another unpublished opinion, my colleagues in Division V were of no use. The justices had their backs up, about whether a cat who bites should be tethered. In *Goldshine v. Lafferty* (2004) the appellate court acknowledged out-of-state authority that holds it is not abnormal for cats to bite under the right circumstances. In *Lee v. Weaver* (1976) 195 Neb. 194 [237 N.W.2d 149] the appellate court found it not surprising that the cat who growled at the housekeeper's vacuum cleaner and broom would one day bite the housekeeper. Opus growled at me and the vacuum cleaner on occasion, but I cannot say she bit me. And this is where George Bush and I are of like mind. I bet he agrees that she would have bitten me if she could. But getting damages for infliction of emotional distress might be a stretch.

Then I found a recent case directly on point. Unfortunately, it is of no use. It's from Texas. In *Willich v. Deastadeai* (Tex.Ct.App. 2006) 183 S.W. 3d 92, defendant found a kitten shivering in the rain and cold in front of their house. He took the cat in and nursed him back to health and incurred vet bills. Two months later, plaintiff, the original owner who lives next door, saw the cat in her neighbors window. Both sides want the cat. Neither will accept money. The justice court ruled in favor of new owner who named the cat "Biscuit." On trial de novo court the County Court ruled in favor of the original owner who named the cat "Sweet Pea" and awards $80 damages. The Court of Appeal ducked the issue by deciding it lacks jurisdiction to hear the case. There might have been a decision if the damages had been at least $100.

I called my friend, the ancient but still wise Miss Anne Thrope who once wrote a legal advice column for the Police Gazette. Her advice was as follows: "Get over it and get on with your life." I don't believe she adequately researched the problem. If you agree with her, please don't bother to write.

THE SHAME OF IT ALL

The other day Boz, my cat, "took a giant dump" on the living room rug. (The colloquial expression in quotes puzzles me. He did not take anything. It is what he left that disturbed me.) I was stunned by this act of betrayal. We have a box in the house filled with unsullied litter for emergencies. Up until the living room incident, Boz had displayed his perversity in less dramatic ways. He does not limit use of the box to emergencies. Better to interrupt his outdoor activities (lengthy siesta is included here as an activity) to pop in the house for a quick visit to the box. Following completion of the mission, he makes perfunctory motions at clean up, rarely accomplishing what I, but apparently not he, consider a thorough job. In the naïve belief that his inattention to details reflects negligence instead of malice, I do not reprimand him. But the living room episode I could not ignore. My disappointment over his unseemly behavior demanded a confrontation. I called Boz into the living room where evidence of the deed was neatly piled in a corner but plainly visible from every part of the living room. "Boz, how could you do this?" I asked. Before he could reply I said, "Bad cat, naughty animal, shame, shame, shame on you." His head was moving up and down, but not in agreement with my assessment of his unbecoming behavior. He was licking himself. It was then that the epiphany struck me like a thunderbolt. He felt no shame. He didn't care, or to be colloquial again, "he didn't give a ****."

In the old days people could endure just about anything but shame. If you felt ashamed, it would be unbearable to look others in the eye. That's why Oedipus switched to Braille. His "shameful" act has become a popular expression of derision, more frequently used by those who have never heard of Sophocles. Like substantial evidence questions, the expression occurs with "rhythmic regularity" in the transcripts of criminal cases.

Today attitudes about shame are different. If I had made my cat wear a sign around his neck that says, "Shame on Me, I pooped in the living room," I doubt that he would have cared, provided the sign did not hamper his movement. That he does not read is beside the point. No one reads these days. But the more pertinent question is: Does anyone feel shame nowadays? If "reality" shows are an indication, the answer is obvious. People eat live bugs and snails, reveal their most vulgar traits, plot against their friends, have sex with strangers, and suffer innumerable humiliations witnessed by millions of enthusiastic viewers. If Hester Prynne were here, she would be doing commercials for the Auto Club.

At first blush (does anyone blush anymore?), shame appears to be an anachronism. But if that is so, why are courts meting out shameful sentences, I mean sentences designed to shame defendants?

In *United States v. Gementera* 379 F.3d 596 (2004) defendant who had stolen mail was ordered to stand in front of a post office for a day wearing a sandwich board sign that said, "I stole mail. This is my punishment" as part of his sentence. At trial, Gementera seemed content with the sentence. On appeal, however, he argued the sentence was not legitimate. It violated contemporary standards of decency and humiliated him. The 9th Circuit saw it differently and affirmed the sentence. The majority acknowledged that the sign condition likely will cause Gementera humiliation or shame, but the condition is reasonably related to rehabilitation, a goal of the federal Sentencing Reform Act. I wonder whether defendant Gementera thought his pilfering letters violated contemporary standards of decency.

In *Demery v. Arpaio* 378 F3d 1020 (2004) the sheriff used "web cams" to stream on the Internet, live images of pretrial detainees in county jail. The 9th Circuit affirmed the district court's grant of a preliminary injunction prohibiting this practice. The appellate court failed to see how turning pretrial detainees into unwilling objects of the latest reality show served any legitimate goal. The practice amounted to unlawful punishment of pretrial detainees. There were dissents in both *Gementera* and *Demery* proving that notions of justice can depend on perception and the right panel. Getting back to Boz, my cat, I require him to wear a collar with a bell. He protests that wearing the collar is humiliating and has filed for injunctive relief. I plan to argue that the bell serves a lofty purpose. It gives unsuspecting birds and mice a warning. It is doubtful the *Demery* court will uphold the constitutionality of the warning bell. The court might acknowledge that the warning bell could save a bird or two, but it could buy into Boz's argument that he is being shamed for a crime he has not even committed. His case is therefore even stronger than that of the pretrial detainees who at least had been arrested for crimes they were accused of committing. True, but I would argue that although Boz is allegedly shamed for a crime he did not yet commit, we can take judicial notice that he most certainly would commit the crime if given the chance. When mice are concerned I think the court will unanimously uphold the use of the bell. I cannot speak to the court's rationale, but I know it will find a way.

If shame is an anachronism, why did Gementera and Arpaio appeal? I think it is because there is a world of difference between choosing to parade one's shameful acts to a jaded public, and quite another to be forced to be shamed in a manner decided by someone else. That can be excruciating. Candid lawyers with unrepressed memories will not forget the humiliating sting inflicted by scornful law professors calling on them with relentless questions for which there were no satisfactory answers. "Shame on the professors," I thought. But were I to shout my indictment from the rooftops it would at best have prompted a yawn.

There is no question that shame can be devastating when one's humiliating act is revealed by others. This happened to me even when I was out of law school and working as a young deputy city attorney. At the time I was trying innumerable "drunk driving" cases. Each morning before court convened, I would stand in the master calendar court and call out the names of the people's witnesses subpoenaed to appear that day. The courtroom was usually filled with police officers, defense attorneys, defendants and witnesses. One person's name appeared on many cases, but he was never there. Day after day I would call out his name loud and clear, "Sid Chemist," (last name pronounced kem-ēast). Police officers invariably cracked up when I called the name of this flakey witness who never showed. My frustration with Sid Chemist was written up in the Police Gazette. That was when I learned that Sid Chemist was the Scientific Investigation Division Chemist who was on call to testify, if needed, to explain the workings of the gas chromatograph intoximeter. Please keep this embarrassing story to yourself.

But judges should be wary of imposing shameful sentences, I mean shaming sentences. One California judge since retired, ordered a beer thief to wear for one year a T-shirt on which was boldly written, "I am on felony probation," and "My record plus two six packs equals four years." The Court of Appeal in *People v. Hackler* 13 Cal.App.4th 1049 (1993) disallowed the order reasoning that the T-shirt just might not favorably impress prospective employers, thus defeating defendant's rehabilitation. In another case, unpublished, the same judge sentenced a woman convicted of beating her children, to wear a contraceptive Norplant device as a condition of probation. The case caused an outcry from civil liberties groups. I was curious to know what Boz thought about the case. To give him a balanced view, I presented the judge's rationale for the sentence. The defendant was a drug addict and already had five children taken away from her. The judge was merely trying to protect a child not yet conceived from brutality and neglect. I asked Boz what he thought about the probation condition. He jumped out of my lap. I heard him scratching away in his box.

THE "WHO'S WHO" BOOK

Everyone's a victim- even lawyers and judges. We, like everyone else, have succumbed to the irresistible pull of the *Who's Who* book.

Enterprising book publishers have pandered to our vanity. A note from the publisher informs us that we are so special that we have been selected (along with 184,000 other important people) for inclusion in this special book.

Lawyers are particularly vulnerable. Lawyers in Los Angeles, who because of their sheer number, feel like just another wildebeest on the Serengeti Plain, will do almost anything for recognition. Some submit their names and a check for inclusion in a book listing out of town lawyers. They rationalize that this will be good for business. You can never tell when someone in Dubuque, Iowa needs a lawyer in Sherman Oaks.

The lawyers create a profile through answers to the publisher's questionnaire. The questions prompt them to sift through all the minutiae of their lives that even their parents find trivial. They convince themselves that offices they held in grammar school, will impress clients. The more imaginative credit themselves with winning once in a lifetime awards. Once the questionnaire is completed, the difference between the profile concocted and the real person makes Dorian Gray and his portrait seem like twins in comparison.

Judges are similarly caught in the *Who's Who* trap. The publisher in Tuscaloosa, for example, will urge you to send in your profile along with $27.95 for your copy of *Judges in the United States*. Well, you can never tell when someone in Salem, Albuquerque or Canoga Park may get the urge to know what you did in high school. Of course lawyers and judges are easy targets. They have big egos and they belong to a group. Anyone associated with a group is a prime target for a *Who's Who* book. It's no use to protest that you hate groups and would never join one. You have already admitted that you belong to the group that hates groups. You are facing the same dilemma as the man who refuses to make a choice. He has made a choice not to make a choice. There is no escape.

It's particularly annoying to belong to a group you would rather forget you belong to. For example, when I turned 50, the American Association of Retired Persons hounded me to join, emphasizing that it only costs $5. Never mind that I am not retired, and don't intend to be retired for years to come.

They sent letters, telegrams and even had an old lady tailing me. They were persistent. I finally joined and now get *Modern Maturity*, a magazine with ads for walkers, bed pans, surgical stockings and vitamin supplements. I also receive announcements for books on such related subjects as impotence, incontinence, and forgetfulness.

Publishers realize that people like to feel important. That's why they buy books in which their names appear. Soon there will be books listing people who have a gold Visa Card. The need for recognition is so overpowering that I fear publishers will soon prey upon people who belong to groups they would not reveal to their analyst or best friends. But seeing one's name in a book, may be worth making the revelation public. We may soon see books profiling people because of their body types or attributes. The Book of: The Fat, The Stingy, The Morose, are just a few examples. Even three seconds of fame may be worth the trouble.

Lawyers and judges are not immune from this primal need. This gives publishers a large base of potential subscribers in the legal profession. Trial and appellate courts have been enforcing the two and three-year statutes so that cases are dismissed with monotonous regularity. This ostensibly reduces the number of cases, but in fact increases them because of the malpractice suits that follow.

From this phenomenon will emerge a new genre, the *Who's Who* books of malpractice. There will be books listing those lawyers who represented plaintiffs, those lawyers who represented defendants and those lawyers who were defendants. As the group expands, one can envision limitless categories into which to divide the books. *Judgments Over and Under $100,000* would make a nice two-book set.

The dark side of *Who's Who* books will touch judges as well. For trial judges, there will be books listing those who have received affidavits of prejudice more than 34 times in one month, or have reversed more than 30 times per year.

For state appellate justices, a book listing judges with more than five opinions depublished in a month would make a nice volume for any sturdy book stand. A book listing appellate justices with 10 or more grammatical errors in a single paragraph during the past year should be a good seller.

I could go on, but I have to get back to my questionnaire.

MEMORIES ARE MADE OF THIS
PART I

Before entering law school I asked a seasoned lawyer who was a family friend for advice about how to succeed in law school. "Sharpen your memory," he advised. "It's all about memory." True, that, and as far as I can remember, a few other things. That was forty-seven years ago. I thought that with over four decades of practice I would have the memory thing down. I'm not so sure. At a bar function a lawyer will come up and talk about a case he or she argued in front of me, God knows when. He or she will either apologize for a gaffe, or boast about a win, and I don't have the foggiest recollection of the case or the lawyer. I can usually get by with a smile and a nod.

When caught in a memory lapse, I usually rely on a dictum of the late Judge Jerry Pacht. "For every case name or statute I remember, I forget a line of poetry." That usually blunts criticism of my forgetfulness.

But however one's memory may lapse or play tricks, there are certain events in one's past that are permanently etched in one's brain. I remember vividly Dean Prosser decapitating a student sitting next to me in my torts class. Prosser's words encased in a trick question (they were all trick questions), flew threw the air like razor sharp blades, followed by others in succession that cleanly sliced through the student's neck so that his head teetered, then dropped silently into his lap. At the end of the class I remember him carrying his head under his arm. I leaned down and asked him how it felt. "Don't ask," he said. By the end of the semester he had learned to answer Prosser's questions correctly and with alacrity. I recall the Dean commenting that the student had finally screwed his head back on.

And I have vivid memories of my jury duty stint some thirteen years ago which inspired my Daily Journal column in 1994 entitled, "We Will Thank and Excuse Juror No. 4." That was an experience hard to forget when you are Juror No. 4. Another article in the Daily Journal about lawyer Tom Rubin, who also does stand-up comedy, reminded me that Tom and I met during that time when he was also on jury duty. Tom witnessed my downcast mien as I ignominiously shuffled out of the jury box. He cracked some jokes about it, which I bet he uses in his act

The foregoing incidents I remember with crystal clarity, but lately my self-confidence is shaken. Because of two recent events, I feel like the protagonist in the movie, *Memento*. This has caused me to question how reliable are witnesses' memories when relating past events.

About ten years ago our traveling judge educator and good will ambassador, Los Angeles Superior Court Judge Judy Chirlin, and I taught a week-long course to Serbian Judges at a judicial institute in Prague. At a cocktail reception the Czech government gave in our honor, I met an elegant lady from one of the cultural ministries. We spent some time conversing about her work, her children and her husband who also worked in government.

Several years later, I attended a concert in Los Angeles featuring the Schulhoff String Quartet from Prague in which my close friend's son-in-law, Jonas Krejci, played the cello. Who was sitting next to me?--the lady from the cultural ministry I met years earlier- or so I thought. She was charming and elegant, just as she had been when we met in Prague. I recalled our meeting but she asserted with certainty, tempered by tact, that we had never met. She protested that she was not in Prague when I was there. "We couldn't have met," she said, and gently squeezing my arm insisted that if we had met she would definitely have remembered me. That little white lie did nothing to ease my apprehension. Was I losing my mind? I remember her so distinctly and yet she insisted we never met. Our faces were locked in mutual smiles, only mine was through clenched teeth. My friends who witnessed the exchange were also smiling. How could I explain this was no smiling matter?

It was so frustrating. There we were, two people with different memories of something that did or did not happen, and there was no one to help resolve the issue. I suddenly knew how frustrating it must be to a witness facing a skeptical fact finder in a trial. Here I was, a witness with a story contradicted by another witness. Yet, I believe my friends who heard the exchange between us found me sincere, but not credible.

Another incident came up a few months ago which left me in a similar quandary. I write about it in the hope that some reader of this column may shed light on the facts which I now relate. Interestingly enough, the event like the preceding one, involves music.

Let's go back to law school in Berkeley where I was honing my memory skills. The year was 1960, maybe 1961. Please dear reader, do not draw hasty inferences. The exact year is not necessary to the story. At various times during that period, three wonderful pianists of the 20th Century each gave concerts at the Harmon gym. The first was Rudolph Serkin. A friend of mine, Adrian Ruiz, had studied with him at the Curtis Institute. To impress my date, I had the temerity to take her back- stage at intermission to meet Serkin. I gained entry by stating I had a message from Adrian Ruiz who in fact I had not seen for a few years. Serkin graciously ushered us into his makeshift dressing room and warmly shook my hand. I told him Adrian sends his regards and he thanked me for stopping by. I don't remember my date's name and Rudolph Serkin passed on years ago, passing the mantle to his immensely talented son Peter. I have no way of proving the backstage meeting occurred, but under most circumstances I would not have to. Most people would be inclined to accept the truth of this unremarkable story.

But the two other concerts left me wondering about a noteworthy incident that occurred at one of those concerts. The pianists were Sviatoslav Richter and Glenn Gould. I attended the two concerts with a dear friend, let's call her D. We have recently renewed our acquaintance and in reminiscing about the past, we have similar recollections about what happened at one of those concerts. We disagree, however, at which concert the incident occurred.

This is what happened. The pianist strode onto to the stage, held his tails behind him as he sat down at the piano bench. He contemplated the keys for a few seconds and then threw himself into a Haydn Piano Sonata. After about 10 seconds he abruptly stopped and began inspecting parts of the Steinway. The audience was silent. Not a sound could be heard other than the creak of the piano bench as the pianist shifted his weight and looked intently at the piano, for what? the source of a vibration? a squeak? Suddenly he tore from the piano a strip of wood just below the keyboard that ran the length of the keyboard. He dropped the board which hit the floor with a clatter. Not a peep from the audience. He began playing the Haydn piece again. After a few seconds he stopped and renewed his search. This time he stood up and peered into the area of the sounding board. His tails were draped over the piano bench, his tall frame bent at a 45 degree angle from his waist so that he looked like a praying mantis. He found something in the interior of the piano which he flung across the stage. A sound like an active beehive buzzed throughout the gym.

For the third time the pianist began the Haydn piece. And again he stopped after three or four seconds. This time he slid the music stand off the top of the piano and threw the unwieldy thing which hit the floor with a jarring bang. I, along with the audience, broke into spontaneous applause. Some cheered. I was in whole- hearted agreement with D who suggested that demolishing the piano could seriously hamper completion of the concert. But the remainder of the concert went on without incident and the pianist received a 10 minute standing ovation at the conclusion of his encore.

So which pianist tore the instrument apart? In my mind there is no question. It was Richter. Dee insists it was Gould. She appears to rely on logic to support her point. "You know how eccentric Gould is," she said with a tone of admonishment. She is right that Gould is eccentric. In fact during his concert, he sang loudly while playing and conducted himself whenever he had a free hand. But I clearly remember that, unlike Richter, he had the music in front of him. It was pasted on large pieces of cardboard stacked on the music stand. He dropped each piece of cardboard noiselessly on the floor as the concert progressed. I reminded D that it could not be Gould, because Richter had thrown the music stand on the floor. She found my point unconvincing.

I approach this dispute like I would a case. Of course I would like to be right, but I am more interested in getting the right answer. That is the responsibility of any good judge. D said I would be hard-pressed to prove which one of us was right. I tried the internet and old newspaper reviews and had no success. But a few weeks ago I was relating the story to a friend, Joan Booke, and she reminded me that she had attended Berkeley in the 60's and was present at the concert where the piano was torn apart. She remembered exactly what happened, because as she pointed out, one does not forget such a unique experience. Could she be mistaken about which of the two pianists abused the Steinway? It is unlikely because she attended only one of the two concerts. I will tell you which concert Joan attended, but I must withhold that information for another column.

Although I take comfort in getting close to the truth, I yearn for something even closer than a near certainty. I would like some corroboration. If anyone reading this column has attended one of those concerts of which I speak, and can provide information leading to the identity of the irate pianist, please contact me at your earliest convenience. He or she will receive honorable mention in a future column, and I will make a contribution to legal aid.

There is comfort in getting close to the truth, what we strive for in our trials. In the meantime, I have been relaxing and listening to Dick Hyman's rendition of a wonderful song by the late Eubie Blake. It's called *"Memories of You."*

MEMORIES ARE MADE OF THIS
PART II

We explored memory's fallibility in the preceding column, remember? We learned that memory carries with it awesome responsibility. It can uplift one to heights of ecstasy, but its destructive force can plunge one into the abyss. It can destroy reputations, opportunities, even life itself. DNA evidence has proven memory wrong. Yet, however faulty and confused, memory often asserts its claim with certainty and arrogance. Judges take note.

In my last column we pondered how to resolve the clash of memories concerning whether it was the pianist Sviatoslav Richter or Glenn Gould who dismantled the Steinway at the beginning of a concert at the Harmon Gym on Cal's campus in Berkeley in the early 1960's. In this column we marshal the evidence that ineluctably leads us to the answer.

As you recall, my friend, who I called D to protect her privacy, and I attended a piano recital at the Harmon gym in 1960 or 1961 (as I shall explain we now know it was 1960),where the demolition occurred. Our respective memories agree on that.

Incidentally, D, who upon reading my last column informed me that the childish use of the letter "D," her nickname, to protect her privacy, which needed no protection in this matter, was unnecessary. Apparently she is not a Franz Kafka fan. So, in this column I shall refer to her as Deena, her name, but with no assurance that after she reads this column, she might have preferred I stick with "D."

Deena acknowledged that I accurately described the details of the manner in which the destruction took place. Up to this point our memories are in, please forgive me, perfect harmony. It is to the question, "Which pianist savaged the Steinway?" that Deena's memory and mine take divergent paths, and that could make all the difference. One memory leads to a faithful recreation of the past; the other to an imagined reality existing only in neurons, synapses and memory cells on sabbatical. Deena says the pianist was Gould, "You know how eccentric he is." I say it was Richter, no buttressing argument necessary; that is what I remember.

We spend two columns on this quirky event because the underlying issues involve the lifeblood of our justice system, memory. This is something of far greater consequence than Maurice Chevalier and Hermione Gingold singing "I Remember It Well" from the musical Gigi. Trials attempt to recreate events of the past based to a large degree on memory. Pity the poor litigants, the facts of whose cases depend primarily on memory. If Deena and I were the only witnesses in a trial to determine which pianist desecrated the Steinway, how would the trier of fact judge our credibility? We are both sincere and certain.

At the conclusion of this column I will render my decision on who was the unruly pianist. In the ensuing discussion I reveal a rare glimpse into a judge's decision making process so that attorneys, litigants, and the public will appreciate the effort and care judges take in reaching the "right" decision. Some might protest that it is unseemly for me to render a decision in a case in which I am a witness, that the decision will be tainted, uncitable, and subject to ridicule. I will not argue the point. I only ask that you consider the facts that I faithfully relate with scrupulous accuracy and decide whether the decision is correct. If the Supreme Court reverses on a technicality, or even worse depublishes it, we still will know what happened.

In concluding my last column, in a plea for help, I tried to resolve this conundrum for the trier of fact. The person or persons who provided information leading to a resolution of the dispute would receive honorable mention in this column and I would make a contribution to legal aid. I received numerous e-mails from a variety of people who were not shy about sharing their views even though most had not been at either concert. A piano dealer said it had to be Gould because the act would be consistent with his personality. Many others agreed with this assessment.

You might also recall that in my previous column I said I was speaking one evening with some friends about the incident, and Joan Booke chimed that she had attended the concert and remembers quite clearly who the pianist was. I withheld disclosing what Joan said because I did not want to influence anyone who might contact me with the information I sought. Now I will reveal what Joan Booke said: "It was Richter." She remembered the event quite clearly and she also remembered that she had not attended the Gould concert.

I sent my column to Deena, and she called me to assert once again that I was wrong about the concert. I told her of Joan Booke's recollection and Deena reminded me that I, a judge, should realize that witnesses' memories are often faulty. I suggested that this insight also applied to her. I acknowledged that recollection is often flawed, but that Joan was an independent witness who had not been coached. Moreover, she had no interest in the outcome of the dispute and gently chided me for pursuing the issue. "Why not just let Deena believe she is right, and leave it at that? Is it so important for you to be right?" I told Joan that however self-serving it may sound, my goal was not to be "right," though it would be a comfort to know my memory was grounded in fact rather than imagination. I was in pursuit of the truth and a decision on the merits.

Another wrinkle in this case is that Deena is relatively certain she did not attend the Richter concert. And Joan is certain that she did not attend the Gould concert. And I am certain I attended both concerts, and absolutely certain that Deena and I had attended the Richter concert together, and moderately certain we had also gone together to the Gould concert.

It is also noteworthy that Deena and I remember exactly what occurred during each of the three episodes when various parts of the piano were removed, and the audience's reactions. She even remembers her remark to me that the piano will be in shambles by the end of the concert.

As the weeks passed after publication of my column more people came forward with the fruits of their research. Joan's husband, my good friend, arbitrator Frederick Booke, informed me that the concert took place at the Harmon Gym on November 13, 1960, at the end of Richter's American tour that began in the New York earlier in the year. Last month I appeared on a CEB panel on Evidence. At the end of the program a lawyer came up to speak to me, not about hearsay, but to inform me that her research revealed that 1960 was the year that Glenn Gould stopped giving concerts. Yes, I was not sure whether the concert had occurred in 1961 or 1960. As you shall see, that small uncertainty is of no moment. Music critic and writer Gene Lees told me that he knew Gould quite well in Canada, and opined that however eccentric Gould was, he would never tear apart a piano. Lees said that Gould was not a violent person and would not commit an act of violence even against an inanimate object, particularly a piano.

But then a breakthrough occurred when I recently received an e-mail from Law Professor Paul McKaskle. He was dean for many years at University of San Francisco Law School where he still teaches a variety of courses. This includes Evidence, which he taught as a visiting professor at Boalt Hall. Now, he ought to know what he is talking about.

He and his wife Ellen attended the Glenn Gould concert at the Harmon gym in 1960. But in 1960 they were not married and did not know each other. They independently remember that Gould, "full of peculiarities," did not lay hands on the Steinway other than to touch its keys. This compelling evidence brings the case to a close. With publication of this column I will send my check in the amount of $200 in honor of Professor Paul McKaskle and his lovely wife to Public Counsel, the law firm in Los Angeles that renders pro bono legal services to the poor.

Deena called me again to see how my research was coming and I told her that I thought the evidence produced by Joan Booke, and Professor McKaskle and his wife compelled a ruling in my favor. Deena graciously agreed. She found it puzzling, however, if not disturbing, that she could be wrong about something she remembers so vividly. That approximates how I would have felt had the evidence pointed to Gould. Indeed, such a revelation can engender acute distress. If parts of our past are the product of mistaken recall or imagination, then that can call into question who we think we are in the present.

I am convinced beyond a reasonable doubt that my decision is correct, but the outcome of this case gives me no satisfaction, other than a momentary sigh of relief. Deena's acknowledgement that her memory had apparently failed her gave me a pang of regret. Would it have been just as well for Deena to believe as she did without my meddling? No. I know Deena, and I am convinced that she, like me, believes the pursuit of the truth is more important than being right.

And that is what judges must do all the time. They must make reasoned decisions even when they are not pleased with the outcome. All we can do is get as close to the truth as possible, and decide whether a party has met his or her burden of proof. And I am not convinced of the correctness of my opinion beyond all doubt. I am not convinced of anything beyond all doubt, including my existence. But if some additional evidence should reveal that it was not Richter after all who violated the Steinway, you can trust me to reverse myself.

PERCEPTION GAP

This was written when John Ashcroft was Attorney General. Not much has changed.

I am not yet eligible for Medicare but people periodically ask, "So when are you going to retire?" How periodic? I don't remember. There are so many things crammed into my brain that require my attention, things like "retraxit," that seldom do I have immediate recall of less important things. Oh, I just remembered how periodic--about two to three times a week. What was the question again?

There is a perception among some that when you reach a certain age you are supposed to retire and do something else, or sit in the park and drool. Not me. I can drool in my chambers just as well as any other place.

Age does not necessarily prevent us from doing our jobs well. Of course it depends on the job. But one thing that may change with age is perception. Besides not seeing or hearing as well as we once did, we see things differently. Take for example, W.E. Hill's drawing entitled, "My Wife and My Mother-in-Law," which appeared in *Puck* magazine in 1915. In his famous illustration Hill merged these two ladies, who no doubt were an important part of his life, into one image. But the drawing depicts two singularly different people. Look at it from one angle and you see a profile of his lovely wife; look at it from a different angle and you see his mother-in-law, an old hag with a long crooked nose and a slit of a mouth. When I had seen the drawing in the past I could discern the two distinct and widely different persons. Not anymore. Now, I see only the young woman. The more I try, the less I am able to connect with the older woman. Maybe that is because I am getting older and don't want to admit it.

Along with many other artists, Jasper Johns has incorporated Hill's drawing into a 1985 painting of his own that is untitled. Recently, I looked at Hill's drawing reproduced in a corner of Johns' painting. I looked at it up close and from far away. I moved from one side to the other. I ordered my mind to relax and not to preconceive. "Just let it happen," I ordered. Stubborn as always, my mind set its limited sight on a narrow focus, folded its arms in defiance, and saw only the attractive young wife.

The ability to perceive may change with age, but often established perceptions become solidified. This becomes problematic when different people perceive things differently. I suppose that is why there are dissents in judicial opinions. My colleagues, who are reasonable, intelligent people (most of the time), do not always see things the same way I do. What is wrong with them?

But some perceptions are truly bizarre- depending on your perception. Attorney General John Ashcroft said he would like to try suspected terrorists who are not citizens in secret military tribunals with no right to appeal. Putting the merits of his position aside for the moment, what is of interest is his perception of those who think this approach might be a violation of due process. He said, "To those who scare peace loving people with phantoms of lost liberty, my message is this, your tactics only aid terrorists." In other words, if you care to preserve democracy then you aid the enemy. Some have perceived Ashcroft's admonition as an accusation that his critics are, in fact, the enemy. Ashcroft, no doubt, perceives his warning as necessary to protect democracy. Others perceive him as choosing to kill democracy to preserve it.

I suppose this shows that perception is in the mind of the perceiver. But a good command of the facts makes misperception less likely, and agreement among the perceivers more likely. This has taught me to be careful before jumping into the embarrassment of a misperception. Here is a case in point: In my neighborhood, film companies often do "shoots." They offer big bucks to shoot scenes around the exterior and within the interior of a homeowner's house. Never mind that they often destroy the house, and that Disney will sell the rights to "Fantasia" before the insurance company pays for the damage. They take over the neighborhood with their trucks, catering vans and mobile dressing rooms.

During the actual shoot, off-duty police officers dutifully block the street and hold up traffic. A platoon of camera women and men, grips, technicians, best boys and assistants to assistants, scurry around the street and surrounding shrubs to help film a few seconds of a person walking out the front door of the house to his car.

Not long ago, it seemed as though a major studio had taken over the neighborhood. I was late for court. The off-duty police officer, sitting smugly on his motorcycle in the middle of the street just around the corner from my house, held up his hand and, with a smile, stopped me. "It will only be a few minutes," he assured me. Wielding the enormous power of a presiding justice, I waited. What else could I do? I support my local off-duty police officers. While waiting, I watched an action shot. An actor opened the driver's door of an SUV. This infuriated me. Was I going to be late for court because of a commercial? Finally the officer waved me on. I arrived at court just in time for a day of grueling oral argument. The lawyers were particularly aggressive, mercilessly taunting the rotating panels of justices. We could hardly get in a question or two. That evening I lectured to a local bar association on the pitfalls of motions for retraxit. At the conclusion of my presentation, the bar president announced to the attendees that they would lose MCLE credits.

I came home dog tired. I couldn't believe it. They were still shooting the movie. The lights and noise would have kept Rip awake. I got ready for bed. I knew that there were rules prohibiting evening shoots in residential neighborhoods and I expected things to quiet down momentarily. They did not. I put on my bathrobe and marched the half block to the house where the movie was being shot. Numerous police officers were milling around the sidewalk and lawn in front of the house.

I swaggered over to them, imagining my bathrobe was a judicial robe. "You are going to have to do something to stop this," I said in an authoritative voice. "We can't," said one of the officers, fingering his baton. "Of course you can," I said. "We really can't," said another. Forgetting the most basic trial lawyer axiom, I asked a question, the answer to which I did not know. "Why not?" The officer with the baton pressed it against the plastic brim of his hat. "Because we are actors and no one will listen to us," he said. If only I had known the facts this embarrassing misperception would not have occurred.

The director came over and asked if she could help me. She was pleased that I had perceived the actors as real police officers. We settled everything right there. I got a part in the movie. I took the part of a judge. I wound up on the cutting room floor. I wasn't convincing.

Here is another example of a misperception involving my wife. She threatened me with great bodily injury if I related this story, so please do not tell her. My wife was in a bank in Beverly Hills where there is a life-like sculpture of a security guard. She asked him a question. She is still offended that he did not answer.

The law, which deals with language and values that are by nature indeterminate, will of necessity be subject to a variety of interpretations and perceptions no matter how well one knows the facts. Last summer, along with others, I taught a course to Serbian judges entitled "Judging in a Democratic Society". Serbia is seeking admission into the European Union. No country seeking admission to the union may have the death penalty. The Serbian judges could not understand how we, with our highly developed notions of due process and constitutional safeguards, could have the death penalty. They perceived a contradiction. Many in this country perceive no contradiction and perceive no need to even consider the perceptions of anyone with whom they disagree.

The years have taught me not to cling too tightly to my own cherished perceptions. Growth comes from an understanding that perceptions can vary. If you are curious to know what it is like not to be aware of this fundamental perception, just ask the security guard.

WHAT GOES AROUND COMES AROUND-SOMETIMES

A few months ago I spoke at the investiture of Federal District Court Judge Valerie Baker Fairbank. One of the other speakers, a retired senior partner from a well-known law firm, praised Judge Fairbank for her intelligence and keen intellect. He admired her work on the Los Angeles Superior Court. He noted that when she had presided in Law and Motion, she read all the cases he had cited in his brief. I can tell you that got me and all the judges in the audience thinking.

After that revelation, I will even glance through a law review now and then. The other day, while leafing through an old issue of the *California Law Review*, I came across a glowing review of Professor John Hetland's book on Real Estate Secured Transactions. Professor Hetland is the world's expert on the subject. He was also my professor at law school. And that got me thinking about the last episode of the Sopranos.

In the final scene we see Tony Soprano and his family dining in an Italian restaurant. From previous episodes we know his life is imploding. He is getting older; he has money problems; he has had a rival killed. Suspicious looking people come in and out of the restaurant and pass his table. Will he be shot right there in front of his family? The tension builds. Just when you think something momentous is about to happen, the screen goes dark. As you curse the cable company, the credits show up on the screen. The dark screen reminds you that this is a show that reflects, but is not real life. And like real life there is no tidy end. Stephan Sondheim explored this experience in his musical "*Into the Woods.*" What happens to some of the characters in fairy tales that seemingly end well? Jack, from *Jack and the Beanstalk*, *Cinderella* and *Little Red Riding Hood* appear to have happy endings. But what about their lives after the "end" of the story? They, like all of us, continue to live in an uncertain world where we are never really out of the woods.

It is the same with trials. They seemingly bring closure to disputes. But even after appeals, reversals, and remands, when the judgment is finally final, is that truly the end? What happens after the lawsuit? Is the judgment collectible? What happens to the parties? For better or worse, their lives go on. So what does this have to do with Professor Hetland? Running across his name reminded me that our lives are more a continuing saga than a series of distinct dramas with discrete endings.

More than four decades ago I was biting my arm in his secured transactions class. That's what I used to do when I was scared. So what was there to be scared of? Hetland, I mean Professor Hetland, was a nice guy, relaxed and easy going. My fear was engendered by the certainty that I did not understand secured transactions. During his lecture Professor Hetland would casually throw a piece of chalk up in the air. It seemed to hang in the air before landing in his palm. It reminded me of an early scene in Stanley Kubrick's film, "2001: A Space Odyssey." A primitive tribe, our ancestors, defeats another tribe in a fight. In triumph, a member of the winning tribe throws into the air an animal bone he used as a weapon to kill a member of the lesser intelligent tribe. The bone rises in the air in slow motion and then becomes a space ship floating through space, millions of years later. This is yet another example that endings are illusory.

But getting back to Hetland. As he lectured he took small steps back and forth in a kind of fox trot, all the while nonchalantly throwing into the air his chalk. I was mesmerized. That chalk was my psyche . . . and chalk breaks easily. One day in the middle of his fox trot he stopped and asked a question. It was about *A* conveying property to *B*, but *C* claims to be a bona fide purchaser. " In a 'race notice jurisdiction,' who prevails?" Instantly I was bewildered. How could letters convey property? There was a short pause after Hetland's question – followed by "Mr. Gilbert?" I muttered two words. The first word was "Oh." My heart raced. My palms sweated. My answer---it was not the right answer. Why did I not have the right answer? Because I did not know what the hell Professor Hetland was talking about. Not his fault.

That appeared to be the end of an inconsequential drama one afternoon in law school. After class that afternoon I went to my job at the Lawrence National Laboratory in the hills of Berkeley. I drove a bus around the complex and picked up astro- physicists, mathematicians, and other smart guys and women with slide rules (that's what they used in those days). I dropped them off at various buildings and at the end of the day took them back to campus. I was sure they could figure out what Professor Hetland was talking about.

I felt bad about not having the right answer to the question. That four other students called on after me also failed to give the right answer gave me little solace. Dwelling upon my poor performance in class, I made a sharp turn around a corner of the building that housed something important --the cyclotron. I bent the bus's fender when I clipped it on a railing adjacent to the building. Damn! Two rotten things in one day. Incidentally, I did pass the class, law school, and the bar.

Would I ever again have contact with Professor Hetland and secured transactions? I thought not, but we are not authors of our life's story. Who would have ever thought I would come to have a hand in shaping the law in California? I bet not Professor Hetland. And who would ever think that some 20 years later Professor Hetland and I would meet up again. I was on the appellate panel hearing a case involving a big land deal. You guessed it. John Hetland was lead attorney for the appellants. Only this time the conveyances were made by real people not letters, and I would be asking the questions. I said to myself, "It's payback time." Of course I would be fair, but I could not help but think that "what goes around comes around." I lay awake nights dreaming up impossible questions for Professor Hetland. There would be no throwing of chalk in the air.

Finally the day of oral argument arrived. We took our seats on the bench and the case was called. And there was Professor Hetland. He looked the same. Doesn't this guy ever age? He looked cool and unflappable. I imagined in Professor Hetland's attic a hideous portrait of him, years older, a twisted depraved visage looking malevolently at the world. I redirected my attention to the courtroom as the ageless Professor Hetland approached the lectern to address the court. Immediately it became clear that that day in class years earlier was not the "end" of the story. And then it happened. It was so . . . so involuntary. My heart began racing and my palms were sweating. I stammered out some questions, but he handled them like Rod Laver returning an easy serve. Nothing had changed. I still didn't know what the hell he was talking about. But later, as I reviewed my notes on Professor Hetland's argument, I understood the issues -- I think. Professor Hetland won.

DOGGONE IT

Doggone it (a euphemism for what I'm thinking). To stay with the metaphor, I am dogged by complaints of people I know unleashing on me their dissatisfaction with perceived misdeeds of the judiciary. Not my misdeeds, mind you, but those of others. They are barking up the wrong tree. Is every law abiding ethical CEO responsible for the Enron scandal? Is any judge responsible for the decisions of other judges? How, I ask you can I be held accountable for the occasional miscreant who appears on the scene?

Case in point. People are still complaining to me about the "judge" who several weeks ago, ordered a victim of spousal abuse seeking a restraining order to leave his court or risk arrest and deportation. Well, first of all, he was not a sitting judge. He was a Pro Tem, an attorney volunteering his time to "help out " the Los Angeles Superior Court with its case load. It appears he didn't help the court, the victim or enhance the public's perception of how the court dispenses justice. But the Los Angeles Superior Court acted with alacrity. It figuratively ordered him to leave the courtroom, or more specifically, it removed him from the list of pro tem judges. The victim who the judge pro temp ordered to leave the courthouse, ultimately had her day in court and another judge granted her request for a restraining order. So a mistake was rectified and justice done. And I hope the public understands that this one isolated incident is not a reflection on the dedicated attorney volunteers who offer their expertise and devote their time to help the court.

Glad to get that off my chest. But on second thought, I know about this incident only because I read about it. Judges are supposed to hear all sides of the story before making a decision and here I am making a judgment without hearing the pro tem's side of the story. True, he used bad judgment, but could his motivation have been benign? He is reported to have mistakenly believed that he was helping the victim by alerting her to the possibility of arrest.

So why have I considered the sliver of a possibility that the ex judge pro tem may have had a plausible explanation for his actions? I think it is because judges of all stripes often take it on the chin for their misunderstood rulings. I remember back some thirty years ago, when I was a municipal court judge. Despite the awesome power we judges wielded in deciding misdemeanors, one thing struck terror in our hearts, the Appellate Department of the Superior Court.

Its presiding judge, now a distinguished judge on the 9th Circuit, Judge Arthur Alarcon reminded us that for all intents and purposes the Appellate Department was our Supreme Court. That alone was enough to scare the daylights out of us. At this time, before word processors were in use in the court system, I thought the opinions were prepared and mimeographed by the typing class at Le Conte Jr. High School. "The left turn was safe. Reversed."

I recall the time a commissioner's finding of guilt on a traffic infraction was reversed by the Appellate Department. The appeal by a pro per defendant stated adequate grounds for reversal. The defendant also alleged that the commissioner made numerous inappropriate comments during the trial. The Appellate Department's opinion stated that if the allegations were true, the commissioner's conduct was unacceptable. But the alleged conduct had not been proved, much less shown anywhere in the record. I knew this commissioner and it was inconceivable to me that he could be guilty of these allegations.

This is just another indication that a judge's judicial life is not a bed of roses. Even judges who have passed away are not free from criticism. The famous Judge Charles Fricke who died in 1958 is still taking heat for the trial he conducted in the famous Sleepy Lagoon case in 1942 on which the musical *Zoot Suit* is based. (*People v. Zammora* 66 Cal.App.2nd 166 (1966). The *Los Angeles Times* recently devoted an article to him. (August 20, 2006) My friend Alice McGrath who assisted the defendants and their counsel during the trial argues that the manner in which Fricke tried the case reflected bias. Enter again my colleague Judge Alarcon who had tried numerous cases before Fricke, and read the trial transcript. He disagreed with this assessment, and points out that the reversal by the Court of Appeal was not based on bias or racism but error in the admission of evidence. The appellate court found the evidence insufficient to show defendants conspired to commit murder. (*Id.*, at pp. 201-202.) The appellate court also chastised Judge Fricke for disparaging remarks he made about defense counsel in the jury's presence. (*Id.*, at p. 215.)

Interestingly Judge Fricke's name appears in an article in the Spring/Summer 2005 newsletter of the California Supreme Court's Historical Society. The engrossing article by Kathleen Cairns is about the conviction in 1935 of Nellie May Madison for the murder of her husband. But for a commutation of her sentence by then Governor Merriam, she would have been the first woman to receive the death penalty in California. Judge Fricke was the trial court judge and actually testified for the prosecution. The Supreme Court in *People v. Madison* 3 Cal.2d 671 (1935) approved of Fricke's conduct. It was proper for him to testify for the prosecution concerning a witness's statements about the interval between gun shots, because that testimony "did not appear in the record and the trial court timed it." (*Id.*, at p. 679.) Lest we be too quick to condemn Fricke, Ms. Cairns points out that the decision tells us much "about judicial attitudes and procedures in the 1930s."

But trial judges can be reversed, and on occasion chided by some uppity court of appeal. Even a graciously written reversal can be devastating to any judge. Recently I was reversed by the California Supreme Court. I was more shocked than upset. When I received the Supreme Court opinion, I said aloud to no one in particular, "Doggone it. How could seven intelligent people all be wrong?"

Just as I was about to howl about my sentiments, I thought back to what I had just said aloud. "Doggone it." Of course that was it. What every misunderstood judge should have. A dog. Dogs don't care about reversals or even affirmances. They are there for you no matter what. Their love is unconditional. For cat lovers, a weakness to which some including this writer have succumbed, it is your unconditional love for the cat that is mandatory. Ask any cat.

But dogs. They are good for judges because they don't judge. A dog's tail will wag for a judge that has been censured by the Judicial Performance Commission. Well that may depend on the breed. I am talking about dogs and judges.

But judges can carry their relationship with dogs too far. Take, for example, Judge Noel Canon. (See *Cannon v. Commission on Judicial Qualifications* 14 Cal.3d 678 (1975).) She was removed from the bench for some bizarre behavior, including having her dog sit in her lap while she conducted trials from the bench. Some of the dog's rulings reflected unfamiliarity if not disdain for the Evidence Code.

When she was removed from the bench, Judge Cannon's dog, a high strung poodle, is reputed to have made commercials to supplement her mistress's income until a dispute with Actor's Equity ended that. But it does show a dog's devotion.

But I wonder if all breeds of dog show such loyalty to their owners. I have no question about Sergeant Preston and his Husky, "King." But do you think a Pomeranian would display the loyalty of Judge Cannon's poodle? I mention this because of an ad I saw in the Los Angeles Times.
In thick bold white letters against a blue background, appear the words, "Pomeranian." Beneath the letters is a photo of an orange Pomeranian sculpture, "actual size 8 3/4 in height. Yours for only $59.60. Allow 4 to 6 weeks for shipping after initial payment."

The ad pitches the "meticulously crafted figurines" as if they were real dogs. It rhapsodizes about a Pomeranian's "intelligent eyes" and "friendly expression." It speaks about how this breed is "outgoing and friendly" and "always ready to play." The ad then urges you to buy a "figurine" to bring the "irresistible charm of this beloved breed into your home."

You can also get a black one if the orange one doesn't appeal to you, or maybe get both. Or maybe get two of a kind. That way one won't get lonely. The photograph of the head of the black Pomeranian is creepy. It looks a bit like a vampire bat. I haven't seen all that many Pomeranians, but I am sure I never saw a black one. There are black labs, black poodles, black cockers, but are there really black Pomeranians? But I'm getting off track.

The ad raises some questions. Has any one seen a Pomeranian lately? Haven't seen any in my neighborhood. Maybe people are embarrassed to be seen with them. Would a misunderstood judge be cheered at the end of the day by a yapping, I mean barking Pomeranian? I don't know, but if the judge pro tem who ordered the victim out of his courtroom does not have a dog, I would be willing to send him a Pomeranian figurine.

THE SHAQ
PART I

My contretempts with Shaquille O'Neal when he played for the Lakers.

After the Lakers lost one of their games to the Sacramento Kings at the Western Conference Finals, Shaquille O'Neal said the only way to beat the Lakers "starts with a C and ends with a T." Sports reporters were speculating about what word or words the big Shaq had in mind. Perhaps the statement was merely an example of Shaq's legendary irony. Before this humiliating defeat, I thought he might be saying "Can't," or "Can't do it." He could not have meant , "Cheat" could he? For some people, Shaq's letters more appropriately meant what he did not intend, "Cheap Shot." In retrospect Shaq's letters seem petty in light of the Lakers winning the NBA world championship.

Although I am not sure of the meaning of Shaq's enigmatic letters, I am sure that speculation about them or anything else often leads one down blind alleys. For example, I have often described certain judicial decisions, with the letters C and S. I was thunderstruck at the astonishing combination of words seemingly thoughtful people believed the letters stood for. No one got it. Why are the words "Common Sense" so elusive?

But why be inscrutable? It only gives journalists and commentators something to ponder and ultimately distort. I think it is better to come out and say exactly what you mean. That assumes you know what you mean and have the means to say it. Shaq's cagey remark seems to reflect his belief that the refs contributed to the defeat. In every game there are questionable calls from the referees, and all teams have a legitimate beef about a "bad call' now and then. After all, referees are simply judges making calls as best they can. But these basketball refs are like the Supreme Court. Their errors may be criticized, but they are the last word, and there isn't much to do about it but gripe. Just ask coach Adelman after losing the Western Conference Finals to the Lakers.

Yet I know how Adleman feels and how Shaq felt at the time of his obscure reference to the "C---T" word or words. Lawyers try to admit evidence and some judge says it is error to do so. That "call" can mean the loss of the case. But even the judges face similar frustration. A reversal from a higher court usually means the judge below screwed up, I mean prejudicially erred. But cryptic alphabetic fulminations may be more the sour expression of a poor loser than the clever retort of a good natured loser. However expressed, just think what emotional invective gives you and your argument. It starts with S and ends with T. That's right-----SHORT SHRIFT.

THE SHAQ
PART II

In my last column we talked briefly about Shaquille O'Neal's response to a question last season about what it would take for the Sacramento Kings to beat the Lakers. Shaq's enigmatic answer that it starts with "C" and ends with "T" caused much speculation. I refused to hypothesize about what Shaq meant, but wrote that for me, "Cheap Shot" seemed appropriate. I have been told that Shaq is (to put it in jock patois) "pissed." And what's more, he's looking for me. Somehow Shaq found out what I said. But how could that be? I doubt he read it. Outside of enlightening Judicial Profiles, I did not think there was much in the Daily Journal of interest to Shaq. I figured he read Sports Illustrated or, because of his interest in law enforcement, the Police Gazette. But sources say Shaq did in fact read my column.

On the ground floor of the Ronald Reagan State Building is a statue of a creature vaguely resembling a California grizzly bear frozen in a perpetual crouch. Rumors in the press suggest that Shaq intends to dribble me around the bear. When asked during an interview with an underground newspaper if this were true, Shaq said, "huh uh, when my hallux gets better." He also mumbled something about his support for case citations in footnotes. Following a practice of many newspapers, there is a box on the front page of this paper called Quote of the Day. In the box appears a quote from Shaq. "When I'm through with him, Gilbert will be—it starts with H and ends with Y." An informal poll has "hamburger patty" running far ahead of "healthy" or "hearty."

This practice of highlighting quotes of the day in daily newspapers reveals our plunge from a literary Everest to a barren Death Valley. Try as you may, you will not find, for example, "Happiness is when what you think, what you say, and what you do are in harmony," Mohandas K. Gandhi. Nor will you find, "Look at all the sentences which seem true and question them," David Reisman, or "Mistakes are the portals of discovery," James Joyce, or "Truth is the most valuable thing we have," Mark Twain, or "It's good to shut up sometimes," Marcel Marceau.

Compare these insights to the quote of a Vallejo criminal defense lawyer that appeared in bold type under the heading, "QUOTABLE" on the front page of the Daily Journal on Wednesday, July 24, 2002. The catchy quote concerns the defense attorney's views about a Solano County superior court judge whose profile appeared in the paper that day. The unassuming defense attorney lavished praise on the judge with a tactful comparison to other judges. The quote, belying the old adage about all the news that's fit to print, is: "most judges I wouldn't piss on if they were on fire...Paul, [the judge in the profile] is really a decent human being."

By seeking attribution for his elegant quote, this attorney must crave notoriety as much as the people who appear on the new "reality" television shows where they stuff raw pig entrails and live insects down their throats. Being seen and heard trumps public humiliation. The analogy is not quite perfect. Unlike the television contestants, here the offal came out of the lawyer's mouth rather than in. His unique judicial encomium contrasted the good qualities of one judge by a disparaging contrast to most others.

I suppose this is just another example of a profession taking it on the chin these days. Who ever thought we would witness seemingly harmless accountants reviled with the same degree of vigor as physicians, priests, historians, lawyers, bar examiners, and even judges, whose repute declined at the conclusion of the last presidential election.

It is easy to ignore a tasteless slight, but when one of your colleagues suggests that appellate justices are not all they are cracked up to be, one has to take notice. Just one day before the graphic quote from Solano County, there appeared an article in the July 23, 2002, issue of the Daily Journal called "Judge-Speak" by retired but not retiring Court of Appeal Justice Robert S. Thompson.

The article appears on the "DICTA" page, which a subheading informs us is devoted to "Notes, Comment, Frolic & Detour." I am not sure into which of these categories Thompson's article more properly belongs. Thompson takes phrases used by appellate justices and offers a translation of what they mean. For example, Thompson says that when appellate justices say they are familiar with the record and the briefs, that means the research attorney drafted the opinion. The admonishment from the court that it is interested in logic not argument means the research attorney has decided against you. Get the drift? Is Thompson saying that appellate justices don't do much of anything but play golf, while the research attorneys do everything? If so, then maybe Thompson's article belongs under the "Comment" subheading. It is noteworthy that two of Thompson's research attorneys became two of our most distinguished appellate justices.

On the other hand, I bet the article belongs under the "Frolic" subheading. Justice Thompson is an incisive thinker, with a penetrating intellect, as conversant with judicial philosophy as he is with hiking trails in the Himalayas. I am sure Thompson drafted many of his own opinions. His article is most likely a gentle satirical rebuke to some appellate courts that he may perceive as becoming bureaucratic and staff dependent.

Yet, for all his accomplishments, fickle history will make Thompson remembered mostly for the much maligned footnote 2 in *People v. Arno* (1979) 90 Cal.App.3d 505, 514. The *Arno* decision authored by Justice Thompson is an extremely well-reasoned decision reversing convictions for possession of obscene films. The footnote was written in response to a derisive dissent that scolded the majority for its opinion. Depending upon how you look at it, the footnote is either outrageous and appalling or innocent and innocuous. That in turn depends on whether you consider the anagram contained within the footnote scatological and repugnant or genial and inoffensive.

Contained within footnote 2 are seven numbered sentences. The first letter of the first word of each sentence spells "schmuck." The footnote points out that a German Dictionary defines "schmuck" as "jewel." The footnote also cites another footnote 6, of Justice Douglas' dissent in *Ginsberg. v. New York* (1967) 390 U.S 629 655-656. Justice Douglas' footnote reminds us that obscenity is in the mind of the beholder. Whatever one thinks of Thompson's majority opinion, I am sure footnote 2 was not written by a research attorney. Because *Arno* involved an issue concerning obscenity, the footnote may have been written only to show how words are subject to a variety of interpretations.

It is ironic that, with all the controversy about footnote 2, the *Arno* decision contains an uplifting grace note in footnote 1. The case had been transferred from the appellate department of the superior court. In footnote 1 Justice Thompson graciously wrote, "We do not denigrate the opinion of the appellate department. It is exceedingly well analyzed, researched and crafted. Our sole reason for not adopting it is a minor disagreement with the manner of expressing the controlling principle." Now that is class. I am sure that Justice Thompson meant no harm by the footnote just as I am sure he meant no disrespect in his Daily Journal article to all the Court of Appeal justices throughout the state who meticulously craft their opinions.

I would love to call Shaq and get his views on the matter. I can just imagine our conversation. Shaq says he really isn't out to get me; he's just joking around. He tells me our little tiff is no different than his brief contretemps with Kobe. I learn that he is an avid reader of the Daily Journal and likes my column about the colonoscopy. He reads the Daily Appellate Report, but thinks many of the opinions lean toward the turgid and may be overwritten. I offer words or encouragement about his upcoming toe surgery.

I bring the conversation around to Justice Thompson. Shaq admires his work. I mention footnote 2. in the *Arno* decision. I suggest it is merely an ironic comment about the use of language. Shaq replies, "It starts with B and ends with….." I interrupt him. "Please, not another guessing game with initials." After a long silence at the other end of the line I hear….. "**B**affled, **U**nsure, **L**aughable, **L**apsing, **S**erendipitous, **H**ectoring, **I**nstructive, **T**umultuous."

Postscript: Shaq did read the column. Attorney Elwood Lui, who once sat as a Justice on the California Court of Appeal, was a member of the Los Angeles Harbor Commission. Shaq was a reserve officer on the commission's police force. Elwood had a copy of the column delivered to

Shaq. Shaq sent me his copy of the column on which he wrote, "Gilbert J.—What makes you think I don't read your column?" Shaq.

BORROWED WORDS

Many people fondly remember our late Senator S.I. Hayakawa. Our memories do not concern any significant legislation. Some remember him as the courageous college president who took on the rioting students at San Francisco State College in the tumultuous 60's. I remember that photo of him standing on the hood of a Chevy, or whatever, tam-o-shanter firmly in place on his head, bullhorn in hand as he shouted down a throng of revolutionaries, or spoiled brats, depending on your point of view. Others remember him for his recreational tap dancing, his association with Duke Ellington, or his penchant for snoozing during Senate debates. I warmly remember Hayakawa for his quotes: "If students are dirty and ragged it indicates they are not interested in tidying up their intellects either," "I'm going to speak my mind because I have nothing to lose," and his book, "Language in Thought and Action, " or as I called it, "Semantics for Dummies." Hayakawa was a lot easier to read than Korzbyski or Wittgenstein. A pervading theme in Hayakawa's book is the word is not the thing. I agree with that notion which has become suspect in this day and age. Indeed, as I have urged on this page before, a word is only a sound or a squiggle on a page. Yet words are the products of pens, or word processors, and we all know how mighty they can be. Wittgenstein had a particular view about a box of matches. This following anecdote may be apocryphal but it makes the point. He is reputed to have held up a box of matches in front of his class and asked the students what he was holding. They said "a box of matches." He flung the matches at them and yelled, "No! A box of matches is a sound."

But sounds or mere squiggles on a page often cause much havoc. Just ask Salmon Rushdie. Or for that matter ask any judge. We say and write things that have been known to create riots, anguish, elation, anger, and boredom. The simple word "reversed" has sent people over the edge.

We must be careful in choosing our words, and in making sure the words we choose are our words. Take for example, the case of two distinguished Harvard law professors, Charles J. Ogletree, Jr., and Laurence Tribe. As reported in the *New York Times* a few weeks ago, six paragraphs in Ogletree's recent book "All Deliberate Speed" were written not by Ogletree, but by a Yale law professor. The six paragraphs lacked quotes and nary a footnote showing that they belonged to the Yale law professor. And portions of Tribe's book "God Save This Honorable Court" published in 1985 borrowed from another professor's work as revealed by identical and similar wording without attribution. Hurried and sloppy research, not malicious intent, contributed to these transgressions.

That these were accidents occurring through the carelessness of research assistants does not excuse the professors. Whether you agree or not with the philosophy of these two legal titans, they are first-rate scholars who face eviction from their airy quarters on Mount Olympus. I appeared once on a panel moderated by Professor Ogletree and was impressed by his brilliance and compelling personality. If this could happen to him, it could happen to me, and I don't live anywhere near Mount Olympus. I was once accused of trying to live there, but the agent refused to show me a condo even on the outskirts. I think the neighborhood petition opposing my setting foot anywhere in the district scared her off. I threatened to sue the agent for discrimination. She convinced me her demurrer would be sustained without leave to amend. But that is another story for another time.

I immediately called in my research attorneys to make sure we had not accidentally written something written by others for which we did not give proper attribution. After exhaustive investigation, we did come across something. In one of my early, very early opinions, I had written this concluding sentence: "Judgment is reversed and the matter remanded with directions to adopt procedures consistent with the views expressed herein in this opinion." That was out and out plagiarism. I will never use it again. The author has not sued me. He does not want to be known.

Another factor crucial to any writer, whether he or she plagiarizes or not, is style. It has to be important because Strunk and White titled their book "The Elements of Style." The final Chapter V is devoted to this most important element. Tone, an element of style, is essential to any writer. An officious or patronizing tone in an appellate opinion detracts rather than enhances.

In a previous column I wrote about my cat's misbehavior in the living room. At the end of the first paragraph I used dashes top refer to a word in a familiar colloquial phrase. My editors at the *Daily Journal* saw it differently and decided not to bleep out the word. We didn't have time to confer, and there it was. I thought the use of the word was jarring and not in keeping with the tone of the article. Some readers of the column voiced similar sentiments while others support the use of what I call the "offending" word. I will admit to a heightened aversion to scatology, but I am anything but a prude, much less a censor. It is simply not always appropriate to be blunt in the name of freedom of expression. This has nothing to do with censorship or a reticence to offend people when they need to be shaken from their apathy. The late columnist Garry Abrams decried the pusillanimity of network television afraid to air the movie "Saving Private Ryan" because of concern about a four letter word uttered by soldiers landing at Normandy. As usual he was right on. The tone there was appropriate. What would soldiers in such a circumstance say, "Goodness Gracious"?

I thought the whole affair over my word had blown over when I was compelled to write the offending word again in another column. Well, it is not exactly the same word although it sounds the same. It all came about when this stranger sat down next to me at Starbucks. He tripped and spilled some of his coffee latte on his hands and what looked like a deposition or an appellate brief. Upon spilling the coffee, he used the quaint expression "Shoot!"

I couldn't help myself. I had to say something. It must have come from subconscious anxiety. "Shoot?" I asked as he sat down beside me with his head slightly cocked. After an awkward pause I said, "Do you want to shoot the shit?"

"Sure, " he said.

"You said 'shoot' not shit," I said.

He nodded.

"Shoot is so quaint," I said, "like a line from the Ozzie and Harriett show. Let me guess why you said 'shoot' instead of 'shit.'"

"Shoot," he said.

"I bet you are a deeply religious person and offended as I am by the indiscriminate use today of scatological expressions."

"No," he replied, "I am an agnostic."

"Well, I suppose agnostics can be prigs," I said meekly.

"They can, but I am not a prig," he said.

"But 'shoot?'" I protested.

The conversation was over. He got up to leave. It suddenly hit me that he looked familiar.

"Don't I know you?" I asked.

He was standing. "No," he said patiently, "you don't know me."

"What is your name?" I asked.

"Jack," he said. "Jack Schitt."

BORROWING OR PLAGIARISM?

My column usually appears on the first Monday of each month. But sometimes my day job gets in the way and I miss a month. On occasion the first day of the cruelest month lands on a Monday. Some of my critics have circulated a petition to prohibit my column from appearing ore than once a year, and only on April Fool's Day. Even I supported the petition. A controversy erupted when the registrar placed the petition at the bottom of the ballot instead of the top. Polls showed the petition had overwhelming popular support and was sure to win no matter where it appeared on the ballot. Indeed those in favor of the petition gushed with enthusiasm, while the few who were opposed, yawned. Nevertheless a lawsuit, *Gush v. Bore* was filed. Ultimately it and the petition were dropped. The petition supporters acknowledged that even with a certain win at the polls, once the courts got involved, they would lose.

In this month of April, the first falls on a Monday. But because Monday is a special court holiday, my column appears on Tuesday. Nuts. I had a great column prepared for April Fool's Day. I had planned to make up this outrageous story about a lawyer who tries to help out his friend, another lawyer, who is in a jam. It seems this friend was appointed by Judge Learned Foote to represent a defendant in a heavy-duty criminal case. The friend dragged his feet on the case so long that the court, in exasperation, ordered that he be hanged and quartered. When the judge's research attorney informed him that this punishment had been outlawed four hundred years prior to our Declaration of Independence, the court then considered jolting him with electricity from a stun belt. That punishment, though of recent vintage, was reserved for obstreperous defendants.

The new lawyer reluctantly substituted in for his harried friend, but did not come up to speed on the case quickly enough to the court's satisfaction. Judge Foote therefore held the attorney in contempt, and confiscated his copy of the Sixth Amendment. It was my hope that I would have the skill to relate this incredible story of horror so that you would believe it actually happened. Then I would end with the exclamation April Fool! Ha ha.

The imaginative incident mentioned above would be insufficient, however, to fill an entire column. If I possessed the genius of Proust so that in minute detail I could expand on the particulars of my spoof to fill more space, even the most dull-witted reader would soon discern the improbability of the events described, and with smug satisfaction, prematurely apprehend the April Fool joke.

I therefore looked up some of my old April 1st columns for additional material. My columns for April 1st, 1991 and 1996 both of which fell on Mondays were dated and therefore unsuitable. What, you think it unbecoming to use material from my old columns? Perhaps, but reuse is not plagiarism. Perhaps I am hyper-sensitive because we hear so much about plagiarism these days. The many books produced by Doris Kearns Goodwin and Stephen Ambrose have made them popular scholars. But they have not always endured the drudgery of original research, or ignited their own creative spark to express an idea. Instead, they have pilfered the hard-earned work and expression of others. Because they have committed multiple offenses, some have lowered their status from copy cats to dirty rats. Author Lynne McTaggart wrote in the New York Times that Goodwin's book, "The Fitzgeralds and the Kennedys," "contained many sections that were copied" from McTaggart's book , "Kathleen Kennedy: Her Life and Times." McTaggart pointed out that passage after passage of her book was "embedded" in Goodwin's book. How can one do something so blatant when detection is almost a certainty?

On the other hand, are we being too harsh? It is true that Goodwin and Ambrose lifted passages from other sources in some of their books. It is also true that neither of them seems all that contrite. But at least they did not steal entire books. And Goodwin settled out of court with McTaggart and others, and is no longer a commentator on public television. She and Ambrose were cranking out so many best sellers that they simply did not have the time to check out all the sources, and so . . . I hear your objection. No excuse.

In some contexts "borrowing" creative ideas is its own form of creativity and is therefore quite acceptable It serves as a tribute to the creative work of another and earns praise for the borrower. The talented filmmakers the Coen brothers, for example, pay tribute to great film directors such as Hitchcock and Wells by copying camera techniques and specific shots developed by these directors in movies from the past. Jazz musicians will often pay tribute to others by weaving into their improvisation, fragments or portions of other musicians' solos. This usually elicits accolades from discriminating listeners.

This all goes to show that in some circles plagiarism is an accepted practice. Take judicial opinions for example. Plagiarizing is so widespread that phrases not worth saying the first time are repeated again and again. Perhaps that is why the originator of the plethoric "at the outset" has not sued those who have passed off this extraneous phrase as their own. What is the need to tell everyone that what you say at the outset is at the outset? The same goes for "preliminarily we note," also written by the originator of "at the outset." I have even found the phrase "at the outset" at the end of an opinion. I queried the author about this anomaly, and he stated it was a typo. The word should have been "sunset."

It is common knowledge that judicial opinions often plagiarize from the briefs. But the prevailing side is flattered to have words lifted from the brief that won the day. Some of us give a feeble attempt at attribution, with something trite like "as appellant aptly points out."

It is also no secret that all appellate justices have a staff of research attorneys crafting opinions that are euphemistically called calendar memos. Often we change more than a word or two, but there exists a collaboration that is not adequately acknowledged. Are we not using their work and passing it off as our own? Of course, that is different from stealing someone else's work. The research attorneys are paid to write memos and draft opinions that are expected to be useful to the judge. Depending on the quality of the work, the judge gets the credit, or the blame.

This reminds me of Paul McCartney, who admits he cannot read or write music. I can understand how that would not stop him from writing original and interesting songs. But he "composed" a symphony in 1997 called *Standing Stone*. How do you write a symphony if you cannot read or write music? Someone else was involved, a composer to whom he "explained" his musical concept.

I think it is better policy to give attribution when it is due. Failing to do so can make one a fool every day, not just April 1st. After all, you can't fool all the people all the time.

THE COLONOSCOPY AND THE ALIEN

Strange things happened during the O.J. Simpson trial.

A short time ago I had a colonoscopy, not a pretty thing to write about, an even less pretty thing to endure. Nevertheless, I was inspired by that superb columnist, Jim Murray, who recently wrote about his heart surgery. Of course what I had was not really surgery, but the extraordinary events that arose from this experience must be told.

A colonoscopy, not to be confused with a sigmoidoscopy, (a piece of cake in comparison), is a procedure that allows your doctor to look inside your intestines. I won't go into the details, but preparing for the procedure is even more arduous than the procedure itself. It's somewhat like preparing for an argument before the Supreme Court on behalf of a defendant in a criminal case: When it's all over, you're not left with much.

A colonoscopy takes place in a hospital. The doctor, with the aid of a machine, sends a tube, on the end of which is a little light and television camera, on a journey through your intestines. It's a circuitous route that goes up up and around and then up some more and so on. As the tube works its way through the 20 to 30 foot labyrinth, following folds and twists and turns, the doctor watches on a television set. The patient also gets to watch, if he or she isn't too doped up.

I have seen many of my friends in the legal profession on TV lately and I figured this was my chance to see some of me on TV. I asked the doctor to do the procedure without the anesthetic. He laughed. He said he could think of only one person in history who got through the entire procedure without an anesthetic. That unfortunate patient now makes the most artistic macramé at the home where he has lived for the past 15 years.

"OK., then give me just a very little bit", I stupidly demanded, or demanded stupidly.

The doctor then did a terrible thing for which I will never forgive him. He complied with my request. This enabled me to supply shrill high sound effects during what otherwise would have been a silent TV production. After awhile the doctor found a way to muffle the sound. But at least I got the chance to see myself on TV, and in color. That's not all. As the scope slid along the smooth shiny walls like a bobsled in an Olympic competition, I saw something strange in its path. The camera almost ran over it.

How can I describe it? Remember the movie, *Alien?* The thing living inside John Hurt's body burst out and caused havoc in the spaceship. I swear I saw one of those things, or something like it in my body. At first I panicked and tried to tell the doctor, but it was hard to speak with the gag in my mouth. The thing,(I came to call him Izzy,) kept reappearing, mugging in the camera like counsel in a televised trial. The camera kept knocking him over, so I concluded he was kind of klutzy and therefore benign, unlike his counterpart who did in John Hurt.

Finally the procedure was over. They got a ladder and scraped me off the ceiling. Then they dumped me on a gurney, and that got me thinking of Sigourney Weaver, only she never showed. All I got was the doctor, who explained with the insouciance that doctors assume when they use medical phraseology, that I was "clean as a whistle." I told him about the alien. He smiled and put the gag back in my mouth.

Make no mistake, there was an alien inside of me. Real life is so unlike fiction: My alien, Izzy, had no intention of leaving. In fact, he was quite fond of me. At first things went along O.K. He liked my column. He got a little nudgy, however, pushing me to get it out, and then trying to find out who was the model for Judge Learned Foote. That was tolerable, but things got out of hand when he began giving me advice on my cases. (I hope cynical readers are not saying, "so that's the reason.")

I told him to back off, but he kept pushing. For example, I would be convinced to go one way on a case, and he would argue, sometimes quite persuasively, to go the other way. It was infuriating: He's more conservative than I. Who can tell how effective I was in resisting him? I was also concerned about violating the judicial canons, however blameless, I was.

Another bothersome thing was that we had different work habits. He wanted to watch the O.J. Simpson trial. I didn't have time. He wanted to know why "we" were not on TV, and kept pressing me to critique Judge Ito. Can you imagine the gall? I tried to explain that Judge Ito has his hands full and doesn't need judges, sitting or retired, to air their views as to how he should rule. Just let him try a case with a couple of billion people watching.

Izzy didn't care. He tried to get me to take phone calls from the press and to appear on TV because cases from my division had been cited in the trial. Izzy started out on TV, and he proved the adage about TV: "Once you're on, you never want to be off." I resisted. Then he got entirely out of control: He began interjecting smartass asides at oral argument, and once even tried to write a dissent-- to one of my own opinions.

I put my foot down. I told him to stop or I would no longer order his favorite food, pepperoni pizza. I was so angry I didn't even give him a chance to comply. I simply stopped eating pizza altogether.

It worked. Somehow he escaped. Don't ask me how. I don't want to know, but I think I was asleep when he left.

I have been carefully scrutinizing the work of other judges and I am almost positive he has taken up "residence" elsewhere in the judiciary. I have narrowed the list down somewhat, but it's still pretty large. I think Izzy is "lodging around."

If you are a judicial officer with a sudden yen for pepperoni pizza, find yourself fighting an urge to appear on television or to suddenly change your rulings, give me a call. Meanwhile, I tried to turn Izzy in to the Judicial Performance Commission. The commission members are not interested. Maybe that's because he is hard to catch, and not very pretty to look at. The hearings are now public. Soon they may be televised: Who knows?

ANOTHER COLONOSCOPY

A person sitting next to me on the plane told me about his recent sex change operation. She and I both knew it was unlikely we would see each other again. I suppose that is why she could talk about this highly personal matter to a stranger. (I wonder if she was as frank with the blind date she had that evening?)

Columnists often write about personal matters. That is because when the columnist writes the readers have not yet been determined. Easier to be revelatory to a faceless inchoate readership than face to face with someone the columnist knows. The act of writing in the columnist's present is past during the reader's act of reading. Einstein no doubt would endorse the principle that "The reader's present is the columnist's past."

This column, involving a delicate personal subject, I have already written and you will soon read. It is intimately related to the federal judiciary. By the way, while you are reading this column, I have already forgotten about it. I am working on something else. But it is not something I knew about when I wrote this column. Get it?

So, to continue, no matter what the function or event, federal judges are always introduced first. Then when everyone is truly bored, they introduce the state court judges. A few months ago I spoke at the induction ceremony of a well-respected state trial judge, Judge Valerie Baker- Fairbank who had been recently appointed to the Federal District Court. Needless to say, many of her state court colleagues were present and joined the admiring audience, the numbers of which were so large they poured into adjoining courtrooms to see the ceremony on TV screens.

The judge presiding over the ceremony graciously welcomed everyone and then began to individually introduce the federal judges present from both the 9th Circuit and the trial bench. The accolades and encomiums made the inhabitants of Olympus envious, "the brilliant, the scholarly, the genius, the distinguished." And then a recitation about the judge's hobbies, blood type, awards and honors dating from grammar school. Then it came to the state judges. "Would you all stand and be recognized"- two seconds later-"that's enough, sit down."

But the real reason federal judges have it made is that unlike state judges, they do not have to run for election. A federal judge can close down the City of Los Angeles with impunity. A rebuke from the press or a higher court may elicit a yawn or shrug, but they are in office forever. Impeachment? Not likely. From the creation of the federal judiciary to the present, only thirteen federal judges have been impeached, and six of those were actually convicted.

Speaking of the federal judiciary takes me to my personal matter. It is my colonoscopy, a subject I had discussed years ago in my Daily Journal column when I was younger and less discrete. (See previous column.) The colonoscopy of which I speak this time is a different one. Lest you think this evidences desperation for material, it is not exactly the colonoscopy itself that is pertinent, but instead, the conversation with the anesthesiologist.

I received a call the day before the procedure informing me that the anesthesiologist would like to talk to me the next morning when I came in. It is the day before when the "prep" occurs. The "prep" is not a picnic. In fact picnics are not allowed. I was reading briefs, but it was hard to concentrate, what with a liquid diet and constant interruptions that reminded me of the quality of some of the briefs.

So early the next morning I was on a gurney with a needle in my arm receiving an IV, waiting for the doctor to do to me what I do to attorneys at oral argument. I was a little groggy when the anesthesiologist came in. He broached a subject of great importance- did my insurance cover his services? I assured him that if it did not I would gladly pay his fee. To prove it, I agreed to sign the form he thrust in my hand. Of course the words were a blur, and for all I knew, my signature could make him the new owner of my house.

As he browsed through the charts he saw that I was a judge. "Oh you're a judge," he said in a higher pitched voice. He took the form out of my hand before I could sign it. He asked what kind of judge I was. "A fair one," I said. He smiled nervously. "What court?" he asked. "The Court of Appeal," I said. "9th Circuit?" he asked. "No," I answered, "my court is the state's counterpart of that court."

In a nanosecond he thrust the form back in my hand and directed my attention to the signature line. It was only fitting that after signing, I should have a colonoscopy. I bet had I uttered the words "9th Circuit" even out of context, I would not have had to sign the form.

But these days I have it as good as federal judges. That is because I am in what state judges call their "federal term." That is a euphemistic shorthand way of saying, " I am not running for re-election." I can assure you that I have never looked over my shoulder when ruling on a high publicity case, or controversial matter. If the public doesn't like or misunderstands my ruling, well that's how it is. It goes with the territory. If there is a chance that I may be turned out of office because of a campaign waged against me by an extremist group with a personal vendetta against me, so be it. But in my "federal term" if those fanatics don't like my rulings they can suck eggs.....

Sorry, I got a little carried away. Where was I? Oh yes. So last year the voters saw fit to return me to office for a 12 year term. This has to be my federal term, right? I mean I am not going to stay that long--am I? I don't want them bringing me orders to sign at the In Need of Lots of Care and Attention Residential Facility. "Here's a writ petition that seeks to close the 405 Freeway. Just give the judge a little shake and wake him up. If he knows who he is, we will ask him if he is going to grant or deny it." That could happen if I stay to the end of my term in 2019.

But in truth I kind of miss the edgy insecurity that comes with running for election. Most of the public have few or no criteria to make an informed vote. You never know what gets or loses votes.

Many state judges engage in a variety of other pursuits when they are not judging. Some sky dive, others crochet. Some run marathons, climb Everest, explore the North Pole, garden, act, sing, box, wrestle, write novels. The people they encounter in these endeavors could be a source of votes.

In off hours I sometimes play the piano in gigs with a jazz combo. The law's seamless web stretches wide. There is a remarkable affinity between jazz and judging - lots of improvising. But when I play the piano, I don't want anyone to know about the judge thing. Wouldn't want to lose votes over a bad chorus of "Stella by Starlight." But I did get a vote in last year's election because of my solo on "Prelude to a Kiss." It was from Charles Embree, a wonderful artist who had studied with Thomas Hart Benton. He is also a talented writer. For many years he wrote short stories for *Esquire* magazine about jazz musicians under the nom de plume, Riff Charles. He wrote me, " Not all judges are piano players, but certainly all piano players are judges. They sit on a bench and hand down decisions to fingers directing them on which key to strike in what order and when. The sound heard is the soundness of the judgment rendered. If the music is select, you must elect! Based on this argument you will be receiving my vote in the upcoming contest."

Embree's incontrovertible logic and his elegant writing convinces me not to be such a malcontent. When I had to run for election I complained, and here I am in my federal term nostalgic for elections. I think I will just settle down and enjoy as much of my federal term as I decide to serve. Why fret? Everything came out all right in the colonoscopy.

Postscript: Embree's eloquent words grace the opening of this book. The illustration is the work of his wife, Barbara Embree.

The three defense attorneys were huddled at the end of the counsel table, whispering while the three defendants sitting behind them fidgeted in their seats. The decision seemed to have been made in a matter of seconds. Their heads nodded quickly in agreement. The tall defense attorney, the one with his hair tied behind his head in a discreet little pony tail, stood up and informed the court that he would thank and excuse juror No. 4. All well and good, so long as you are not juror No. 4.

A recent event compels me to explore a universal theme as common in Greek tragedy as it is in modern tabloids. It is an inescapable part of human experience. It is what we wish to avoid at all costs yet we often embrace unwittingly, giving it access to our hearts where we can feel its sharp cutting edge. It is what makes us feel diminished, incomplete, and self-consciously aware of our imperfections whether real or imagined. It is rejection.

I have known it. Glenda Sue Thompson turned me down for the high school junior prom. So what if I asked her out the night before. Rejection pressed against my chest like an implacable weight that even Arnold Schwarzenegger could not budge. Of course, in those days Arnold Schwarzenegger was in grammar school. (This column was written in 1994. Today in 2008, Governor Schwarzenegger is proposing a budget from which he is reluctant to budge.)

I decided never to be in that predicament again. I asked Betsy Jacobs to the high school senior prom when we were still in our junior year. She had to check her calendar. Yes, she would be free the coming year. Unfortunately, nine months later she moved away and transferred schools. That left only three months until the prom. I wasn't going to take any more chances with rejection, so I volunteered to tend bar at the prom. The trustee in bankruptcy for the school district settled the last lawsuit just last week.

No matter how many precautions you take to avoid it, it sneaks up behind you, then jumps in front of you so you are face-to-face with it. And it doesn't care who you are or what your station in life.

Take the legal profession, for example. Every trial lawyer knows what it's like to have an argument rejected by a judge. But don't think for a moment that judges are insulated from rejection. If you doubt me, just ask trial judges who have been reversed by courts of appeal; ask appellate court judges who have been reversed by the Supreme Court; ask judges on the appellate courts who write dissents. Yet these types of rejection are to be expected and there is some comfort in the company that misery keeps. But there are other less expected ways in which even a judge must face rejection.

I was called for jury duty. I went. The notice said to be there promptly at 8 a.m. I drove to the Santa Monica courthouse where I used to sit in Department G. I felt the warm glow of nostalgia as I pulled into the lot. I was at the courthouse steps at 7:58 a.m. right on time. The courthouse was locked.

I joined a small crowd waiting outside in the cold for the doors to open. Some people grumbled. I suggested that perhaps the recent earthquake had something to do with it. Some lawyers spotted me and asked what I was doing there waiting outside the courthouse on a chilly morning. I told them. One of them said, "Good for you."

"Was it?" I wondered. And would it be good for him if I were on a jury on a case he was trying? Of course, it would…if the facts and the law were on his side.

The doors finally opened at 8:20 a.m. I waited in line and went through the metal detector. The alarm sounded. It was the steel rim on my glasses. People in line behind me were irritated with the delay. I saw it as an omen. The earthquake had rendered the jury room unusable, so we went to a courtroom. The jury clerk told us about our duties and responsibilities. She was explicit in her instructions, efficient but also courteous. She gave us forms to fill out. I filled out my form and handed it in. A few minutes later she called my name. I felt my heartbeat quicken. Was it over already? No, I forgot to sign the form.

We were then excused to the hallway where we were to wait to be called for a case. I propped myself against the wall and read some briefs in a criminal case. When I got bored reading, I did something else useful, like finding words that rhyme with jury – furry, surrey, curry, blurry, hurry, and… WORRY. That's the word that stuck. But, what was there to worry about?

A few days later my panel was called for a case in Judge Rex Minter's court. Three defendants had been charged with possession for sale and transporting cocaine. There they were with their attorneys at one end of the counsel table, the prosecutor at the other end, and Judge Minter presiding, with the appropriate demeanor and bearing of a fair and wise judge. This was a scene in which I had participated thousands of times before, but now I was seeing it from the other side of the bench and I felt a sense of awe.

The clerk swore in the jury venire and then began calling prospective jurors to take seats in the jury box. I was juror No. 4. Judge Minter treated everyone in the courtroom with respect and dignity. He introduced the defendants, their counsel and the prosecutor. He began the voir dire questioning. When he got to me he did a double take. "Justice Gilbert?" he said. "Didn't expect to see you here." We both forced a weak smile.

I thought I did well on voir dire. First, a little banter. I promised not to pass judgment on Judge Minter's rulings. (Chuckle, chuckle.) No, I would not believe the testimony of a police officer just because he was a police officer. I didn't think the defendants had to take the stand. I would be fair and impartial, and I had absolutely no bias or prejudice against anybody – well, maybe Adolf Hitler. I revealed my past, law school, city attorney's office, private practice, municipal, superior court, my old courtroom upstairs in Department G.

But as I talked, I began to feel clammy, just the way I did when I was dialing Glenda Sue's number to ask her to the prom. Oddly, for a moment I thought of George H. W. Bush as a thousand tiny lights of doubt began flashing in my brain. Once again I was setting myself up for the big fall. The lawyers regarded me with noncommittal eyes, but I detected a vague look of horror on the faces of the defendants.

The People passed for cause and then accepted the jury panel. "A sagacious prosecutor," I thought to myself. It was next the defense's turn to pass for cause. They then exercised their peremptory and excused juror No. 1. So what if he had had a bad experience with a meter maid over a parking ticket and has ever since hated law enforcement. A new juror was called into the box. She passed voir dire with flying colors. Her answers were snappy and direct. The people again accepted the jury panel. A pathetic little bubble of hope began to grow in my heart.

The judge then said "peremptory with the defense." And now we are back where we began, with the three huddled, whispering defense attorneys. I can't tell you what they were saying but it must have been something like "better now then later. Just do it." They nodded. I pictured them giving each other a mental high five. The tall defense attorney with the little pony tail rose up from his seat. He had a commanding presence, but also a warm engaging manner. He cleared his throat. His tone was apologetic. "With great embarrassment the defense would like to thank and excuse juror No. 4." Damn you, Glenda Sue. He shrugged his shoulders as if to say, "Sorry, I had to do it." Judge Minter gave me a sympathetic smile as I picked up my things and left the hushed courtroom.

There are countless ways to rationalize rejection. Here is my way: No matter how we may try to alter the sequence of events and circumstances of our lives, we cannot alter the grand design that was specially conceived just for us. It was simply ordained that I not be on this jury. I'm glad I had the experience. I've learned how to better deal with rejection, and my respect for the court system remains solid and strong.

Important writ matters in my court required that I cut my jury duty short. I have to complete the remainder of my jury service in the future. Although I'm more philosophical about rejection, I still might use the technique I employed for the senior prom. Instead of being a prospective juror, maybe they will let me serve as a courtroom attendant.

Postscript: A week or so after my jury experience I attended the Criminal Defense Bar Association dinner. I ran into the defense lawyer who had exercised his peremptory challenge to remove me from the jury. He said he was sorry that he had to "kick me off the jury." I said that

I understood and that he was doing what he thought best for his client. We each took a sip of our respective cocktails. Then I said, "You must have had a shitty case." He took another sip and said, "You don't know how shitty."

LIBERALS ARE EASILY FOOLED

I felt like an actor in a commercial. It was a bright clear Monday morning at the end of October, and my drive up the coast highway to the court in Ventura was exhilarating. The sun sparkled on the ocean where, in synchronicity, dolphins cut graceful arcs out and into the water. My hands gently held the wheel as the Jaguar stretched its limbs and bounded up the coast, the double wishbone design providing the suspension that offered perfect balance and nimble handling. I was listening to Joseph Conrad's Heart of Darkness on tape, but in preparation for the day's work, I also thought of a multitude of legal subjects. *Neary vs. Regents of University of California* (1992) 3 Cal.4th 273 popped into my mind, and I heard the voice of Kurtz -- "The horror! The horror!"

Neary held that while a case is pending on appeal, the parties may stipulate to a reversal of the trial court judgment as part of their settlement. I was working on a case involving newly enacted Code of Civil Procedure section 128, subdivision (a)(8) which provides, among other things, that an appellate court shall not reverse a judgment unless there is no reasonable possibility the interests of nonparties or the public will be adversely affected, and the reason for reversal outweighs the erosion of public trust that may result from nullification of the judgment.

The statute was enacted in response to the acrimonious debate that *Neary* engendered. Some writers opined in the Daily Journal that *Neary* critics were liberals, more concerned about stating broad principles for the so-called good of society than in permitting individual litigants to resolve their disputes as they saw fit. I thought *Neary* was a bad decision, but if I am a "liberal," it has nothing to do with my disapproval of *Neary*.

Just up ahead I saw a bedraggled hitchhiker, squinting in the sun and holding a cardboard sign on which was written in crude black letters, "Santa Barbara." I drove right by him, ignoring his contemptuous stare. But if I am a "conservative," it has nothing to do with my disregard for the hapless hitchhiker. Our court bailiff pointed out the obvious danger in picking up strangers and asked me to abandon the practice. As a compromise, I picked up old, infirmed hitchhikers, but also ended that practice after my experience with one such elderly gentleman.

He had settled himself in the car and, as soon as we gained speed, began yelling innocuous phrases at the top of his lungs: "WE'RE ALL GOING TO DIE! DEATH IS HERE! THERE IS NO WAY OUT." I was terrified but persevered, and he directed me with gesticulations and barely comprehensible directions to his destination, an alcoholic rehabilitation facility in Oxnard. It was an unsettling experience, and I decided it was too risky to pick up hitchhikers, a conservative approach, but not necessarily an essential characteristic of a "conservative."

Jaguar and I arrived at the courthouse and we turned gracefully into the driveway. I gave a slight press of the button on the side of the door and the driver's side window slid effortlessly into the door. I reached for my magic card sitting in a holder between the seats, and pressed it against the metal plate attached to a concrete post just outside the entrance to the exclusive VIP parking for justices and their staff. The large protective metal gates slowly swung open and the Jag, purring after its romp up the coast, crept into the partially covered parking area, then inched its way into its assigned parking space. It would rest for about 10 hours while I, in my chambers, would ponder and then write about important legal issues impacting the lives of millions of people.

I pulled the ornate key from the ignition, and the faint hum of the Jaguar's 4.0 litre, 281 horsepower aluminum engine fell quiet. Just at that time, one my colleagues pulled into his driving space. We got out of our cars and greeted one other. He prefers that I not use his name; in fact, he threatened me with grievous harm should there appear in this column even a trace of a hint as to his identity.

Within a moment, the eerie sensation of a presence cast a pall over our warm salutation. In this restricted, private spot, the shadowy figure of an outsider emerged from nowhere. The Jaguar slumbered, but for a moment we became dogs; our lips curled and the hair on our backs stood on end. The stranger was pudgy and wore a black stocking cap under which curled, like so many worms his hair, black with wanton streaks of gray. His clothing was layered. He wore a raggedy jacket; underneath that, a loose, ill-fitting sweatshirt from the bottom of which hung shamelessly, a grimy T shirt. His beard was a patchy stubble, and his dark glasses hid whatever intent was reflected in his eyes. He approached with outstretched hand.

Who spoke first? It is hard to recall, but one of us offered a greeting. "Who are you and what are you doing here?" His answer to this compound question was non-responsive: "Hey, can you guys help me out?"

We told him that he was not supposed to be there and that he would have to leave. He asked, "Can't you just help me out a little?" My colleague told him to leave or he would be arrested. He did not leave. My colleague went into the court to get the bailiff. In the meantime I gave him two bucks and showed him a side door which would provide his escape. I implored him, "Leave before they come. You will be arrested. Come on dude, it's time to split." My anxiety was mounting. Why didn't he just leave?

"Do you think they might help me inside?" he inquired. "Help you inside?" I said in disbelief. Suddenly he smiled. "I can't take your money," He handed me the two dollars. "Why not?" I said, offended. "Well if you don't want it now, I can give it to you at the Halloween Party this afternoon." He pulled off his wig. It was

V., one of the court clerks. His disguise was perfect. He had everyone fooled. Secretaries and research attorneys had run from him.

"You're the only one who gave me money," he said. I sheepishly took back my two dollars. My colleague, who was not in on the joke, came out with the bailiff, who was in on the joke. My colleague exclaimed, "It's you, V. Great disguise." They warmly shook hands. V. looked in my direction and said, "he gave me two dollars." "It figures," said my colleague, "He thinks *Neary* was a bad decision." "You're damn right I do," I shot back defensively, "and I like the new statute."

They all regarded me with disapproval. "Are we not here to help others?" I asked. Someone said, "If that's true, what are the others here for?" I couldn't think of an answer.

Since the incident, my life has changed somewhat. V. and the bailiff have been a little less friendly. The Commission on Judicial Performance is looking into allegations that I had conspired with a trespasser to evade the law and had tried to give him succor and comfort. The old bromide, "No good deed goes unpunished," keeps rolling around in my head. I'm less inclined to give money to people on the street. And now that the holiday season is approaching, I say, "Peace on Earth, and Goodwill to, to . . . men and women everywhere . . . I guess."

THE FUTURE IS NOW

Things are not what they seem. A short time ago newspapers carried an obituary that Arthur Gilbert died. Although at times I feel like it, I am not dead. The papers were referring to the other Arthur Gilbert, the wealthy one who was knighted by the Queen of England. That will never happen to me. I don't want to get that close to a sword. And besides, unlike the late Sir Arthur Gilbert, I never owned a priceless silver collection. The closest I have come to precious silver was petting the Lone Ranger's horse when I was a kid. Years later I was disappointed to learn that the horse was a stand- in.

Sir Arthur Gilbert lived in Los Angeles the last half of his life, and occasionally I would receive his mail. Of course I opened it; it was addressed to me. I'm sure he did the same with my mail. To avoid confusion I considered changing my name to Gilbert Arthur but thought better of it. Gilbert Arthur sounds literary, and hardly anyone reads literature any more.

The recent proliferation of chain bookstores might suggest the opposite. But as I said, things are not what they seem. The lawyer who wrote in his appellant's brief that defendant is a person of "Mexican American dissent" probably had not been to the literature section tucked away in a dark corner of his local chain book store. There are dozens more out there just like him. We can be charitable and attribute solecisms to typos, but the truth is we are not now a literate society. Remember the touching and eloquent letters that were read to us on Ken Burns' Civil War series? I recently asked a student I know if he writes letters. He said that he did, and proceeded to print a "B," "C," and "D," on his notebook paper.

Today people do not write letters; they e-mail memos along with stupid jokes. And forget about punctuation. How can we be literate if we do not read literature? Why do we not read literature? The stock answer is that there is no time. Even Evelyn Woods will concede that reading literature requires time, only, she would argue, less of it. What with professional journals, advance sheets, newspapers, magazines, *Buffy the Vampire Slayer*, and *Malcolm in the Middle*, there is no time even for Evelyn Woods to curl up with *"Finnegan's Wake."*

The gurus of our continually changing technological age tell us that the only businesses and institutions that will survive are those that continually change. They warn that we must change or die. The Greek philosopher Heraclitus said, "All that endures is change." But today the pace of change has become so rapid that the most we can grasp of the present is a few strands of the slippery rope of time, yanked through our hands by the irresistible pull of the future. Accelerated change has caused us to mistake the future's indistinct and shifting contours for a structure with a sturdy foundation in the present.

Ads for new products and services announce that "The Future is Now." This seeming contradiction may be true. The mania for change has trapped us in an indefinable haze in which the present and the future are merged. How can any idea or activity be sustained, when the very word "permanence" has become an anachronism?

Enslaved by the future, our shaky and uncertain present affords us barely enough time to sleep, perchance to dream and nourish poetic creativity instead of Hamlet's horror over death. And in our waking hours there is no time to achieve maximum skill and accomplishment in our endeavors, which are in a constant state of change. It is not surprising that we are anxious and troubled. This all-consuming insecurity has in turn engendered the creation of chain book stores.

Millions of people are reading, but not for the joy and the wisdom derived from literature. Motivated by the twin tyrannies of fear and greed, they are reading self-help books. How else to cope with the future which is now? But the dislocation of the present has so deprived these millions of readers of their self worth that they eagerly purchase books that brazenly insult them. "Gardening for Dummies." "Cooking for Dummies." "Accounting for Dummies." "Tai Chi for Dummies." The only acceptable title I found was "Astrology for Dummies."

No matter what the subject, we need help understanding an ever-increasingly complex world that will not sit still long enough for us to comprehend it. Change has so radically transformed the innumerable mundane activities of our lives that we lack the confidence to do the most basic things. It is one thing for Emily Post to give us pointers on etiquette, but now we have books telling us how to make love, how to order in a restaurant, how to impress a date, and how to relate to your cat.

Books are read for their pragmatic value, not for insights about life and human nature, not for the appreciation of the written word or a descriptive phrase, or for the sheer pleasure of reading. In our obsession to survive, we read books that promise to reveal the secrets that will ensure success in the future - which is now. This phenomenon is particularly widespread in the professions. Whatever the issue, there is a book with immediate and practical advice. The legal profession, for example, has a plethora of books, tapes, or CD ROMs, telling lawyers how to get clients, how to keep them, how to impress them, how to bill them, how to socialize with them and how to collect receivables from them.

The American artist John Baldessari satirizes this phenomenon in his painting "Tips for Artists," which perhaps may more properly be called a "painted text." It lists in bold print "Tips for Artists Who want to Sell."

His painted text advises the use of light colors, the avoidance of morbid props. The painting lists subjects that sell well. These include Madonna and Child, landscapes, flowers, and still lifes. On one level the painting is an indictment of commercial art. On another, it offers with tongue in cheek what actually sells. Literal readers of Baldessari's painting who follow his advice might in fact sell well.

On this level, Baldessari's painting serves as a model for anyone wishing to write a professional article for the legal profession. For example, "Tips for Lawyers Who Want to be Judges." Depending on the appointing authority, the applicant's views on the following subjects, which for many may be expressed in abbreviated form as "I do support" or "I do not support," will either guarantee or exclude from consideration possible appointment to a federal or state judgeship: the death penalty, abortion, victim's rights, mandatory sentencing, strikes (the entire gambit from one to three), takings, civil and property rights (differences if any between the two), victim's rights, defendant's rights, wrongs, the use and abuse of habeas corpus, restraint, activism, rehabilitation vs. punishment, judicial discretion, judicial independence vis-à-vis the appointing authority's "philosophy, vision, and bias." I could go on, but I'm sure you get the point.

But these quick fixes with their superficial answers provide no solutions to difficult problems. That requires sustained reflection. And that in turn requires time, time in the present. No wonder many judicial opinions and statutes are often incomprehensible. They have been drafted in a vanishing present, overpowered by an ever-encroaching future.

Change is inexorable, and it is a good thing to be open to it. But when we ignore the other tenses of time, we lose ability and stability. With time on fast forward, I favor a thumb on the pause button. If the only way to survive is to embrace constant change without a breath, then maybe the obituary for Sir Arthur Gilbert applies metaphorically to yours truly. Old fashioned I am, reading a good book in the present. That's my way, a silent swan song. I am in the middle of volume I of " Remembrance of Things Past." Only five volumes to go.

A CHOICE:
MADONNA'S BOOK, "SEX"
MY BOOK, "LEX"

"Is Madonna amazing or what? She sings, dances, and acts, and now it turns out she's a writer, too." Caption from a cartoon in the *New Yorker*, Nov. 9 1992.

I'll come right out and admit it. I read Madonna's new book, *Sex*. No I didn't rush down to the bookstore and buy it. They were sold out. You will probably never believe this, but I came by the book fortuitously when I was getting a haircut. My barbershop had purchased the book for certain customers to read while getting their hair cut.

When I arrived for my haircut last week and learned that Madonna's *Sex* was available for my perusal, curiosity got the best of me, and I put aside my copy of *The Meditations* by Marcus Aurelius.

The barber yelled, "Do you want to see Madonna's '*Sex*'?"

Despite the whir of hair dryers, everybody in the shop turned. I whispered that it might be interesting to take a gander.

"What?" the barber yelled. "Can't hear you. Do you want to see it or not?"

"I'd like to see it," said the lawyer sitting in the adjacent chair. "I can read this anytime," he said, waving a copy of "Blackstone's Commentaries."

"I think it might be interesting to see," I said hoping to preempt the lawyer.

"That's the understatement of the year," said the lawyers. "Why don't we share it? We can pass it back and forth."

I begrudgingly agreed, provided I got to see it first. The barber handed me the book. Can you believe it, the cover was metal? The pages were held together by metal rings. The cold unyielding cover seemed so at odds with the title. One would have expected the book to be flexible, pliable, soft to the touch. But I guess that's just me, kind of old-fashioned.

I opened the book. Hairs fell out. Maybe that was because I was in a barbershop, but with Madonna, you never can be sure. A lawyer obviously had a hand in writing the introduction. It contains a disclaimer that any similarity between persons depicted in the book and real persons "is not only coincidental, it's ridiculous." That ought to keep bothersome lawsuits in check.

The book is ostensibly the fantasy of a fictional character who, if real, would never have worked in the presidential campaign of Pat Buchanan or Pat Robertson. At times it uses the epistolary form, but it is hardly Richardson's "*Pamela.*"

You probably won't remember it for the writing. Maybe because it is so richly photographed. Lots of crowd scenes. A photographic fantasy is an oxymoron. It's really happening.

The lawyer sitting in the barber chair next to me and I passed the book back and forth. We later discussed our reaction to it. It stimulated us both to indulge in our own fantasies, only they were very different from Madonna's. She fantasized about the most important subject in her life and wrote about it. We fantasized about the most important subject in our lives, and this inspired me to write my own book. I call it *Lex*.

"*Lex*" is more of a fantasy than "*Sex*." That's because it has no photographs. It contains, however, fanciful, richly textured creations of the mind that make Madonna's imaginative foray seem prosaic by comparison. Without restriction I unleashed the creative forces of my imagination so that they could concoct phantasmagoric visions. The result is a book that reveals, without expurgation or shame, the unbridled and daring fantasies of lawyers and judges. I'll reveal just a few

I The judge's fantasies include the following:

- A lawyer cites a case for a legal principle, and the case actually stands for that principle.
- A judge asks a dumb question during the argument, and the lawyer's response does not begin with the words, "With all due respect…"
- Attorneys laugh at a judge's joke because they really think it's funny.
- A judge is invited to a large firm's Christmas bash because its members actually like the judge's company.
- Prosecutors assist a judge in computing the sentence of a defendant convicted of multiple charges with enhancements.

II Some of the attorney's fantasies are as follows:

- A justice on the court of appeal finally writes an opinion on conduct credits that everybody understands.
- A lawyer appears before a judge who, on more than one occasion, can be talked out of a tentative ruling.
- When appearing in a crowded courtroom with a client, the judge says, "You know, counsel, your excellent brief has convinced me that my earlier ruling was incorrect. I was wrong and your insightful argument has convinced me to reverse myself."
- Clients truly appreciate an attorney's efforts on their behalf and gladly pay their bills on time.
- A partnership dissolution is amicable, with all parties treating one another with civility and generosity.

- A lawyer never has to confirm an understanding in writing.
- A lawyer always gets a continuance when needed.
- The Supreme Court holds that a criminal case cluttered with innumerable little errors, which are harmless when standing alone, added together equal a reversal.
- A lawyer who is three minutes late to court because of stopping to help an elderly woman fight off five gang members trying to steal her purse—and then getting stuck in the courthouse elevator between the seventh and eight floors – is listened to by the judge, who believes the excuse and agrees to vacate the default judgment just taken.

You can see that "*Lex*" is a true fantasy, and in many ways quite unlike "*Sex.*" There is, however, one characteristic they have in common. Any similarity between actual persons or events is – well, "ridiculous."

PUTTING WORDS IN THE MOUTHS OF INTERVIEWEES
PART I

A few years ago, writer Janet Malcolm got off her couch and wrote a two-part article in *The New Yorker* magazine about the psychoanalyst Jeffery M. Masson who had been fired as projects director of the Sigmund Freud archives. The article, which later appeared in book form, portrayed Masson as a self-aggrandizing, arrogant, braggart, who seemed to be desperately in need of an analyst himself. Much of the material that made up Masson's unflattering portrait appeared as quotes taken from Masson's own mouth. This made the depiction of his personality, or lack of one, all the more devastating.

Masson filed a libel action in federal court alleging that Malcolm misquoted him. Masson lost his case on a summary judgment in the trial court, and the Court of Appeals for the Ninth Circuit affirmed.

The Court of Appeals held that even if Masson had been misquoted, there was no libel. The court reasoned that some of the quotations attributed to Masson did not alter the substance of his actual comments, thus ruling out malice. Other misquotations were justified as rational interpretations of Masson's own ambiguous remarks.

A blistering dissent by Judge Kozinski pointed out that "an unqualified quotation attributed to a third party is commonly understood to contain *no* interpretation; by using quotation marks the writer warrants that she [or he] has interposed no editorial comment, has resolved no ambiguities, has added or detracted nothing of substance."

The dissent opined that Masson's words were manipulated so as to place him in an unfavorable light. Thus, the issue should have gone to a jury. Kozinski concluded that "Masson has lost his case, but the defendant [Malcolm, The New Yorker and Alfred A. Knopf, Inc.] and the profession to which they belong have lost far more."

Ironically, while the case was pending, Janet Malcolm wrote another two-part article for *The New Yorker* concerning the book *Fatal Vision*, written by Joe McGinniss. McGinniss believed that Jeffrey MacDonald, a physician who had been convicted of brutally murdering his pregnant wife and two daughters, was in fact guilty. Malcolm's article, in its analysis of the relationship between journalists and interviewees, touched on profound moral, philosophical and epistemological issues. Malcolm excoriated McGinniss for the way in which he deceived MacDonald in order to gain information. The hint of mea culpa that Malcolm offered in the article must have enhanced the satisfaction she felt about her victory over Masson.

The Masson opinion, of course, does not necessarily sanction misquoting by reporters, but it lets them off the hook for libel when the misquoted material constitutes a rational interpretation of what was said, or is substantially the same as what was said.

Most self-respecting editors would sack a reporter who misquotes, but the Masson opinion may lead some reporters to misuse quotation marks. This practice misinforms the reader and can be unjust to the interviewee.

Imagine an interview with Gertrude Stein conducted by a reporter not concerned with accurate quotes.

The Actual Interview

Reporter: It's a pleasure to be here Mrs. Stein

Stein: That's Ms. Stein.

Reporter: This is 1924. We haven't even heard of "Ms." Yet.

Stein: I'm ahead of my time.

Reporter: I'm curious to know about the oft-quoted phrase of yours, a rose is a rose is a rose.

Stein: What I said was, "Rose is a rose is a rose..." The first "rose" is not preceded by the indefinite article "a," and the word "rose" is repeated four times, not three.

Reporter: In any event, you must have a great fondness for gardening.

Stein: I hate gardening, and I'm not all that crazy about roses, either.

Reporter: Well, you are certainly repetitive when it comes to roses. I mean, after all, a rose is a rose or it isn't.

Stein: Roses are not the issue. I'm trying to revitalize worn-out nouns. A rose is now red for the first time in 100 years.

Reporter: So you like red roses, do you?

Stein: No, I told you I don't particularly like roses. I detest the way we have bastardized the English language. We don't even know what is a rose.

Reporter: Hmm, roses are red, violets are blue- might be a good lead for my story.

Stein: Alice, give her another brownie to munch on with her tea.

The Article

GERTRUDE STEIN- WRITER OR HORTICULTURALIST?

"This writer, in Paris last week, had an exclusive interview with Gertrude Stein at her salon. Her aide-de-camp, Alice B. Toklas, served brownies during the interview. I practically ate the whole tray and have been feeling giddy for days. She promised to send the recipe.

"Miss. Stein is obviously obsessed with roses. She rationalizes this preoccupation by stating, "People just don't know what roses are. A person could look at a tulip and think it's a rose. A rose should be a rose, not a daffodil or a marigold. People are forgetful, and I'm reminding them what a rose is. Its funny I take the trouble to do it, however, because I hate roses, although I guess red roses are okay. But roses haven't been red for 100 years. I hope they don't say that about my book, 'Three Lives,' 100 years from now.'

"I munched on a new brownie as I tried to figure that one out. As much as Mrs. Stein hates roses, that's how much she hates the English language. 'The English language is a bastard,' she said gruffly. Perhaps her contempt for the language stems from her inability to use it effectively. Repeating a thing over and over again doesn't make it important. Mrs. Stein, however, says, 'How are people going to know anything about roses unless you drum it into their heads. Since words, and particularly nouns, are worn out, I see no problem with wearing out a few people now and then. Here, have another brownie.'"

Some reporters argue that a little touch-up work in quotes is legitimate. They argue that if you are interviewing, for example, a recent winner of the Nobel prize for literature, and in a momentary lapse he says, "Irregardless," and you quote him as saying, "regardless," what's the harm? The harm sneaks up on us when we start wrestling with the question of where to draw the line. Who is worth protecting and who isn't?

Misquotes Just Aren't Right

Did Neil Armstrong say, "That's one small step for a man, one giant leap for mankind," or did he actually say the redundant, "That's one small step for man, one giant leap for mankind"?

If we can't believe in quotation marks anymore, what is there left to believe in? Have we actually reached that point where anything goes? A misquote is like Beethoven's Ninth on a synthesizer. It's not right, and it does not belong. Words that appear in quotation marks should be a verbatim transcription of what was said.

Let's not aggravate the misinformation epidemic by abandoning punctuation. The easy way for a reporter to tidy up a rambling response from an interviewee is to scratch the quotes. If the reporter is looking for a more elegant response than he or she gets, a substantially similar phrase will work provided there are no quotation marks. As far as I'm concerned, the practice of misquoting grosses me out.

Please don't quote me on that.

142

MISQUOTING IN QUOTES
PART II

Courtroom scene: Prosecution bearing down on witness and waiving a sheath of papers back and forth. "Isn't it a fact that you told Officer Quitgate...and I quote," (now reading from one of the sheets), "I did see the defendant do it.'?"

"That's not what I said," replies the witness with conviction.

Prosecutor, trying to decide whether to ask the next question that all the books on trial practice say never to ask. "What the hell," he says to himself. "Dog brains, the defense counsel, will ask it anyway." He asks it. "Well then, what did you say?" The jury leans forward. A hush envelopes the courtroom.

The witness in all earnestness says, "I said I did not see the defendant do it." The prosecutor, feeling like a dejected Mr. Berger in the closing scene of the Perry Mason show, says, "No further questions."

Defendant is acquitted. Defense attorney Stuart Racehorse No. 1, a.k.a. S.R.1, is interviewed by the press on his 487th win.

"To what do you attribute yet another win?" asks the reporter, now known as a staff writer.

"I can't take all the credit," says S.R.1 with false modesty. "Quotation marks won the case for us. You can quote me on that."

Quotation marks carry the imprimatur of accuracy. They provide a rationale for admitting into evidence a declaration against interest. A damning self-portrait carries authenticity. No concern about hearsay here. If that's what the witness says the person said, it must be true.

Quotation marks. Today they are like wasps buzzing around the head of Janet Malcolm. This is the subject of the preceding column, "Putting Words in the Mouths of Interviewees." In 1989, she was celebrating her recent victory in the 9th U.S. Circuit Court of Appeals. She had written an unflattering book about psychoanalyst Jefferey M. Masson, who had lost his job as projects director of the Sigmund Freud Archives. Masson sued Malcolm for libel and charged that she had misquoted him.

The court of appeals affirmed a summary judgment in favor of Malcolm. The majority held, among other things, that Malcolm had not libeled Masson. Her alleged misquotes were only a rational interpretation of what Masson had said. Judge Alex Kozinski, in his dissent, pointed out that quotation marks are understood to have no interpretation.

That's what I thought. It's a writer telling his or her readers, "This isn't what I'm saying. This is what dorkhead said." Indeed, the quotes are objective evidence the journalist uses to support the thesis that dorkhead is a real jerk.

Malcolm's victory prompted her to write an essay in the New York Review of Books, March 1, 1990. Her piece, seasoned with appropriate erudition, argued that quotation marks do not necessarily represent what was actually spoken. If they did, we would be lost in a thicket of mangled syntax, repetition, contradiction and fragments that make up everyday speech. The tape recorder is not of much use. It only fuels the flames of a lawsuit. The argument rages over whether a journalist functions as a writer or a stenographer.

Malcolm also touched on a theme she has written about before, that journalism can be a dirty business.

There are the expectations and hopes of the interviewee, to be favorably immortalized. It is in the atmosphere of false friendship between journalist interviewer and subject interviewee that these expectations thrive. The impressions of the journalist, however, form and grow in secret, under cover. When they come to fruition in an article, the interviewee may meet Rosemary's baby.

Malcolm's essay had a wistful tone. She seemed to be saying that journalism can be exploitive and a dirty job, but somebody's got to do it. She even expressed some sympathy for Masson, the gracious gesture of the victor to the defeated "whose efforts had come to nothing." But among Malcolm's learned references was the omission of Yogi Berra's thoughts. They would have been a reminder that the case is not over until it is over. Masson won the next round in U.S. Supreme Court. (*Masson v. New York Magazine Inc.,* 111S.Ct.2419 (1991).)

The Supreme Court acknowledged that quoted material may be changed for the correction of grammar or syntax, but rejected the 9th Circuit's holding that an altered quotation is protected so long as it is a "rational interpretation" of the actual statement. It's one thing to rationally interpret an ambiguous statement, but as Kozinski pointed out, quotation marks are a sign that the author is not interpreting but reporting.

Presumably, a jury will ultimately decide whether Malcolm misquoted Masson, and if so, did she libel him.

What irks people, such as Deirdre English, who wrote about this in the Daily Journal on July 11, 1991, is that Malcolm apparently thinks that even if she misquoted Masson in the way he suggests, it was perfectly legitimate. It is encouraging that journalists like English, and many others with whom I have spoken, deplore the practice of misquoting.

The ethical implications of the Masson case touch lawyers and judges, as well as journalists. The parallels are striking. The factual portion of a judicial opinion, or a lawyer's moving papers, is much like a story written by a journalist for Page 1. Whether the subject is a flood, a meeting of foreign ministers, or the details of a personal injury accident, the relevant facts should be stated with scrupulous and painstaking care. The discussion portion of the opinion, the argument, however, is only as good as the facts upon which it is based. A seemingly well-reasoned argument is deceitful when the facts are manipulated to make the argument work.

What is frustrating to journalists, lawyers and judges alike is that facts are seldom so tidy that they lend themselves to a particular argument. All of us often find ourselves wedded to a particular position. What to do? It's simple —direct our efforts toward modifying our position, not the facts.

We have to meticulously guard against misusing the facts, unconsciously or otherwise, in the cause of a belief or thesis. A position, whether propounded by a journalist, judge or lawyer, that is based on distorted or skewed facts has no foundation. The position, along with the person who propounded it, ultimately disappears in the wind.

If Masson ultimately prevails over Malcolm, then will her efforts have come to nothing?

Postscript- Janet Malcom went to trial and won.

THE WHOLE TRUTH AND NOTHING BUT . . . .
PART III

Judges who preside over high profile cases find that their comments, offhand or otherwise, whether made from the bench, or at the barber shop, will be subject to intense scrutiny. Commentators on the O.J. Simpson case, for example, most of whom are lawyers who find working in the media more alluring than practice, analyze every utterance Judge Lance Ito makes. Suddenly there's a hidden meaning in "You may proceed counsel."

A statement the judge made in ruling on a motion was recently reported in an article in the *New Yorker*, "The court must always remember this process is a search for truth." The article went on to discuss the merit of truth seeking in trials, and the abolishment of the exclusionary rule to achieve that end.

It's hard to quarrel with Judge Ito's statement as a general proposition. In any trial we would like to know the truth, but at what cost? Most people have rejected beating the "truth" out of someone. Often it gives a false answer, and besides, being a barbarian is unseemly. I suppose we could get right to the truth in some cases if we dispensed with the bothersome rules that create obstacles to achieving that end.

We could scuttle the Miranda Rule or simply abolish the exclusionary rule. Some argue the exclusionary rule is moribund already because of the Leon decision. It permits officers in certain cases to conduct searches in violation of the Fourth Amendment so long as they do so in good faith.

In our goal to get to the truth we could give the exclusionary rule another nudge in the direction of oblivion with a new rule, "the good faith hunch." Here's how it works. Police officers are patrolling a neighborhood. They notice a sleazy looking guy walk up to the front porch of the house, suspiciously look over his shoulder and then surreptitiously slide his key in the front door lock. He enters the house and a few minutes later motions for someone waiting in a parked car to come in.

Is this a burglary? Is it a drug deal? Or is it merely a husband sneaking his out-of-town father-in-law into the house, a surprise for his wife's birthday? The police have a hunch this has something to do with drugs. They break into the house and search it without a warrant and find drugs. The "truth" wins out. But what if all they ultimately find is a terrified father-in-law who was waiting to yell "Happy Birthday" to his daughter when she walks in the door? The cost of a mistaken hunch may be too high a price to pay for the truth.

Our yearning for the truth should not compel us to so tamper with the rules that govern our justice system that we undermine the protections we have spent centuries building. Even if we abolish rules that frustrate our quest for the truth in a trial, finding the "truth" is still problematic. Most of the time the best we can hope for is an approximation of the truth by the end of a trial. Seldom do we know what really happened.

Truth lacks certainty because it's often colored by appearance. Take the case of writer Janet Malcolm who wrote a scathing article in the *New Yorker* about psychoanalyst Jeffrey Masson, former director of the Freud Archives. He sued her for libel. The jury searched for the truth and found that Malcolm had libeled Masson. The jury could not, however, come to a decision on damages. The trial judge considered retrying the case solely on the issue of damages, but then decided it was better to retry the entire case.

In the second trial a new jury searched for the truth and found Malcolm did not libel Masson. The jury did find that some of the quotations Malcom attributed to Masson were false, and one was even defamatory, but determined she was not guilty of libel because she lacked the necessary intent or malice.

So why the different verdicts? Isn't truth supposed to be absolute? Something happened between the two trials. If trials are theater, as some have suggested, then Malcolm did what any capable actor would do: She hired a speech coach. Rex Bossert reported in the Daily Journal that after the first trial, Malcolm worked for eight months with a noted speech coach, the same one who taught Robert DeNiro to learn an Appalachian accent for the movie "Cape Fear." But DeNiro was doing what actors do, playing a role. He was learning to speak like somebody on screen other than Robert DeNiro off screen.

What was Malcolm learning between the two trials? Malcolm's coach taught her how to speak to the jury, and how to avoid distracting and annoying mannerisms. He told her how to dress. She even had a full dress rehearsal in the form of a mock trial at New York University. This preparation proved the cliché that practice makes perfect.

I'm not suggesting there was more truth in one trial than in the other. Malcolm's coaching may have simply helped her communicate more effectively with the jury. But being a better speaker or making a good appearance doesn't make one more truthful. In which trial was the truth obscured and in which one was it brought to light? I can't say, but I'm sure Malcolm and Masson have different views.

The truth (pardon the expression) is that neither jury knew the truth better than the other. If either case had come up before an appellate court, I suspect that under a substantial evidence standard of review, either verdict would be upheld, absent instructional or evidentiary error.

Truth is just more elusive than we wish to acknowledge. When judges make sure that parties prove their cases by the correct burden of proof, and when they apply the law evenly and fairly, they do justice and most often, but not always, get to the truth. That is the stunning achievement of our system of justice.

Nevertheless, people are still concerned about what they perceive as a preoccupation with protecting rights at the expense of finding the truth. Having lunch in a restaurant the other day, I couldn't help overhearing the conversation of two people at the adjacent table. They were talking about an upcoming criminal case. One person opined that the defendant will probably get off on a technicality. The other said, "Ain't it the truth." Their cynicism was misplaced. They obviously hadn't heard of harmless error.

TO SPEAK OUT OR NOT TO SPEAK OUT-
THAT WAS THE QUESTION IN 1993
IT STILL IS

We were at the dinner table with several guests.

My parents' close friend, Mrs. Grabow was sitting opposite me. She had pencil-thin eyebrows that danced when she spoke. The fine delicate hairs on her upper lip formed a subtle but noticeable mustache that seemed to crawl like a caterpillar when she spoke. I had seen her several times in the past, but had been so fascinated by the dance of her eyebrows that this was the first time I had actually noticed her mustache. "You've got a mustache," I blurted out.

"Inappropriate," you might say. Perhaps, but what do you expect from a five year-old? My shins still ache from the kick I got under the table from my parents.

This was my first introduction to the notion that we do not always get to say what we want to say. As we mature, we say less of what we are truly thinking, less of what we would like to say. These constraints stem from a variety of sources which include a code of personal or professional ethics, notions of good taste, or simply a realistic sense of self-preservation. Think of the countless number of bosses who will never know what their employees really think of them.

Like most things, these constraints have their benefits and burdens. Some thoughts are better left in the silence of our hearts, half formed and unexpressed. Like chickens that never break out of their shells, they will not come home to roost. But, as "talk radio" proves, there are so many issues on which to speak out, that keeping one's thoughts bottled up can be frustrating.

These call-in radio shows provide a safety valve to relieve the pressure for people who need to get things off their chests. Some people simply speak out about how their "rights" relate to the universal themes of our time: abortion, minorities, life, death, mothers, fathers, sons, daughters, lovers, ferrets, smoking in restaurants, violence on television and Madonna.

But not everyone gets to speak out. Officers in the armed forces must button their lips when they get the urge to criticize their commander in chief, or they may fade away before they become old soldiers. Newspaper reporters (they are now called staff writers), are also subject to restrictions on speaking out. For example, a reporter who speaks on an issue at a political rally loses the appearance of objectivity if he or she writes a news story on the same issue. The same principle applies to judges who must not publicly speak about pending cases or issues that pertain to those cases.

The subject of judges speaking out prompted a respected judge on the Ninth U.S. Circuit Court of Appeals to speak out about judges speaking out. Judge Arthur Alarcon spoke out about some of his colleagues who had spoken out.

He did not think they should have spoken out, so he spoke out about it. Now judges are speaking out about Judge Alarcon's speaking out about his colleagues speaking out.

You can see how this thing can get out of hand.

Judge Alarcon no doubt recognized that important public figures often use a university speech to air their views on crucial issues. For example, Winston Churchill in a speech to Westminster College in Fulton, Missouri, on March 5, 1946, spoke about the Soviet Union's attempt to isolate itself from the West. He characterized that isolation with the term, "iron curtain."

In a similar fashion, Judge Alarcon used the occasion of a speech to the graduating class of Loyola Law School to speak about an issue crucial to both the public and the judiciary: under what circumstances may judges make public comments pertaining to the judiciary?

Judge Alarcon scored some of his unnamed colleagues because they publicly spoke out about their dissatisfaction with the manner in which the U.S. Supreme Court handled the Robert Alton Harris execution. Is it appropriate for judges to publicly criticize their colleagues' decisions? Judge Alarcon thinks not, and suggests that the judges who spoke out may have violated the code of judicial conduct by undermining the public's confidence in the judiciary. Judge Alarcon thinks such judges should be subject to discipline and publicly criticized by the State Bar.

Should judges express unflattering views about the judiciary by holding press conferences, giving speeches, or even worse yet, writing a column? If they violate the code of judicial conduct by doing so, then do they violate the code any less when they lambaste a colleague in a judicial opinion?

U.S. Supreme Court Justice Antonin Scalia, for example, cannot abide those numbskulls who don't see things his way, and he is not shy about saying so in his opinions. Does not this also undermine the public's confidence in the judiciary? Maybe not, because who reads judicial opinions? OK, I suppose some people have to read them, but considering the way opinions are written these days, how many people actually understand what they are reading?

Even assuming they do know what they are reading, the problem with attacking colleagues in judicial opinions is less pronounced in California. Although justices on the California Supreme Court have been known to disagree with one another, dissents speak to the issues rather than to personalities. The reply in a majority opinion to a dissent also reflects civility and a concern with the issue rather than the character or intelligence of the judge who has a different point of view.

As for the court of appeal, an inflammatory opinion can easily go up in a poof of smoke – depublished. In fact, since beginning my column for the Daily Journal, there is a move afoot to depublish my birth certificate.

But getting back to Judge Alarcon's point, he has a legitimate concern about judges airing their criticisms in public, rather than in an opinion, or from the bench. By venting their spleen in public, judges may bring the judiciary into disrepute, and may give the impression of being biased. This is not the best way to instill confidence in the judiciary even though everyone knows that judges do in fact have views on issues like the death penalty, abortion and welfare.

What the public does not always understand, however, is that a judge's view on an issue does not necessarily reflect the way the judge will rule on a case involving that issue. On the other hand, if a judge has strong feelings about an issue, perhaps the public might have more insight into the character of that judge than if he or she were quiet. This prompts another question: is the false appearance of bias as big an evil as bias itself?

I do not have an answer because it is not always easy to draw the line that separates what may be talked about publicly from what may not. I do not feel, however, that a judge should automatically be disciplined for making critical comments in public about the judiciary or the laws the judiciary must enforce.

For example, I think U.S. District Judge Terry Hatter's public comments about the federal sentencing guidelines are appropriate. His comments concern these laws in general as opposed to their application in a pending case.

Judge Hatter has spoken out about what he considers to be the unfairness of the federal sentencing laws which give judges no flexibility in sentencing. Whether you agree or disagree with Judge Hatter's point of view, his comments have provoked a healthy public debate about the fairness of the federal sentencing laws, and about the proper role of the judiciary.

My recommendation to judges or anyone else for that matter, who wishes to express an opinion to the world: listen to your inner voice. It usually reflects your best judgment. First think about what you intend to say. Then ask you inner voice the crucial question, "So what do you think?" If your inner voice says, "Are you serious?" Whatever you do, under no circumstances – I mean no circumstances whatsoever – should you even utter this comment in private let alone in public," then it is a good idea to follow the advice.

THE DIFFICULTY WITH DIFFICULT JUDGES AND LAWYERS

There is much talk these days about obnoxious lawyers. Ask any judge. The favorite topic around a judges' lunch table is how to cope with obnoxious lawyers-pass the Alka-Seltzer. These are the lawyers who have developed expertise in sidetracking a trial with endless, mind-numbing, irrelevant, and incomprehensible questions. This in turn has pushed more than a few judges into the abyss of error. This unfortunate event is memorialized by a higher court bamboozled by the upstart attorney.

Some lawyers are not even concerned about forcing a judge into error. They like to drive judges crazy just for the fun of it. Their arsenal includes double speak, tardiness, sneers, badgering, haranguing, begging and the worst of all, motions for reconsideration. These lawyers don't always get away with it. Sometimes a court of appeal affirms the imposition of sanctions. But, trial judges also have other ways of dealing with difficult or obstreperous lawyers. Rumor has it that there is a secret judges' list of troublesome attorneys. It is not appropriate for me to comment on this alleged list or the significance of alleged asterisks next to the names of some attorneys. Suffice it to say some things are hard to forget.

But enough about obnoxious, difficult lawyers. What about judges? Is there such a thing as an obnoxious, rude, or difficult judge? Apparently so, because I have been asked to be on a panel sponsored by the State Bar at its upcoming annual meeting in Monterey to discuss ways in which lawyers can effectively deal with difficult or obnoxious judges. It's going to be one of those demonstration type panels. I wonder why they were so eager to have me on the program.

To get ready for the program, I looked at a transcript that reflects an exchange between a lawyer and a justice during oral argument at a court of appeal.

Attorney: It appears to me-
Justice: What appears to you is of no interest to me. Appearances are deceiving and as irrelevant as what you think. Let's get down to what *is* rather than try to make sense out of your apparitions.
Attorney: But your honor, I only wanted-
Justice: Don't sass me back. Just get on with the argument.
Attorney: That's what I'm trying-
Justice: My patience is wearing thin. What about *People v. Flotsky?*
Attorney: That's a criminal case your honor.
Justice: That enlightening comment is not responsive.
Attorney: But *Flotsky* is an embezzlement case, and my case involves pretermitted heirs.
Justice: Don't patronize me.

Attorney: But your honor I don't see how *Flotsky* applies.

Justice: That may be why your argument is falling on deaf ears.

Attorney: But Probate Code section...

Justice: That's right, throw up the probate code when you're in trouble.

Attorney: I'm in trouble?

Justice: That starts with a T.

Attorney: This is mind boggling.

Justice: Boggle is an intransitive verb. Nothing can boggle the mind. It's the mind that boggles. It's like the refusal of an ass to move. Just as the ass does its own refusing, because no one can refuse for the ass, so too, a mind does its own boggling.

Attorney: Speaking of asses...

Justice: What was that?

Attorney: Nothing your honor.

Justice: Anything further?

.Attorney: I don't see how...

Justice: What was that?

Attorney: Nothing further your honor.

Justice: I see. Nothing further.

Attorney: Nothing your honor.

Justice: Very well. Thank you.

Attorney: Thank you your honor.

This is a transcript from a hearing I recently conducted. I will use it for the panel discussion on difficult judges. Of course I will have make extensive changes. After all, I have to make the judge rude, obnoxious, and maybe even a little foolish. Got any suggestions?

TRAFFIC SCHOOL
PART I

True or False?: Judges don't get traffic tickets. False---particularly if the judge doesn't reveal his identity. Last month I got a traffic ticket on Pacific Coast Highway (PCH). I was on the way to work. The officer said . . . . forget what the officer said, I was going 62 in a 45 mph zone, O.K.? It's hard to believe, but around Big Rock there actually is a 45 mph zone on PCH. Never mind that in the morning, PCH northbound is the Indianapolis speedway, and everyone was passing me. I was driving sufficiently over the speed limit to warrant (pardon the expression) a ticket. A sheriff's deputy pulled me over. He was professional, polite, courteous, even a bit sympathetic.

This was embarrassing. A few decades ago I had been the supervising judge of the Los Angeles Municipal Traffic Court, the largest traffic court in the world. My conduct did not set a good example.

The officer must have sensed my discomfort. "You can go to traffic school," he said cheerfully. An excellent idea. I applied. You make arrangements with the Malibu Municipal Court. No need to go in person. You can do it through the mail, provided you understand the mailing instructions. If you do, you can prepare a 1040, and probably pass the bar exam.

One thing, however, is crystal clear. You have to send in lots of money. But as the instructions cogently point out, if you are eligible for traffic school and decide not to attend, your automobile insurance **may** be adversely affected. No doubt a timid bureaucrat surrounded by a phalanx of city attorneys inserted the word, "may." In the patois of my fellow traffic school students, "give me a break."

There is the cost of bail, and through the use of a lucrative concept employed in all escrow instructions, an administrative fee, and still other fees to pay later on. I got a second mortgage on the house and sent in my money. Waiting for the response was nerve-racking. I remember when I presided in Traffic Court, the clerks in the master calendar could never find the file I needed. I was convinced my application would be lost. It wasn't. A response came in the mail. I was instructed to send in a $5 money order to the traffic school referral agency to get a "validation certificate" and a list of traffic schools. The municipal court trusted me to send in a check, but not the traffic school referral agency. Have you ever tried to get a $5 money order at your bank? It only costs $4.

I signed up for one of the many Comedy Traffic Schools. The only joke turned out to be on me. I called to make an appointment, and picked what turned out to be the nicest Saturday of the year. Over the phone I was told what they tell buyers in drug deals-bring cash and be on time. On the way there, I panicked over the thought of getting a traffic ticket. This, I later learned, was a common phenomenon.

The class was held in a cramped room in a small hotel in Santa Monica where the air conditioning either worked too well or not at all. The teacher had long stringy hair, and small fierce eyes. His protruding stomach was covered by a black T-shirt the front of which displayed a skull and cross bones surrounded by indecipherable illustrations. It refused to stay tucked into his black jeans. His Brooklyn accent seemed to rule out an affiliation with the Hell's Angels. As for his comedy, there was only one thing it failed to elicit--laughs.

Most of the students were of college age. Some actually went to college, only you wouldn't have known it, or believed it. There were a few older people, like me, who looked at the floor a lot. The teacher went around the room and asked each of us about our violations. I confined my answer to the traffic ticket.

One of the students, an attractive young blond woman told us of her past drunk driving experience. She spoke in the universal argot of her peers, every declaratory sentence ending with a question mark. "Umm . . . I got busted for a duce? Only I wasn't really drunk? I inhaled fumes from the newly painted walls of my boyfriend's condo? And like it registered on the B.A? My lawyer said it was a bummer?" That was the only laugh we had all day.

Much like hostages who grow to like their captors, I grew to like my instructor. He was conscientious and wanted us to be better and safer drivers. He knew a lot more about the Vehicle Code than I knew or would ever know.

Think it's O.K. to drive with bare feet? Seizing upon my past knowledge of traffic court, I said it was against the law. "It was, about 20 years ago," said a know-it-all in the front of the class. It's O.K. now.

Did you know that you can't have headphones plugged into both ears while driving, but that you can have a plug in one ear, so long as the other end of the headphone is dangling, but not resting against your cheek?

The instructor and I wound up having lunch together. He is the current version of a Renaissance man. He is a loan broker (I have his card), a rock musician(oxymoron-the CD is coming out next week), a tennis instructor (for the unfit?) and of course a traffic school instructor. A woman sitting at an adjacent table recognized me and came over. She had been a public defender in my court when I sat in traffic. The jig was up. He thought it was very funny and mercifully did not blow my cover when class reconvened.

The afternoon session went slowly. We watched some videos and talked a lot about drunk driving. We also took a test. I missed one. What a bummer. The class was beneficial and it changed my driving habits. If some weekday morning you bear down upon a car slowly proceeding northbound on PCH, waive to me as you go by.

Postscript: Shortly after writing this column, both my colleagues in Division Six received speeding tickets. They both intend to attend traffic school. I offered to write them recommendations. They declined.

TRAFFIC SCHOOL
PART II

Another traffic ticket five years later.

Judges are human. They screw up just like everyone else. Clinging to the cliché that to err is human, five years ago I confessed in my column to speeding on the insidious Pacific Coast Highway. It happened again. A behemoth they call an SUV, sucking up gas, its insouciant driver on a cell phone, was poking along in the lane ahead of me. Jaguar and I had enough and we changed lanes and passed on the left just as a sheriff's deputy going in the opposite direction zapped us with a radar gun. I did not even challenge the accuracy of the radar gun, which I learned in traffic school might have won the case for me. To demand that the officer show me his radar gun at the scene did not occur to me.

Justice William O. Douglas's imperfections were of mammoth proportions according to a recent biography, *Wild Bill: The Legend and Life of William O. Douglas* by Bruce Allen Murphy, Random House, 2003. So you can hardly expect me to be perfect. I had to give up a beautiful Saturday afternoon for traffic school at the Improv Comedy Club, a hole in the ground off an alley in Santa Monica. I joined my classmates in the serious study of the subtleties and nuances of the Vehicle Code.

My results on the traffic test are embarrassing. I expected to receive a perfect score this time. You, prescient reader, have already deduced that I did not pass the test with flying colors. My test score accounts for my stressing the "judges are human" theme in this column. I expect to do much better on the make up-test.

The manner in which the test was given made the pressure unbearable. The instructor couldn't have just given us a written multiple choice test at the end of the class. Oh no, he had to go around the room and ask impossible to answer questions. I had legitimate handicaps. First of all, the current Vehicle Code is not the one I used when I was reigning king of traffic court back in the 1970's. Furthermore, the instructor had it in for me. He spent the first half of the course telling us how to beat traffic tickets. Can you imagine? Without revealing my identity, I suggested that perhaps this was not the best approach to promote traffic safety. "Should we not own up to our traffic transgressions instead of devising ways to avoid punishment?" I asked innocently. Instantaneously, I became the class pariah. You expect me to do well on the test?

Try this question. "When you turn left from an intersection, into which lane should you go?" Would not any reasonable person say, as I did, "the left lane"? Wrong. You can turn into any lane provided it is safe to do so. I wonder. When I have time, I'm going to look it up. Do you know what color car gets the most tickets? I said, "red." Wrong again. It is white. Question—"What color car gets the least traffic tickets?" Answer—"Black and White." Remember, this is comedy traffic school.

This experience has made me so obsessed with human error that I have come to believe I am responsible for the blunders of others. My wife ascribes this condition as a perverse form of megalomania. When I go to the bank and the computers are down, I apologize to everyone waiting in line for the teller.

Shortly after my matriculation from traffic school, my self-confidence was below sea level. I had dreams of headlines screaming "Ex traffic judge caught speeding." Because misery loves company, I felt whole again after receiving something interesting in the mail.

Federal Magistrate Judge Andrew J. Wistrich sent me his fascinating law review article which he co-authored with Professors Chris Guthrie and Jeffrey J. Rachlinski. It is titled, *Inside The Judicial Mind*, Cornell Law Review, Volume 86, May 2001. Once you accept the basic assumption made by the title, the article tactfully reveals what the cynical among you may have suspected.

To quote from the introduction: "Judges, it seems are human. Like the rest of us, their judgment is affected by cognitive illusions that can produce systematic errors in judgment." Now that got my attention. Speeding on the highway is one thing, but speeding on the bench is quite another. The authors arrived at their conclusions after conducting an empirical study of 167 human federal magistrate judges who agreed to serve as guinea . . . I mean volunteers.

Like all humans, judges make many decisions on complex issues through what psychologists call "heuristics," a fancy word for "mental shortcuts." This in turn can lead to "cognitive illusions" which lead to errors in judgment. Oh dear! If the federal magistrate judges are an example, not just one, but five formidable cognitive illusions influence the way judges make decisions. They include: "1) anchoring, (making estimates based on irrelevant starting points); 2) framing (treating economically equivalent gains and losses differently) ; 3) hindsight bias (perceiving past events to have been more predictable than they actually were); 4) the representativeness heuristic (ignoring important background statistical information in favor of individuating information); and 5) egocentric biases (overestimating one's own abilities)." The latter is a trait I have observed in abundance.

Examples abound. Judges, like juries, may be influenced by an "anchor" when assessing damages. The request for a specific amount may influence the result by setting the standard of reference for the judgment. Higher requests may get higher awards. Framing the decision options can significantly influence the decision whether it be to help settle the case or decide issues. The study shows that in disputes over ownership of property, for example, the possessor of the property usually wins even when "possession is arbitrary." Arbitrary according to whom?

Judges, like everyone else, are prone to "hindsight bias," an illusion that one has the ability to have predicted past events before they occurred, and that others should have been able to do so. Easy to say after the event has occurred, but in reality often impossible to do. And of course there is that insidious "egocentric bias" which can be a blinder to the recognition of one's limitations. But the authors point out that overall the benefits of having a confident decisive judge are outweighed by an "occasional erroneous decision." Although an inflated belief in one's abilities may be the most difficult illusion to overcome, going to traffic school is a good step in the right direction.

Inside the Judicial Mind should be required reading for all judges. I would prefer lawyers not read it, but I'm sure they will with glee. So we are all human and subject to cognitive illusions. No system of justice is perfect, and Judge Wistrich and his colleagues have made us aware of our shortcomings. We are all human and from self-awareness of our human limitations comes the likelihood of better judging and more insight into our concept of justice. It also might make us safer drivers.

UNDER SUBMISSION-THE EASY WAY OUT

January 1991

I asked a psychiatrist friend of mine, an avid skier, if he were going to vacation on the slopes this month.

"Not a chance, this is the time of year when business picks up. You of all people should know that."

I knew he had a point. I never bought into the notion that April is cruelest month unless you're living in a wasteland. For most people it is a time of joy, a time of renewal and growth. Birds sing, butterflies wiggle out of cocoons, and flowers open their buds. It is a hopeful time of change. I realized what my psychiatrist friend was talking about. I, of all people should have known that in the legal world, January is the cruelest month.

The first of January is when most of the changes take effect. There they are: new statutes with shorter limitation periods, more rigorous requirements for an array of motions and complaints, new court rules, which, for those who can understand them, seem to contradict the new statutes.

And January is the month when new presiding judges, eager to wield their newly acquired power, make new judicial assignments. The judges who hope to stay in their previous assignments, and those who hope to get new assignments are on edge. The affable and easygoing become bullying tyrants and vice versa. The uncertainty of who will decide their cases send attorneys into shock.

I told my psychiatrist friend he was right, "We have it rough in January."

"What is this 'we' business?" he asked. (The word "business" is a euphemism.)

"All of us people in the legal world."

"You judges are in a world of you own."

"We have plenty of stress too," I protested. "And not just in January, but all year long."

"Hardly. You, unlike the lawyers, have a safety valve."

"We do?"

" ' Gimmick' is perhaps a better word. You use it whenever there is even a hint of pressure build-up."

"What is he talking about?" I asked myself.

"And what's more," he went on, "when you use this device to decrease you own tension, you correspondingly increase the stress of lawyers."

"What is the device?" I blurted out.

"Oh, come now, you know what it is. Its very name conjures up the specter of oppression. It's called 'under submission.' "

"Oh that," I said weakly.

We ended out conversation. It was time for another lawyer to take the couch. I hated to admit it, but he was right again. "Under submission" was a judge's way out of many a mess.

Lawyers must adapt quickly to change. A judge can postpone a decision by taking a matter under submission in order to have the time to contemplate the issues and thus make a correct decision. Unfortunately, it prolongs the agony of the litigants and the lawyers, and it can be one of the cruelest weapons in a judge's arsenal.

But just because it's a way of buying time while trying to figure out what the case is about does not make it a gimmick. It has other uses as well. For example, it's a way of not having to face the parties in open court when you make your decision.

The practice, in the interest of courtroom safety, is often employed in small-claims court. Judges Judy and Wapner, incidentally, hold their matters under submission for the shortest time of any judge in history- just a couple of commercials.

The more I thought about it, the more "under submission" had me under the weather. I took momentary solace in other uses of the word "under": *Under Milk Wood, Twenty Thousand Leagues Under the Sea,* and *Notes From the Underground* gave me a momentary lift.

But even these great works could not overcome the negative connotations of "under." No one sets their sights on reaching what's under the rainbow, and few people strive to under-come a problem.

To make matters worse, we cannot underestimate the negative synergy caused by the juxtaposition of the "under" with "submission." That truly sounds oppressive.

No one wants to be under submission, whether it be to a government, a master sergeant, a judge or a columnist.

While we are rejoicing in the new-found freedom gained by countries in Eastern Europe, it's hardly the time to be talking about "under submission."

"Under submission" is insidious. It has worked its way into other parts of my life. When at a restaurant the other night the waiter asked me if I wanted my potatoes baked or mashed, I took the matter under submission. Maybe "under submission" is out of date in this age of fast track and fast answers. Maybe it's an anachronism like pheasant under glass. When was the last time you ordered that?

Because January is the month of change, maybe its time to make some changes in the use of "under submission." After all, January is also the month to make New Year's resolutions, and they invariably involve change. In order to make life a little less stressful for lawyers, particularly in this cruel month of January, I'm seriously thinking of taking fewermatters under submission. I'll let you know what I do. I have the matter under submission.

LET'S HANG THE JUDGES- THEIR PHOTOGRAPHS

Robert Jones, often wrote about the changing social landscape in California. In 1991, he wrote in the Los Angeles Times about a changing phenomenon in Los Angeles: the display of celebrity photographs in business establishment. It got me thinking that there was something of value here for judges.

Back in the '30s and '40s, movie stars had class and grace, even when they said, "My dear, I don't give a damn." You wouldn't find their signed photographs on just any wall. You would have to go to the most exclusive restaurant to see a glossy black and white of Lana Turner, or better yet, a caricature of her just above your booth at the Brown Derby.

It's different now. The stars of today lack the glamour and savoir-faire of their predecessors. They belch, burp, scratch and scream. They pick their noses and grab their crotches, and the fans go berserk.

And as Jones points out, celebrity photographs no longer just appear in fancy restaurants, elegant tailor shops or posh haberdasheries. Your local muffler shop, gas station or cleaners is apt to conspicuously display rows of signed photos. Recently, I was munching a veggie-tofu supreme on pita at my local sandwich shop, when I noticed a young woman gazing dreamily at me from a photograph mounted just above my Formica table with an indention for my drink.

I squinted to read the inscription. It said, "Dear Abdul, your egg salad is divine. Love, Kim." I discovered that she was Kim Davidson. Who's that? She had a walk-on last year as an emergency room nurse on "General Hospital."

But it's probably a good thing that the famous and the not-so-famous have their signed photographs displayed in a variety of establishments. It's good for the star or the aspiring star because it increases their exposure. It makes the owners of establishments feel good; they let you know that they know somebody who is somebody. This in turn, they think, enhances the prestige of their business.

We faceless members of the public probably get something out of this as well. Maybe on an unconscious level we feel good about bringing our laundry to a place where on the wall we see a photo of Madonna with the inscription "To Sid, With Best Wishes." We don't even care that the owner of the laundry is named Burt. What matters is that Madonna's signed photograph is there in our laundry. When we drop off a bundle of clothes, we feel, in an ineffable way, a connection with Madonna somewhere deep in our imagination.

But the display of photographs need not be limited to show business personalities. Let's not forget the myriad categories of politicians. Photographs of city council men and women, water district members, senators, congresspersons and sometimes members of their staff adorn the walls of Laundromats, hardware stores and pizza kitchens. This gives elected representatives a tie, with their constituents, albeit a tenuous one.

Now it's time for judges to also get in touch with the public. The public display of their photographs can be a bridge from the quiet sanctuary of their chambers to the bustling world outside. Most judges have an official photograph, and many judges have their photographs hanging in the silent corridors that lead to their chambers.

For the few of you who have gained entry into the inner sanctum, of the California Court of Appeal or the Supreme Court, you will recall seeing photographs of justices who sat during the early days of this state. Their collars are high in starch, and they look at you with grim, inscrutable faces. More recent photographs reveal changes in hair styles, and occasionally you see a smile. Today the photographs are in color, often with an added touch of inadvertent symbolism, the California Reports significantly blurred in the background.

These photographs would look just as impressive in the local barber shop. Judges, whether trial or appellate, should not resist the trend. It's better than getting exposure over which they have no control.

A restaurant in Malibu, for example, has a sandwich on its menu named after the local sitting trial judge. I ordered the sandwich once. I don't remember the ingredients, but it was tasty —and no, it wasn't a turkey burger.

If judges can have sandwiches named after them, they can certainly have their photographs hanging in a shoe store, a yogurt shop or a dentist's office. For the photograph, to have an impact, it should have an appropriate inscription. If the judge's photograph is to hang on the wall of his dentist's office, the inscription might read, "Dear Dr. Mole —We have a lot in common. You fill cavities and I fill jails. Best always, Judge Farnsworth."

Signed photographs of judges will be particularly significant in law offices. Of course we might have to revise the ethical canons a bit. A photograph of a judge with an inscription to the senior partner of a law firm prominently displayed in the reception area would not hurt business.

Initially plaintiffs' firms would have photographs of their favorite judges, and defense firms would have their favorites. This, however, would not last long. A client, for example, would walk into the law firm and see the photograph of the judge that just imposed sanctions of $10,000 against him and $25,000 against his lawyer. Down comes that photo.

This practice should not offend judges. On the next case, this same firm might be on the winning side. That would mean that photographs would be coming on and off the walls of law firms all over the state. As photographs come off the wall of one firm, they would be traded for photographs that have come off the wall of another firm. The trading of judges' photographs would be much like the trading of baseball cards.

It's true that some alterations would have to be made in the inscriptions, but there is a value here. The public would see that judges are fair and unbiased and that there is no such thing as a defense-oriented or plaintiff-oriented judge.

Trial and appellate judges would enjoy enhanced prestige as their objectivity became known to more and more people. The hanging and trading of judges' photographs could extend to all states in the union. The third branch of government would win respect and admiration as citizens everywhere realized that judges truly have no preconceived notions about how they will rule on cases.

And this brings me to the group photo of the U.S. Supreme Court…well, that's another story.

IN THE BEGINNING THERE WAS ERROR
AND IT WAS HARMLESS
PART I

You hear a lot of complaints these days. As a rule, when people complain they look back nostalgically to the way things used to be. Criminal defense attorneys, particularly those handling appeals, complain that things are the way they used to be. Apparently, they are not talking about how things were 25 to 30 years ago, but instead are looking farther back in time.

How far back? : The Old Testament. You get a clue by listening to two or more criminal defense attorney talking about error. Familiarity with the Bible helps you get their drift. You will hear references for example, from Ecclesiastes: "All is vanity," "The sun rise, but now it goeth down," and "I despair of all the labor which I took under the sun."

If you were to inquire why such gloom, one of them might respond, "The thing that hath been, it is that which shall be... and there is no new thing under the sun." This is all about error, mind you.

If you should ask, "When was the thing that hath been?" you'll usually get the following answer: "In the beginning...the very beginning."

I asked a criminal defense attorney friend of mine more specifically what was meant by "...the very beginning." He answered with the alacrity of a trial judge denying a continuance, "Genesis."

"Oh, that beginning," I said. "I would have never believed you would be interested in original sin."

"Not original sin, original error. It is part of the human condition," he said.

"But why is this of interest to lawyers?" I asked.

"Because the courts have gone back to Genesis, and this makes criminal appeals difficult."

The subject of error has been of immense interest to me. That must be because I am always stepping into one of those infuriating puddles of error. I skillfully circumvent one puddle, only to find myself stepping into another. That's why I walk around with my trousers rolled.

I discussed the error phenomenon with Judge Learned Foote. He pointed out that errors are the very reason we have judges, and that errors are what give existence meaning. "Errors each day are why judges get paid," he said with a smile. I wondered whose errors he was talking about, theirs, or his? He must have read my thoughts. "Of course, I allegedly make errors too, but what do vindictive out-of-touch appellate judges know?" he asked.

I had to admit, he had a point. "Errors are my lifeblood," he went on rubbing his hands. "But I never go hungry because lawyers are a walking Fort Knox of errors."

His imagery threw me for a moment, but then he told me he was about to publish his multivolume work, "Foote on Sanctions."

I thought to myself, a better title would be "Sanctions on Foote."

I chuckled silently until I thought once again about the countless errors I make each day. For Foote, errors conjured visions of profits, but all I could see were puddles. I'm not talking just about errors in my work. On that subject alone, Witkin could bring out an entire new set of books. There would be "Gilbert's Errors in Secured Transaction," "Gilbert's Errors on Torts," and the new two-volume set, "Gilbert's Errors in Family Law." The updates alone would fill a wall of shelf space.

I'm talking about those other errors, the kind we all make in our everyday lives. Of course lay persons (nonlawyers) don't call them errors. They call them "blunders," "boo-boos," or "screw-ups" (a euphemism). Professionals, who like to inflate the ordinary into the profound, call mistakes "errors." Secretaries make mistakes, but a judge's mistakes are called errors.

The peccadilloes we commit each day, like forgetting to take out the garbage or teasing the cat. are really nothing to worry about. We might apologize, but deep down we say, "so what." A judge would call these "so what" errors, harmless errors.

This helped me to understand the enigmatic religious comments of the criminal defense attorneys. Courts are tolerant of mistakes, or harmless procedural errors. After all, we all make them. A crime, on the other hand, is something much more than a mistake, and that, we cannot tolerate. We have indeed gone back to the very beginning, to Genesis.

The current trend in criminal law goes back to Adam's pro per appeal. Adam pointed out the numerous errors in his case. He urged the defense of entrapment. He argued that diminished capacity prevented Eve from possessing specific intent. After all, she heard a snake speaking. He advanced the equal protection argument; the snake, which had not been prosecuted as an aider and abettor, got off scot-free. Adam also pointed out neither he nor Eve had an attorney or jury trial, and they were never given a chance to cross-examine the snake.

Moreover, they were not advised of their rights against self-incrimination, and their confessions were not free from coercion.

The Lord considered the argument and issued an opinion. It was a majority – all three signatures. The good news was that the Lord conceded the case was replete with error. The bad news – it was all harmless.

The lesson then and the lesson now – harmless errors will not save you from the consequences of sin or (in modern day parlance), crime.

172

It's no wonder that defense attorneys are reading Ecclesiastes. Nothing is new under the sun. Eve urged Adam to try habeas corpus, but that was as helpful then as it is today.

Nevertheless, criminal defense attorneys need not be so depressed, and so preoccupied with somber reflections on Ecclesiastes. Just think, if Adam had won..?.

SON OF HARMLESS ERROR
PART II

April is the cruelest month, isn't it? For judges and lawyers, it's hard to tell because all months are cruel these days, and some are downright ruthless. Maybe that is because the law is so consuming. When one gets bogged down it is a good time to put aside the advance sheets for a moment and switch to something else for diversion.

The trouble with me is that no matter what else I read, it still reminds me of the law. The other day, for example, I was reading T.S. Elliot's *The Wasteland*, and no sooner had I read the title than, for some reason, I was reminded of the California Reports. So I switched to something else, what we used to call a dime store novel.

Today it costs about 200 times as much and is a bestseller at a chain bookstore at the mall. This one was a horror novel about vampires and international intrigue.

Certain lines in the book caught my attention: "A thousand tiny legs of error began to crawl in my brain"; "Swarthy and sinister armed errorists surrounded the ambassador's limousine"; "The entire city was gripped by error." "The renegade political faction used error as an instrument of policy."

It finally occurred to me that the word "error" was itself an error, a misprint. The word should have been "terror." This mistake, or error, in the text, however, got me thinking about error in general, and error in the legal profession in particular. There I was again, back in the law. But in this case, it was not surprising; after all, error is the very foundation of our legal system, isn't it?

Why are the courts in business? Because people make errors. People make errors when conducting their business, when getting married and divorced, when driving their cars, when buying and selling houses, cars, animals, junk bonds, franchises, and computer software for legal research programs. Practically all intentional and negligent acts are simply the product of errors in judgment.

Of course, the very lifeblood of appellate courts is error. Trial courts provide a vein of continuing nourishment. This gives appellate justices their sustenance. That, no doubt, is why we search for error with the single mindedness of Ahab in pursuit of Moby Dick.

It would be unseemly, however, to display our zeal in public. Therefore, we disguise our passion. You may have noticed that at oral argument some justices appear to have no vital signs. Don't be fooled. Off the bench, in the privacy of their chambers, the passion for error erupts.

It typically works in this fashion: A justice is doing what everyone knows justices do each day hour after hour. He or she is laboriously but quietly poring over a voluminous record. The justice suddenly spots an error. That is when the calm breaks. If you happen to be strolling down the hells of the Court of Appeal at just the right time, you might hear muffled behind the walls ecstatic shouts of "Eureka," or an exuberant "Geronimo!" It has been said that at this moment of discovery, some justices begin a Dionysian dance which is performed in a kind of giddy, unrestrained rapture. This extraordinary exhibition, never seen on 60 Minutes, is reputed to have occurred on desks, sofas, chairs, and in the one case of a particularly small justice, on a bookcase.

The dance of justices these days, however, is more restrained. Like hardy fishermen, their efforts invariably produce a sizable catch of errors, but lately they have been throwing most of their fish back into the sea. This is because of the doctrine that has now become de rigueur in judicial circles these days, harmless error. In a previous column on this subject, I outlined the multiplicity of procedural errors that occurred at the expulsion hearing of Adam and Eve and pointed out that higher authority in a majority opinion held the errors were harmless. A transcript can be found at Genesis.

My colleague, Judge Learned Foote, also conducted research on the matter and concluded the doctrine surfaced in ancient Greece. He cites the Venus De Milo as an example. He missed the point. The doctrine I'm talking about has reappeared again in recent times, creating an epidemic that has afflicted criminal defense attorneys. The symptoms are depression, a sense of futility, and a proclivity to quote from Ecclesiastes. These attorneys see criminal cases with the texture of a moonscape covered with unsightly craters of error. Nevertheless, to their dismay, convictions are affirmed because of harmless error.

So what if a trial judge gives a negligence instruction concerning what a reasonable person would do in a criminal case instead of the reasonable doubt instruction? Such an error can create a legal conundrum for stickler, but what if the evidence of guilt is overwhelming? Error, after all, is part of the human condition, isn't it?

I tried to get back to my novel, but my thoughts kept coming back to the significance of error in the law.

What if the same kind of error that occurred in my novel also occurred in appellate opinions, only the word "terror" was mistakenly used instead of "error"?

This kind of error may be more difficult to detect. An opinion might read, "Defendant complains that most of the trial judge's rulings were terror." "The transcript of the trial was a study in terror." See what I mean? Some people would not catch the misprint. In other cases, the misprint would be obvious, e.g., "The judge committed terror, but it was harmless." There the misprint is obvious. After all, "harmless terror" is an oxymoron. "Harmless error," on the other hand, is an entirely different matter – isn't it?

TO OFFEND OR NOT TO OFFEND
A CONTINUING STUDY IN ERROR
PART III

It has been said that the only things certain are death and taxes. As is evident from the last two columns, I must add "error" to this short list of indisputable truths. When one assumes the role of "teacher," the lapse into error can be as awkward as an ex-traffic judge getting a traffic ticket. But a column offers a therapeutic outlet in which to reveal one's gaffes and blunders without excessive wincing. Mercifully, one does not see the disapproving eyes of the audience. So let's get it over with. I was teaching this course to new judges at CJER (Center for Judicial Education and Performance), California's famous Judges College. The spellbinding curriculum included jurisprudence, standards of review vis-a-vis the trial court, and Shakespeare's "Measure for Measure."

The calamity that happened in a nanosecond came just after my exegesis on the nuances of error. The irony was grossly magnified because I had been discussing harmless error. I concluded my remarks on this peculiar category of error, which the criminal defense bar finds so odious, with what I thought at the time was an apt if not ingeniously clever appellation. I called it "Venus de Milo" error. The look of bewilderment on the student judges' faces should have alerted me that something was amiss. I blurted out "armless error" and saw instantly that the sobriquet was, as they say in legal circles, "inapposite."

But it was too late to suck in, like a Hoover, the words that had escaped my lips. The students' derisive laughter, not to mention their boos and hisses, was unnerving. Nevertheless, I pressed on to give them my piece de resistance on the least understood and most abused form of error, "abuse of discretion." Well consider, if you will, the definitions I gave the students. "'[T]he term [judicial discretion] implies absence of arbitrary determination, capricious disposition or whimsical thinking. It imports the exercise of discriminating judgment within the bounds of reason, '" (*In re Cortez* 6 Cal.3d 78, 85-86, (1970).) My heavens.

Abuse of discretion occurs when the court exercises "it in an arbitrary, capricious or patently absurd manner resulting in a manifest miscarriage of justice." (*Baltayan v. Estate of Getemyan* 90 Cal.App.4th 1427, 1434, (2001).) Gracious. You can just imagine how off base a judge has to be to abuse his or her discretion. No doubt I was rattled by the students' outburst. In an attempt to capture the significance of abuse of discretion in a graphic, forceful way, I fell into the most terrifying error of all, "error per se." I said the judge had to be out of his or her "cotton pickin mind." I then moved on to other topics.

At the break it was tactfully called to my attention that the phrase, "cotton pickin" could be offensive to some people. I was unable to determine if anyone had in fact been offended by the remark, but as I reflected, it occurred to me that the remark could call to mind a shameful part of our history when slaves picked cotton. On the other hand, many people other than slaves also picked cotton and still do.

I decided right there and then to erase that phrase from my lexicon. Although I disavow membership or even a casual association with the political correctness club, the likelihood that the phrase legitimately has offensive overtones for some led me to my decision.

After the break, I expressed regret if that term had offended anyone, and related my decision to find more suitable adjectives to place in front of the noun "brain." At the end of the class, a number of students from a variety of races and nationalities came up to me and weighed in on the issue. They told me they did not find the phrase offensive and would continue to use it even if I did not. They said one student thought the term could be offensive.

Nevertheless, I wished to learn from where the expression came, and checked numerous etymological references but could not find its origin. What I did learn through an exhaustive search on the internet is that there are numerous web sites that boldly if not baldly adopt the moniker "cotton pickin." These include a square dance organization, antique fairs and cotton manufacturers.
Whether the phrase I used was in fact error per se, or an error in judgment, I thought my airing the matter and acknowledging it as an error would give me absolution. But that night during a restless sleep I had a disturbing dream. It began like a scene from a movie of the 1930's. I saw twirling before my eyes the front page of a newspaper that became bigger and bigger as it got closer and closer. And then it stopped spinning. Covering my entire field of vision was the front page of the Daily Journal.

The headline screamed, "Court of Appeal Presiding Justice severely punished by rioting judges at Judges' College." The article penned by the editor said: "It is with regret that we report that the Daily Journal's own noted columnist, Justice Arthur Gilbert, teaching a course that included of all things, Shakespeare, to new judges at the Judges College caused a riot when he used offensive adjectives to describe a brain. Gilbert, who many have opined tends to push the envelope to the limit, clearly went too far this time. His use of the adjectives, too abhorrent to be reprinted here, would have made Eli Whitney hang his head in shame. The offended students ordered Justice Gilbert to spend an entire day picking cotton in fields in the Central Valley of Fresno.

"Our reporter confronted Justice Gilbert toiling in the 110 degree sun laboriously extracting the white lint from the bursting pods. When asked by our reporter how he felt about his punishment, Gilbert ignored her and zombie like, robotically continued his arduous toil. It was later learned that Gilbert had not heard our reporter's question because his ears were stuffed with cotton.

"Los Angeles Superior Court Judge Veronica Simmons McBeth, who made international headlines when she sentenced a slum landlord to live in the squalor of his own dilapidated tenement, had this to say about the sentence meted out to Justice Gilbert: 'Art is a good friend of mine, but even friends have to pay for their misdeeds. I cannot deny that the sentence was innovative. But had I been sentencing him, I would have closed his text of Measure for Measure and sentenced him to read the entire works of Danielle Steele.' Gilbert is now in seclusion rewriting the lyrics to *Dixie*."

I awoke with a start, got out of bed and washed up, hoping that was not a description of my career. I had breakfast and drove to work, a chastened individual with heightened sensitivity. As I drove up to the on ramp to the freeway, I noted the sign naming the freeway after a former Israeli prime minister. This is perfectly acceptable to me, but with tensions in the Middle East and all, I had hoped that other freeways would bear names of other heads of state. I could find none. Instead, I discovered that many freeways had the same name. That was not fair, so I wrote to my state representatives urging them to discontinue use of the name "Begin Freeway."

The dream obviously had had an enormous impact on me. But the next day reason returned and I realized how foolish I had been to write my state representatives about the matter. I must have been out of my higgledy-piggledy mind.

180

There were six of them this time. They straggled out of a side door of the courthouse and blinked in the glare of the noonday sun. Oral argument for the morning calendar was over. Their minds were numb, but the two justices and four research attorneys had to decide where to go to lunch. The question of how to apportion liability in a multi-defendant toxic tort case was rudimentary compared to the question now before them--where to eat. But, like the innumerable issues they decided daily, for better or worse, a decision would be made, and, miraculously, they would all end up eating at the same place.

They began walking. They stopped in front of a small Mexican restaurant where they had lunched several times in the past. Outside was posted the special of the day, Sopas, a favorite of at least three of them. One of them said, "Let's eat here." Five seconds passed and no one objected. This was a waiver. They entered the restaurant, a long, narrow corridor with tables against the opposite walls on which were painted colorful hacienda scenes.

The hostess smiled and ushered them to the rear of the restaurant where, she, with the help of two of the research attorneys, pushed two tables together. They sat. Moments later the waitress appeared with two bowls of chips. She took their orders.

What follows purports to be a transcript of a portion of the luncheon discussion. The names have been changed, not to protect the innocent, because there are no innocent, nor to protect innocence, it having been lost in the second year of law school. The names have been changed because the transcript is not altogether authentic. Neither is it certified, nor stenographically recorded. See *Court Reporters v. Judicial Council* (1997) 59 Cal.App.4th 959.

Donald: (Stuffing chips into his mouth.) The last lawyer seemed a little testy today.

Della: A little testy? He was unduly contentious and downright rude.

Huey: He argued over every little point, no matter how insignificant.

Daisy: Perhaps his argument would have been better if we had bothered to tell him what we consider to be significant.

Louie: I don't think it would have mattered. After all, contentiousness lies at the heart of the adversary system.

Huey: (To Donald) Would you mind leaving a few chips for the rest of us?

Della: I would not equate rudeness with forceful advocacy.

Louie: It's a thin line.

Daisy: Are you suggesting that for lawyers, civility is a mere pipe dream?

Louie: I don't know if I want to go that far.

Dewey: Can't unscramble the eggs now.

Louie: I did not rule out civility...

Huey: Can't put Humpty Dumpty back together again.

Donald: What does Humpty Dumpty have to do with it?

Della: He means Humpty Dumpty is an egg.

Donald: An egg?

Louie: In case any of you eggheads missed it, just a few seconds ago, Dewey said I could not unscramble the eggs.

Donald: I don't think Humpty Dumpty is an egg.

Della: Of course he is.

Donald: Do you have authority?

Della: What? I need authority? (Sips her iced tea. Then rolls her eyes in mock horror.) Heavens! I don't have authority.

Donald: What is missing from the Humpty Dumpty rhyme, you silly goose, is the word "egg."

Della: Literalism spawns absurdity. "Egg" is implied.

Donald: Not so.

Dewey: You call that a sentence?

Louie: The words "that is" are implied. (Laughter.)

Della: "Not so" is rude, and it is grammatically incorrect.

Donald: Humpty Dumpty could be a porcelain vase, or a china doll.

Huey: The name "Humpty Dumpty" fits an egg. You wouldn't call a vase "Humpty Dumpty." The logic of the poem points to an egg.

Louie: You find logic in horses trying to put an egg back together?

Donald: You have all been influenced by the illustrations you have seen in children's books that depict Humpty Dumpty as an egg. But that does not make it so.

Dewey: In the Middle Ages, "Humpty Dumpty" was a term describing a numskull, a person whose brains were scrambled.

Donald: That doesn't make Humpty Dumpty an egg.

Louie: True. Maybe he's Simple Simon.

Dewey: Not likely. Simple Simon's got his own poem and he's with another studio.

Donald: I think Humpty Dumpty is a particular person, but not a simpleton. All the king's horses and all the king's men would have no interest in putting some oaf together again.

Daisy: He's got a point. I read somewhere that Humpty Dumpty is King Richard III. He was hunchbacked, hence the word "hump." His horse, the wall upon which he sat, was slain and thus he fell or, if you like, was dumped to the ground. This also symbolized his fall from power. While frantically offering to exchange his kingdom for a horse, he was cut to ribbons. This fall was so total, so complete, so irrevocable that "All the King's Horses and All the King's Men couldn't put Humpty Dumpty together again."

Dewey: Not a bad exegesis.

Daisy: I could give you a dozen more.

Donald: That's the trouble. A statute, or a rule, should be read for what it says, not what we or some quack thinks or wishes it said. But a vague statute lends itself to creative reading which leads to a variety of interpretations which in turn leads to uncertainty and chaos. It breaks apart society's shell.

Huey: But "Humpty Dumpty" simply does not lend itself to a literal interpretation.

Della: Has everyone here forgotten that "Humpty Dumpty" is a poem, not a statute?

The check came. It took awhile to compute what each person owed including his or her share of the tip. Huey gathered the money and put a saltshaker on top of it.

Dewey: We had a good discussion, and, for once, it was about something other than the law.

Huey: Someone should write a column about it.

Louie: No, it would be too off the wall.

Dewey: It would be a column about nothing.

Della: We could call it the Seinfeld column.

Huey: It deserves a web site.

They got up and straggled out of the restaurant. They stood a moment on the sidewalk, once again adjusting their eyes to the sun. Then they made their way back to the courthouse for an afternoon of stimulating oral argument.

EVEN THE POLITICALLY INSENSITIVE
ARE ENTITLED TO COUNSEL
PART I

Lawyer W.M. Grendel, in one of his less circumspect moments, greeted the smiling, smartly dressed woman approaching him on the street. "Hi Honey," he said warmly. Before she had a chance to react, he felt a strong, leather-gloved hand on his shoulder. A voice behind the glove said, "Going to cite you for uttering a demeaning remark to a member of the opposite sex."

Grendel turned and saw the badge with its dread initials, PCP. He looked up to see the humorless face of an officer of the Political Correctness Patrol.

"You should know better than to address someone with such a patronizing term. Got any priors?" the officer asked.

The young woman interrupted. "That's all right officer, he's a friend of mine. . . ."

"All the more reason to show respect," said the officer, beginning to write in his citation book.

"I don't think you understand officer; my name is Honey Hudson. Everyone calls me by my name, even strangers."

Grendel was dumbfounded. He had never seen this person before.

"I do appreciate your concern officer," she said, still smiling.

The woman's self-assurance and charm dissuaded the officer from further inquiry. He regarded Grendel for a minute. "I'll let you off with a warning this time," he said, tearing up the citation and walking away. They watched the officer enter the vehicle he had exited just moments before.

"Each officer has his exits and entrances," said Grendel, trying to impress his benefactor. "Thanks for saving my skin, Honey."

"That's not my name," said the woman.

Grendel was astonished. In a thoughtless moment, he had addressed a perfect stranger in a degrading and demeaning manner, and she had lied to protect him.

"What is your name?" he asked.

"Babe Sugarman."

"Wow, Babe, you're quite a gal . . . ."

She interrupted him and spoke in a somewhat less friendly tone. "Listen, brick head, don't talk to women in that fashion."

"Who are you really?" he asked.

"I'm the Fairy God Protector for the Politically Insensitive . . . provided their obnoxious conduct is unintentional and not habitual. I'm in charge of the legal profession, that's why I carry the largest caseload. As I recall, your specialty is . . . ."

"P.I.," he answered.

"Mr. Politically Insensitive, you are about to be enlightened," she said, pulling him down with her into a dark void that suddenly opened beneath them.

Like Virgil leading Dante through the circles of the Inferno, Ms. Sugarman led Grendel through the circles of exile where the miserable souls who had been sentenced for bias, boorishness and blasphemy cried out in agony. A sign over the entrance read, "Abandon Hope All Ye Who Believe the First Amendment is Absolute."

In the middle of the foul-smelling mist that hung over the landscape like a diaphanous curtain stood a drab building over the door of which were the letters, COR. This was the Court of Offensive Remarks.

"Imagine, in the middle of Hell, a court just like the ones at home," said Grendel.

Once in the building, they entered a large courtroom and saw a defendant complaining to Judge Learned Foote, presiding, that he had been railroaded.

"That's what you get in a fast track court," said Foote, to the delight of the court watchers. "You used the word 'Shylock,'" said Foote, hot with anger.

"I was just referring to the character in Shakespeare's 'Merchant of Venice.' I had no intent to offend anybody."

"You have a prior. Four years ago you referred to chicken soup as Jewish penicillin. Your mother didn't think it was funny. You are sentenced to hard labor. Over the next six months you are ordered to delete all sexist and offensive phrases from the entire works of Shakespeare, the Bible and Pilgrim's Progress."

Foote called the next case. The defendant was a prominent lawyer charged with using the term "Chinese Wall" in a case where a potential conflict existed between the lawyers. In arguing against disqualification of one of the law firms, he used the offensive term to describe a screening mechanism to protect confidentiality.

Grendel turned to his Fairy God Protector. "He's a lawyer, defend him."

"I'm knocked out. The air down here is bad. You do it." She pushed him forward.

"He didn't mean to offend anyone, Your Honor," said Grendel, who found himself standing before the podium. "He was only referring to the Great Wall of China, one of the world's great architectural marvels, designed and built by an illustrious civilization primarily as protection against invading Huns and Mongols. This term has been used in the title of an important law review article and had appeared in numerous trial and appellate cases."

"That doesn't make it right!" thundered Judge Foote. "Read the concurring opinion by Presiding Justice Harry Low in *Peat, Marwick, Mitchell & Co. v. Superior Ct.*

(1988) 200 Cal.App.3d 272, 294. The term has a discriminatory flavor and reflects insensitivity on the part of those who use it."

Foote was right. Justice Low's opinion was unassailable.

"You are absolutely right, Your Honor, but how far do we go in correcting these offenses? A stinging indictment against an inadvertent offender who has no malice or intent to injure is as bad as the offense itself. Educating the public as Justice Low did will ultimately result in more understanding and more sensitivity. Public reproval, however, for an inadvertent remark fosters resentment and stifles spontaneity. Wariness and fear makes for a staid and stodgy world where inhibition dominates the landscape. My client has learned. Let him off with a warning."

The Fairy God Protector said, "Not bad."

There was a long silence as Judge Foote pondered the issue. Finally he spoke. "I'll take the matter under submission.

BREAKING THROUGH WALLS OF INSENSITIVITY
PART II

In 1980, a note in the University of Pennsylvania Law Review discussed the use of screening mechanisms in conflict situations. The title of the article was *The Chinese Wall Defense to Law Firm Disqualification* (1980) 128 U.Pa.L.Rev. 677. The article had the unfortunate consequence of perpetuating the term "Chinese Wall" in opinions and subsequent articles. In *Peat, Marwick, Mitchell & Co.* v. *Superior Court* (1988) 200 Cal.App.3d 272, Justice Harry Low remarked that the ethnic focus of the term, an obvious reference to the Great Wall of China, is "singularly inappropriate." Indeed it is, despite its use by many who have no malicious intention. With education and awareness comes sensitivity.

Moreover, Low pointed out, the metaphor is not apt because The Great Wall was a one-way barrier designed to keep outsiders out. The wall to protect confidentiality, on the other hand, is a two-way barrier designed to prevent communication between two groups.

In the previous column, W.M. Grendel, a P.I. lawyer (Politically Insensitive), was touring the lower circles of the Legal Inferno with his fairy godmother, Babe Sugarman. With no time for preparation, he argued a case in the accelerated fast track Court of Offensive Remarks, Judge Learned Foote, presiding. His client, a lawyer, was charged with using the term "Chinese Wall" when arguing a case involving attorney conflict. We left our friends just after Judge Foote had taken the matter under submission.

While waiting for the decision, Grendel and Babe decided to explore lower circles of the Lex Inferno. The air was close, stifling, and putrid, the odor sour and acrid. The lost souls, wandering between the circles, were moaning softly and had the vacant stares of automatons. People with briefcases scurried to and fro among the damned, paying them little attention.

"We could just as well have strolled through the county courthouse and seen the same thing," said Grendel, stifling a yawn. He was roused out of his lethargy as they entered the circle of the Activist Judges.

The scene was almost too horrible to describe. The judges, like thousands of black robed hamsters, were running on wheels which squeaked, clattered, and jangled with frightful intensity and a deafening din. As they ran, they threw from their wheels hastily drawn decisions, which cluttered the floor in a chaotic profusion of paper.

Half the circle was filled with LAJ's (liberal activist judges), the other half with CAJ's (conservative activist judges). With a relentless ferocity they attempted to outrun one another, although not one of them advanced an inch. Their determined resolve not to rest for a minute ultimately caused them to fall exhausted and gasping for breath onto the cold steel grating of their wheels upon which they struggled to get up once again to resume the race that would never be won.

Babe led the shaken Grendel yet lower into the circle of the Vindictive Legislators. In one section of the circle were legislators and their aides, their hands badly crippled and misshapen by writer's cramp, scribbling at a furious pace, legislation to counteract judicial decisions they disliked. In another part of the circle were other legislators and their aides wearing oversized green eye shades that hung over their heads like ominous shadows. Each sat before reams of paper. Their large unblinking eyes were extended on stalks that followed with slow meticulous care, every phrase, every word, every comma, ever written by a nominee for a judicial position.

A formidable sign hung overhead said, "Snare the Nominee." Every now and then an aide would cry out, "Here's something. In a 6th grade essay on government, the nominee said, 'the courts are a coequal branch of government and their job is to interpret the law.'"

Someone yelled, "Subversive activism." "We can use it!" everyone cried out in unison.

"When will they use it?" asked Grendel, distraught and appalled.

"They could use it now or on the morrow," answered Babe.

"Morrow?" said Grendel in disbelief.

"Luckily, they don't always succeed."

Babe and Grendel proceeded down to yet another circle, the one reserved for The Unrepentant. In the center was a boxing ring. The preliminary events were one boring discovery fight after another. The two sides beat up each other with jabs and punches, but all bouts ended in draws. The crowd booed.

Then came the main event, C.I. Sheriff vs. the challenger B.M. Counselor. C.I. cast a penetrating glare at the raucous crowd. They cheered and booed.

The referee called the combatants to the center of the ring. Just then, word came that Judge Foote was ready to rule on the Chinese Wall case. Babe and Grendel left before they had an opportunity to witness or discuss the pending match. They looked forward to obtaining a report and analysis on the outcome at a later, more appropriate, time.

Babe and Grendel returned to Foote's courtroom, hoping that he would show mercy for what Grendel perceived to be an innocent blunder. Grendel's client was pacing nervously back and forth as Foote took the bench. Foote said he would place the defendant on probation provided he promise never to use the offensive term again, nor ever describe ordinary nouns with an ethnic adjective.

"He promises," said Grendel.

"But what if I have to cite the article?" asked the defendant.

Foote narrowed his eyes.

"He promises, Your Honor," said Grendel, as Foote stepped down from the bench.

"I'll never be able to cite the article again," said the lawyer. "Nor will I be able to use cases that mention the term."

"Yes, you will. You can cite the article and the opinions without using the forbidden term. Use something more appropriate, like 'impenetrable wall.'"

That sounded like a reasonable solution. The client cheered up.

"It will be easy to follow the conditions of probation," said Grendel. "We came out O.K. Let's go to lunch."

"Great, how about Chinese food? I mean . . . ."

They stood fixed in their tracks as a sickening fear numbed their senses.

192

A lawyer and a judge compare notes on whose life has more stress. Who do you think makes the best case?

Wrong! It's not the lawyer. Before I make the judge's case, however, I will first present a fair and objective argument for the lawyer.

She might say, "God, it's rough out there. Barracuda City! An avalanche of litigation, a Malthusian explosion of lawyers. Opposing counsel won't give you an inch. The client expects perfection. If you give less than 110 percent, there's a hungry competitor waiting to take your place. And if somehow another lawyer does take your place and screws up, he will convince the client it was your fault, and he will draft the client's complaint against you.

"And that's not the half of it," she will say, gathering momentum. "Associates in the firm are waiting like jackals to tear you down from your shaky position as a partner. The management committee is looking at your time sheets and wondering whether you're worth the trouble. Your financial commitments multiply like amoebas. There's the payment on the spouse's Bentley, my Lamborghini, the weekend Jag (when it's not in the shop), the kids' tuition for myriad schools and payments for countless lessons. That does not include the balloon payments on the home, the beach condo and the desert retreat. The pressure gauge needle perilously quivers in the red zone.

"Courtroom appearances are sheer hell because you have to appear before smug, self-satisfied judges whose ignorance could fill Dodger Stadium. There's the five-year statute, the three-year statute, which will soon be the two-year statute, and there's discovery, with innumerable interrogatories containing infinite subsections, requests for admission and the constant threat of sanctions. It's no bed of roses."

As she catches her breath, I would say to my imaginary friend, "No need to go on." Then I would point out that, no matter how long her list of miseries, the stress a lawyer suffers is as inconsequential as a warning label on a mattress, as uninspiring as the printed ingredients on a package of beef jerky, compared to one excruciating horror, one unspeakable terror for judges, one looming dark dread that turns their blood to ice, that stabs their hearts with a thousand spears of fear – their profile in The Daily Journal.

Can They Be Fair?

The interview with the reporter is not so bad. The problem is not knowing which lawyers the reporter is going to interview and quote in the profile. Will it be the lawyer who just lost in your court, the one who jabbed his pencil into his hand and ground the lead into the wound when you said, "Motion denied"? Do not expect him to give a fair and even-handed view of your ability, or to be objective when asked to appraise your talents. More likely, he will drag your name through a toxic waste dump and he will be sure not to give his name.

How many nameless lawyers are going to be dropping the guillotine on your reputation? The agonizing wait from the time of your interview to the appearance of the profile in The Daily Journal is worse than waiting for bar results.

When the profile finally appears, it can be devastating for a judge to read: "An attorney who wishes that his name not be used said, 'Judge Squirrelly is lazy, stupid and arrogant.'" Another attorney who requested anonymity said, 'Judge Badger doesn't know res judicata from radicchio. He is intemperate, egocentric, and irritable. And now let me touch on his bad qualities.' Another attorney who would only give his blood type said, 'When they put Judge Gerbil on the fast track, he became derailed.'"

Who are these courageous lawyers who desire anonymity? Can there be such a thing as a lawyer who wishes not to be known? Is it not a contradiction in terms? Do these lawyers even exist? Perhaps I'm getting paranoid; of course they exist. They have to exist. Journalists would never create an imaginary cadre of nameless assassins, would they?

Lawyers do not give their names because they think that what goes around comes around. This groundless fear of retribution has made judges anxious. There is no easy solution to this dilemma. For example, we cannot require journalists to divulge their confidential sources because that would have serious constitutional implications. With such a rule, much of the news would not be printed, and Nixon would still be president.

For a moment I thought the problem could be alleviated by having profiles include views of persons other than just lawyers. I thought that in this way the reader would get a more balanced view, but I quickly rejected the idea. Such an approach might in fact compound the problem. For example, a profile might read: "Judge Mongoose's neighbor says, 'He throws loud parties and blocks out driveway.' The judge's wife says, 'He snores, won't walk the dog and rarely takes the garbage out.' The judge's barber says, 'He's fussy about his sideburns and is a lousy tipper.'"

Here's the Answer...

Then, the solution hit me. Why not give judges the choice of anonymity. If the judge were anonymous, then the attorneys could identify themselves.

A typical profile would start as follows: "Today we profile a judge who wishes not to be identified. Lawyer Smerdley Tapir says that Judge X is a pompous ass whose IQ wouldn't register on the Richter scale. When asked to rate the judge on a scale of 1 to 10, attorney Malcolm Mongoose asked if a fraction was okay. Lawyer Harry Hamster said, 'The inquisition was a study in due process compared to what goes on in Judge X's courtroom.'"

I suppose lawyers will complain that such an approach would not give them the insight they seek into how a particular judge ticks. Not having this vital information, they argue, would make a lawyer's life more difficult and therefore more stressful than it already is.

Maybe so, but I have my own stress to think about.

COMES NOW THE LAWYER- WITH AN AD

It's easy to find a lawyer these days. They set up shop in high-rises, storefronts and even department stores.

With so many lawyers, more than 200,000 in California, the consumer is in a quandary over which one to choose. Some lawyers try to "aid" the consumer by advertising. The more enterprising skywrite their messages in the clouds or paint them on park benches. The more conventional use the yellow pages. What information do lawyers make available for prospective clients? Last week I thumbed through the phone book to find out, and I declare under penalty of perjury that I actually saw the following ads. I have only changed the names of the lawyers. Let's call them all by the same name- something easy for the reader. How about Melvin Zeitgeist?

One lawyer announces that two prominent bar associations have declared days in his honor. Do banners hang from buildings on Rodeo Drive proclaiming Melvin Zeitgeist Day? Do schools close?

Another lawyer boasts that he is recognized by the governor and the mayor. I can see the governor and mayor who happen to be together at a ribbon-cutting ceremony. The mayor grabs the governor by the arm and says, "Quick, down this alley. Here comes that jerk Zeitgeist."

In another ad, a lawyer promises that he will come to your home or hospital bed. I assume that also includes intensive care. Another lawyer in his ad displays two photographs. One shows him reclining in a snazzy Naugahyde chair; the other photograph displays his 45-foot yacht. This should be a real inducement for clients who wish to help out with slip fees.

But who needs the yellow pages when an ambitious lawyer can reach millions of insomniacs with television? One sleepless night at 2 a.m. I switched on the TV and happened to catch one of the 37 commercials during the movie break. I saw a lawyer I knew from my trial court days. At first I didn't recognize him. All the law books neatly shelved in the background threw me off. How could the unsuspecting viewers know that he had never opened one of those books in his life?

His eyes were glazed as he asked the Tele Prompter if it had been involved in an accident. He removed his glasses the way he imagined Raymond Burr might do it, got up from his desk, and walked with the gait of C-3P0 to a chart showing the percentage of recovery an enterprising plaintiff who hired him could make. His voice was flat and dull as though he were reading for a part in "Invasion of the Body Snatchers." As the commercial mercifully drew to a close, a voice-over repeated his name and said in English, "Interpreters are available for foreign born." This was a little like asking everyone who is deaf to please raise their hands.

I have also heard the audio portion of this commercial on the radio. This got me worried. These ads, which tell you nothing about a lawyer's skills but a lot about his lack of taste, are reaching more and more people. If you want to buy a can of soup, you can at least read the contents on the label. Many lawyers' ads, however, suggest that the lawyer's role is to invent a lawsuit. With the focus on greed rather than justice, it is no wonder that the legal profession is not held in high repute today. This also may explain why the public apparently supports the trend toward reduction in available tort remedies.

I fear that for some lawyers the dwindling number of theories to support tort liability may spur them on to make even more brazen advertising claims. In an appeal to potential litigants, they will boast of their skill in making a complaint stick. They will try to improve their ads by emulating commercials for other products like that exotic beer commercial which used to be on the air. The announcer got your attention with his narration of a short, dramatic episode usually written by the person who came in last in the Hemingway imitation contest. A macho-type character relates his perilous or life-threatening experience in some exotic location. "Pepe and I scrambled out of the river as the piranhas ripped our kayak to pieces. Later that night we relaxed and drank our San Miguel beer with the Kaukau Pygmies. Whenever I drink a San Miguel, it brings back fond memories of the kayak and the Kaukaus."

Here's how a lawyer might use an adventure story to sell his services:

MUSIC-Appropriate sound effects. "Pepe and I ran hard. Close behind were the pursuing process servers. It was hot as we prepared to cross the Los Angeles River. Rays from the indistinct sun shone down on us through a smoggy sky as we climbed down the side of the graffiti-covered embankment. We tried to read the graffiti, but the script was too ornate. As Pepe leaned forward trying to make out a word, he said, 'My neck hurts. It's not so good.'

"I knew what he meant. Then suddenly I remember Melvin Zeitgeist, Attorney at Law. A reassuring smile played across my face. 'I have a lawyer,' I said.

Pepe looked doubtful. 'Who do we sue, a river that doesn't run?'

He had a point. Zeitgeist would think of something. 'Maybe we can sue the city,' I said, knowing that Zeitgeist would not blow the notice requirement.

'We may be up against government immunity,' said street-wise Pepe.

'Zeitgeist will find an exception,' I said. 'Maybe we can sue our carrier under the insurance Code.'

Street smarts only go so far. I didn't tell Pepe about *Moradi-Shalal*. But, who knows, there still are some causes of action left.

Pepe kept on romanticizing. 'Maybe we can even get punitives.'

'Don't hold your breath, Pepe,' I said to myself. Zeitgeist knew how to squeeze juice out of a complaint, but could he stop trends that have gathered too much steam?"

VOICE-OVER- "Don't give up hope. Punitives bad faith, emotional distress- Melvin Zeitgeist, the lawyer who knows his way around a cause of action."

Maybe judges should get equal time. A short commercial now and then might be salutary:

Sound of gavel coming down hard. "BANG!"

Voice No. 1- "Demurrer sustained without leave. Now let's discuss sanctions."

Voice No. 2- "This sound bite brought to you by Judge O.R. Roughy, the judge who knows what is a cause of action."

TO TELL THE WHOLE TRUTH AND NOTHING BUT....

What you hear the trial judge say at the conclusion of the witness's testimony: "Thank you. You may step down." What you would hear if the judge gave voice to the raging thoughts he tied to a post in his mind: "You lying piece of offal." The judge ultimately enters judgment against the party for whom the witness testified. On appeal the appellate court affirms the judgment because substantial evidence supports it. The trial judge has said nothing about witness credibility, but that doesn't matter. The appellate court relies on the trial judge's implied findings that he did not believe the witness. The trial judge's thoughts can now be safely unleashed from their tether to frolic at will.

Trial judges have enormous power. I once was a trial court judge, so I know. Their findings on credibility are given great deference by appellate courts. Trial judges instinctively know a liar when they see and hear one on the witness stand. Similarly they have an unerring sense of when a witness is truthful and forthright. From where do they get this superhuman power? There is no such course offered at the Judges College. A few years ago a judicial education program offered a course purporting to teach one how to tell whether a witness is lying. The course was cancelled, however, when my wife decided she was too busy to teach it.

Up until recently I gave little thought to credibility findings. When I was invited to speak to a group of Administrative Law Judges (ALJ's) about credibility findings, I accepted on condition that no one eat turkey for 24 hours prior to my talk. L-tryptophan would not enhance audience attention to this seemingly dull topic.

In fact, the topic was not dreary. It prompted me to question how judges in fact judge credibility. How do we know whether someone is telling the truth or lying? Sometimes we just know it in our gut. There is that ineffable quality that exudes from some people and forms these words encased in a bubble over their heads, "I am a sleazy scum bag for whom the truth is as welcome as West Nile virus." But who knows whether the trial judge has it right? Certainly not appellate justices. I suppose in rare cases an appellate judge might question credibility findings, when, for example, a trial judge credits the testimony of Stevie Wonder and George Shearing, each of whom swear they saw plaintiff stumble on the curb and hold his ankle in pain.

But what would happen if trial judges had to document their credibility findings based solely on demeanor? How would they articulate such findings for a reviewing court? I broke out in a cold sweat at the thought. But no judge has to do this, right? Wrong. No one except . . . ALJ's. They make important decisions that have a profound effect on the public and on the lives of the parties appearing before them. They adjudicate a plethora of decisions made by state and local governmental agencies. These decisions concern, among other things, professional and vocational licensing, professional and employee discipline, payment of disability and retirement benefits, and land use issues. They write their own detailed decisions stating their findings. And of course they routinely make decisions based on the credibility of witnesses. On writs of administrative mandamus heard by the superior court, are credibility findings of the ALJ entitled to deference? In many cases the answer is yes, but it comes with a price.

Government Code section 11425.50 (a) requires ALJ's to write a statement of the factual and legal basis for their decisions. And when their decisions include a determination based substantially on witness credibility, section 11425.50 (b) provides that the ALJ's written "statement shall identify any specific evidence of the observed demeanor, manner, or attitude of the witness that supports the determination." And to show how valued these findings are, subdivision (b) goes on to tell courts they must give "great weight" to these credibility findings. *California Youth Authority v. State Personnel Bd.* (2002) 104 Cal.App.4th 575, 588, citing the Law Revision Commission's comments to section 11425.50 (b), concludes that the ALJ's credibility findings are **not** entitled to great weight unless the determination derives from the judge's observation of the demeanor, manner or attitude of the witness.

So, to get deference, the ALJ has to identify or describe what it is about the witness that leads to the conclusion of truthfulness or prevarication. I thought back on the innumerable cases I had heard as a trial judge when I was certain a witness or two lied through his or her teeth. I have not forgotten the testimony of an expert statistician. Lies and damned lies paled in comparison to his statistics. If I had been an ALJ, I would have gotten no deference on that one because my determination was not based on his demeanor, attitude or manner. But what if it had been? How does one go about describing why a witness is a lying S.O.B.? Does this not involve a creative recitation of the judge's perceptions, something not reflected in the record? With great empathy for the ALJ's, I tried to fashion credibility findings from another case I had heard when I was a trial judge.

"The witness was perched on the edge of his chair like a trapped condor hoping for an updraft to carry him away. Tiny beads of sweat formed on his forehead like drops of condensation inside an old refrigerator. As the noose of cross-examination tightened around his neck, he blurted out an answer that sounded like a scream. His wild eyes bulged as tentacles of terror closed round his heart. I have noted the witness's nervous twitches and discomfort. In my view the witness is . . . ." The witness is what, a liar or highly credible?

Could not either conclusion apply? A nervous and fidgety witness may simply be exhibiting discomfort in a courtroom where he is the center of attention. His uneasiness may have nothing to do with his truthfulness. The witness who hesitates and stammers may be searching for the truth as opposed to the cool and collected witness whose pat answer is a packaged lie.

Identifying aspects of credibility can be particularly dicey in novel cases, say, for example, when someone sues himself. That is what happened in *Lodi v. Lodi* (1985) 173 Cal.App.3d 628, a case written by a distinguished jurist, Justice Richard Sims, who coincidentally also authored *CYA v. Henderson*. If Dickens had written about the *Lodi* case, he might have titled his novel, "The Best of Times—The Worst of Times." Lodi's complaint alleges that he, Lodi, as a defendant is the beneficiary of a charitable trust, the estate of which should revert to him, Lodi, the plaintiff. Apparently plaintiff and defendant could not agree to settle the matter. Defendant Lodi was served but failed to answer. Plaintiff Lodi sought a default judgment. The trial court's dismissal of Lodi's complaint was affirmed by Justice Sims and his colleagues. Justice Sims with characteristic insight noted the even-handed application of justice accorded Lodi. True, Lodi lost, but he also won. Driven by unwavering rectitude, Justice Sims ordered each party to bear his own costs. It is rumored that after the decision the Lodis reconciled, made dinner at home and watched a movie on television, "The Three Faces of Eve."

I shudder to think what would have happened if the Lodis had gone to trial. I can envision plaintiff and defendant Lodi, each telling his respective lawyer to "sue the bastard" and show no mercy. No doubt discovery would have been an ordeal, but the trial would have been a nightmare. Imagine the difficulties facing the trier of fact if he or she had to identify credibility findings. What if the judge believed Lodi, but disbelieved Lodi? The findings might read as follows: "Plaintiff Lodi was the only credible witness. His answers to defendant Lodi's convoluted questions were forthright. Lodi was patient and reserved. In contrast, Lodi was fretful, evasive, and hostile. He refused to look Lodi in the eye, slumped in the witness chair and stammered when answering the most simple questions. For Lodi, the truth is a pendulum, which under Lodi's careful cross-examination, sliced Lodi's lies in half."

Credibility findings, whether articulated or not, can have serious repercussions. About 35 years ago, a Municipal Court Judge sitting in traffic court found his wife guilty of speeding. After rejecting her defense before a packed courtroom, he questioned her veracity, lectured her on traffic safety, and fined her $100. Before calling the next case, he said, "See you at home for dinner, honey." I have been unable to verify the rumor that he was hospitalized that evening for ptomaine poisoning.

It occurred to me the other night while listening to Fred Astaire's version of Gershwin's "Anything Goes," that sooner or later there will be a case where a judge appears before himself. I would hate to appear before me. I am tough on myself and put little stock in my credibility. I would no doubt impose a heavy sentence on me, and this is in a civil case. In a criminal case, I would definitely file an affidavit of prejudice.

For the time being, trial judges do not appear before themselves. Nor are they required to do the heavy lifting required of ALJ's and explain credibility findings on witness demeanor to get deference from higher courts. But I no longer feel sorry for ALJ's. I have heard that many supplement their income by selling the movie rights to their credibility findings.

THE NAME AND THE THING ARE NOT THE SAME

What was a great present for a bright kid in 1953? A Gilbert chemistry set. My name happened to be Gilbert. It still is. When I was in high school, everyone thought I would be a wiz in chemistry. That's how stupid people were in those days. Thank God my name was not Einstein. Is Ernest Hemingway's brother, the accountant, a brilliant novelist? I proved everyone wrong when I took high school chemistry and coined the phrase, "Worse Things Through Chemistry," in defiance of DuPont's slogan which defined chemistry as the road to Shangri-La. DuPont labs manufactured napalm used in the Vietnam War. In 1996 Fatboy Slim made an album entitled "Better Things Through Chemistry." One of the tunes was called "Next to Nothing." That's what I knew about chemistry. I was a total klutz in the lab. One day I mixed the wrong chemicals. The explosion was not all that powerful. No one was hurt. I received minor burns on my arms. The ointment helped. Within a week the scars had cleared up. The teacher was sympathetic. I passed the course. In college, chemistry was a prerequisite for medical school. That's why I opted for law school, thereby saving the lives of innumerable potential patients and avoiding being sued in a medical malpractice suit.

My name created further difficulties for me in law school. The less astute students thought I had authored the Gilbert Law School Outlines. Professors held the Gilbert outlines in contempt and saw them as the counterpart to Classic Comics in Literature classes. But then not many of my law professors seemed to know much about literature. The more malevolent law professors would call on me in class, prefacing a convoluted question with, "Kindly enlighten us, Mr. Gilbert, with an outline to the solution to this apparent conundrum." I didn't have the solution. The chemistry just wasn't right.

We give names much importance, but a name is merely a sound or a squiggle on a page. It should not be confused with the actual thing. Call a weed a rose, it still won't have the fragrance. Just ask Shakespeare. Jude Law is an actor, not a lawyer. I bet he doesn't have the slightest idea how to draft a living trust. That our birthdays fall on the same day has no significance. Sometimes names get close to the mark. Take Michael P. Judge, for example, the Los Angeles County Public Defender. His office represents the poor and the disadvantaged charged with criminal offenses. Although not deciding cases as a judge, he and his deputies pursue justice for their clients. Judges dispense justice, don't they? So there is a connection. But if he should ever become a judge, that is, if there should ever be a governor who will appoint a criminal defense attorney to the bench, he would be known as Judge Judge. Sometime ago a state senator sought to change his first name to senator. It is rumored that his favorite dish was mahi mahi. My computer thinks these are spelling errors.

Judge Minor Wisdom, the courageous judge of the 5th Circuit Court of Appeals who protected and guarded civil rights and steadfastly implemented *Brown v. Board of Education*, was anything but minor, and in all respects wise. There the name worked. The same with Judge Learned Hand, one of the most learned jurists of our century. Can't say the same about Judge Learned Foote, who has appeared in this column on many occasions. He often steps into trouble. I met a man whose last name was Cool. He would have made a Cool Judge.

But names conjure up images that can enhance or detract depending on our goals. Some of the candidates running for judicial office refer to themselves as "criminal prosecutor." They no doubt believe that such designation resonates better with voters than the simple "prosecutor." I wonder if the voters know that these "criminal prosecutors" cannot be prosecutors on the bench. A plaintiff's personal injury lawyer I know wants to run for judge as a "civil prosecutor." Many years ago I knew a judge who was up for reelection. She drew a challenger. The judge designated herself "incumbent" on the ballot statement. That was the kiss of death. She might as well have called herself "criminal defense attorney." She lost.

Going further back in time when women judges were a rarity, a judge named Nancy changed her first name to Noel, which apparently won her the male chauvinist vote. And in other ways she copied men. Xavier Cugat, the famous Latin band leader of the 1940's, led the orchestra in sambas and mambos with a Chihuahua nestled in his arms. The judge conducted her trials with a poodle nestled in her arm. That was a bad idea. The poodle was a tough sentencer. He has taken issue with a recent 9th Circuit Court of Appeals case, *Cetacean Community v. Bush* (9th Cir. 2004) 2004 WL 2348373, which holds that the "Cetacean Community," the world's whale, porpoises and dolphin population, does not have standing to sue over the Navy's use of sonar to detect "quiet submarines" at long range. The high strung poodle with a strong aversion to water nevertheless felt a kinship to the laid back cetaceans because "we are all mammals."

Titles and names mean nothing. The title "Judge," for instance, carries little weight. Many, many years ago (the statute of limitations has run), I called a popular restaurant to make reservations. I wanted a good table, so I told the person on the phone that I was Judge Gilbert. He made the reservation for Judd Gilbert. I performed a wedding ceremony and at the conclusion pronounced the couple married by virtue of the authority vested in me as a justice on the Court of Appeal. During the toast to the newly married couple, a well known actor referred to me as the "Justice of the Peace." I would just as soon not use the title. But "retired" judges who become active private judges want to be known and introduced as judges. For some reason you will find them in abundance at bar functions they rarely attended in their pre-retirement days. And those who were not the most congenial bench officers have suddenly learned to smile and be ingratiating with members of the bar.

Names and titles are deceiving. I know someone named Small who is 6 feet tall. I know someone named Short and he is short. There is even someone named Jack Schitt. I don't know him.

We should all do and be our best and forget about our names and titles. They say nothing about who we are. This is particularly true for judges. The best appellations a judge can carry are "fair," "objective" and "unbiased," for example. Because they must be earned, they are the ones that count.

As for me, no need to call me "your honor." Like the poodle, I favor the cetaceans. Call me Gilbert.

MILITANT INTERPRETATION

My friend, Judge Janice Brown, with whom I often disagree, sits on the Federal Court of Appeals for the District of Columbia Circuit. I wrote this column in response to a speech she made in 1997 when she was a sitting justice on the California Supreme Court.

I caused a scene at the hardware store the other day.

People from my generation are not supposed to cause scenes. I, who came of age in the fifties, belong to the Silent Generation. In truth, I more properly belong in the previous Lost Generation because I could never find myself. The label "silent" was a gross exaggeration. You wouldn't find my generation hanging out at the Christian Science Reading Room. And, if you listened carefully, you could hear us softly bitching in our gray flannel suits. In comparison to the sixties, the fifties were quiet, but they saw revolutionary changes in the arts and in the law. Take, for example, *Brown* v. *Board of Education* . . . but I'm getting ahead of myself.

Back to the hardware store and an incident that elicited clamor, not silence. I was waiting in line at the only open register. The patron ahead of me was purchasing half of the store's plumbing supplies. The clerk was computing the prices of the innumerable pipes and cylinders on the counter before him with the alacrity of a three-toed tree sloth. Another clerk arrived to open a second register and said or mumbled, "I'll take the next person in line." That was me. Some of the people behind me at the very end of the line simply moved over and formed a line at the second register. I was left waiting in line at the first check stand steaming at this gross injustice. The clerk in the new check stand began to wait on a young woman who had been behind me in the first line.

"She's not quite the next person in line," I said sarcastically.

"I've been waiting in line too, you know," she said staring me straight in the face with the self-righteous air of unearned indignation. Of course it wasn't entirely her fault. It was the clerk who understandably would rather serve her than me.

I directed my comments to the clerk. "It's not fair to take the people at the end of the line first. They are not the people who are next in line. They are not even close to being next in line."

There was a momentary lull as everyone considered the merit of what I had said. For a moment time stopped.

The customer behind the woman broke the silence with an abrupt slam of reality. "This discussion is not worth the time," he said flatly.

"Not worth the time, indeed," I thought. Inspired by Hugo Black, I pulled out of my pocket a dog-eared copy of the Constitution and tried to find an article, or an amendment, that would support me. I whistled softly to myself while flipping the pages.

An elderly man looking over my shoulder said, "Son, that document isn't going to solve this problem." His words hit me like an injunction prohibiting discrimination. I had been groping in the penumbra, but his words, a beacon of light, illuminated the truth. The Constitution was not meant to solve my problem. It was not designed to correct every injustice in the world.

The woman narrowed her eyes in anger. The man behind her said, "He's next," motioning to me. The clerk looked my way and said, "You're next Mr." The line moved back to let me through.

I stuffed my copy of the Constitution back into my pocket. The clerk in my line was holding up a ball-cock assembly and a float ball. As I moved a little sheepishly into my rightful place in the next line, I thought of the speech recently given by Supreme Court Justice Janice Brown at the California Club reported in the Daily Journal, December 12, 1997.

According to the article, Justice Brown deplored what she termed the "judge militant." These are the judges that seek to solve society's social problems "by constitutionalizing everything possible, citing constitutional rights which are nowhere mentioned in the Constitution." She was puzzled by "the conceit of judges who claim infallibility and shrug off the Constitution like a worn suit and never let tradition stand in the way of a desired result."

I know what Justice Brown was talking about. I had momentarily fallen into the Constitutional trap in the hardware store. But I was able to achieve justice without the use of some vague constitutional phrase like "due process" or "equal protection."

Justice Brown cites *Brown* v. *Board of Education*, the famous 1954 school desegregation case, as a "philosophical turning point." Since that opinion was decided, Brown states the public has appeared less interested in the "classical virtues" of its judges, which include "impartiality, prudence, persuasiveness and self-restraint."

Her comments brought to mind a couple of examples of "judge militants." In *First English Evangelical Lutheran Church of Glendale* v. *County of Los Angeles, California* (1987) 482 U.S. 304, the U.S. Supreme Court ignored the legislative will of the people of Los Angeles. Because of a terrible flood the county enacted an interim ordinance temporarily prohibiting construction within a flood protection area for the "immediate preservation of the public health and safety." The majority opinion authored by Chief Justice Rehnquist held that this temporary restriction on the development of the property could constitute an unconstitutional taking. In his dissent Justice Stevens argued that the majority opinion ignored both precedent and legislative will by creating a constitutional right to compensation where none existed before.

In *Lucas* v. *So. Carolina Coastal Council* (1992) 505 U.S. 1003, another "takings" case, Justice Scalia acknowledged that before the 1922 case of *Pennsylvania Coal Co.* v. *Mahon*, it was generally thought that the "Takings clause reached only a direct appropriation of property." But now, the court was looking at the Takings Clause in a different way. Again, Justice Stevens deplored the majority's lack of judicial restraint, and the illogical expansion of the constitutional concept of regulatory takings. (Pg. 812.)

Were the *First English* and *Lucas* decisions examples of an arrogant judiciary, ignoring precedent and manipulating the Constitution to achieve a desired result? The answer perhaps depends on one's values and perceptions. Just as the unanimous court that decided *Brown* v. *Board of Education* thought it was embracing the Constitution, not shrugging it off, so did the majority that decided *First English* and *Lucas*.

Without the *Brown* decision our nation would have been deprived of some of its most capable leaders in all branches of government and the professions.

Indeed were it not for *Brown* v. *Board of Education*, and the cases that followed in its wake, I would probably not be writing this particular column about Justice Brown speaking at the California Club. That she was there expressing her views about the Constitution is not something to shrug off.

"It's good luck." That's what Judge Learned Foote said about the horseshoe nailed above the doorway to his chambers. But for many of the lawyers who appeared before him, it was bad luck to be in his courtroom. Judge Foote, however, did not measure his fortune by the complaints of whiney lawyers, but lately even he questioned the efficacy of his horseshoe.

Judge Foote recently had been reviled by colleagues and the bar for denying an attorney's motion to continue. The attorney's father had died a few days before the hearing. He called opposing counsel and asked for a brief continuance. Opposing counsel immediately responded with the characteristic professional courtesy that's so prevalent today. "Forget it," he said and hung up. When the attorney asked Judge Foote for a short continuance so that he could attend his father's funeral, Judge Foote said, "Denied."

This prompted the attorney to write a poignant letter to the Daily Journal about the incident. The lawyer spoke of his personal hurt and his profound disappointment about the low state to which the profession had fallen. This in turn prompted Judge Foote to write a letter to Miss Anne Thrope. (You may recall I have written about her in a previous column. She's the ancient lady who lives in a Hollywood bungalow, and who, when she's up to it, gives advice on matters relating to the legal profession.) Judge Foote wrote her the following letter:

Dear Miss Thrope,

A lawyer came before me the other day and asked for a continuance because his father had died. Before ruling on the motion, I thought for a moment about some of the motions for continuance I had denied in the past: Counsel's house had burned down, counsel had to give blood for a transfusion for his brother who had just been in an accident, counsel's wife and children were being held hostage for ransom.

Since these motions were not sufficient for a continuance, why should this one be? I'm tired of being blamed for everybody else's problems. The no-continuance rule has to be followed if we are to run an efficient court. The rule would be meaningless if we allowed it to be swallowed by exceptions.

"I am, however, tired of being ignored at bar functions and of eating alone in the judges' luncheon room. All the uptight lawyers in my courtroom are making me feel uptight also. I'm restless and misunderstood. Maybe I need a change. What should I do?"

Anne Thrope wrote the following reply:

"Dear Misunderstood,

I think you need a change. You are not interacting well with human beings. Maybe you should get away from them for awhile. Take a brief assignment on the

Court of Appeal. They have lots of writ petitions. You will have the opportunity to do what you do best – deny them."

Shortly after receiving Miss Thrope's reply, Judge Foote's canary died. He took a few weeks off and then began his assignment at the Court of Appeal. Despite his horseshoe, his bad luck persisted. He could not get concurring votes on the first opinion he wrote. He therefore wrote the dissent.

He urged the majority to publish the opinion so that people who read the dissent could see how the issues should have been decided. The majority stubbornly refused to publish it. Judge Foote tried to reason with them, but they wouldn't budge. In desperation he once again turned to Miss Anne Thrope for advice.

Although she was terribly weak, she managed to offer the following wisdom:

"Dear Dissent,

We cannot always get what we want. Sometimes half a loaf is better than none. Compromise with your colleagues. Ask them to publish every other paragraph of the opinion. In this way, everyone gets a little and gives up a little."

Judge Foote put this proposal to his colleagues. To foster collegiality, they agreed to publish every other paragraph of the majority opinion, together with the dissent in its entirety.

Judge Foote thought his luck had changed, but he was wrong. The majority opinion was hailed as one of the few literary masterpieces to come out of the Court of Appeal. It was praised for its structure, its organization, and its clear, unencumbered style. The dissent, however, was depublished. As his stint on the Court of Appeal drew to a close, Judge Foote grew more and more apprehensive about returning to the trial court. He feared that the stress he caused lawyers would again provoke his feelings of anxiety.

Once again he wrote to Miss Thrope and asked for her advice. She barely had the strength to write back. She could only manage to scribble one faint word with her unsteady hand – "Christo."

Judge Foote knew that Christo was the fabulously wealthy avant-garde artist who continually shocked the world with his unorthodox creations. He was the Ross Perot of the art world. But what could Christo have to do with the tension and stress in his courtroom? Christo's Umbrellas. They dotted the landscape and gave people a feeling of peace and serenity – although one did topple over in the wind and kill a spectator.

Lawyers who entered Judge Foote's court on the day he returned to the trial court were astonished to find in the middle of the courtroom a large orange umbrella. They were also puzzled because the umbrella was closed. After Judge Foote had taken the bench to call the law and motion calendar, one of the attorneys gathered enough courage to ask him why he didn't have the umbrella open. Judge

Foote smiled patiently and gave a quick glance at his horseshoe: "Because that would be bad luck."

AN ATTORNEY CLOSE BY

Picture if you will, a law firm where the attorneys say, "say ahh," along with "we'll sue"; where they wear surgical gowns over their three piece suits; where they take your pulse along with your deposition; where they are as quick to reach for a stethoscope as they are the Civil Code; where when taking an oath they mean the Hippocratic one.

No, I'm not talking about a frustrated group of lawyers who had once flunked out of medical school. The vision of this law firm came to me after reading the case of *Life v. County of Los Angeles, 227* Cal.App.3d 894 (1991). The case dealt with the stimulating topic of compliance with the claims statute. As you all know, before suing a governmental entity, you must timely file a claim with the entity before you may sue it. If you suffer from insomnia, I highly recommend browsing though sections of the Government Code pertaining to the filing of governmental claims. Do it just before turning the lights out. You'll thank me.

The *Life* court tells us that the purpose of the claims statute is to give the public entity sufficient information so it can adequately investigate the claim and settle it, if appropriate, without expensive litigation. Don't hold your breath.

The plaintiff in the *Life* case wished to sue doctors and personnel at a county hospital for medical negligence. His attorney had never filed a claim against a government entity before. Already you can smell trouble. He made his first mistake when he called the hospital to find out to whom he should present his claim for medical malpractice. He apparently forgot the old adage, "And you will be deceived." An employee told him to file his claim with the legal department and to just address his claim to the medical center, Attention Legal Department.

Maybe I'm jumping to conclusion, but this led me to believe that the offices for the attorneys representing the hospital are right there in the hospital…probably in the cardiac-care unit.

The well-meaning attorney mailed his "timely" claim to the legal department. Upon receiving the claim, the legal department snapped into inaction…like a patient etherized upon a table. Perhaps the lawyers came and went, and spoke now and then of Rembrandt or maybe David Hockney, but they apparently ignored the claim.

Plaintiff filed his action, but defendant county hospital won its summary judgment motion on the grounds that plaintiff had failed to comply with the filing requirements. The Court of Appeal affirmed the trial court. Filing the claim with the legal department instead of the appropriate county officials did not constitute substantial compliance with the claims statute. And so another case bit the dust, perhaps only to reappear in another form sometime in the future.

What interests me about the case is the location of the lawyers' offices. Think how convenient it is for them to be right there in the hospital with their clients, and their potential opposing parties. Lawyers can pop up into patients' rooms just before surgery and have them sign informed-consent forms. Paralegals can scrub for surgery and be there working up potential defenses while the malpractice is actually taking place. A firsthand observation beats a muddled explanation months after the fact. The lawyers also can work with the doctors in preparing patients' medical charts. That can reduce the number of embarrassing answers on cross-examination.

Preventative law is important for businesses because prevention means protection. In this litigation-happy society, all businesses, big and small, need their lawyers in close proximity ever minute of the working day. Having a lawyer around is akin to getting a flu shot.

Even a very small-business person feels it useful to have a lawyer close at hand. Just the other day my handyman came to my house to do some work, fix a few things, wash some windows and haul away some trash. He said he would be there at 7:30 a.m. He showed up at 8…with his lawyer who had expertise in workers' comp and P.I. The lawyer did some checking before the work began.

He asked questions, like how sturdy was my ladder and how high were the windows. I said I thought the ladder was just fine. The lawyer and the handyman conferred off to the side. I started worrying…the ladder was a little rickety.

They ended their conference, and the handyman agreed to do the windows. I got the ladder, and he climbed up it. I started to sweat, "Maybe you ought to get down from that ladder," I said. The lawyer's eyes narrowed. "There's a problem with the ladder?" he asked coldly.

"No, of course not. I just don't think the windows are all that dirty."

The lawyer beckoned the handyman, who had already soaped up part of the windows. The handyman shrugged his shoulders and started down the ladder. I held my breath. His foot slipped on one of my rungs.

"Whoa!" he shouted. I held the ladder firm and uttered some kind of wish under my breath. The handyman regained his footing and continued slowly down the ladder.

"Doesn't look too sturdy," said the lawyer. "You're not just kidding," said the handyman touching the ground.

I was relieved. True, I wouldn't be able to see out of my soapy windows, but I had avoided a possible lawsuit. There was a lesson here. The presence of lawyers makes us all cautious. Just as a highway patrol officer's car in the lane next to us slows us down, so, too, does a lawyer on the scene modify our conduct.

Of course, the lawyer was of immense benefit to the handyman. Had there been an accident, the lawyer would have had the facts immediately at his command,

and could have decided whether this would be a comp or a P.I. case. That a lawyer under such circumstances might have to be a witness in his own client's case, necessitating bringing in another lawyer to try the case, would only help spread the work around.

These thoughts brought me back to the *Life* case. It proves that having a lawyer around gives a client a justified sense of well-being. A county hospital with its legal department on the premises puts the minds of the doctors at ease. After all, claims against the hospital occasionally are sent to the legal department. Now that's a comfort.

CITE UNSEEN

A shocking thing happened to me. Although not easy to discuss, it is de rigueur to reveal the most embarrassing details of one's life to a wide audience. I declined an appearance on Geraldo. I prefer instead, a more narrow, sensitive audience. That is why I am using this column to disclose my disquieting experience.

Some background will help illuminate the significance of my ordeal. It goes back to my first column in July of 1988. It was then that the editors of the Daily Journal asked me if I would write an article about depublication. I agreed and wrote it. The Supreme Court tried to depublish it. They failed.

Flush with victory we launched my column. It became a vehicle to express my views and alienate a modest assortment of otherwise phlegmatic readers.

Of course the Supreme Court still depublished my opinions from time to time. I fooled them for a while by writing under an assumed name. They caught on and tried to depublish my birth certificate. The order was defective and I persevered. I'm not sure if there was a causal relation, but as the number of columns I wrote increased, there was a corresponding decrease in the number of my opinions depublished. There was, however, a slight increase in my reversal rate.

I didn't think the statistics were all that important until I went to the law library one day a few weeks ago. I told the law librarian that I wished to check out the four volumes of Coke's Institutes of the Lawes of England. In keeping with Supreme Court tradition, I wanted one of my opinions to contain the historical antecedents for a legal principle. I felt this would be important to the general practitioner.

You may view Coke's work only in a special room with a security guard standing over your shoulder. It's much like the scene in Citizen Kane when the reporter looking for insight into the meaning of "Rosebud" views Kane's papers with a guard standing nearby.

You may not even see this work unless your name is on a special list. Justices with more than three depublications in a year are removed from the list with the alacrity of an affirmance in a criminal case.

The law librarian gave me a cold glare and looked to see if my name was on the list. I knew that if they counted depublications by the calendar year rather than by the fiscal year, my name would be there. Apparently it was still on the list, because the librarian asked me in a haughty tone if I had an appointment. I reciprocated in kind and said, "No, are the books busy?"

To my astonishment he informed me that they were. They were attending a funeral for several opinions that had been recently depublished.

I was relieved to learn that none of the cases I had authored were in this group of recent opinions that had been laid to rest. I thought I was in the clear until the law librarian discovered an obituary for one of the decedents. It caught his eye because it noted that the deceased had the smallest shroud in the history of depublication. It went on to say that the deceased was small and delicate, young and innocent. I noted a tear in the librarian's eye.

With a flourish of his pen he crossed my name off the list. He gave me a sneer and quickly walked away. He left the obituary on the counter. I grabbed it and read its contents. I was stunned to learn that the waif who had passed on was intimately related to me. What I next realized caused darkness to spread over my heart and I gasped, ". . . the horror." I had been depublished.

"Why such distress over a mere depublication?" you might ask. Most Court of Appeal justices with an imagination at one time or another have been depublished by the Supreme Court. That is true, but this case was extraordinary and alarming. You see I was depublished by-the Court of Appeal.

You may well question whether it is possible for such a thing to occur. To my consternation I discovered it is possible, but it takes enormous effort.

Here's how it happened. One of the divisions in the second district partially published a celebrated family law case, Cochran v. Cochran. In the opinion, the justices referred in the following manner to a family law case I had authored: "As Justice Gilbert's erudite 'digression' in Harris v. Superior Court etc…" The next page of the opinion read, "Viewed from the perspective which Justice Gilbert's entreaty requires, the inapplicability of (citations omitted) becomes apparent."

I was flattered that distinguished colleagues had referred to me in such laudatory terms. The shattering blow came, however, when they granted a rehearing. They still cited the Harris case, but deleted all references to me, including my "erudition" and my "entreaty." After I looked up "erudition" in the dictionary I cooled off a little. Nevertheless, the deletion of my "entreaty" I consider an unacceptable affront. What could be more insulting than to relegate a person's entreaties to oblivion?

No sooner had the Daily Journal appellate report published the modification in its Daily Appellate Reports than I had to contend with an avalanche of imposing inquiries and comments. A reporter wrote an article about the incident. Numerous colleagues wrote or e-mailed me with their gratuitous observations.

The noted humorist Justice William Bedsworth, whose witty column appears in another publication, had little sympathy. He would have accepted a special assignment just to vote for the deletion of "erudition." He did, however, understand my chagrin about the deletion of "entreaty." He recalled that some of his entreaties had been rejected with extreme prejudice--a drink in the face. This, he pointed out much to my discomfort, paled in comparison to a depublished entreaty.

It was as though the entreaty had never been made. He implied that an entreaty rejected is far better than an entreaty never made.

Others questioned the motivation for the court's quirky maneuver. Why state an encomium only to recant it? One distinguished retired judge opined that one of the party's publicity agents urged the modification. One can only speculate about what caused the change of heart. Did the concurring justices work on the author of the opinion to delete the offending language? Did they employ gentle persuasion to turn her around, or did they strong arm her? Who knows?

There is a bright side. I submitted the modification that depublishes me, along with all my other depublished cases, for publication to an underground publishing firm, East's Oxymoron Publishing Co. The company accepted the submission and published it. It comes in a handsomely bound five volume set. Although it provides interesting reading, my royalties are low. Nothing in the set is quotable or citable.

A QUICK TRIAL

A neighbor of Judge Learned Foote, who had just lost a small-claims case, cornered him in the supermarket. "Why is it so hard to get justice in the courts?" she asked.

"Because the courts are inefficient," he answered while pulling a 60-second frozen dinner out of the freezer.

"Why are they inefficient?" asked the persistent neighbor.

"Too much time on trials," he said backing down the aisle toward the Hamburger Helper.

"They hardly spent any time on my case," said the neighbor holding on to the front of Judge Foote's shopping cart. "It was over in seconds. The judge never let me explain how the cleaners discolored my curtains."

"Good for him," muttered Judge Foote not quite under his breath.

"You mean good for her," said the indignant neighbor giving a backward push to Foote's shopping cart. "But not good for me. That judge didn't give me my day in court." She turned in a huff and made for the potato bin.

"That judge ought to be hearing criminal cases," Foote thought to himself. He watched his neighbor frantically grabbing and rejecting potatoes. "What does she expect?" he thought. "She probably believes in that half-baked idea that too much efficiency means too little justice. People can't expect perfect justice in an imperfect world."

On the way to the check stand he stopped for a moment and spoke to the manger about the sign over the potato rack, "POTATOES." "You should pay attention to that produce sign. By now everyone in the country knows that an 'e' does not belong in potato."

"But we're selling more than one," said the manager.

Judge Foote had no time to argue. He did not want to be late for the theater that evening. He did not realize it at the moment, but the play he would see that night would inspire him to solve the trial court's congestion crisis.

That evening Judge Foote experienced the ultimate in efficient theater. He saw Tom Stoppard's play, "The 15 minute Hamlet." In fact, the production was so efficient that the play took only 11 minutes to perform. Stoppard's version featured only the important and significant portions of Hamlet.

It doesn't waste your time with unnecessary details.

"The play's the thing, wherein I'll catch the conscience of the…Hyperion to a satyr…Frailty thy name is…Alas poor Yorick…To be or not to be that is…To thine own self be true… Out damned spot, out I say" oops, that's Macbeth, but you get the idea.

Foote decided to do for trials what Stoppard had done for theater. He reasoned that a condensed and tightly controlled trial would force lawyers and judges to get to the point and pursue only the essentials. There would be no wasted time with needless questions.

Here's the transcript of the auto theft case that was tried in Foote's court the following day.

Voir Dire

The first 12 jurors are in the box. Judge Foote addresses them. "You will all be fair won't you?" he nods his head up and down and the jurors (well, at least nine of them) nod with him

Opening Statement

Prosecution: The defendant did it.

Defense: No, he didn't

Direct Examination of People's Witness No.1

Q: State you name for the record please.

A: Justine Balthazar.

Judge: Let's move it along.

Q: Do you live at 1958 Mountolive?

A: I lived there when my car was stolen.

Q: Was that a 1957 Chevrolet with the personalized license plate, Bitter Lemons?

A: It sure was

Q: And…

Judge: (interrupting) That's quite enough. (Turning to defense counsel)- you may cross.

Prosecution: But you honor, I…

Judge: (raising his voice) Cross-examination.

Cross Examination

Q: Now Ms. Balthazar.

A: That's Mrs. Balthazar.

Q: All right, you say your name is Mrs. Balthazar.

Prosecutor: Objection, asked and answered.

Judge: Sustained.

Q: You really don't own that car do you?

A: What?

Q: The pink slip says the car is owned by Justice Clea.

A: That was my maiden name.

Q: So when you bought the car you were Miss Clea?

A: That's Ms. Clea.

Q: Did you…

Judge: (interrupting) Redirect.

Defense counsel: But you honor…

Judge: Don't make me warn you.

Redirect

Q: You were Ms. Clea, but now you're Mrs. Balthazar, right?

Defense Counsel: We've been over this before.

Judge: Is that an objection?

Defense counsel: Yes, it certainly is your honor.

Prosecutor: I'm rehabilitating the witness your honor.

Judge: Overruled.

Q: And do you have a driver's license?

A: Of course. I need it to drive my car.

Q: And the name on that driver's license is…

A: Mrs. Balthazar.

Q: And you need the license to drive the car…

A: That was stolen.

Defense counsel: Objection!

Judge: Overruled. (Turning to the witness) Thank you, ma'am, you may step down.

Witness: That's Mrs. Balthazar.

The remainder of the testimony took three minutes and 42 seconds. The police broke into the defendant's garage and found the car. They had a warrant. The affidavit was written on the back of a registered warrant to a state employee issued during the budget crisis. The warrant was signed by a retired judge from Tehran.

Foote upheld the warrant under the *Leon* good-faith exception. The opening and closing argument was an abbreviated version of the opening statement.

Foote edited and combined the tedious jury instructions into a half-page which he read to the jury without taking a breath. Total time: 26 seconds.

After deliberating for 2 ½ weeks, the jury said it was hopelessly deadlocked. Foote told them that a jury with conviction would reach a verdict. They got the hint and found the defendant guilty.

The appeal also was handled efficiently. The opinion issued by the Court of Appeal consisted of one word.

The retrial took even less time than the original trial. Ms. Balthazar had moved to Alexandria and was beyond the process of the court. The People decided it would be hopeless to try to admit her testimony from the prior trial. The case was dismissed.

Judge Foote reread Hamlet to find out what went wrong. He got a clue from Act II, Scene 2:   "Find out the cause of the effect."

Or rather say, the cause of this defect,

For this effect defective comes by cause."

Judge Foote thought about the cause. He wondered whether "something is rotten." He decided not to pursue the matter further because he had another case to try, and there was simply no time.

HALL OF FAME

I know someone who has a place of honor in the prosecutors' hall of fame. No, it's not J. Edgar Hoover; it's not Thomas E. Dewey. It's a defense attorney. "How could this be?" you ask incredulously.

Well, remember Roy Riegels? He played in the 1929 Rose Bowl game between Cal and Georgia. He ran 80 yards and almost scored a touchdown for Georgia. The only trouble was, he played for Cal. That's why he has a place of honor in the University of Georgia's hall of fame.

In a similar fashion the defense attorney I'm speaking of gained his entry into the prosecutors' hall of fame. This attorney was the subject of a Los Angeles Times feature story a few months ago. He tries death penalty cases. Nothing unusual about that, but he tries them a little differently than most defense attorneys. A death penalty case usually takes several months to try. Not with this lawyer. He knocks them out in a day or two, and when he's dragging a little, three or four days.

That may be the reason he has the distinction of having the most number of clients on death row. Not many prosecutors can make that claim. No wonder he has a place of prominence in their hall of fame.

Of course there really isn't a prosecutor' hall of fame, at least not in the sense that there's a baseball or football hall of fame. But you know what I mean. All of us have our private halls of fame, and every group has its unofficial hall of fame. I bet the morticians' hall of fame, for example, honors those colleagues who have been the most creative with their cadavers. Bus drivers, taxidermists and even judges have their peculiar halls of fame.

Well, actually judges need something a little more impressive than a prosaic hall of fame for truly special accomplishments. Take, for example, the E award. The E does not stand for mere excellence or for extraordinary effort or even for ecstasy. It combines all these qualities under what has become today's most important attribute – EFFICIENCY.

Judges who run the most efficient courts are potential candidates for the coveted E award. For some, it has become like consent for the judicial academy award. Of course, it's not a big televised spectacle, no running down the aisle, no breathless thanking of producers, agents, spouses, parents and the dog. There is no Oscar, but there is an appropriate commendation by a harried P.J. and some envious glares from winded colleagues trying to keep up with the backlog.

Efficiency can be a good thing. There is no need for a case to drag on forever, and the judge who handles cases with dispatch does a service to the litigants, the lawyers and the public. But when efficiency becomes the paramount value, other values like fairness and justice suffer.

A judge concentrating on efficiency was presiding over a high-publicity murder case. He desperately wanted the E award and kept the trial going each day into the early evening hours. Several of the attorneys asked to leave before 5 p.m. on one afternoon because it was a religious holiday that comes just once a year. The judge, who apparently was of a different faith, said "nothing doing." The attorneys threatened to leave anyway and to contest his threatened contempt by way of a writ petition. The judge relented. He suddenly rediscovered other values when he considered the repercussions of trying to keep the attorneys in court after 5 p.m. The E award receded into the distance.

This takes me back to our speedy lawyer who tries death penalty cases faster than it takes a judge to conduct voir dire in a criminal case. Many of his cases are on appeal, and one has been reversed because of his lack of adequate preparation. He apparently had been so concerned with efficiency that he may have missed some points here and there, like, for instance, whether the defendant committed the crime, or whether he had the intent or mental capacity to commit it.

When efficiency crowds justice, reversal raises its ugly head and guess what suffers? Efficiency. Of course reversal has its positive side. It keeps us in touch with other values and does provide work for appellate judges and their staffs. Ultimately, trial attorneys get to try the case again. That, however, is not always the case.

When the Court of Appeal reversed a murder case because our speedy lawyer did not competently represent his client, it ordered a new trial. But the prosecution witnesses were no longer available. The defendant may or may not have been found guilty of the crime. In either event, the rush to judgment in the name of efficiency did not serve justice, and it gave efficiency a bad name.

Our first priority is to do justice. Our second priority is to do it efficiently. Whoever achieves this has a place in my hall of fame.

RAISING MONEY

There are few years when the courts have not faced a budget crises. 1993 was no exception.

Ask anybody for money these days – not an easy thing to do if you can't take rejection. No matter who you ask, a parent, a friend, a banker, or a government official, it's a daunting task. You're lucky if you get a simple "No." I would prefer that to "Get serious," or the question, "Why are you so special?"

But if the question were put to me as a member of the judiciary by a member of the Legislature, I would have no difficulty in answering. It is not the judiciary alone that is so special, although it is a co-equal branch of the government that, incidentally, uses a microscopically small amount of the total budget. What is so special is the people who use the courts. Pardon the expression, but these people are being short changed. Some of them have forgotten what their case is about by the time they get to trial.

Judicial resources are simply too meager to accommodate the burgeoning number of cases.

The courts have done all they can to handle the crisis. To ease the burden caused by increased case filing, trial court judges have taken on backbreaking caseloads, put in long, arduous hours, and because of fast-track demands, have had to make decisions without adequate time for reflection. To ease the financial burden of decreased funding, court employees have taken unpaid vacation days.

Unfortunately, these commendable sacrifices have not solved the crisis. If the legislature cannot, or will not, adequately fund the courts, then it's time for the judiciary to take control of its own destiny. It must find alternate ways to raise money for the judiciary. Where else to find innovative ideas but from members of the legal community?

I have solicited ideas from the many segments of this diverse community and offer for you consideration some of the suggestion I received.

- Miss Anne Thrope, the aged columnist who, when she is lucid, offers advice to the legal profession.

"Recently, certain court employees made an economic sacrifice by taking unpaid vacation days. Now it's time for the Robes to bear the burden. Take criminal judges, for example. Assess fines against them whenever they are reversed. The more reversals, the higher the fine. This plan has another benefit. It should keep liberal judicial activism in check."

This was a good idea, but I also asked Miss Thrope about keeping conservative judicial activism in check. "Forget it," she replied. "You can only fine a judge for reversals, not affirmances."

- Harvey Parataxis, linguist, Brachiator, paralegal, parapsychic and pari-mutuel bettor.

"Charge lawyers and judges for every participle they dangle, for every modifier they misplace, and for every infinitive the split. Zap them for every obscure thought they utter, and for every ambiguous phrase they write. If you add to my list every absurd proposition they advance, you'll have enough to cover the national debt."

I told Harvey I thought he might be too much of a purist. "Not a chance," he said. "I even endorse slang so long as it accomplishes what lawyers and judges don't do – communicate. "Hey, I'm out of here. It's time for me to simply split."

That will be $20 Harvey.

- Sylvester Stark, criminal defense attorney.

"Criminal convictions are being affirmed despite dozens of errors that have occurred during the trial. The courts have labeled them 'harmless.' Harmless to whom? Certainly not to defendants. Why not make them harmful to lazy prosecutors who pay no attention to them. Assess hefty fines against prosecutors for every error they commit. Double it when they look the other way every time a judge commits an error. The people will still have their convictions, but the courts will make a fortune.

I immediately ran this idea by a prosecutor I know, Sans Merci. She dismissed Stark's idea with a summary sneer. "You want to raise money?" she asked. "Assess fines against defense attorneys every time they argue prejudicial error. Someone clears their throat, and they are objecting. In the face of overwhelming evidence of guilt, they get exercised over the admission of a little inadmissible hearsay. Assess fines every time a defense attorney makes a meritless prejudicial error argument. "That will put a stop to this odious practice. You won't need more money because trials will be over in one-third the time, and the problem of court congestion will be solved."

She left before I could raise the incompetence-of-counsel argument.

The trouble with these solutions is that they forcibly take money from people working in the court system. Something less coercive would be preferable.

A novel suggestion to raise money came from attorney Jim Christiansen. Employing a keen sense of entrepreneurial ingenuity, he has devised a remarkably simple plan in which people will gladly part with their money: gift shops in the courts.

In the Supreme Court or the Court of Appeal alone, innumerable items would be hot sellers. Autographed photos of the justices containing a personal salutation to the attorney purchaser. A must for every law office – "To Sol, Best wishes to an attorney who knows how to avoid a hard question. Yours, Justice – (Justice's name here)."

It's hard to think of a better way to impress the client than such a photo on a lawyer's desk.

Also available will be recordings of an attorney's oral argument. For an additional charge, insults and excoriating comments from the bench will be edited out. By use of state-of-the-art technology, gratuitous comments may be added, complimenting counsel on an excellent presentation and reviling counsel's opponent.

Another sure-fire best seller would be T-shirts with a judge's photo on one side, and counsel's photo on the other. The same can be done with shorts.

Cardboard cutouts of judges sitting on the bench should be a popular item. Because the cutouts would be indistinguishable from the real thing, the cutout could be put to use for rehearsing oral argument. Also, creative lawyers could use the cutouts in other ways unimaginable in real life – a good source of therapy for the frazzled practitioner.

Bumper stickers with catchy mottos specifically tailored to a lawyer's case would be a real attention grabber. For example, the new cases in biotechnology offer innovative ways to flaunt victory. Can't you just see on the bumper of a new Mercedes:

> **"The court said affirm – I keep the sperm."**

There are even slogans for losers:

> **"Why can't they see what we clearly meant – no one got it, except the dissent."**

I ran these ideas by my colleague Judge Learned Foote, and asked him if he would endorse any of them.

Without taking his eyes off a sanction order he was working on, he said, "Get serious."

What if a panel were convened to discuss civility and in the heat of the discussion the panel members began punching each other out? This churlish thought crossed my mind at the beginning of summer in 1998. I wasn't feeling all that civil, and in June I was about to participate in a panel on civility at the Ninth Circuit Judicial Conference in Santa Barbara. In fact, what I thought would be the summer of my discontent turned out to be a summer of content, in two senses of the word: contentment and substance. Also, the absence of "dis" as in disrespect made it all the more agreeable.

Take, for example, the civility panel. The panel members, some of whom, like myself, are not known for their reticence, included Leslie Abramson, Thomas V. Girardi, Michael E. Tigar, Ronald L. Olsen, Judge Charles B. Renfrew, Judge Marilyn Hall Patel and Chief Justice Thomas A. Zlaket of the Supreme Court of Arizona. Although forceful in expressing our opinions, we were all quite civil to one another. The deft questioning and finesse exercised by our learned moderator, Professor Charles Ogletree, assured that a mood of affability prevailed.

I took the view that judges set an example of civility by their treatment of lawyers in court and by the tone of their written opinions. In criticizing Justice Scalia for some of his acerbic opinions, I confess to a minor lapse in civility myself. A circuit court judge for whom I have profound respect chided me for referring to Justice Scalia as "Scalia."

Most of the panel members expressed the view that rules of civility are more than mere rules of etiquette, and that civility is not inconsistent with vigorous and forceful advocacy. Many of us felt that legislating civility in the form of court rules that punish lawyers for saying unkind things about judges was ill-advised (a euphemism for blatantly unconstitutional.)

Imbued with a renewed sense of civility, a few weeks later I attended a symposium at the University of Kansas on the Restatement (Third) of Torts: Products Liability. Wisely, I left Toto at home with Dorothy. He would never have been able to stand the oppressive heat or the humidity of Lawrence, Kansas. In summer in Kansas, you move in slow motion through a translucent curtain of wet heat. Luckily, the symposium took place in the air-conditioned law school.

The Reporters of the Restatement, Professors James A. Henderson, Jr. and Aaron D. Twerski, began the program. After culling cases from all over the country, they concluded that in a majority of jurisdictions, courts generally decide products liability cases in a certain way even though they do not always articulate their decisions in the same way. Some courts speak of a consumer expectation test, when in fact they use a reasonable alternative design test (RAD). To quote the professors at the conclusion of their law review article "Achieving Consensus on

Defective Product Design," Cornell Law Review, Volume 83, No. 4, May 1998, at p. 920, "Both normative analysis of what courts should do and empirical analysis of what they have done support this conclusion. By adopting risk-utility balancing with a reasonable alternative design requirement as the general design standard, subject to the exceptions for demonstrably defective and egregiously dangerous designs that this Article describes, the Restatement (Third) reflects the consensus views." In a concluding sentence anchored in assurance, the authors conclude that "[t]he few jurisdictions that remain in the minority on this issue may be expected to join the majority, given time for reflection on what has transpired."

Of course there were other points of view. Some professors and practitioners see the Third Restatement as a enormous step backward from the Second Restatement. They consider RAD as a threat to consumers whose cases may never reach a jury, but instead will meet an untimely death in a summary judgment motion. They argued that RAD discourages the filing of small products liability cases because of the expense in obtaining experts, that it serves to separate the victim from the manufacturer, that it dispenses with strict liability and that it gives an edge to manufacturers of defective products. RAD eliminates corrective justice because juries know what a reasonable consumer expects.

The discussion was vigorous and contentious, but quite civil. It was so much more refreshing and stimulating to be dealing with arguments and logic than with personal attacks. The noticeable presence of civility allowed us to better focus on the issues.

We had a group dinner after the first day of the symposium at Lawrence's luxury hotel, the Holiday Inn. In the conference room next door was a taxidermist convention. After dinner some of us sneaked in to view the exhibits. Lined up on the walls were plastic forms of various animals: foxes, possums, birds, raccoons. A skilled taxidermist demonstrated that after gutting his animal, he stretches its skin over the appropriate sized form. Next comes artificial but extremely realistic eyes, claws and tails that closely match those of the actual eyes of the victim animal. (I consider a stuffed animal a victim even it dies of natural causes.) Trapped in a frozen moment, the "completed" animals looked authentic, but seemed eerily unreal. Somehow they reminded me of the Third Restatement.

On the way out I noticed one animal in the corner and for a moment gasped in horror. I thought it was Toto. A closer look revealed a West Highland terrier. Toto is a Cairn terrier.

The conference ended and I drove back to the airport at Kansas City, Missouri. A stop on the way at the Truman Library in Independence grounded me in the wholesome past when we didn't talk so much about integrity or civility, because we seemed to have more of it.

While waiting for my flight in the airport lounge, I overheard a conversation which I doubt would have occurred at Kennedy International. A smiling, young freckled-faced woman walked up to two elderly ladies who were sitting next to me. "Thank you all for watching my suitcase. It didn't try to run off did it?" (Chuckle, chuckle.) One of the elderly ladies replied, "Mercy no. We gave it a stern look and it stayed put."

While flying home I got to thinking about what I would do if my suitcase had run off. I would bring suit. I don't think I would have much trouble making a case for reasonable alternate design. But I would do it in a civil way. There would be no rancorous remarks or snide epithets at depositions as there were in *Tylo v. Superior Court* (1997) 55 Cal.App.4th 1379, or *Green v. GTE* (1994) 29 Cal.App.4th 407.

To questions about the suitcase, I would say something like, "Certainly I expected to buy a suitcase that knew it was supposed to stay put and not just skedaddle whenever it gets a mind to." I must have been dozing when I became aware that the plane was already landing at LAX. I tried to hold on to my sense of civility, but I knew the deposition would never go the way I had imagined, not when litigating in the big city. Perhaps I was not fully awake, because, as the plane taxied to a stop, the lady sitting next to me gently nudged me and said, "We're home." I turned to her and said, "Oh, Auntie Em, there's no place like home."

FREEDOM TO EXPRESS ALL POINTS OF VIEW

This column was written in 1991. Historian and critic, Nat Hentoff quoted portions of it in his book "Free Speech for Me But Not for Thee. How the American Left and Right Relentlessly Censor Each Other." Harper Collins, 1992.

"Stamp out Bigotry." "Down with Discrimination." Most of us support these noble sentiments.

We've made some progress in combating bigotry and discrimination, but we have a long way to go. The people who fought the hardest for these ideals had to overcome the fierce resistance of those would keep them silent. Those who fought for minority rights and against the evils of discrimination have a lot to be proud of. So do the lawyers who represented those involved in the cause.

Because of these efforts, the more accepted view today condemns the evils of discrimination. So what about the imbecile who favors discrimination, whether it lie against gays, women, or racial minorities? He can crawl back into the woodwork as far as I'm concerned. But, does he or she have a right to be heard? Heard by whom?

There are indications today that the very people who once championed an unpopular cause want to make sure their old adversaries are silenced. Obnoxious views should not have a forum, so goes the argument. There seems to be a lot of support for "the shoe's on the other foot" mentality.

There's a certain irony here. There's also a lot of pressure to make sure one subscribers to the "politically correct" point of view. A recent issue of Newsweek , and an article by Nat Hentoff that appeared last month in The Daily Journal ("These Days, Even Moot Court Has to Be Politically Correct," Dec 21, 1990), discussed the phenomena. Pressure is being placed on students and faculty in some colleges to express the correct views or suffer the consequences. I know how that pressure feels. In my high school and college days, "McCarthyism" was rampant, and anyone who expressed an "unacceptable" point of view was in deep trouble. Failure to take a loyalty oath before signing up for mandatory ROTC was a good way to be branded a communist and thrown out of school.

I thought all that was behind us. But, if some of the people who fought against discrimination and prejudice, for example, are now the ones enforcing the new rules on conformity, we've all lost something. Isn't the idea behind the First Amendment that the views of the minority, no matter how odious, may be expressed? The attempt to suppress thought ultimately promotes the very ideas that are sought to be suppressed. When used against any group it backfires.

I remember an incident when I was in high school. School authorities had rented the auditorium one evening to Gerald L. K. Smith who was running for President of the United States as a candidate for the Christian National Party. His platform was based on white supremacy, bigotry and hate. Although my candidate was Adlai Stevenson, I went to hear Smith. My rationale was that it would not make a difference- after all, I couldn't vote.

The truth is, I knew that someone- not me mind you- would raise some hell, and I wanted to see what would happen. Smith walked up to the microphone. A large American flag was stretched out behind him providing the appropriate patriotic background. Smith uttered a few words. A group of protesters in the balcony cheered in mock support. Smith would utter a few more words, and the same thing would happen again. Soon the cheers turned to jeers. The group in the balcony was now shouting and screaming. Things were getting out of hand. A police sergeant came up to the microphone and dispassionately urged the protestors to be quiet. Things quieted down a little.

Then Smith approached the microphone again. In a remarkable lapse into logic and common sense, he reminded the protesters that everyone in this country had a right to express his or her views. He pointed out that the people who were attempting to disrupt the meeting were in fact undermining the very Bill of Rights they claimed to protect.

After this sobering insight the audiences fell quiet. The pro-Smith forces (mostly elderly people) and the anti-Smith forces (mostly high school students) were reflecting on the same principle. I was about to score one for the bigot, but then Smith blew it.

He raised his fist and started to scream into the microphone that this was all the work of communists, radicals, foreigners and other subversives trying to destroy the American way of life. The place erupted into pandemonium. The old and the young were shaking fists at each other. Smith made sure these two groups would have nothing to say to each other.

Of course, all the ruckus (mild by today's standards) gave Gerald L. K. Smith more publicity than he had ever hoped for. It encouraged a few more Neanderthals to support him for President.

The presence of self-appointed enforcers to compel the expression of the politically correct point of view can have a devastating effect on the law profession.

Hentoff expressed his regret about the refusal of some law students at N.Y.U. to participate in moot court competition. They balked when given the assignment to argue against the petition of a lesbian couple seeking custody of a child. The students thought it offensive to deny the lesbian couple custody because of their sexual preference. Of course it is. That's why we need lawyers. They are there to protect all points of view, however offensive. The Bill of Rights was enacted just so that politically incorrect points of view could be expressed.

If lawyers become intimidated by the enforcers of correct thought, then we are in big trouble. The students who refused to participate in the moot court competition because they disagreed with the principle they were assigned to argue, unwittingly sabotaged the very principles they professed to support. When certainty of the correctness of your position causes you to silence the opposition, you have undermined your own position. You have become like your enemy.

If lawyers forget this, we will ultimately have a society where ideas are crimes. *Fahrenheit 451, Brave New World, and 1984* will have been written in vain.

Those who fight for minority rights, whether they be the rights of gays, blacks, Jews, women, or atheists, should be particularly sensitive to preserving the right of others to be heard, no matter how loathsome the point of view.

It was hard for Jews in Skokie, Illinois, to countenance Nazis marching in their neighborhood. Nothing could be more understandable, but it was even more understandable that Jewish lawyers defended the rights of the Nazis to march. If the Nazis don't have that right, neither will Jews, or any other group.

Whether it be Madonna singing a passage from the Bible, or Brett Easton Ellis denigrating women in "American Psycho," the more we stifle, the more we strengthen the resolve of the opposition. If the Nazis had marched and no one complained, the incident would have been a great non-event.

No one is forcing us to watch or listen to Madonna's video, or to read Ellis. Speaking out forcefully for what we believe is the best way to fight bad ideas. When all ideas are allowed expression, the good ones ultimately endure.

By allowing the free expression of bad and even offensive ideas, we insure that good ideas flourish. It is this way that we preserve the American freedom of mind and spirit. It's something law students must learn , and lawyers must never forget.

A COMPELLING SCREENPLAY

Like a river, a theme runs through my last several columns. It is the painful but important recognition that judges, like all humans, are subject to foibles, prone to mistakes, and liable to fall on their faces. My frank exploration of this phenomenon has stimulated an interest in some of my readers that borders on the obsessive. Diverse in their backgrounds and philosophies, this group of readers share two characteristics: 1. they are not judges, 2. they take a morbid delight recounting the concrete example I provided of the prosaic maxim that no judge is above the law. Why such exhilaration over the knowledge that speeding judge gets traffic ticket and attends all day traffic school where know-it-all instructor lords it over him?

Whatever the reason, I have thoroughly examined the existential dilemma of the judge as authority figure, decision maker, and arbiter of right and wrong on the one hand, and floundering, insecure dolt on the other. How best to bridge the gap between omnipotence and ineptitude? I have the answer. It can be summed up in one word: awareness. Judges must be cognizant of their shortcomings. The seeming simplicity of my solution is complex in application. In the infinite variety of situations in which judges find themselves, one cannot reasonably expect them to be aware of everything they do or say each and every moment.

As just one example, judges who decide cases involving important and sensitive issues regarding bias and sexual harassment could themselves be unwittingly guilty of the very conduct that gives rise to the lawsuit they are deciding. It is like the basketball referee who double dribbles when he and his buddies play basketball on his day off.

To heighten the self-awareness of judges hearing cases involving workplace harassment torts, and to make them more sensitive to their own employees and litigants, I have written an instructive yet artistic screenplay. Oddly, investor interest has been tepid. I have pitched my script to various studios but not one has bitten. If you are over 12 years of age, no one in this business will give you the time of day. The studios could learn something about age discrimination, but obviously they are not aware of their own biases.

The Center for Judicial Education and Research has a copy of the script. I still haven't heard anything from them. I think they are mulling it over. They have had it for 8 years. If I don't hear from them soon, I'm going to shop it elsewhere. Space and time do not permit me to reproduce the script in its entirety, but here are some highlights. The discerning reader will note the influence of French New Wave cinema. The working title is simply "Bias," Un film de Artur Gilber.

Throughout the film an on screen narrator functions as a Greek chorus. Dressed in judicial robes, he or she is the embodiment of judicial awareness, a sort of judicial Every Man or Woman. Most of the time the characters are unaware of the narrator's presence, but on occasion there may be interaction between a character and the narrator.

Scene I

(Justice Grendel pulls into his reserved parking space at the courthouse parking lot. Narrator and Justice Grendel walk from the parking lot into the building.)

Narrator

(Putting his hand on the shoulder of Justice Grendel and speaking to the viewer.) This is Justice Grendel coming to work. He's fair. Well at least he thinks he's fair. (Justice Grendel is oblivious to the existence of the narrator.) They walk into the building and into the justice's chambers. Justice Grendel walks by his secretary and says "Hi Babe." The Narrator is shocked. (He speaks to the secretary.) Madame-weren't you offended?

Secretary

No, and please don't call me Madame.

Narrator

Sorry, but may I ask your name?

Secretary

Babe Henderson.

Narrator

So you don't mind being called . . . .

Secretary

By my name, certainly not.

Narrator

Do you have a good relationship with your justice?

Secretary

I really like working for Justice Grendel, but sometimes he is sarcastic when I make a mistake.

Justice Grendel

(Calling Babe. He sounds irritated.) Babe you have a remarkable talent to type while asleep. No doubt your comatose condition accounts for your omitting the changes I noted on page four.

Secretary

(To narrator.) See what I mean?

Narrator

Have you discussed your complaint with the justice?

Secretary

Should I have to?

Narrator

(Speaking to the viewers.) The way in which the court treats its staff reflects on its image. One never knows what staff say about the court to family or friends.

Scene II

Cut to Babe Henderson at a large family Thanksgiving dinner. She is at the head of the table about to carve the turkey. The mood is festive and gay. Uncle Jake yells, "It's Thanksgiving. First thing we do, let's kill all the turkeys." Everyone laughs. Babe begins carving with the expertise of a neurosurgeon. She is intent and seems to be relishing her work. "You sure know how to slice up that turkey," someone remarks. Babe looks up and says, "I just pretend its Judge Grendel, the turkey I work for." Raucous laughter from the guests.

Narrator

See what I mean? In public it is important to keep your awesome power in check. Remember Teddy Roosevelt's admonition and keep your voice down. Wearing your robes to dinner parties is not recommended. Nor is it advisable to hold members of the public, merchants, service personnel and the like, or even family and friends with whom you have disagreements, in contempt. Such conduct tends to erode public confidence in the courts.

Scene III

(Narrator follows Justice Grendel into a conference room for a writ conference. The writ attorney enters the room.)

Justice Grendel

(Acknowledging the writ attorney.)   Hi Sweets.

Narrator

(To the writs attorney.) I suppose your name is Sweets.

Writs attorney

No, it's Honey Holloway.

Narrator

They shouldn't talk to you in that manner.

Honey

Are you trying to stir something up?

Narrator

No, but calling you Sweets . . . .

Honey

It beats calling me by my name. I have told everyone not to call me Honey. I always bring candy to the court. That's why they call me "Sweets" and that suits me fine. Get it, dork head? So do me a favor and butt out.

Narrator

(To viewers.) Some people cannot appreciate legislation for their own good.

Scene IV

(In the courtroom. An attorney is arguing a case to the justices. Two of the justices are conversing on the bench while the attorney is arguing.)

Narrator

(Interrupts the justices. This time the narrator is invisible to the attorney but engages in conversation with the justices.) You know you are talking while the attorney is arguing.

Justice 2

We hear him. He's not saying much. In fact he's just repeating what was said in his brief.

Narrator

He probably thinks you are prejudiced against him.

Justice 2

We aren't prejudiced against him, just against his position.

Narrator

But it looks to him and to his clients, who incidentally are in the courtroom, as though you do not care about his case. You owe him your undivided attention, no matter how bad his argument is.

Justice 3

(To the narrator.) Mind your own damn business.

Justice 2

(To Justice 3.) Smartest thing I've ever heard from you. You won't get a dissent from me on that one.

Narrator

(To all the justices.) Your insolent and demeaning conduct is rude and boorish. You should treat all attorneys with respect and civility.

Justice 1

(First turning to his colleagues.) This guy is some kind of radical. (Now to narrator.) We have heard just about enough of you. Take this as a warning.

Narrator

You wouldn't treat lawyers like this if you were private judges.

Justice 1

Bailiff! (Bailiff pulls the screaming narrator out of the courtroom.)

I have to stop here. I don't want to give the trick ending away. I don't have a release date, but when the film comes out, you are all invited to the premier.

A RULE HARD TO ENFORCE

This column was inspired by the response in 1993 of some federal judges to an outspoken lawyer who had publicly accused a judge of bigotry.

Judge Letha L. Killer is a tough no nonsense judge. She moves her calendar with dispatch and does not suffer fools or sentence lightly. Her name puts people off, particularly repeat offenders, but what's in a name?

"A heck of a lot," you might say. "Look at Judge Best, Wisdom, and Real, for example. And if first names count, Judge Learned Hand."

Others might counter by quoting, "What's in a name? A rose is a rose by any other name." But one could counter with yet another quote: "Rose is a rose is a rose."

Whether Judge Killer's name has any significance is beside the point. Whatever anybody thinks about her, she is who she is. But who she is became an important question with epistemological significance. People who did not know much about the judge, other than knowing she was a judge, would say in an imprecise way, "I know who she is, but I don't really know who she is, I mean, I don't know much about her."

One lawyer, Lucious Left, who also happened to be left handed, thought he knew who the judge really was. He was convinced Judge Killer disliked lawyers in general, but had an outright dislike for left handed lawyers.

To better understand how Left arrived at this impression, we have to get a clear picture of him in Judge Killer's court.

Left is sitting at the long counsel table in front of the bench with a look of vague indifference as Judge Killer expostulates on the law before making a ruling. The judge is commenting on the law of search and seizure after Left has argued a suppression motion. Left's client, sensing the inevitable, jabs him in the side and whispers, "I can't stand it, what's she waiting for, Lefty? I can feel it; we're going down the tubes."

Left, still looking blasé, whispers, "Sometimes a good rule is hard to enforce."

As the judge begins to announce her ruling, Left's passivity dissolves, and his attention suddenly shifts to the legal pad in front of him. His right hand, inert, merely holds the holds the pad in place, but his left hand moves along the page in a kind of agitated paroxysm of busy scribbling, a ragged claw, "scuttling across the floors of silent seas."

The convulsive movement of that insistent left hand along the page, could drive an opposing counsel, or even a judge, to distraction.

Left contended that his habitual practice of frenzied left handed scrawling was normal and innocent.

Left noticed, however, that Judge Killer often ruled against him. On occasion she thundered and raged against him. And once in awhile, she sanctioned him. Left concluded that the judge had it in for him because he was left handed. Right-handed lawyers seemed to get off easy.

Whether because of pique, frustration, revenge, or plain short-sightedness, Left went to the press. He gave an exclusive interview to the radical underground journal, "Left Bank," where he told the interviewer "once Judge Killer gets a hold of a lawyer, there is nothing left." He followed this statement with a remark that in print seemed to drip with sarcasm, "Killer is always right."

Just after this remark was made at the interview, there was an unsettling pause. The interviewer, known in newspaper jargon, as a "staff writer," and being adept at his trade, knew that the pause was significant. Although it took no more than 10 seconds, it seemed like an eternity. Left was looking intently into the interviewer's eyes. The interviewer could stand it no longer. He broke the silence.

"Your pause," he said in a tone that hovered between a declaration and an inquiry. "My pause," said Left ruefully. Another pause. "That's the point!" he exclaimed.

"Judge Killer has it in – for southpaws."

The staff writer, no Janet Malcolm, got the quote exactly right. And so there it was in black and white.

It was this last comment which most observers believe gave rise to the unprecedented judicial hearing. Left's charge, if unfounded, could unfairly hold the entire judiciary in disrepute. The court, pursuant to its rules which prohibit attorneys from holding the judiciary in disrepute, held a hearing which sent shock waves throughout the legal community.

The five-judge court had to determine it Left had violated the rules. Was this a false claim brought by a manipulative lawyer against an innocent judge to get the judge off his case, or did this judge have sinister intentions towards the left handed? If Left did not prevail, he could suffer severe sanctions.

Representing the court was an influential lawyer from the powerful Right Handed Bar Association, Dristane Droit (pronounced drew-it, rhymes with do it.) Left, on the other hand was represented by counsel from the less influential Left Handed Bar Association, Prudence Port.

The lawyers soon discovered that the case was not as simple as it at first seemed. They had to wrestle with a multitude of issues, the First Amendment, slander, and whether judges as opposed to other public figures should be immune from public scrutiny, to mention a few.

Stating that someone has it in for south paws is an easy charge to make, and a difficult one to prove. Attorney Port realized this, and planned her strategy around the good faith belief defense. Port reasoned that if police officers can violate the Fourth amendment so long as they act in good faith, why cannot lawyers criticize a judge so long as they are in good faith? For example, what if the evidence established that Judge Killer did not have it in for south paws, but attorney Left had a good faith belief she did? Would this be cause to acquit Left of any wrongdoing?

The court reasoned that if Left were going to raise a good defense, he should have the burden of going forward with that defense. The prosecuting lawyer, Droit, asked Left if he thought Judge Killer was against him just because he lost so often in her court.

Left answered by stating that most lawyers in town knew that Killer favored right handed lawyers. A Mona Lisa like smile played across Droit's face. "Name names," he said.

Left refused. He would not jeopardize their careers.

Was he bluffing, or did he really mean it? This further show of defiance created a quandary for the court. They could hold him in contempt, but this would make him a martyr. It would also leave unresolved the question of the truth of his accusation. A ruling on the matter was deferred, and the court recessed for several weeks.

By a remarkable coincidence, during the recess, the leading legal periodical in the state ran a judicial profile on Judge Killer. The thorough staff writer responsible for the profile, sought out the opinions of various attorneys about Judge Killer. Needless to say, the publicity surrounding the Left hearings prompted the staff writer to ask the attorneys if they thought the judge had it in for left handed lawyers.

The results of this informal poll were inconclusive. Not surprisingly, most of the lawyers asked to remain anonymous. Some avoided a direct answer by simply saying they supported Left. Others said they thought Killer was against the left handed, but gave no further details. Seven lawyers said they thought the judge loved left handed lawyers. Two of those lawyers asked to be identified.

Curiously, the profile revealed that Judge Killer is ambidextrous and that two of her children are left handed, although one is adopted.

After the profile appeared, lawyers quoted in the profile wrote letter to the press, all of which were published, excoriating those lawyers quoted in the profile who expressed views contrary to their own. The Bar Association immediately launched an investigation pursuant to its new rules which prohibit bringing into disrepute members of the legal profession. These new rules were enacted in response to the proliferation of lawyer bashing jokes.

The investigation faced insuperable hurdles – none of the letters were signed. The Bar's prosecution team was stymied, and concluded that sometimes good rules are hard to enforce.

When the judicial panel reconvened Left's hearing, both lawyers stipulated that the article on the profile of Judge Killer could be entered into evidence. The judges furrowed their brows. No one knows what they were thinking. Perhaps they were silently reflecting, "Sometimes a good rule is hard to enforce."

JUDICIAL ELECTIONS 1990
IT IS THE SAME TODAY

There's a warning sign flashing in California and in other parts of the country. It says "Legislators Beware." A concern about the influence of so-called "special interests" and corruption has prompted some states to pass initiatives that limit legislative terms.

The manner in which Congress has tackled the budget may have given these measures a boost in the polls.

Another warning sign is also flashing in parts of the country. It says "Judges Beware." Look at what happened in the state of Washington. A few weeks ago, Keith Callow, the Chief Justice of the Washington Supreme Court was defeated in an election. The chief was held in high esteem by his colleagues and the bar.

So then how could he have been defeated by a little known lawyer named Charles Johnson who handled only minor cases, who mounted no campaign, and whose only quotable remark was "I'm a blue-collar attorney?" No one has the answer. The experts could only speculate. Johnson was a more popular name than Callow. Perhaps voters thought Callow was callow. Washington did not provide voter pamphlets for its primary. Judges on the ballot were not identified by job title, incumbency, or political party.

Maybe all these facts contributed to the defeat of Callow, but the warning sign that judges or legislators should beware inexorably leads to yet another warning sign. "Voters Beware!" The people of Washington are not well served by the new "blue-collar" attorney who will soon be sitting on their Supreme Court. How is he going to handle white-collar crimes? Johnson's sole reason for running was his belief that judges "need to be challenged." That's no reason for him to be sitting on a state Supreme Court in place of a competent and highly respected jurist.

The need to challenge an incumbent is the same reason that many voters will be casting their vote to limit legislative terms. Because of a rotten apple in the barrel, they want to throw everybody out of office. In our anger at the improper conduct of a few, the principle of guilt by association has prompted us to punish everyone. If we adopt Johnson's attitude and challenge everybody, we shortchange ourselves. If, for example, we limit the terms of legislators, we stand to lose a large number of capable, dedicated and ethical people in public office.

When it comes to judges, voters in California are less likely to be deceived as were the voters in Washington. We do have voter pamphlets for our primary, although it costs a candidate dearly to file a candidate's statement. And our ballot at least identifies incumbents in judicial elections. Further, Appellate and Supreme Court justices do not have the worrisome problem of an opponent to contend with as Chief Justice Callow did.

Nevertheless, the average voter knows little about judicial candidates. Even when voters know something about the judge they still may be in a quandary as to how to vote. Take, for example the confirmation hearings of David Souter. Sen. Joseph R. Biden Jr., D-Del., chairman of the Judiciary Committee, wondered out loud what you have to do to get inside the brain of someone to find out what he is thinking. The unflappable Souter did not remove the top of his head to give the senator a peek inside. When voting for appellate judges, particularly those on the Supreme Court, we want to know how that judge will vote on particular cases. Whether it be a voter in California deciding whether to retain in office a state Supreme Court justice, or a U.S. senator voting to confirm nominee for the United States Supreme Court, the curiosity is the same. However burning that curiosity may be, we will just have to wait and see whether Justice Souter will vote to overturn *Roe v. Wade.*

Tomorrow the electorate will be voting for several judicial candidates. Are our voters enlightened when casting their vote for judges? Years ago, when I was a municipal court judge, a couple of my colleagues were challenged in an election. One contender urged the voters to vote for him because the incumbent he was challenging had never sent a criminal defendant to state prison. Never mind that municipal court judges lacked the jurisdiction to do so. Another municipal court judge had an uncommon last name. His unqualified challenger ran against him in the apparent hope of capturing the vote of those open-minded people who pick their candidates by the sound or spelling of their last names. Fortunately, the public saw through these reprehensible tactics and voted to keep these highly qualified judges in office, both of whom are now respected superior court judges.

But California voters have not always been so enlightened. The defeat of Los Angeles Superior Court Judge Alfred Gitelson by his unprincipled opponent, who ran on a platform to end busing, made us aware that legislators are not the only ones who are vulnerable at election time. Maybe Gitelson's seat was jinxed. His opponent lost in the next election, but then his challenger lost the seat to yet another challenger. The current judge in that seat is extremely competent. Let's hope he breaks the chain.

Appellate judges take note. What happened in Washington cannot happen in California. Yet, we all know from recent history that appellate judges are not invulnerable. Three Supreme Court justices have been turned out of office. During that same election year, a right-wing political organization mounted an unsuccessful campaign to defeat any appellate justice appointed by Gov. Edmund G. "Jerry" Brown Jr. without regard for the justice's competence or integrity.

To prevent unfair tactics from deceiving the public, various bar organizations throughout the country have formed evaluation committees whose goal it is to keep the voters informed. Bearing in mind that voters often have no idea which judicial candidate to vote for, these committees will evaluate judges up for election. To compile as much information about the judge as possible, these committees often send out questionnaires for the judge to answer. The committee may be well intentioned, but sometimes the questions are intrusive and irrelevant to the issue of whether the judge should be in office. They seem to reflect that compelling desire that Senator Biden had to delve into the candidate's mind. It's that quest for certainty that makes us pry so relentlessly.

A judge's record should be held up to public scrutiny, but the judge should not be subjected to a voir dire examination. It is not necessary to know the judge's blood type, astrological sign, or which team the judge rooted for in the World Series. It's not necessary for evaluation committees to contact former partners, former spouses, or former research attorneys. So he had to be nagged to take the garbage out. So she fired 5 research attorneys during the past four months. So when he was in law practice didn't bring in enough business. What does that prove?

On the appellate level, each justice gives the public a guide to determine whether that justice should be retained. Simply read his or her opinions. If they do not enlighten on the issues involved in the particular case, they will perhaps shed light on the question of whether to retain the justice in office. If the opinion of a justice distorts the record, his or her colleagues will take appropriate note.

Speculation about what a judge might do in some future case belongs in a rare transcendental realm. It's a poor guide as to what to do down here in the real world. The voter or and evaluation committee need only written opinions of a justice to make an informed decision at the voting booth. These opinions reflect the philosophy, writing skill and legal acumen of the author. As Keats said, "…that is all Ye know on earth, and all ye need to know."

BEHIND CLOSED DOORS

What goes on behind closed doors? Everyone wants to know. Columnists and commentators make their living guessing what's being said behind closed doors.

Decisions concerning employment, advancement, demotions, acceptance, war, peace, survival, happiness, despair, wealth, life, death, and what the superior court assignments for next year will be, are made behind closed doors. It is no wonder that for those of us shut out, the closed door taps into our anxieties and fears. It confronts us with something far more terrifying than our ultimate fate-uncertainty!

All institutions have their closed doors, but the legal profession has the most. That is why a law career is so stressful and angst-ridden. Those lacking in fortitude, spirit and endurance opt for other professions- like dentistry or taxidermy. Future lawyers are up against the closed door before they even get their license to practice. A closed door separates them from the sadists who have devised that exquisitely brutal initiation into the law profession: the bar exam. It was behind a closed door that "they" determined what the correct answer is in the multiple-choice section. Every listed answer could as easily as apply as not.

Lawyers experience the same problem in their own offices. They never know, for example, which side of the door they will be on during the formation and dissolution of partnerships.

The courts, however, offer the most striking example of the closed-door syndrome. What are the jurors talking about during deliberations? Those muffled shouts coming from the jury room make you wonder. The plaintiff and defendant don't feel that strongly about the case, so why are the jurors so hot?

But there is another closed door that is the most ominous of them all: the one that separates the judges from the lawyers. Attorneys have confessed to me that they are dying to know what my colleagues and I say to each other during our conferences. They apparently believe me when I tell them we are talking about the case, but they want to know the manner in which we talk about the case. Do we use slang? Do we shout at each other? How do we characterize each other's position? How do we make our points?

I will let you in on a little secret. Even judges like to know what other judges are talking about behind closed doors, particularly when those judges sit on higher courts. We therefore all share that maddening blend of insecurity and curiosity. Those cases of mine, for example, that find their way to the California or the U.S. Supreme Court cause me to wonder and speculate about what "they" are saying about my opinion. When the court is divided, I like to think that the justices who supported my position put up a good losing fight.

As for the conferences in my division, I cannot tell you much, other than to say they are spirited, thought-provoking and fun. Whatever the outcome, no one is angry, at least not for long.

Not to disappoint you, I will share with you some specifics of an appellate court conference in another state. I was visiting as a guest, and took some quick notes on a portion of their conference. For obvious reason, I have changed the names of the judges. Let's just call them Manny, Moe and Maxine. Here's how the conference went:

Manny: I think we should affirm

Moe: That's like a juror saying, "Guilty" before the foreman is even selected.

Manny: I see it as I see it. What else can I tell you?

Moe: Tell me your reasons.

Manny: Oh, you want to get cute. Reasons, he wants. What about the memo?

Maxine: You mean the document written in Sanskrit that was entitled "calendar memo"? I read it but I don't understand it.

Moe: You didn't understand the calendar memo?

Maxine: That's what I said. Did you?

Moe: What?

Maxine: Read the calendar memo?

Moe: Yes, and…

Manny and Maxine (in unison): And…

Moe: And… I don't think I understand it.

Maxine: You don't think, or you don't know…

Moe: Whether I understand it?

Maxine: Yes

Manny: Wait a minute here. What's the exact question?

Moe: Whether I understand the memo or not.

Maxine: No. We already know that.

Manny: No. We don't know whether he thinks or whether he knows that he doesn't understand the calendar memo.

Moe: You think or you know?

Maxine: Don't start that again.

Moe: That's the problem. I don't know.

Manny: We are at a total impasse.

Maxine: This is what happens when we don't understand your reason.

Moe: I only said that I didn't think I understood his calendar memo, that's all.

Manny: So should I rewrite it?

Moe: I can't tell you that until I understand what your reasons are.

Secretary (entering the room): Here's some goodies for you to munch on during your conference.

There is a lesson to be learned here. It's better not to know what goes on behind closed doors. Imagination is so much more interesting than reality.

NO TIME TO READ

Self-storage buildings are taking over the city. Those ubiquitous, windowless monoliths could double as Gestapo headquarters.

How can there be so many people who need to store their belongings in an empty room off an empty corridor? The answer came to me while I was browsing through a gigantic file from the law and motion department. The file's capaciousness provided the clue. Self-storage buildings must be the places where lawyers store the old files they are too lazy to scan.

It makes sense. Enormous amounts of paper are required for important files. These are files that impress well-paying clients. They usually contain motions and all the responsive declarations and points and authorities required for an appropriate opposition, and more of the same for the motions that follow once the motions to make the motions are granted in the first place. These multiplying files have to be stored. Not many lawyers can afford to expand their office space for this purpose. Some enterprising genius, therefore, came up with the idea of self-storage.

Does anyone actually read the contents of these voluminous files with their infinite variety of motions and endless interrogatories? That all depends upon what you mean by read and by whom. Presumably, opposing counsel and the judge read what they have to. If this is true, then when do they have time to read all the other material submitted to them daily?

That's not easy to answer. Consider what you, the average judge or lawyer, have to read each day. In the morning there are the *Los Angeles*. and *New York Times*. Other home reading material usually includes dozens of publications you once impulsively subscribed to and don't know how to discontinue. A typical list includes: *Newsweek, Time, The New Republic, The National Review, Police Gazette, The New York Review of Books, Seventeen, Architectural Digest, National Geographic, Saga, Rolling Stone and Better Homes and Gardens.* There's also *Crime and Punishment* that has to be finished for the book club which meets next Tuesday evening.

Once you get to work, it doesn't stop. You have to read the advance sheets, various bar and law journals, and law review articles of interest.

While the fast track judge is pouring over 1,000 files, you, the lawyer, have to get back to work on that summary judgment motion. To assist you with the points and authorities, you have to read the Rutter book, Witkin, various treatises culled from the index to legal periodicals and dozens of densely written cases.

For the facts, you, of course, must read the other side's 90-page verified complaint,. the 340 pages of evasive answers to interrogatories, the 30-page unhelpful response to request for admissions and the 13 volumes of deposition testimony consisting mostly of "Would you repeat that?" and "I don't recall."

Ultimately, you will also have to pore over the opposition papers and attached exhibits and be prepared to refute them. This, of course, is only one case. The 230 other cases you are working on also demand attention.

Don't Forget Court Rules

It doesn't stop there. You also have to keep up with the court rules. There are those that apply to all courts in this state, those that apply to the court system in your county, those that apply to the courts on the third floor of the courthouse where your motion will be heard, and those that apply to the individual judge who will be hearing your motion. Of course, all these rules usually conflict with one another so you have to spend some time trying to reconcile them, which you have as much chance of doing as balancing the national budget or even prevailing in your opposition to a motion to dismiss for failure to prosecute.

There's just too much to read. It's humanly impossible to read it all, let along comprehend it. I first recognized this problem when I started law school. That was when I first saw, you should pardon the expression, the writing on the wall. And that even took some time to read.

One evening while reading *Pennoyer vs. Neff,* I wondered if I could ever cut through the dense verbal forest contained in the cases and hornbooks I had to study. As if in a dream, a beautiful woman appeared before me; she said she had a magical solution to my dilemma. "Who are you?" I asked in astonishment. "I am Evelyn Woods," she said beaming like Billie Burke.

She inspired me to enroll in her speed reading course from which I graduated with honors. I was able to tear through *Prosser on Torts, War and Peace"* and *Paradise Lost* during a coffee break. Just don't ask me any questions about these works. Their meaning is buried in my subconscious. Hypnosis or primal therapy may bring it to the surface. After I paid for the course, Evelyn Woods never again appeared before me again, in or out of court. She was too busy opening reading schools in shopping malls.

I even tried enhancing my comprehension by listening to tapes on the law while I slept. Applying the Evelyn Woods concept to a different medium, I played the tapes at a faster speed. They sounded like Woody Woodpecker analyzing the *Palsgraf* case. It didn't work. The tapes kept me up.

I have concluded that there is simply no way to read it all. The best we can do is to allocate priorities for our reading material. Unfortunately, the priority is not determined by what we wish to read. In fact, our favorite choice is usually at the bottom of the list. Maybe that's why Tolstoy is not the topic of discussion at most cocktail parties.

Mountains of Briefs

For most lawyers, the opposition to the motion for summary judgment is usually at the head of the list. After all, the lawyer is being paid to read, comprehend and destroy the motion. The more the lawyer has to read, the more she or he has to concentrate to keep the threshold of comprehension at an acceptable level.

It's no easier for judges. Those sitting in law and motion, or those on the appellate bench, have to struggle though mountains of briefs that appear to be written with the intention of putting the most alert mind in alpha mode.

To make this forced reading regimen more interesting for judges, I suggested in a past column that lawyers draft their motions in the style of various writers. No doubt, the idea caught on because many lawyers, when remarking about their opponents, have adopted the style of Nancy Reagan in her book, "My Turn."

So now its time to be honest. Nobody reads everything all the time. Sometimes we (euphemisms spring to mind) skim, peruse, consider, scan, run though or look over material. You know how it goes:

"Have you read my article?"

"Yes, I looked over it. Very interesting."

That's a way of saying, "Are you kidding? I don't have time to read warning labels, let alone your article."

Yet, the burning question for every writer, whether a novelist, or a mom leaving written instructions for the babysitter: "How can I be sure the reader will read every word of what I have written?" The answer is simply to make what you write worth the reader's while. The next question is, "How do I do that?"

Mmmm. Good question.

LOYALTY AND SOCIAL COHESION

Professor George Fletcher and I were classmates at Hollywood High School. At that time, neither of would have believed we would wind up in our respective professions. There is one trait George retained all his life that can be summed up in one word. Provocative. Here is a review of a provocative book George wrote in 1993.

George P. Fletcher, Professor of Law at Columbia University has written a provocative book. It is entitled "Loyalty: An Essay on the Morality of Relationships" (Oxford University Press, 1993).

Professor Fletcher examines how loyalty affects out lives and our relationships. Commitment borne of loyalty, whether to an individual, a group, an organization, a religion, or a nation has a profound affect on how we define ourselves and how we behave. Our sense of duty is often borne of loyalty. It is intensely personal and varies with the individual. Notions of betrayal, commitment, support and friendship are intimately connected to loyalty, and our individual moral universe is often defined by our sense of loyalty. When we act out of loyalty we may suspend our judgment about right and wrong; we may even act in ways that seem to be against our best interests.

Fletcher looks at individual cases of loyalty drawing upon literature and real life. The philosopher and writer Sartre said that if he had to choose between his mother and the French Resistance, he would choose his mother. The fierce loyalty that one may feel for his or her mother is understandable, although I guess it depends on you mother. On the other hand, if Sartre's sentiments had been to choose the French Resistance over his mother, to many, that choice would have been just as understandable.

Fletcher analyzes the three dimensions of loyalty. The loyalty of love is portrayed in such works as Antigone, King Lear, and Peer Gynt. In Antigone, for example, we are shown how a choice dictated by loyalty may have tragic and profound moral consequences. The necessity of making a choice, no matter what that choice is, may involve the sacrifice of a value.

The duty of loyalty one feels towards a brother to tell a lie to protect him, for example, conflicts with the value he places on honesty. On the other hand ignoring his brother's request amounts to the antithesis of loyalty: betrayal. Group loyalty on the other hand is based on membership, instead of relationship. We see this type of loyalty expressed in acts and attitudes towards corporate or other employers, labor unions, armies and nations. The relationship one has with God is yet another dimension of loyalty.

Conflicting and competing loyalties can make our choices agonizingly difficult. God's request of Abraham that he sacrifice his son Isaac compelled a choice that could have had tragic consequences. Just as irreconcilable differences may break down a marriage, one might wonder whether irreconcilable and conflicting claims of loyalty can cause an individual to break down. The government recognizes the overriding importance that loyalty has in certain relationships. The marital privilege, for example, which allows spouses not to testify against one another insures the stability of the family. Fletcher even suggests that it would be appropriate to extend this testimonial privilege to brothers.

Fletcher stresses that the legal system should not intrude upon relationships grounded in loyalty. He speaks of the need for the state to show deference to existing loyalties that stem from friendships, families, religious practices or that relate to groups asserting their cultural autonomy. Of course, there are limits to this deference. If Abraham actually sacrificed Isaac, obviously such conduct could not be tolerated as an expression of free exercise of religion. Taking into account reasonable limits on the government's deference, Fletcher critiques Supreme Court decisions dealing with the free exercise of religion and concludes that the government should defer to those religious loyalties that are based on beliefs grounded in community practices. Yet it is also legitimate for the government to claim a bond of loyalty from its citizens.

We Americans live in a multicultural society, but as diverse as we are, we are bound together "on a deeper level in a common culture." What greater symbol of our culture is there than the American flag? It is the shared duty of respect we owe to our national community that underlies our government's interest in protecting this symbol of our nation. Fletcher prods us into looking at the issue of flag burning in a new way. Laws banning the destruction of our flag reflect a duty of self-restraint citizens must exercise as a commitment of loyalty to their nation, rather than as an individual right to expression. In this way our society achieves cohesion and stability. The government recognizes it must show deference to groups expressing their cultural individuality, but it also recognizes that all citizens have duties to the nation. These shared duties emphasize what we have in common despite our differing and particular loyalties.

This is a time when many feel that our society is fragmented and coming apart. Fletcher makes us reexamine our values concerning individual rights, and to direct our focus to those values that preserve our society and give it stability and cohesion. Fletcher's provocative ideas make us question our assumptions about an abstract impartial morality that is far removed from the particular morality borne of loyalty which permeates our relationships and which creates bonds between individuals and groups. This makes for a more complex world in which a right answer is illusive.

Whether one agrees with Fletcher or not, he makes a compelling argument at the end of his book. He posits that what is even more important than loyalty is the need for people to treat one another with respect, and to pursue their arguments by way of reasoned discourse rather than an emotional appeal based on personal loyalty.

REEL DILEMMAS
TWO UCLA LAW PROFESSORS EXPLAIN

What follows is a review of the first edition of Reel Justice: The Courtroom Goes to the Movies, published in 1996. In May, 2006 the authors, Professors Paul Bergman and Michael Asimow published their 2nd edition.

For a change let's start with an impertinent question. What is the one thing you wish you had more than anything else in the world? It could be anything: the Hope diamond, the Nobel Prize, a night with Madonna, box seats for the Laker games, praise or recognition from your father, your dog, or whoever. So what is it? Your failure to speak up is not surprising. This is a personal question and nobody else's business. Few people will disclose this secret to anyone, not even their priest, best friend or nutritionist.

Like you, dear reader, I too am reticent to make such a revelation. Nevertheless, for reasons that will become apparent if you choose to read the remainder of this column, I will reveal my secret wish in the next sentence. What I never have had, and what I wish I could have more than anything else in the world is---the answer.

From earliest childhood on I have never had the answer. "Arthur, where's Blackie?" How does a two-year-old know where he left his stuffed dog? I still don't know where he is. In grammar school, Mrs. Grabble asked me before the entire class, "Master Arthur, would you please divide 134,216 by 12 and give us the answer." (No calculators in those days.) Why not ask me to scale Half Dome?

In law school the art of asking for answers that were as elusive as the unified field theory was refined to an exquisitely cruel art. I can still hear in my mind's ear a voice both sarcastic and derisive, "Perhaps you could enlighten us on the Rule Against Perpetuities, Mr. Gilbert." I couldn't. The effects of law school interrogations still linger.

If you think judges are immune from this ordeal because they get to ask questions, you are mistaken. I ask questions, but the answers I get only prompt more questions. Ultimately I have to supply the answer.

In fact the strain is particularly hard on judges because they are expected to know everything, when in fact the opposite is usually the case. At a dinner party the other night, just as I was placing a generous spoonful of vichyssoise in my mouth, someone at the other end of the table said in a voice a little too loud, "Judge, in the movie, 'The Star Chamber,' was the evidence the police found in the garbage really inadmissible? And why wasn't the bloody shoe found in the van admissible?"

There were three, maybe four lawyers at the table. In the second or two that it took the vichyssoise to fight its way down my throat, everyone stopped eating and looked at me. I had a fleeting thought about Einstein's theory that time is relative. Was it two seconds, or a hundred million years later that I said, "Well that all depends . . . ." The pause following this well-proven escape hatch gave the lawyers an opening to scream, I mean voice, their opinions on the subject. I concentrated on my vichyssoise.

I could have said, "the suppression motion may have been properly granted when the film was made, but in California v. Greenwood, decided by the U.S. Supreme Court after the film was made, police officers may search a person's trash can without a warrant. And today, police may arrest a person based on their good faith reliance on information obtained from a computer database, even if that information turns out to be wrong. (Arizona v. Evans.) Today the arrest of the scuzz-bags in the van would be valid, and the bloody shoe would have been admissible. Not so when the film was made. And by the way, 'The Star Chamber' was an English court created in 1347, which later became known for its severe punishments and arbitrary procedures . . . and after dessert, I would be happy to talk about 'Witness for the Prosecution.'"

How could I have had all this information at my finger tips and made such a penetrating and incisive analysis? By simply reading a marvelous book with the catchy title, "Reel Justice, The Courtroom Goes to the Movies." It is written by Paul Bergman and Michael Asimow and published by Andrews and McMeel, a Universal Press Syndicate Company, Kansas City, 1996. What is so astonishing is that both authors are law professors. Think of the irony, two highly respected U.C.L.A. law professors giving answers. It's like Rockefeller giving money to public causes.

Bergman and Asimow review, rate, and analyze sixty-nine "trial movies." Four gavels are equivalent to a blockbuster verdict, one gavel is a dismissal with prejudice. They consider many classics such as "Judgment at Nuremberg," "Twelve Angry Men," "Paths of Glory," and "To Kill a Mockingbird." They also review more current fare such as "My Cousin Vinny," "Presumed Innocent," and "Losing Isaiah."

Bergman and Asimow discuss not just legal issues, but when relevant, the moral and ethical questions that legal issues often implicate. Did it ever occur to you that defense attorney Paul Biegler played by lovable Jimmy Stewart in "Anatomy of a Murder," probably committed a number of ethical violations? Bergman and Asimow make a persuasive argument that he did. They also explore important issues such as the right to refuse treatment for mental illness in their discussion of "Nuts," and the right to die, which was central to the movie, "Whose Life is it Anyway?"

They also provide comments on the background which served as inspiration for some of the movies. "A Few Good Men," "Breaker Morant" and of course "The Life of Emile Zola" were based on actual cases.

"Reel Justice" is entertaining and informative. As Judge Alex Kozinski points out in an engaging forward, the book is a good guide to bring with you to the video store. Even if you are not interested in answers, "Reel Justice" offers the opportunity for a spirited discussion, or if you like, a vicious quarrel about your most and least favorite films. I wish I had read it before that last dinner party. I'm not all that crazy about vichyssoise

GOD'S LAWYER

This column was inspired by a sign on the freeway at the time of the O.J. Simpson criminal trial.

A few weeks ago as I traveled eastbound on the Santa Monica freeway approaching downtown I saw a sign rising high above the roof of a nondescript building. The sign read, "GUILTY," black letters against a white background, stark, implacable, certain. I tried to avoid looking at it, but I was irresistibly drawn to it. It made me sweat. Maybe that's because I often feel guilty. Nothing specific mind you, just a vague disquieting feeling of guilt, a milder version of what Kafka's hapless victim experienced in *The Trial.*

Similar signs were popping up all over the city. The signs were thought to express an opinion about the O.J. Simpson case. Never mind that the prosecution had not rested yet. That's supposed to happen in July-I'm not sure which year. Most of the signs turned out to be advertisements for a local radio station. I still think they are a cynical exploitation of the case.

But just as the meaning of a poem is not dependent on the poet's intention, the sign has a special meaning to me quite apart from the intention of the maker of the sign. Although I don't know how others responded to the signs, there is one person who I'm sure did not respond the way I did.

He is the lawyer mentioned in an article in the Daily Journal a few weeks ago who represents the Hemet Unified School District in a law suit over the teaching of sex education. He's against it. The article points out that because of all the cases in which he has waged battles over morality issues embraced by the so called "Christian Right," he is known as God's lawyer.

No doubt God's lawyer would be so anchored in moral certainty that he would not give the sign a second thought. One might think such a lawyer would have no worries about guilt or anything else. After all, the lawyer who represents the ultimate client, indeed the ultimate judge, is in his own right, (pardon the expression,) the consummate rain maker. It's hard to find anyone comparable. Imagine representing Oliver Wendell Holmes, Samuel Goldwyn, or George Burns. This is even more awesome. True, it would do wonders for any practice, but representing Him or Her could bring with it a host of other problems.

I won't even go into the retainer agreement. What about client control? Lawyers give clients advice on a number of issues, like for example, the best way to testify. In the early part of the O.J. Simpson case, (if you can remember that far back,) the limousine driver was called to the stand. His mother, an attorney, gave him a wise admonition: Don't drink soda pop before testifying; it makes you belch. Good advice. I remember from my own days in practice passing along similar helpful hints to my clients: Make sure your fly is buttoned; don't shoot up before testifying.

Well and good for the ordinary client, but what are you going to tell God? Be humble? Be sincere? Don't come on strong? And how does God take the oath? The problems go on. We all know what the code says, but should God be required to sign a declaration under penalty of perjury? I can see room for an exception here, but some fool appellate court would probably interpret the statute literally and say "a rule is a rule." And then there's an ethical problem. God is omniscient. Therefore God knows how the case is going to turn out. Is that fair? And since God is omnipotent, why does God need a lawyer in the first place?

I see another difficulty. If one side represents God, where does that leave the other side? All these difficulties point to the obvious. God should not be a party to a law suit. Litigation over differing views on important issues is not a battle between good and evil. Furthermore, whatever one's conception of God, anthropomorphic or otherwise, God does not need a lawyer. Some might argue it's the other way around.

If God represents what is good and positive in human beings, then our ability to reason, to settle disputes, and resolve controversies, is a more convincing indication of a divine presence than is the certain belief of such a presence on one side or the other of a particular controversy. What is worthy of praise is the machinery we have devised to accomplish this end, our unique legal system. When appropriate, it accommodates to meet changes in values of our society, but its essential mission to promote justice in accordance with the Constitution has remained constant. Despite occasional and vociferous criticism, it has survived and endured.

Today, however, it may be in jeopardy. Many people originally thought the "GUILTY" signs reflected an unsettling impatience with a case that is perceived to reflect shortcomings that permeate our legal system. Some are exploiting that impatience to institute so- called reforms that would bring drastic changes to a legal system that in the vast majority of cases works remarkably well. It would be tragic if an extraordinarily unique and atypical case causes us to tamper with and thus weaken a legal system that is a model for nations throughout the world.

Of course it's not perfect. Neither are we who devised it. Our legal system gives us some degree of predictability, but it can never give us absolute certainty. But there's a virtue in lack of total certainty. It makes us consider the other side of an issue and reminds us that we are not perfect.

These thoughts give me some comfort. I don't feel quite so guilty now when I pass the "GUILTY" sign. I will probably feel even less guilty when I drive in other parts of the city. There one can see other prominent signs that also demand attention. They say "INNOCENT."

JURIST LANDS ON HIS FEET
PART I

At the end of 1995 relations between the courts and the legislature were strained.

It's 5 A.M. and I'm asleep, floating in the void of a REM cycle. Vivid images from the subconscious coalesce to form fantastic dreams far removed from reality: the O.J. Simpson trial engendered public admiration for the justice system; lawyers value civility over billable hours; the great writ and the 4th Amendment are vital and alive.

Something intrudes on these reveries. I'm dimly aware of a cold nose touching mine. It's not my wife's. Her nose is warm. There is the sound of distant aircraft. The images fade. I'm awake, nose to nose with my cat. He is saying, "Good morning. Time to get up. I'm ready for breakfast."

If it were not my cat there could be no punishment too cruel or too unusual for this intrusion. His immunity derives from a simple truth - cats get to do things like that. Only people who know and understand cats appreciate what I'm talking about. Such undemanding persons of refined sensibility know the limits of power. They make excellent judges. Such a person is Justice Armand Arabian who recently announced his retirement from the California Supreme Court.

His spirited dissent in *Nahrstedt v. Lakeside Village Condominium Assn.* (1994) 8 Cal. 4th 361, 390, offers an example of what I mean. In *Nahrstedt*, plaintiff shared her condominium with three cats, all of whom she adored. The condominium association's CC&R's provide that "No animals (which shall mean dogs and cats), livestock, reptiles or poultry shall be kept in any unit." The CC&R's permit residents to keep "domestic fish and birds." Presumably the restriction applies to wild fish, to gerbils, and probably even to those innocuous green turtles no bigger than a thumb that sit on a rock in a bowl of water for hours on end. Absurd.

Plaintiff, who had two cats, sued the homeowner's association to prevent it from enforcing the restriction. The majority held that plaintiff's complaint failed to adequately allege the restriction was unreasonable.

In his dissent, Justice Arabian pointed out that the cats are kept only in the plaintiff's unit, and that they are noiseless. Moreover they create no nuisance, other than perhaps to wake plaintiff in the middle of the night if her cats' habits bear any similarity to mine. (Actually I have two cats, but the one who rises earlier than 5 A.M. is barred from the bedroom at night. Even cat owners have their limits.)

Justice Arabian concluded that the plaintiff's pleadings sufficiently alleged that the pet restriction was unreasonable as a matter of law. He cataloged among other things, archeological findings that cats were household pets in Egypt 5,000 years ago, and were mummified and entombed with their owners. He also cited the English Nuns Rule of 1205 which prohibited nuns living in a nunnery from keeping a pet except a cat.

In a wan attempt at levity the majority pounced upon this historical note to pronounce that "pet restrictions have a long pedigree." Not to be backed into a corner, Arabian's dissent concluded with the somewhat fustian, yet inspiring commentary that the majority "view, shorn of grace and guiding philosophy, is devoid of the humanity that must temper the interpretation and application of all laws, for in a civilized society that is the source of their authority. As judicial architects of the rules of life, we better serve when we construct halls of harmony rather than walls of wrath." *Nahrstedt* at pp. 396-397.

If I should ever commit a crime, (other than writing this column, or committing a capital offense,) I would want to be sentenced by Justice Arabian. A judge who understands, and therefore loves cats, could be moved to demonstrate compassion and flexibility at sentencing. This is just one of the many reasons I'm disappointed he is leaving the court. He has an independent streak. His writing style, though leaning towards the bombastic, according to one disagreeable academic, is nevertheless refreshing. In short, he made the court interesting.

So why leave after only five years? And why have so many others left after a short tenure on the court? On announcing his retirement, he spoke of strained relations between the legislative and judicial branches stemming from *Legislature v. Eu* (1991) 54 Cal.3d 492, the decision which upheld "The Political Reform Act of 1990," or Proposition 140, the term limits initiative.

It's hard to say whether it was the actual holding, or the court's penchant for quoting from the initiative that engendered the hostility. The court spoke of the initiative's goal "to restore a free and democratic system of fair elections, and to encourage qualified candidates to seek public office by limiting the powers of incumbency." The case spoke of "unfair incumbent advantages" which "discourage qualified candidates from seeking public office" and which "create a class of career politicians." The court concluded that the compelling interests set forth in proposition 140 outweighed the narrower interests of legislators who wish to perpetuate their incumbency.

The *Eu* decision did not exactly endear the court to the Legislature. It probably would not have made much of a difference if the court had couched its opinion in more tactful language. The Legislature responded with attempts to cut court funding, and even to move the court's headquarters to Siberia, I mean Sacramento. The Legislature would have even tried to impose a term limitation on Supreme Court justices, but with all the retirements, the justices beat them to it. Many have imposed on themselves so short a "term limit" that it's over before the term is.

Despite the *Eu* case, the Legislature is not justified in retaliating against the courts. Less funds for the courts reduces the public's access to the courts. With too few judges to handle a burgeoning caseload, litigants who can afford it use private judges. And who are the most sought after private judges?-retired Supreme Court justices, who are more likely to command the highest fees. The Legislature should act quickly to adequately fund the courts. That's the best way to get even.

A MUTE COURT
PART II

You may recall I have written about the eminent jurist Learned Foote, who, after his many productive years on the bench, made a fortune selling sanction insurance to lawyers. The incidents I speak of today also involve Judge Foote, but only indirectly. If you see this as a clue that the story I'm about to relate is bizarre, I applaud your perception. In fact, I don't doubt that you, the discriminating reader, will question the veracity of this odd little tale just as I do.

To make matters worse, my knowledge of the details is sketchy at best. Nevertheless, I will share with you the little I know of the incident, because whether true or not, there may be a lesson here for anyone concerned about the administration of justice.

Judge Foote had several children. How many are several? I cannot say, but I believe there were more than three and less than nine. Whatever their number there were boys and girls.

As I have described in my last column, Judge Foote was enamored of the law. Not surprisingly, he wanted his children to be thoroughly familiar with the institutions that make and interpret the law, to wit, the legislature and the courts.

"How," Judge Foote thought, "can I interest my children in the law?" He knew that children, like attorneys, can be obstinate. Therefore, he concluded, he would have to accomplish his goal though subtlety and cunning. He hit upon a scheme. He would reach his children though their stuffed animals. Of course, this meant he would have to substitute his imagination for theirs, but this was a small price to pay to achieve his goal.

He went into his childrens' rooms and gathered together all of their stuffed animals. Without much fanfare he pronounced each stuffed animal a member of the legislature. I'm afraid I can't tell you how many animals were involved, but I know they included Poof, the pedantic ponderous panda bear; Chicken Chant, the corruptible, chatty chicken; and Tobias, the tedious troublesome turtle. As to the others, I confess complete ignorance of their names or species.

Each night, while the children slept, the stuffed animals came to life (in a manner of speaking) and did their legislative work. What laws did they enact? I can't say, but I've been told they enacted such extraordinary laws that we would find them incomprehensible. Cynical readers might find apt comparisons to other legislators.

The members of the newly created legislature were pleased with their roles, and in fact, were a bit smug. It was obvious they needed a court to interpret some of their outlandish statutes. Foote thought it would be inappropriate to put stuffed animals on the court.

"Who would be the best candidates?" Foote thought as he searched his childrens' rooms again, much like a president with vacancies to fill.

After looking through their various rooms, he realized he had the perfect court. Each of his children had several Raggedy Ann and Andy dolls which they adored. A Raggedy Ann-Andy court would be perfect. It would reflect the valuable contribution of women to the justice system, yet it would he homogeneous. It would be a dignified court, but most important of all, it would be a happy court. Judge Foote at first called the court the "moot" court, but because he was an inveterate punster, he decided on the "mute" court.

The congenial Raggedy Ann-Andy court did its best to resolve disputes that came before it. The court interpreted the laws with fairness and objectivity. Some laws, such as those excluding certain animals from the legislature, whether live or stuffed, for example, were quickly overturned by the court as unenforceable.

The children of course were not happy with the new roles held by their stuffed animals and dolls. Poof, who had been a loveable panda bear before taking office, changed considerably. He threw his weight around in the legislature and lost touch with the children.

The children also found it disquieting to know that while they slept, their stuffed animals were busy enacting legislation. They found it galling that their own imaginations had been bypassed. They could endure this situation only so long.

They met and conferred and were determined to reach a decision on what to do about their stuffed animals. Of course, they were unruly, as children are known to be. After much shouting and interrupting, they managed to vote on all issues.

This is what they decided: their stuffed animals would simply be turned out of office. The legislature would be disbanded. Each child would take back his or her stuffed animals and do with them what they wished. Some of the older children, who had outgrown their animals, threatened to give them away, or even worse, throw them away.

To assuage the concerns of the younger children, however, they also decided that if a child wanted to keep a stuffed animal, that was his or her choice. Moreover, a child who kept a stuffed animal could pretend it was whatever the he or she wished it to be, including a legislator. No one was too concerned that that would happen, because even the dullest child had more imagination than that.

For some reason, the children forgot about the doll court. Maybe that was because judges are less visible than legislators. Besides, very few children outgrow their Raggedy Ann and Andy dolls.

When the stuffed animals heard of the vote, they reacted with fear and anger. That night, Poof called an emergency meeting of the legislature. After much discussion and argument, the animals concluded they had only one place to go—the court.

They argued with all the eloquence they could muster that the children's vote should be overturned. Their basic argument boiled down to this: Judge Foote had bought the stuffed animals for the children; therefore, the children did not really own the animals and had no say over their future.

The court listened to the arguments and gave them due consideration. Then the court ruled. The children had spoken, and there was no basis upon which the court could invalidate their vote. It did not matter who had purchased the stuffed animals. They belonged to the children, and the children could decide what to do with them. This was a political question over which the court declined jurisdiction.

Upon hearing the ruling, the stuffed animals went into a frenzy. They began shouting, "The children don't know what is best for themselves. They are just a bunch of spoiled brats." Then they yelled insults at the court itself. "You are just as spoiled and unreliable as the children."

The court tried to reason with the animals. "We serve the children just as you do. They may vote as they please, even if their decision is a foolish one. We can do nothing about it."

Poof pointed an angry paw at the court. "You have made a foolish decision, and we will do something about it," he growled.

The smiles on the faces of the members of the court reflected their patience, but one could detect more than a trace of exasperation and regret behind those smiles.

The court tried to speak one last time on the issue. "Children may be unpredictable but…"

"But nothing," interrupted Poof. "Is this your final ruling?"

The court didn't answer. It had ruled. There was nothing more to say.

The stuffed animals roared their disapproval. They told the court to watch out, that it too could be thrown out just as they were. The court accepted that as a possibility, but it knew that could not be a reason to change its ruling. And then the unthinkable happened.

The stuffed animals actually threatened the court. I do not know the nature of the threats, but it might have had something to do with funding.

The stuffed animals made threatening moves toward the court. Poof was the leader. Chicken Chant began to chant Poof's name. The others joined in.

The children, awakened by the clamor, confronted the angry animals. The angry group of stuffed animals strained forward, but before they could touch a freckle or shout the panda bear's name, "Poof!" They were gone.

CANINE TALE

It happens quite often. I'll be at a social function, or maybe at the frozen food section of the market. Someone will come up to me, always a non-lawyer, and mention the name of one or another of the recent high publicity cases that has consumed our attention. In the next breath he will say "The courts are going to the dogs."

I don't appreciate those comments. I've always felt that the juxtaposition of courts and dogs is a goofy notion. Recent scientific discoveries, however, led me to the opposite conclusion. We need dogs in court.

I do however remember an incident involving a dog in court that did not have a happy ending. The following story illustrates my point, but I also use it to make my case.

Many years ago, a judge in Los Angeles often kept a small poodle on her lap while court was in session. In fairness to the judge, she didn't mimic Xavier Cugat and ostentatiously cradle a Chihuahua in her arm. Of course she wasn't leading a Latin band at the time either. At any rate, no one questioned this practice, but that was understandable. She had also threatened to give a police officer a .38 caliber vasectomy.

Everything seemed to be fine, until she made a particularly bad ruling against either a litigant or an attorney. Whoever it was possessed both a creative sense of humor and an extraordinary sense of retribution.

Shortly after the bad ruling, the judge was conducting a trial in another case, while gently stroking the poodle resting peacefully in her lap. It was during vigorous cross examination. Our phantom (I hesitate to use "culprit"), who was crouched in the hallway outside the courtroom, imperceptibly opened the courtroom door a smidgen. Then, he/she, with ferocious intensity, blew a dog whistle. It's piercing, high pitched sound was heard by no one . . . other than you know who.

What followed was not pretty. How to best describe the manner in which the dog reacted, followed in turn by the judge? Using current patois, the word "freaked" comes to mind. More specific details are too unseemly for this refined readership. Suffice it to say the judge got a new robe and was later removed from the bench.

This story takes me back to my point about the usefulness of dogs in the courtroom. It proves that dogs have certain sensibilities we humans lack. Dogs, for example, can sense up to 30 minutes beforehand when a person is going to have an epileptic seizure. According to an article in a recent edition of Newsweek magazine, certain dogs in Britain have been trained to bark and fetch the phone for a person they sense is about to have a seizure. This gives the person a chance to call for help.

No one knows exactly how a dog can tell a seizure is about to take place, but I suspect that just as a dog is equipped to hear high pitched sounds that we cannot hear, so too is a dog equipped to sense changes in a person's body that we cannot.

We could use a dog's special senses to improve our system of justice. Take harmless error, for example. It is a legitimate and useful analytical tool that helps us separate cases that should be affirmed from those that should be reversed. Unfortunately, its current ubiquity encourages sloppy lawyering and judging. A lawyer asks improper questions, or turns an opening argument into a closing one. There's an objection. The judge uneasily overrules the objection. Somewhere in the back of his mind he knows he's wrong, but he also knows a higher court will probably rule the error harmless. The judge's outer calm, however, is betrayed in some fashion by his body, much like a person whose lie is betrayed by the polygraph recording his body's reaction.

Maybe he sweats, or secretes a hormone. Whatever it is, a well-trained dog could sense this change and in an appropriate manner notify the judge. Barking in the courtroom would be disruptive, but the example set by Toto in the Wizard of Oz is instructive. A gentle tug on the robe would be unobtrusive. In such a circumstance most virtuous judges would change their rulings.

I decided to discuss the idea with Judge Learned Foote. Remarkably, he was working on a case involving an ex-judge who sued to keep a pet Chihuahua in her condominium. The association's CC&R's prohibited pets. Nevertheless, he was going to rule in her favor. I reminded him that *Nahrstedt v. Lakeside Village Condominium Assn.* (1994) 8 Cal.4th 361 upheld such restrictions. "So what," he growled. "The dissent was right; it was brilliant." I agreed, but pointed out his ruling would be error. "There's a way around it," he replied. *Nahrstedt* involved cats." A trickle of sweat ran down his cheek.

Judge Foote liked the idea of dogs in the condominium but flatly rejected my idea of dogs in the courtroom. "Got enough of them already," he said, pointing to a stack of cases on his desk.

If anyone needed a dog at his heel it was Foote, so I persisted. "Better to have dogs going to court than the other way around." He was alert and unleashed yet another objection. He read me the ordinance which states that except for Seeing Eye dogs, animals in public buildings are prohibited.

He had me. I quickly thought of a way to interpret the ordinance . . . but then I felt something like a gentle tug at my robe.

A MESSY JOB

WARNING! Portions of this column depict violence and gore. Reader discretion is advised.

I have often devoted this column to provocative issues. The death of the Fourth Amendment, the strangulation of the great writ, and the grievous harm of harmless error, are just a few that come to mind. These lugubrious topics have engendered letters from faithful readers ranging from unctuous praise, (a couple) to scurrilous castigation. I have collected these letters over the years; today their number fills the pouch of a large marsupial.

Several months ago, however, my column about Justice Arabian's dissent in the case of *Nahrstedt v. Lakeside Village Condominium Ass'n.* (1994) 8 Cal.4th 361, 390 garnered the most letters of any single column. At the time, Arabian was retiring, although that term hardly does him justice.

In his dissent, Justice Arabian spoke of the right of a condominium owner to possess three harmless cats despite the association's CC&R's which prohibit the harboring of cats but not criminals. I sympathized with Arabian's position, even though my cats, unlike Ms. Nahrstedt's, are not confined indoors. They are, however, in possession of a full set of claws, but missing other basic accoutrements.

I received more comments from this column than most others, with cat lovers predominating over cat haters three to one, although one letter made a credible argument supporting dogs. Appellate lawyer, Susan Wolk sent me a magazine piece which spoke of an abominable cruelty to cats. A storage company in Stockton has been recycling old legal briefs into kitty litter. If there were as much concern about cruelty to judges, the briefs would have been recycled way before they ever got to storage. I've heard a rumor that the Supreme Court intends to recycle some of my opinions in the same manner.

The significance of the *Nahrstedt* case and Ms. Wolk's letter led me to an epiphany the other morning shortly after I fed my cats their morning meal on the back patio.

While pouring into their bowls the little pellets they find so irresistible, I foolishly asked, "How come you guys haven't caught anything lately?" Dumb question. As I turned to go on my morning run, I almost stepped on the remains of a partially decapitated rat with most of its entrails exposed. I stifled a gag.

The day had not started yet, and here I was at work, cleaning up another mess. It was then that the insight pounced on me. This is what appellate judges do, survey the remains of mutilated cases and clean up the mess. The trick is not to leave the guts lying about. Skilled judges know how to do it neatly and with dispatch, to make it look easy, despite the arduous work. Although unpleasant, my disposition of the rat will give you an idea of what I'm talking about.

The cats, of course, are a metaphor for the judicial system. Cats can be friendly and rub against you. They can also destroy with a savage fury. But that's in their nature. They had done what was expected of them, and I did what was expected of me.

I got a bag and a long shovel. It was extremely windy. No sooner had I set the bag next to the rat and began scooping its body onto the shovel, than the wind knocked the bag over and blew it shut. I set the bag upright. It stayed still for several seconds while I tried to scoop the rat and its parts onto the shovel. All the while the capricious wind toyed with the hapless bag.

This was typical judge's work. Getting the rat into the bag was like getting ideas into an opinion. You just can't drop them in. Things often work against you, like logic, a recalcitrant colleague, or the Supreme Court.

After many tries I was finally able to work the rat onto the shovel. There was a lull in the wind and the bag did not fall over. There was, however, a breeze with sufficient strength to blow the sides of the bag quite close together. This made it difficult to angle the shovel into the bag. I gingerly raised the shovel on which was now resting the remains of the rat's body. I moved the shovel over the bag and lowered it at a slight angle, so that the rat's body would remain on the shovel without falling off. I gently pushed at the top of the bag with the tip of the shovel and was finally able to nose the tip a fraction of an inch into the bag. Then, by gently jiggling the shovel I was able to separate the two sides of the bag and slip the shovel in. I increased the angle so that the rat slid off the shovel into the bag with a mild thud. Just then a gust of wind blew the bag to one side, but the rat's body provided sufficient weight to prevent the bag from toppling over.

The wind gusted again, but the bag remained upright. I took a peek inside. The rat's head hanging by a mere thread stared up at me. I folded the side of the bag shut and then cleaned the shovel by sliding it back and forth over the grass. Another opinion put to bed.

When I arrived at my chambers, I found it hard to begin work. I thought that perhaps there really was no analogy between cats, rats and the law. I tried to get my mind off the unpleasant incident. I reached for the Daily Journal and randomly opened it. I broke out in a cold sweat. The first thing I saw was a column entitled, "The Rodent."

A CAT IN THE BASEMENT

Last October, the voice of Cleveland Amory, fell silent. Mr. Amory died at the age of 81 and animals throughout the realm, along with many humans, mourn the loss of one who did so much to protect the welfare of animals. Although he was reputed to have a special fondness for cats, Mr. Amory had an abiding concern for all animals, whether they be monkeys, whales, seals, horses, elephants, donkeys, or mice.

Although I believe we should give a priority to human suffering, we should still do all we can to alleviate animal suffering as well. A legal background can be most helpful in accomplishing this end. Not too long ago, my in-laws were convinced a cat was trapped under their house. My mother-in-law had heard a faint meow coming from the basement. She related the incident to me one evening when my wife and I were there for dinner. Through my relentless cross-examination, she admitted she thought she had heard a faint meow. "How could a cat be trapped under the house?" I asked with the arrogance of a first year law student. "If he can get under the house, he can get out."

I went down into the cellar to investigate. My in-laws have one of the few houses in Los Angeles with a cellar. You get there by descending a dangerously steep flight of stairs that takes you to a small rectangular room which remarkably lacks even a single bottle of wine. Two of the cellar's cement walls extend to a seven foot ceiling. The other two walls are about five feet high, on the other side of which extends a large amount of crawl space level with the height of the wall and coextensive with the square footage of the first story. It was somewhere in this dark, inhospitable area that the cat was "thought" to be trapped.

Once in the cellar, I felt like I was working on a case. Often one has to use one's wits when trying to resolve issues that are hidden beneath the surface. I called out, "Here kitty, kitty, kitty." Nothing. I went upstairs, opened a can of tuna and placed it in a dish which I left on the top of the four-foot wall. I left. When I returned about an hour later, the tuna was gone. I deduced that an animal had eaten the tuna. I went back upstairs and got a flashlight. Luckily it worked. I flashed the light into the foreboding black space, and at the farthest end my beam caught the iridescence of two eyes. I called, "Kitty?" This time I got a response which led me to the conclusion that my mother-in-law was right once again.

The cat would not come. I went upstairs and told my mother-in-law of my discovery. She was not surprised. "The cat cannot get out," she said with certainty. "A few days ago, I hired someone to replace the small screens that cover the vents that lead to the space under the house. The workman removed the old screens and replaced then with new screens which he cut to sizes that covered the vent holes.

No doubt the cat crawled into one of the open holes. The workman replaced the screens before the cat could get out."

My legal training told me to act upon, not argue against, irrefutable facts. I went outside to locate the vent holes. I then came back in to get the flashlight which I had left in the cellar. The beam was now weak but shed sufficient light to enable me to find one of the vent holes hidden behind some bushes which were wet with the evening dew. The vent hole, a small rectangle about six by twelve inches, and no higher than eight inches above the ground, was covered with a screen held in place by four screws which had been drilled into the plaster of the wall. I went back to the house to get a screwdriver.

Once I had agreed to take my muddy shoes off, my mother-in-law let me into the house. I found a screwdriver in the service porch. I went outside, put my shoes back on, and made my way back to the vent hole. The beam on the flashlight was becoming even weaker, but still gave me sufficient light to arrive at yet another inescapable conclusion. I would have to return to the house and get a Phillips screwdriver. Of course I took off my shoes again, and after much rummaging in the cabinets on the service porch, and various kitchen drawers, I concluded there were no Phillips screwdrivers in the house. I then went outside, put on my shoes again, and continued my quest in the garage. After much searching and many expletives, I found one.

I returned to the vent hole. The last faint beam of light from the flashlight provided just enough momentary illumination to reveal that the Phillips screwdriver might be slightly too large for the screws. Before I could definitively confirm this supposition, the light gave out. Through what I will call for lack of a better term, the Braille method, I was able to turn a screw approximately 1/16 of a turn with the ill-fitting screwdriver - that is when I was able to turn the screw at all. I doubt that anyone can imagine the time and patience this enterprise required for not just one, but all four, screws. I cannot. Searching in the dark for the screwdriver, which I had thrown on the muddy ground now and then, intolerably lengthened the time and shortened my patience.

Finally, I was able to unscrew all the screws - - well not exactly. Let's just say, I got the screen off. I went back to the house, took off my shoes, went inside and opened yet another can of tuna which I placed on the ground just outside the now open vent hole. I left with a "Here kitty, kitty, kitty," and felt the eerie presence of Cleveland Amory.

The next day we took in the empty plate and replaced the slightly torn screen.

I was proud of my efforts on behalf of the unfortunate feline and related the incident to my old friend, Anne Thrope, whose advice has appeared in this column in the past. Miss Anne Thrope loves animals.

As you may recall, the aged and infirm Miss Anne resides in Hollywood near the Vedanta Temple. Her belief that animals have souls is just one reason she has provided refuge to ferrets, opossums, dogs, bob and domestic cats, raccoons, and assorted humans, a number of whom she believes have no souls.

She was unimpressed with my tale of the cat under the house and denounced the courts for not having the courage to protect the rights of animals and their owners. I remonstrated against this unjust indictment, but she cited *Nahrstedt* v. *Lakeside Village Condominium Assn.* (1994) 8 Cal.4th 361. In *Nahrstedt*, our Supreme Court, over a vigorous dissent by Justice Arabian, upheld condominium rules which prohibited pets. No exception was allowed for plaintiff, an elderly woman who kept three harmless cats in her unit.

I countered with a case I had authored on behalf of animals, *Philips* v. *San Luis Obispo County Dept. Etc. Regulation* (1986) 183 Cal.App.3d 372. Missy, a black Labrador, had been sentenced to the gas chamber. Despite my contempt for people who quote themselves, I read the opening line to Miss Thorpe to prove my point: "This is a death penalty case. We reverse." Missy was allowed to live and "go out in the midday sun," because she had been condemned to die under an ordinance that failed to provide a noticed hearing.

Miss Thorpe seemed unimpressed. Her critical comments about the judiciary, however, caused me to reflect that only an independent judiciary can protect rights. But judicial decisions are not always popular. Although there was wide community support for Missy, no doubt some thought she should have bitten the dust.

But Missy, who "nipped" when teased, was a pussycat compared to the zealous hounds who wish to censure judges with whom they disagree. Attempts to censure judges for their decisions, whether right or wrong, undermine the independence of the judiciary and inhibit its ability to protect all our rights. We must keep the dogmatic hounds of censure at bay. Their chase must end whether it be with a bang, or a whimper. See *Phillips* at 381, and "The Hollow Men" (1925). Thanks Thomas.

THE TELEPHONE IN COURT
PART I

Scene: The living room of a suburban home in1991. Wife is cooking dinner. The front door opens. Enter husband.

Husband: "I'm home, sweetheart."

The phone rings.

Wife: "Honey will you get that? My hands are full." So far this sounds like Ozzie and Harriet, but wait, there's more.

Husband: "Oh gosh, sweetheart, I'm afraid to get it. I think it's my boss."

O.K., it's Blondie and Dagwood. The conversation is kind of dated. It does not reflect our perception about reality today. What in fact happens when Dagwood and Blondie arrive home from their separate jobs? The phone rings as they come in the house, but neither answer it. Instead they let the automatic answering machine do it. The caller is Dagwood's boss, Mr. Dithers. The machine plays a few recorded bars of Home Sweet Home. Then it tells a lie.

Mr. Dithers hears Blondie and Dagwood say, "Hi," then he hears them recite alternate lines of a limerick:

"That you have called makes us so glad. We're not here right now, but don't feel bad. Just leave a message, what a treat. Wait a moment for the beep."

If Mr. Dithers doesn't hang up after the first verse, but waits an eternity for the beep (he has heard the limerick 73 times before), he will shout into the phone, "Bumstead, what did you do with the Farnsworth file?"

It's a little easier to shout when the other person isn't there. That's the way it is in this technological age. Technology has transformed the telephone and our lives. It has changed the way we deal with people at home, in our offices, and in our courts. Like most technological advances, it has given us more efficiency, but less compassion.

I have always had problems with machines. I still haven't mastered the escalator, for example. I don't get a cozy feeling when I turn on my computer and see, "Good Morning Arthur Gilbut." Remember Hal in 2001? I have the same uneasy feeling about these technologically advanced telephone systems.

We yearn to talk to a human being. How else can we retain some humanity in a world with precious little of it? We lose our empathy, our ability to communicate when we don't have to face, or at least talk to, another human being. It then becomes easier to withdraw from human connection. If judges in law and motion, for example, only communicate with lawyers through an answering machine, they may become aloof and distant. Okay, more aloof and distant.

The message idea breeds fear and mistrust. For the caller, the answering machine can be a gnawing source of insecurity. You're about half way through leaving your message after the beep, when a voice yells, "Don't hang up." That means the other party just got in and grabbed the phone, or they listened for awhile and then decided you were worth talking to. How flattering. Now you get to repeat part of the stilted message you have already left. The next time you call this person and there is no interruption, you wonder if he is really there, snickering while you stammer out a message.

I also have difficulty with the recorded salutation. What I prefer is, "We're no at home, leave a message," and an immediate beep. I'm infuriated when I have to listen to a two-minute comedy routine which isn't funny the first item and deadly the 75th.

People who do accents or impersonations should be shot. Those who team up with their spouses to do a short dramatic piece should be whipped. People who leave messages for those from whom they are expecting a call should be censured. "John, I have to meet you at 8 p.m. rather than 7 p.m., because Cynthia has to first pick up Claudia, and by the time we get to Jamie's, we'll never make it. Susan, leave the file with Mark at the office. I'll pick it up later. Everybody else, leave a message."

The courts have become an even greater source of alienation than ever before because they have been touched by the automatic phone system. If you want information about the warrant for your arrest for failing to appear on a traffic ticket you never got, just try calling the court to talk to somebody about it. You get a recorded message that's not all that enlightening. Try pressing zero to talk to someone. That usually gives you two options, disconnection or a busy signal. In desperation you go to court and tell the judge your story. You sold that car last year, and you are not responsible for the new owner's parking tickets. The sympathetic judge immediately dismisses the case against you. Of course the warrant is re-issued—against you.

You could try the phone again, and let's be fair, there are times, although less frequent than winning the lottery, when you get a real person on the line. He will tell you to come to court and talk to the judge.

In some courts you can call the law-and-motion department to hear a humorless recorded voice tell you the tentative ruling in your case. Some attorneys say this is a useful practice. That assumes you have the endurance of a caller to a late night talk show. The satisfaction of triumphing over the busy signal often compensates for losing. The next call is usually to your insurance carrier whose answering phone asks you to leave a message at the beep.

That is not to say the telephone does not have a useful purpose in the court system. The Court of Appeal in Fresno gives attorneys the option of presenting oral argument over the telephone. The justices tell me it works just fine. It saves the state money that otherwise would have to be paid to court-appointed attorneys who must travel long distances to attend the court hearing. At least there is an exchange, albeit over the phone.

You do lose, however, the other components that go into the communication, like body language, facial expressions and gestures. The attorneys don't get to see the judges nod in approval, or just nod off. The judges don't get to see the sweat pouring down the attorneys' cheeks.

The Fresno system, however, does give the attorneys a subtle benefit. A snide remark is heard over the speaker phone in the courtroom. One of the justices says, "Who said that?" Silence.

The next step is going to be some kind of automatic answering system in the Court of Appeal. Resist as I may, it's bound to happen. If its use is inevitable, why not use it in what is the most distasteful part of appellate practice for both judges and lawyers—petitions for rehearing.

Instead of reading a rehearing petition, I can listen to one. The opinion has been issued. The attorney representing the loser calls the court. A recorded message says, "You have called the rehearing hot line. Leave a message at the beep." Then the attorney can say what's on his or her mind. I can listen to the message at my leisure. "You're wrong, wrong, wrong. You don't understand the facts, and you don't understand the law. You completely missed the point."

I'll use an automatic phone device to call them back, like the ones that call you at home to take a market survey. "Hello, this is the court appeal calling. We have listened to and considered your petition for rehearing. We are unavailable to discuss it, but it is denied. If you wish to hear this message repeated, please hit the pound key." Beep.

292

THE TELEPHONE IN COURT
PART II

Today we use videoconferencing when conducting some of our oral arguments. Back in 1997 we first used speaker phones to conduct oral argument for attorneys in far away locations. The practice had some hang-ups which I outline in the following column published in May of 1997.

Ring, Ring, Brrriinng, Ring, Brrrinng. "Will somebody please answer the damn phone."

The clerk answers the phone. "Good morning- All rise. Division 6 of the Court of Appeal is now in session."

The clerk has just called the court into session on a speaker phone. The spectator section of the courtroom is empty. So are the chairs behind the bare, implacable counsel tables. The lectern looks like an uncompleted art piece, a wee tower without someone standing before it, pounding it, holding it, leaning on it, or clutching its sides. The priapic microphone, in this setting a useless appendage, reaching up like a sightless antennae.

The bailiff, always alert for potential trouble, has his eyes glued to the speaker phone.

The judges are at their places on the bench staring out at the vacant courtroom. Two are wearing their robes.

"Please be seated," says the clerk.

The parties at the other end of the line sit down--if in fact they were standing when the clerk called the court to order. The bailiff's eyes, still fixed on the speaker phone, narrow.

Welcome to the Alexander Graham Bell approach to oral argument. For some time I had cradled the idea of holding oral argument via the telephone in appropriate cases. We tried it last month. How did we come to emulate the practice of our colleagues in Fresno who view this novel approach to oral argument as significant as the invention of the telephone?

It may have its genesis in the column I wrote in February on civility. In last month's column I told you about a letter I received from a family lawyer who complained that some judges were uncivil to lawyers. Much like Claude Rains in Casablanca, I found the revelation shocking.

I am confident that the judges to whom my correspondent was referring had no intention to be rude, impatient, arrogant or peremptory-- all right, maybe peremptory. For those who confuse discourtesy with efficiency, judges on occasion may seem overbearing.

I know a judge who uses a time clock to help attorneys focus on core issues and present their cases and arguments concisely and quickly. The judge's calendar runs like an airline without a flight controller in the tower. Sometimes a hoped for take-off doesn't get off the ground. Here's an example of a colloquy during an argument. "To respond to your honor's question about the principal issue in this case, the definitive answer is in this new case that just came down this morning which states . . ."

"Your time is up counsel . . . sit down."

Some attorneys might mistake this for brusqueness. But irrespective of a judge's intent, does the quest for efficiency rule out civility? Are these mutually exclusive conditions? Is there not a way to combine the two?

The answer came when I heard a bell ring in my head. Luckily, the line to my brain was open. I didn't put the call on hold. The message was a signal for a busy court: "Try oral argument by way of telephone. Fresno does it."

The efficient part of the program is obvious. It drastically reduces time spent by lawyers traveling to court to argue on behalf of indigent defendants. This in turn benefits taxpayers.

Civility is also built into the package. The attorneys who argue cannot see the judges grimace, yawn, whisper to each other, nod, or nod off. And it's almost impossible to interrupt someone who is speaking a mile a minute over a speaker phone.

Of course there are drawbacks. Judges do not see counsel's body language indicating subservience or cowering. Nor can they read facial expressions reminiscent of Munch's "The Scream." They cannot see the anxious rivulets of sweat trickling down the face of counsel, who under relentless questioning hears the roar of the falls just ahead.

I remember vividly, if one can remember vividly what one hears, a particularly tedious argument over the telephone. Counsel was beating a dead horse so far into the ground that only the protruding hoofs were visible. I recall the argument in exquisite detail. "Yap, yap, yap, and moreover, yap, yap, yap, yap."

"Counsel . . . " we tried to interject.

He didn't hear us. Maybe he did.

"Counsel . . . "

"Yap, yap, yap, yap, yap, yap . . . ."

The bailiff got up and approached the speaker phone with his hand tightly grasping his baton. Undaunted the attorney continued. Whatever our intentions, counsel perceived no incivility from us.

Counsel's argument finally drew to a close. I blurted out a question.

From the speaker I heard something that was just barely audible. It sounded like, "ask (something muffled) question" or was it, "stupid ass question?"

"Who said that?" I asked.

The bailiff's muscles tensed. Silence.

"Anything further?" asked the P.J.

"I would like to respond to the issue about laches," someone said over the speaker phone.

"Who said that?" one of us asked?

"I did."

"Please identify yourself for the record," said the clerk.

No response.

"I have a question," I said.

"What question? someone asked.

"About laches?" I answered.

"I'd like to respond to that," said a voice.

"Haven't we covered that?" said somebody.

"I believe our time is about up," said the P.J., "but would you respond to the laches argument.

The clerk said , "I believe one of the parties has been disconnected."

"Or hung up," I said softly.

"What?" said a voice.

The clerk tried to call the disconnected party. A recording said the number was no longer in service.

"Case submitted," said the P.J.

My colleagues insist that oral argument is better with "live" persons instead of disembodied voices. Nevertheless, I'm installing a rehearing hot line to replace the traditional written petition.

There is a menu. Counsel presses the appropriate numbers depending on the grounds for rehearing. These are: (1) Alleged misstatements of facts, law and issues; (2) Outrage, or bewilderment over faulty or inexplicable reasoning; and (3) Uncontrolled frenzy due to a blatant subversion of established law to reach a desired result.

Counsel may leave a message at the beep. Significantly, there is no option to press 0 to speak to an operator. We know how to reach you.

PREDICTIONS

This column was written shortly after the verdict in the O.J. Simpson criminal case.

Remember Criswell? He made predictions. In the days of early television he had a show called "Criswell Predicts." He referred to himself in the third person, and with the dramatic flair of an actor who had been in too many melodramas, he would say, "Criswell predicts . . . women will wear shorter dresses next year." Picking ourselves up off the floor after that bold look into the future, we would wait for the next startling revelation.

On occasion he did go out on a limb, but I suspected he had a knack for being wrong most of the time. But I couldn't be sure. Who remembered months or years later whether his predictions were true or not? What mattered was his flickering image speaking to us at the moment. He could have been a commentator on the O. J. Simpson case.

Remember the commentators' predictions? "The case should take about three or four months to try"; "the jury will be out at least two months"; "the Court of Appeal will never intervene."

There were so many lawyer commentators on radio and television that Harry Shearer, the satirist, remarked that you couldn't get a criminal lawyer in Los Angeles because they were all busy commenting on the O. J. Simpson case. They signed autographs in the supermarket, and the next day in their television interview they criticized O. J.'s lawyers for craving publicity.

Some kept a scorecard on the lawyers in the courtroom, designating winners and losers for particular days. They probably forgot that it was the trial the lawyers were trying to win, not a Tuesday or Wednesday in the courtroom. They criticized F. Lee Bailey's cross-examination. Why didn't the witness shrivel up and wither on the witness stand? No doubt they had confused the televised trial with a television program. In fact the witness did shrivel up. It just happened later.

Some people saw the trial as a soap opera that replaced the ones it pre-empted. The scorecard was no less offensive. It trivialized the tragedy that gave rise to the trial.

Nevertheless, some of the commentators were quite good. Who cares if they never tried a case? After all, I suppose there are responsible movie and literary critics who have never directed a film or written a novel. But there were also excellent commentators who were experienced trial lawyers and academics. They enlightened the public. Professor Erwin Chemerinsky, whose insights on any legal subject are of value, offered informative and illuminating commentary. So did Stan Goldman, a professor at Loyola Law School who served many years trying criminal cases as a public defender.

Roger Cossack, who offered a down-to-earth analysis sans the arrogance displayed by some of his colleagues, wound up with his own show on CNN. Retired Superior Court Judge Jack Tenner became a media personality with numerous radio and TV appearances. He often challenged his listeners and viewers with thoughtprovoking questions. I must admit, however, he gave me a scare the first time I saw him on CNN, hosting a show on the O. J. case. He was wearing colorful suspenders, a striped shirt and no coat. For just a terrible instant I thought, "Larry King, Not Alive?"

But now that the case is over, the criminal case that is, in a naïve moment I wondered: What would happen to all the commentators? Would they have to go back to practicing law, where analysis and predictions do make a difference? Would people hold it against those whose predictions were wrong? Not a chance. Depositions have not even begun in the civil case, and they are out there again with off-the-cuff analyses and insouciant predictions.

If the world is still listening, I hope the commentators will direct their energies to enlighten rather than to titillate.

I hope they will point out the errors of those who are misusing the O. J. Simpson trial in an attempt to bring harmful changes to our justice system. I hope they will point out that mistakes in the trial do not reflect deficiencies in the criminal justice system.

I hope they will speak against a proposal for "new restrictions" on a defense attorney's closing argument. There are sufficient limitations now on closing argument for all attorneys, defense and prosecution.

The outcome of a single criminal case did not demonstrate the need to depart from the requirement of a unanimous jury to convict. Let the commentators speak out against such a measure, which was proposed in anticipation of what many, except the prescient Ira Reiner, thought would be a hung jury.

There is even talk of a nitwit proposal that seeks to keep from the jury the identity of defendants in criminal cases. Putting aside one major obstacle, the Constitution, do you not think this proposal would make it hard to observe the defendant's demeanor if he or she testified with a bag over the head? Still, better not to talk too much about this one; the idea just might catch on.

Should cameras be prohibited? Not necessarily. Cameras do not do anything wrong. They just record what happens. Their presence in the atypical O.J. Simpson case should not necessarily result in their banishment from courtrooms from now on. Granted, the "media" is generally interested in the sensational case, but in all instances, the public benefits from exposure to its court system. Under our present system, state court judges decide whether or not to permit cameras on a case-by-case basis. Maybe it should stay that way.

A trial is like a living organism. It evolves and changes and is not always predictable. When a particular trial is over, those involved on the winning and losing sides often have differing perceptions about what was right or wrong with the trial. If, to quote the defense witness Dr. Henry Lee, "something was wrong" in the Simpson case, changing the system will not necessarily change what was wrong.

I hope the commentators will persuade the public to reject attempts to tinker with a justice system that is the envy of the world. I hope they will succeed, but I hesitate to make a prediction. I don't want to wind up like Criswell.

CIVILITY IS A TRAIT
NO LESS IMPORTANT TO JUDGES THAN TO LAWYERS

A few weeks ago while taking a shower, I succumbed to a sudden impulse of judicial activism and shaved off my mustache of thirty years. My wife was blow drying her hair at the time. I emerged from the shower. It took a few minutes before she saw materialize in the mirror through the dissipating steam a strange naked man standing in the middle of the bathroom (to be more precise, what appeared to be a different strange man in the middle of the bathroom). She turned with a start. When she realized who I was she said, "You really are naked."

We went out to dinner that night. It was like a first date. But of course I wasn't a new guy. I was still me, only now revealing a prominent simian upper lip. My wife adjusted quickly, and observing the doctrine of separation of powers, did not press me to disclose the reason for the change. I wouldn't have had an immediate answer had she asked, but prior and subsequent events gave me a clue.

It may have started with my February 1997 column which touched on the paucity of civility in the legal profession. I received a letter from a family law attorney who complained that lack of civility was a problem lawyers suffered more at the hands of trial judges than from other lawyers. He complained that many trial judges were crabby and discourteous while commissioners were just the opposite.

My correspondent went on to observe that judges never write about judicial rudeness, but instead aim their criticism at lawyers. No doubt that is because judges do not appear in front of other judges--unless they have been indicted or live in another county and are contesting spousal support.

I decided to broach the subject of judicial incivility with Judge Learned Foote. When I entered Judge Foote's chambers he was tinkering with a time clock. "When lawyers chatter, better that time be in my hands than on theirs," he said with dramatic timing. "With this baby," he said, massaging his clock, "I moved a case along so quickly that plaintiff didn't have time to make a closing argument."

I suggested that maybe that wasn't fair. His eyes narrowed. "Defendant came in under his time allotment with two hours to spare. I let plaintiff's lawyer bargain with defendant's lawyer for the additional time. He offered ten grand for it. I bet if he had come up with another five, he would have had a deal . . . . Got something against free enterprise?"

Before I could answer, he mentioned an article which appeared in the California Political Review in 1997. The author, a conservative legal columnist rebuked the California Supreme Court, and its Chief Justice for heading in the direction of "liberal judicial activism."

He wrote that the Chief was neither making the "right" decisions in his opinions nor in his capacity as Chair of the Judicial Council. He criticized the Chief for succumbing to political correctness by investigating reports of racial bias in the courts, and by encouraging gender fairness; in other words, for treating litigants and lawyers with dignity and respect. I thought this was the goal of all qualified judges whatever their judicial philosophy or political affiliation. Indeed, I thought this enlightened approach would eventually cure the problem of judicial incivility which had so disturbed my correspondent.

The columnist also chided me for what he considered to be my misguided perception that our high court was conservative. He even labeled me with the "L" word.

Judge Foote emphasized the forlorn epithet. But I protested that the "M" word more accurately described me.

"'M' word?" he asked. "Mustache? No, you don't have one anymore. You must mean mediocre, mealy-mouthed, Milquetoast, or mushy."

"No," I replied. "Moderate."

"Same thing," he snorted. "But you did take a step in the right direction and removed the carpet from your upper lip."

"I just felt maybe a change was in order."

"Felt," he said with contempt. "Rearrange the letters and you get 'left.' Liberals like facial hair. It masks their expression. Harder to detect traces of empathy or compassion, when those annoying pests scamper across their pained physiognomies. Qualified judges know how to decide cases without a lot of extraneous considerations. So what's on your alleged mind?" he finally asked.

"I wanted to talk to you about civility," I said.

He searched my countenance and then hit the button on the top of his clock. "Time's up."

As I was leaving his chambers he yelled out the door at me, "I'll give you two weeks before you grow it back."

I went back to my chambers with a dozen thoughts spinning in my head. Were judges rude? Did sympathy for a victim or a defendant, or even a lawyer, make a judge less qualified? It was hard to get back to work. I started to write my traditional April Fool's column, but put it aside and worked on a case. The appeal concerned a litigant who complained that the trial court placed unreasonable time limits on him thus preventing him from adequately presenting his case.

As I pondered the issue I noticed that appellant's argument suffered from a significant handicap. I absent- mindedly felt my bare upper lip. No one was around to see the subtle expression of sympathy that momentarily stole across my face. His brief exceeded the page limitation.

ANIMALS IN COURT

Do we truly see ourselves as others see us? Do judges, for example, mistake a lawyer's sneer of contempt for a crooked smile? Do scathing judicial profiles in legal periodicals force judges to see themselves as they truly are? How should I know? I am as guilty of self-deception as any other person or judge. But whatever they may say about me, one thing I can say about myself with certainty: I am not a tyrant.

How do I support this bold assertion? By a simple proclivity: I like cats. Biographers tell us that Hitler and Napoleon despised cats. Psychologists opine that tyrants hate cats because they cannot control them. I'm sure Saddam Hussein hated cats. The three villains I have just mentioned would have been terrible judges. People who like cats make good judges because they do not need to lord it over people . . . or cats.

I cannot say the same thing about people who love dogs, unless the dog is a Basenji. Basenji dogs are much like cats. They do not bark, they lick themselves, and are fiercely independent. They do whatever they damn please. Basenji owners make good judges. I'm not so sure about dog lovers of other breeds. The "roll over," "play dead," "get me the paper," mentality does not lend itself to forbearance when passing judgment on some poor defendant.

Yet, domestic animals have a soothing effect on irascible humans. That is why I support cats in court. Dogs too. Unfortunately, judges who bring their animals to court get in trouble. (See *Cannon* v. *Commission on Judicial Qualifications* (1975) 14 Cal.3d 678, 684, fn. H-3, 704.) The mechanical canary chirping away in Judge Cannon's chambers during court hours was disruptive. But that should not count against a real canary who I'm sure would have been quieter.

The judge also brought a real dog to court, which among other things, got her into big trouble with the then Commission on Judicial Qualifications. But what is so wrong with having a tiny poodle sit on a judge's lap while she or he tries a jury case? (This is a serious subject, so I forgo lame jokes about a dog of a case; see *Phillips* v. *San Luis Obispo County Dept. etc. Regulation* (1986) 183 Cal.App.3d 372.) Xavier Cugat, the Latin band leader, famous to anyone over 60, led his band with a Chihuahua cradled in his arm. The dog was not all that distracting, not with Cugat's vivacious wife Charo gyrating to a compelling beat.

Judge Cannon's Poodle was not any more distracting than Cugat's Chihuahua, that is until the Poodle was distracted. An attorney bearing an animus against either the judge or her Poodle, or both, created havoc with a diabolical prank one morning during a jury trial. The Poodle was resting comfortably in the judge's lap during an agonizingly protracted cross-examination of an expert witness. Unnoticed, the miscreant attorney standing in the hallway opened the courtroom door just a crack. Taking a deep breath, he placed a dog whistle between his malevolent lips and blew. If this was a joke, its effect was not practical. To describe the disorder that followed in current usage, the Poodle freaked out.

From one end of the dog came hysterical yapping, the sound of which resembled a chicken with laryngitis. What came out of the other end produced a similar but louder response from the judge. At the judge's hearing before the Commission, the Poodle, who was reputed to be a heavy sentencer, marked not a drop of contrition. His damaging testimony helped bury her career as though it were a mere soup bone. She was removed from the bench after which she disappeared into obscurity. The dog went on to make a fortune in television commercials.

I submit that this unfortunate incident was neither the fault of the judge nor the dog. Nevertheless, the *Cannon* case stands as a precedent for banning pets from chambers and the courtroom. How foolish. Pets have a calming influence. Pets that visit patients in convalescent hospitals promote recovery and good health. At one time cats lived with prisoners in San Quentin. Their presence helped reduce violence.

Animals in the courthouse would make domineering judges more amicable. It would help reduce hypocrisy. Of the many judges who retire to graze in the green pastures of private judging, there are a few who have disagreeable temperaments. In the private sector, they have to live down their dreadful reputations. How often do we see them at bar functions unctuously glad handing, working the tables with smarmy demeanor, while trying to effect warm personalities? This shameful ruse would be unnecessary had they been allowed to have a cat on the bench. A cat would have softened their oppressive natures. They would have been mellow and genial, obviating the need for the six f's: False Friendly Face For Finding Fortune.

If I brought my cat to court, the Judicial Performance Commission would be on me like a vexatious litigant. But as I cannot take my cat to court; I take the court to my cat. That is, I used to. When I worked at home (on weekends and nights of course), my cat Oge assisted me. Oge was his nickname. His real name was O.G. (Other Guy) to distinguish him from Boz, the cat who was the first to establish residence with me. Oge is recently deceased. The circumstances of his demise is a painful story that I will reserve for another column. Oge would sit on my desk and help me decide cases. Please do not report this to the Judicial Performance Commission.

While I was drafting at my word processor, Oge would, at times, simply walk on the keys and delete material. Seldom would I strike the undo button but instead take his sage advice and start anew.

Unlike Oge, Boz is not an intellectual. He preferred watching T.V. while Oge and I worked. Oge, on the other hand disliked T.V., except for the Sopranos. Boz and Oge had little use for each other but were compelled by circumstances to arrive at an uneasy truce. They were much like two justices of widely differing judicial philosophies and temperaments in the same division. They learned the value of tolerance and coexistence.

Incidentally, for you skeptics, cats do watch T.V. and even have favorite shows. On National Public Radio, Ira Glass, host of *This American Life*, interviewed a producer of video programs for cats. Not surprisingly, the videos featured the sounds and movement of birds, squirrels and lizards. I did not buy the video for Boz, as he was content with animal shows on Public Television and the Discovery Channel.

Even dogs like television. In the 1950's my friend Lewis Barth, who is now Dean of the Hebrew Union College, had a dog named Peaceful. Lewis was extremely popular. After all, he was the first kid on his block to have a television set. During the first few weeks that this miracle with a ten inch screen appeared in Lewis's living room, Peaceful kept running to the back of the set. Lewis said that Peaceful was looking for the people on T.V. . . . and this was in the days of black and white grainy television. Lewis attributed too much intelligence to his dog. People are simply not that short.

Since Oge is gone, some people have hinted that my work has suffered. I was hoping that Boz would take his place. Unfortunately, he has little interest in the law. Because he likes T.V., I tried to use that medium to provoke some curiosity, hoping it would not kill him. He found Judge Judy abrasive and rude and refused to wait for the outcome of a landlord tenant dispute between two solipsists.

I finally induced Boz to watch Animal Court with me. We snuggled together on the couch as the redoubtable Judge Wapner presided over his kingdom. Boz and I hoped to see a heated disputes involving hamsters, parakeets, and mice. All we got were arguments about the value of a Schnauzer. We fell asleep.

SPEAKING ONE'S MIND HAS ITS COSTS AND REWARDS

This column was written in 1995 when Newt Gingrich was speaker of the House of Representatives.

What do lawyers want more than anything else; what would they kill to have? The answer is obvious, a legal secretary with a high IQ. Most lawyers would agree that such a person is even more valuable than an associate with a high IQ. And partners? Everyone agrees, a high IQ is a detriment.

But getting back to our ultra-bright legal secretary, there is such a person. Her name is Nikki Frey, and her IQ is in the stratosphere. That's why she belongs to Mensa, the organization for the self-consciously brilliant. You don't get to belong unless your IQ is over 132.

Until recently she was the editor of the Los Angeles chapter's newsletter. Not anymore. That brings me back to killing. All she did was publish an article that advocated we kill the homeless, the mentally retarded, the aged and the infirm. I'm not sure whether this included Stephen W. Hawking. The article also opined that Hitler's greatest offense was giving a bad name to the concept of a master race.

What with recent attacks on the intellectual elite, Ms. Frey picked an inopportune time to air these controversial views. The executive committee of the local Los Angeles chapter put its collective gray matter together and ousted Ms. Frey from her non-paying position as editor.

Isn't there a moral issue here? Doesn't Ms. Frey have a right to express a point of view, however offensive it may be? I suppose so. But when she expresses that point of view on behalf of an organization whose membership has a radically different point of view, perhaps she should be out of a job.

Please understand, I'm only raising an issue here. My purpose is not to defend Mensa. After all, I'm not a member. I hear the entrance exam is a bitch, and besides, they didn't ask me to join. I had hoped to qualify for membership under an affirmative action program, but it didn't work.

Speaking of Newt Gingrich . . . I know we weren't speaking of him, but this incident reminded me of him.

The articles Ms. Frey published contained ideas that would go far in reducing government expenditures—after incurring the cost of rounding up the suspects and exterminating them. But Newt found himself in the same position as Mensa, and had to do some firing of his own.

Gingrich, ever watchful for governmental waste and corruption, hired a loyal supporter, political science professor Christina Jeffrey, as House historian. As Gingrich's office spokesperson put it, "This is the historian for the House of the whole United States of America."

She and Newt must have a lot in common, being professors and all. Both taught at the same distinguished institution of higher learning: Kennesaw State University in Marietta, GA. I don't know if she belonged to Mensa, but like Ms. Frey, she was fired from her job because of her point of view.

Wouldn't you know it, Hitler popped up again. Professor Jeffrey felt that if schools were going to teach about the Holocaust, they should be fair and objective and also teach the Nazi point of view. She also stressed that the Ku Klux Klan has a point of view. That's true. So does Charles Manson. But so far we have been talking about ideas that were born from the womb that produced Rosemary's baby.

What about ideas that are not despicable and grotesque, but just controversial? There's a price to pay for expressing those ideas as well. Judge Bork comes to mind. His critics, who kept him off the court because of those ideas, may have only a Pyrrhic victory to celebrate. If subsequent prospective appointees are reticent about expressing their points of view, we could wind up with someone who makes Bork look like Che Guevara in comparison. Or what about an appointee who has no views? We can be sure he or she will be mediocre.

The best way to deplete provisions in the marketplace of ideas is to punish those who express a reasonable point of view. Please keep in mind you don't have to agree with an idea for it to be reasonable. We should encourage people to express their ideas and to clarify the facts upon which those ideas are based. That makes it easier for us to make intelligent decisions about issues.

Whatever the consequences, there are people who believe that an open and fair airing of the facts is the only way to approach an issue. Such a person is Robert Baker, one of the nation's most eminent defense attorneys. His skill as a trial lawyer is matched only by his integrity and courage.

He offered his views to the House Judiciary Subcommittee on Economic and Commercial Law. The subcommittee was considering legislation on the federal level that would change the law in medical malpractice suits. The subcommittee looked to California, which has always been a leader.

In the days when Roger Traynor was our Chief Justice, California led the nation in expanding the rights of consumers. In recent times those rights have been more circumscribed. Our Supreme Court has upheld California's MICRA, (Medical Injury Compensation Reform Act of 1975.) Congress is looking to enact similar legislation on the federal level that limits the amount juries may award to plaintiffs injured because of a doctor's negligence and limits the amount of contingency fees lawyers representing such plaintiffs may collect. The more serious a plaintiff's injuries due to a doctor's negligence, the less his or her proportional recovery.

Plaintiffs' lawyers have argued that "tort reform" measures such as MICRA make it economically impossible for lawyers to represent plaintiffs in medical malpractice cases. Baker told the subcommittee that these so-called reforms were of significant benefit to doctors and insurance companies, but were not all that helpful to injured parties who now find it hard to obtain representation. He also pointed out that less than one percent of total medical care costs can be attributed to malpractice. Thus, it follows that these laws have hurt consumers with legitimate lawsuits, but have had practically no effect in holding down health care costs.

Baker paid a price for expressing his point of view. It's been reported that because of his comments, his firm has lost some of its big clients, such as the Kaiser Permanente health plan.

Lawyers usually lose clients when they do a poor job in representing them, but Baker's win record is phenomenal. He racks up one defense verdict after another. He is a vigorous advocate for his clients' cause and exhibits a skill and tenacity on their behalf that is unmatched. The Daily Journal reported that his colleagues have remarked how many doctors owe their practices to him. In other words, they owe their livelihoods to him.

Baker sets an example for all of us. He had the courage and the strength of character to speak his mind. Cynics might say that his integrity and self-respect do not pay the overhead. Others might counter that the momentary loss of some business is insignificant when it comes to preserving those invaluable attributes. This may be beside the point, but in my view there will always be plenty of business for a lawyer of Baker's ability. And when Baker spoke his mind he made the public understand why lawyers have cause to be proud of their profession.

310

PERESTROIKA
TEACHING AMERICAN JURISPRUDENCE
IN POST-SOVIET RUSSIA 1995

The tea and bread was good, but I had trouble with the frankfurter and the salami streaked with fat: not the ideal breakfast. I couldn't complain though, because this was a typical Russian breakfast, and I was in Russia.

I looked across the table at my breakfast companion, Judy Chirlin, and managed a weak smile. She took a slice of salami onto which she had placed a large dollop of cheese and popped it into her mouth with gusto. Judy, a judge on the Los Angeles County Superior Court, was used to this. This was her sixth trip to post-Soviet Russia. She had traversed the country from Krasnodar to Altai, leading seminars and enlightening Russian judges on American jurisprudence.

The high-cholesterol breakfast had just been served in the dining room of a hotel located at Solychnaya Polyana, a bucolic location that is a two-hour drive from Moscow. We were about to begin our seminar with a group of Russian judges who were among the first to conduct jury trials in criminal cases in the "new" Russia. Many of the judges had received previous training from some of their U.S. counterparts led by Judge Chirlin. Most of them had visited the United States and observed jury trials conducted in federal courts in various cities throughout the United States.

Our program was organized by the Central and East European Law Initiative (CEELI), sponsored by the American Bar Association. We were there to discuss the structure of a typical U.S. criminal jury trial and to explore ways to ensure that trials are fair to both sides.

I wanted to begin our program with a few comments about diet, but Judge Chirlin thought I would be more successful discussing double jeopardy. She finished the last of her salami and assured me that when we got back to Moscow, she would treat me to a hamburger and shake at McDonald's.

Our American panel consisted of Judge Chirlin; John Radson, a prosecutor working on the U.S. Department of Justice Organized Crime Initiative in Russia; Nicholas Arena, a criminal defense attorney from New York with a passion for Russian literature; and myself. The Russian participants were judges from regions outside Moscow, two professors from the Institute of the General Prosecutor's office and a journalist.

Our exchange was frank and informative. The Russian judges were intelligent, sophisticated and eager to establish an independent judiciary as a coequal branch of government. Jury trials had not been a part of the judicial system under Soviet rule. In those days the public had little faith in the independence of the judiciary, although lay assessors would sit with judges on criminal cases.

In 1991, the Russian parliament passed laws that recognized the supremacy of the individual instead of the state. These included the Concept of Judicial Reform, which acknowledged the advantages of jury trials. A Law on Juries was adopted in 1993 over fierce opposition from the general prosecutor. The law reduces the prosecutor's authority over criminal trials.

For the time being, jury trials are being tried only in certain regional courts, and only for serious felonies. The judges desperately want jury trials to become a permanent part of the entire Russian legal system. They believe this will give the public faith in the integrity of the courts and will ensure continuing public support.

The new Russian constitution also changed the role of the judge, who used to be an investigator and often aided the prosecution in a search for the truth. Now, trials are moving in the direction of adversary proceedings modeled after those in our system. The judge operates more as an impartial referee than an investigator.

Even as Russia looks to the U.S. justice system, I was struck by how our system in some ways is leaning toward theirs. For example, jury verdicts in Russian criminal trials must be unanimous—but only if the jury has deliberated for less than three hours. After three hours, a simple majority vote is sufficient to convict. It puts one in mind of the proposals in our country and state to eliminate the requirement of a unanimous jury vote for conviction in a criminal trial. This is a giant leap forward or backward, depending on your point of view.

Schools of thought in our country argue that a trial, above all, should be a search for the truth. The Russian system is also concerned with finding the truth. Russia's Criminal Procedure Code speaks of the task of exposing crime and convicting the guilty. Perhaps that is why the Russian system affords an equal opportunity for all parties to appeal a decision, whether it is a conviction or an acquittal. If the prosecution doesn't get it right the first time, with a successful appeal it may get the opportunity to investigate more thoroughly the next time around. There is no double or even triple jeopardy.

The quest for the truth in Russia is served by fewer restrictions on the admissibility and presentation of evidence. Narrative testimony is allowed, and there is no formal direct examination or cross-examination. Often, testimony of reputation and prior bad deeds find its way into the evidentiary mix. Russian judges wish to effect changes to tighten the rules of admissibility—while some in our country would argue for a relaxation of these rules.

The Russian judges take pride in their efforts to create an independent judiciary designed to protect the individual. They respect and admire our system and look to emulate it. In our understandable yearning to discover the truth, we must not forget what makes our criminal justice system the envy of the world. Justice is found in the procedural safeguards accorded the individual, which are more important than finding the truth at all costs. As many Russians discovered during the Soviet era, the price was too high.

Postscript- The optimism expressed in this column, written in 1995 has given way to disappointment in 2008.   The emasculation of the democratic process has seriously undermined its judicial institutions

IT'S NOT THE LAW THAT IS A ASS

This column was inspired by a lawsuit brought against an aggressive criminal defense attorney who almost got into a fight with a prosecutor after the conclusion of a criminal case. I did not mention the names of the lawyers when this column was written in 1997. As I look over this column in 2008, I think it still is better not to mention their names.

"But laws, in their more confined sense, and in which it is our present business to consider them, denote the rules, not of action in general, but of human action or conduct; that is, the precepts by which man, [and woman] the noblest of all sublunary beings, a creature endowed with both reason and free-will, is commanded to make use of those faculties in the general regulation of his [her] behavior." Blackstone, Sir William, Commentaries 44-46, 1765-69.

Blackstone would have been chagrined to know that over two hundred years later, his sublunary beings have not always exercised their faculties to reflect nobility, despite the laws they enacted to regulate their behavior.

But an instance now and then of a particular lawyer's imperfections is no excuse for the current cinema to be so blatant in depicting lawyers in an unfavorable light. In *Jurassic Park*, for example, the lawyer was a slimy, greedy money grubber who wants to commercially exploit guileless dinosaurs. In a skewed sense of justice without trial, Tyrannosaurus did the hapless lawyer in while he was in the outhouse, not the courthouse. The defense lawyer in *The Verdict*, was cruel, heartless, unscrupulous, and unethical. The movie may have given the uninitiated the impression that all defense lawyers are like this. A recent movie I have not rushed out to see, is *Devil's Advocate*. Its message is not exactly subtle. The reviews say that it portrays the senior partner of a large law firm as Satan, the very quintessence of depravity and evil. Notice, he's not a surgeon. Moreover, there is a cameo appearance by Senator Alfonse D'Amato. This film from hell depicting a successful lawyer as the Fallen Angel, should do wonders for the legal profession.

These unflattering portraits do not reflect the overwhelming majority of lawyers, they, the noble beings dedicated to their profession, who seek the resolution of disputes through the civilized application of reason. That is why we must combat the alarming and unjustified assault on the legal profession. We must inform the public of the truth, but not by way of a Pollyannaish gloss over the occasional embarrassments that do occur. A frank and open disclosure of the good and the bad will ensure credibility and best educate the public. This in turn will restore faith in our splendid profession.

Start with the children. True, they are impressionable, but they also have an unerring sense of the authentic. Tell them of the fair but forceful prosecutors who bring the lawless to justice. But also tell them of the courageous defense attorneys who protect the constitutional rights of their clients and thereby also protect all our constitutional rights. Tell them of the Watergate prosecutors and the defenders of Sacco and Vanzetti; tell them of the organized crime prosecutors, and the defenders of those who fought racial discrimination. But lest we paint too majestic a picture that to some might seem unrealistic, we should not shrink from revealing what on occasion happens at the other end of the spectrum. Stout hearted children can handle it.

A recent incident that thankfully has been brought to a conclusion is an example of what Blackstone did not have in mind when writing his commentaries. It inspired me to write the following children's story:

Lawyer John Goes to Court

See lawyer John. See lawyer John go to court. John is a lawyer for a man who did some bad things. The lawyer on the other side is a lawyer for all the people. Hear lawyer for the People tell the judge he wants man who did bad things to go to jail a long time. The judge is wise and fair. The judge says the man did bad things, but not real bad things. Hear the judge say the man goes to jail a short time. Man is happy. Lawyer John is happy. Lawyer for People is mad. Court bailiff is mad.

Lawyer John thinks bailiff and lawyer for People look at him with mean faces. See the mean faces. John does not like bailiff and lawyer for People to stare at him with mean faces. See John go to lawyer for the People. See bailiff go quickly to stand next to lawyer for the People. See John look with mean face at lawyer for the People and at bailiff. Hear John call lawyer for People a bad name. Hear John say lawyer for People is an animal with four legs and long ears. Hear John say to bailiff to come outside of courtroom and fight with him.

Other lawyers for the People say John is a bad man who broke the law. See lawyers file lawsuit against lawyer John. Hear lawyer for People say he will make lawsuit go away if lawyer John says he is sorry. Can you hear lawyer John say he is sorry? Listen. It is quiet. You cannot hear lawyer John say he is sorry. Lawyer John is not sorry.

The lawyer for the People files lawsuit against lawyer John. It costs much money. See everyone go to court. See the jury listen to the case. See the jury not able to decide if lawyer John is wrong. See wise judge make lawsuit go away. Is John wrong? The end.

I sent my story to several publishers of children's books. They all rejected it as too improbable and inane for kids. Several producers, however, expressed an interest in the story for a network movie of the week. There was, however, one criticism that can easily be rectified with minor revisions. The judge has no flaws.

EXPRESSING THE TRUTH
PART I

As a child I learned to recognize different types of vegetables. Then I was forced to eat them. Then I had to learn to spell them. And now I could be sued if I insult them.

Mississippi law, gives producers of agricultural products a cause of action for damages, and other relief the court deems appropriate, against those who even imply that an agricultural product is not safe for consumption. The statement must be shown to be false. "False" is defined to mean the statement is not based upon reasonable and reliable scientific inquiry. The battle of the experts to decide whether a statement is false could leave a lot of husks and peels on the floor. California farmers are proposing a similar law for our state.

Therefore I'm loath to insult broccoli, cabbage, asparagus or cauliflower on or off the field. And as for cows, the lawsuit against Oprah for her off-handed remark about mad cow disease taught me bovine respect.

If vegetables and cows receive shelter from calumny and obloquy, judges should enjoy the same protection. It is true that in court judges have ways to deal with obstreperous attorneys who cannot tolerate those inevitable rulings that decimate their cases and their egos. The redoubtable Judge Learned Foote remarked that in his court "no disparaging remark goes unpunished."

But what about degrading comments uttered out of court? Some attorneys think they have free reign to denigrate judges. Should a radish have more protection than a judge?

Federal judges in the Central District do not think so. In their understandable distaste for unfounded criticism, they have developed a new pesticide in the form of a proposed change in their local rules as reported in the Daily Journal. Rule 2.5.2 makes lawyers think twice before yapping about a judge's conduct on or off the bench. The rule prohibits them from making comments which degrade or impugn the integrity of their federal judges. A discipline committee reviews charges and investigates. A three-judge panel has the power to suspend a lawyer who it finds in violation of the rule. The message is: "Open your Mouth, Close your Practice."

You may recall that about five years ago such a panel tried to suspend attorney Stephen Yagman for his critical remarks about a district judge. The Ninth Circuit set aside the decision of the discipline committee. See *Standing Committee v. Yagman* (9th Cir. 1995) 55 F.3d 1430. The appellate court characterized Yagman's comments as opinions and also ruled that the discipline committee had the burden to prove Yagman's statements were false. The proposed rule change shifts the burden to the attorney to prove the statement is untrue. (I mean, true. See next column - Part II.) This makes the discipline committee's job much easier. An attorney charged under the rule must prove that any statement that he or she made about a judge which impugns the character or integrity of the judge, or degrades the judge, is untrue. It's like making a defendant in a criminal action prove his or her innocence. Because he inspired the rule, Yagman thinks it should be named after him. "The Yagman-Gagman rule" is a catchy double rhyme.

The rule could present problems for lawyers such as Jan Schlichtmann. He was the tortured lawyer in Jonathan Haar's gripping masterwork, "A Civil Action," winner of the National Book Award for non-fiction. In a Herculean struggle, he represented a group of families whose children died of leukemia allegedly caused by the contamination of a city's drinking water by two powerful corporations. His adversaries were not just the corporate defendants, but Federal Judge Walter J. Skinner, whose rulings drove him to distraction. He refers to him as "that arthritic old bastard," and decries "the false and corrupt pretense of justice" in his courtroom. In considering a motion for sanctions against the defense for allegedly withholding crucial evidence that tended to establish the liability of one of the corporate defendants, Judge Skinner found Schlichtmann guilty of misconduct for filing his action without having competent evidence to establish a case against that very same defendant. Schlichtmann is quoted as saying "The man is demented!...the man is a f------ monster."

Legal scholars may argue about the merits of Judge Skinner's ruling, but Schlichtmann would be hard pressed to meet his burden under the proposed rule. Although some of Skinner's rulings were questionable, the Court of Appeals affirmed his decision on the sanctions issue. Indeed, the appellate court commended him for tackling "so thankless a task with incisiveness and vigor." Actually he had no choice because the court had ordered him to hold the hearing. But the court's remarks about Skinner's findings would leave Schlichtmann immobile from the weight of the insuperable burden he would have to overcome. The court concluded that the findings were "sound, well-substantiated, and free from observable legal error."

Judge Foote thinks that if Schlichtmann had been subject to the proposed rule, "A Civil Action" would have been a different book, or perhaps not even written. Before I could voice an objection, let alone an opinion, he told me of his proposal for a similar rule for state court judges.

He was incensed by what one writer said about one of his recent decisions. "Militant Judge Foote displayed his affinity with dishonesty by once again reaching a result he knows is contrary to law. Surgical stockings provide more support than the reasoning for his holding. Foote is at least democratic. He shows equal disdain for logic, common sense, and the Constitution." Although the remarks were made by Foote's wife, he still felt they should be prohibited.

I was prepared to support Foote's rule, but, being a judge and all, I felt I should consider the arguments against the rule. They were voiced by what Foote called "the cry babies." Some of the opposing arguments are as follows: The rule violates the First Amendment. The rule is overbroad. There is no requirement that an attorney censured under the rule be guilty of malice. The attorney may suffer the loss of his or her livelihood without the right to a jury trial. There is no way to ensure the independence of the committee which is usually comprised of lawyers who regularly appear in federal court. An attorney who actually defames a judge is better dealt with in state bar disciplinary proceedings. The rule is an affront to the public, who in a democracy expect their public officials (that includes judges) to be held up to scrutiny.

Much to Foote's chagrin, I had to admit these arguments have merit. On the other hand, no one likes to take unjustified criticism, especially judges who have no effective way of defending themselves. Maybe this troubling inconvenience just goes with the territory. But having to take abuse when there is no way to fight back is like being forced to eat your vegetables. This childhood memory calls to mind something else I learned as a child. It was a rhyme about sticks and stones. Some things are worth remembering from childhood. They keep you from acting like a child when you are an adult.

EXPRESSING THE TRUTH
PART II

Like most sensible people I hate typos. Those infuriating scoundrels march like army ants across your work wrecking havoc and destruction in their path. They try to humiliate and discredit you, but with wariness and vigilance you can defeat them. Of course now and then one or two will succeed in blending in with its surrounding like a chameleon.

As much as I detest these abominable creatures, on occasion I will deliberately drop one in the middle of my column in order to test the acuity of my readers. I did so in my last column. We discussed the proposed change in local Rule 2.52 of the U.S. District Court for the Central District. You may recall this rule prohibits attorneys from impugning the integrity of federal judges. I pointed out that the new rule places a burden on the offending attorney to prove the truth of the allegation. Two sentences later, I inserted the typo that said that the offending attorney making a degrading statement about a federal judge has to prove the statement is "untrue." The word should have been "true."

Some of you wrote me about the error. I caught the tone of smug satisfaction. I acknowledge your resourcefulness, but ask, how many believe I deliberately placed the typo in the column? What . . . not one person? You are right. Not even my mother would have believed it. The truth is that the sentence in which the typo occurred came from an earlier draft that I negligently failed to omit from the final draft.

My fib about the typo illustrates a point. We seem less willing these days to take responsibility for our actions and to admit our mistakes. Now that I have faced the truth about my mistake, I might as well admit to other such mistakes. Once I created havoc by the omission of just one little word in an opinion. The word was "not." It was supposed to go in front of the word "guilty." On another occasion I offended someone by writing of their "bawdy" language instead of their "body" language. Once I dogged a Jack Russell terrier, typing him as an inebriated canine. I called him a Jack Daniels.

To call these gaffes "typos" treats the typo as though it has an existence independent from its creator. A person should be accountable for creating or for not catching it. Instead we bend the truth to avoid responsibility for the blunder. A common example is the so-called computer error. You were billed 14 times for a bill you paid three years ago. The letter from the company that has relentlessly dunned you finally concedes there was a mistake but explains it was "computer error." The implication is that it is not the company's fault. Perhaps the computer was distracted with worries about its future after the year 2000. The truth is that the computer error was a person error. Someone screwed up.

Bureaucrats are notorious for avoiding responsibility. A typical agency letter reads: "It was decided that your request for a license to operate a Turkish bath should be denied." Who made the decision, and why the denial?

If we will not be truthful about our mistakes, then it is unlikely we will be truthful about other things. As pianist and songwriter David Frishberg reminds us, we are living in a "Blizzard of Lies." The persuasiveness of this phenomena would have pained George Washington. "The check's in the mail." "Of course I will respect you in the morning." "Your president is not a crook." "I was not the least bit rude to defense attorney Blum." This in turn fosters cynicism and skepticism even if someone may be telling the truth. "I have never had an affair with her."

Of course the legal profession must constantly deal with perceptions about the truth. We require witnesses in legal proceedings to tell the truth, the whole truth, and nothing but the truth, but do we exact the same promise from ourselves? Do we not mold and shape the truth when we fear its sharp unyielding edge may cut into us?

Attorneys sometimes cite cases for propositions that bear about as much relation to the case as Eli Whitney to Tanqueray on the rocks. The Palsgraf rule is not limited to railway stations. We cannot find a recipe for heart patients in a Julia Childs cookbook.

Some lawyers are so eager to wiggle around the truth that they test positive for a negative pregnancy. The client is defiled when the attorney answers: "Defendant denies that he stole $500,000 from plaintiff." Actually he stole $493,000.

Attorneys argue for harmless error when the error is so harmful that the case should be on life support. And what happens when small insignificant errors accumulate like tiny flecks of paint on a pristine white canvas? When the canvas looks like a Rorschach test, does the sum total of all the individual harmless errors still equal harmless error? At what point is it disingenuous to argue that it does?

Our concern with truth and falsehood is reflected in our defamation law which punishes those who spread harmful lies. As we discussed in a previous column, one court has enacted a rule that prohibits attorneys from impugning judges. These prohibitions work in some cases, but they may also encourage reproofs by way of indirection and insidious subtlety. Take for example Mark Antony's speech to his friends, Romans and countrymen. An honorable judge may be dishonored when an attorney answers the judge's question in an unmistakable tone with the words, "with all due respect." Respect is locked in a safe deposit box.

I know of a lawyer who had a client named Justice. Mr. Justice skipped bail. When the case was called, the attorney looked around the crowded courtroom and announced to the judge that there was no Justice here.

A rule that prohibits one from degrading you may in fact facilitate the very thing you are trying to prevent.

Being truthful with ourselves about the truth may make life less complicated: no tangled webs to weave. Lawyers can be vigorous advocates for their cause and achieve more success by urging a reasonable extension of the law instead of misstating it. Cynicism wanes when telling the truth becomes habitual. Telling the truth ultimately makes us feel better, even when at first it hurts a little to do so. That is how I feel now that I have disclosed the truth about my typo. I was wrong not to catch it and was wrong not to immediately fess up to it. After all--two wrongs won't make it write. I mean . . . .

A CURRENT OFFENSE

This column written in 1998 was inspired by the conduct of two judges. One, devised a unique method to control an obstreperous criminal defendant during his trial. He was forced to wear a "stun belt." When he got out of line, the judge would nod to the bailiff, who through a remote control device, delivered volts of electricity to the belt. The other judge almost got in trouble when as a matter of conscience, he refused to follow Supreme Court precedent.

To practice ones calling with integrity is to honor it. Rigorous standards ensure rectitude. One's motto should be, "Practice no legerdemain on those who trust us." That's why I take scrupulous care in writing this column. My readers deserve no less than the unmitigated truth.

Those who use their words to dissemble are justly condemned. Stephen Glass fabricated numerous pieces for the New Republic. He fooled readers with gripping stories that grew out of his imagination. Time and CNN collaborated on what turned out to be a fanciful story about our own military forces using nerve gas on American military defectors during the Vietnam War. Patricia Smith, a well-known columnist for the Boston Globe, wrote about characters who lived within her brain, but not anywhere else.

These revelations make me doubly determined to be absolutely faithful to you in commenting on people and events. That is why I hesitate to write about events that seem stranger than fiction.

For example, I was going to write about a violation of the First Amendment by federal judges sworn to uphold the amendment. The judges were thinking of enacting a rule designed to punish lawyers who made degrading comments about them. Lawyers charged with violating the rule would have to prove the truth of the comment. I was going to suggest the rule itself would engender the very ridicule the judges were trying to avert.

But would anyone believe me? Would my readers dismiss me as another Glass? Luckily, the judges decided not to adopt the rule, and will be content to protect their dignity by disciplining lawyers who violate the State Bar's Rules of Professional Conduct.

That was a close call. No sooner did that crisis pass than I was faced with the following story, one that will strain my readers' credulity, a story that even Ripley would have hesitated to include it in his "Believe It or Not."

I was in my study musing that judges like journalists are held to high standards of accuracy. To maintain credibility and trust they must be scrupulously honest when discussing or writing about the facts and law in legal proceedings. My reflections were interrupted when I received a frantic call from Judge Learned

Foote. "Come over quick," he gasped over the phone. "The Judicial Performance Commission is after me."

I dropped everything and rushed over to his courtroom. He was in the middle of a two defendant criminal case. One of the attorneys rose from his seat. "Objection your honor," he thundered. Before he could utter another sound, Foote gave a cue to the bailiff, and 50,000 volts of electricity flowed from a "stun" belt strapped around the lawyer's waist and surged through his torso. His body jerked like a puppet doing the Lindy Hop. He moaned and slouched back in his chair. A wry smile played across Foote's lips. The other defense attorney, his face flushed with indignation, leapt up from his seat, but before he could do or say anything, Foote once again gave the cue. An inhuman shriek came from the lawyer's mouth before he slumped over the counsel table. One of the defendants yelled, "Oh no!" Foote gave the cue yet again. "I think it's time for a recess," he said thoughtfully regarding the defendant whose body twitched at three second intervals. He motioned me into chambers as he descended the bench.

His expression changed. "The Judicial Performance Commission is after me," he moaned. "I feel hunted."

"You look haunted," I replied.

"Hunted, haunted, . . . whatever. I'm in trouble."

"No wonder," I said. "Electrocuting defendants and their counsel is conduct that is . . . ."

"Oh that," he said nonchalantly. "That conduct is positive."

"Negative," I countered.

"They won't charge me for that conduct. If you can zap obstreperous defendants, you can certainly give a few jolts to their rambunctious attorneys. This promotes efficiency and protects victims' rights, principles I believe the Commission supports. "You know the motto, 'Better things through electricity.'"

"You mean chemistry."

"Chemistry, electricity, whatever . . . . I have been charged with misconduct because when ruling on a motion to dismiss, I said that the Supreme Court decision which compelled me to dismiss the case was wrong and I would not follow it."

"So you didn't dismiss the case?" I asked.

"No, I did dismiss the case, but for a different reason."

"So your statement about not following the law had no effect."

"None whatsoever. My ruling was like a swimming pool without water."

"But why did you say you would not follow the law when you could have simply dismissed the case for another reason?"

"Or come up with a reason to distinguish this case and not dismiss it at all?" Foote chimed in.

"Yes. Why, for God's sake didn't you do that?"

"Because it would have been deceitful to piously pretend to follow the law by making a facile but insignificant distinction to avoid the law."

"But had you done that, the Commission would not have touched you."

"Precisely. Be dishonest and it leaves you alone. The Commission seeks to punish candor. Judges do not just say what the law is, but on occasion say when it should change and why. This keeps our law vital and dynamic. Many dissents have become majority decisions."

"But what if you made an error?" I asked.

"Let the Court of Appeal do its work. It loves to expose errors."

"How odd that the Commission should treat errors as misconduct," I said. "The Commission is giving a strange performance."

"Is it possible that all eleven (11) members voted to proceed against you?" I asked in disbelief.

"Can't tell. They are hiding the ball."

"They certainly seemed to have pulled a boner this time."

Foote grabbed at my lapels. "You've got to write about this in your column. You've got to tell the world of this injustice."

"I don't know if anyone will believe me," I stammered. A pool of terror began to seep through my brain. "What if the Commission tries to silence me?" I asked.

"The First Amendment lives . . . in some quarters. Others will speak out while the Commission proceeds with its hunt."

"What do you mean by hunt? Give me a hint?"

"It hunts judges who speak out; it hunts to uncover the beliefs that reside within a judge's inner house."

"One's haunt?"

Foote ignored my question but said, "The Commission is a lonely hunter."

"Had he stepped over the edge?" I wondered.

Then he began speaking again, but in a monotone. "It hunts for ways to assert its power; it hunts for reasons to invent misconduct; it hunts for judges who express unpopular points of view; it hunts for reasons to erode the judiciary's independence." He looked up at me with desperate eyes. "And I am the object of the hunt."

His heavy breathing broke the silence.

I cannot say how much time passed before I asked him, "Which hunt?"

MOLECULE MAN-A SYMBOL OF JUDICIAL IMPARTIALITY

An imposing work of art sits in front of the Roybal Federal courthouse in Los Angeles. Made of flat pieces of aluminum, four immense human figures riddled with large holes tower some 40 feet or more above us mortals. Unlike "Godzilla" or "The 50 Foot Woman," they do not threaten us.

The figures stand equidistant around a circle, facing the center so that each figure also directly faces another figure. The four figures lean forward embracing, or pushing against the one opposite it. There is force and energy in this movement. The left leg is bent at the knee and the right leg is extended behind the body with the heel raised, thus giving power to the forward movement.

This impressive piece, the work of renowned artist Jonathan Borofsky, was completed in 1991. He calls it "Molecule Man." Federal District Court Judge Robert Timlin has his own name for the piece. He calls it "Drive by Shooting." Was he influenced by the location of LAPD headquarters, Parker Center, which is just down the street? Federal District Court Judge Dickran Tevrizian, who has been an outspoken critic of other art work outside the federal courthouse, has given the piece a favorable verdict.

But how does it relate to the law? Elwood Lui, a former California Court of Appeal justice, and now a prominent attorney, thought the piece represented four men coming to a decision. A play on words took him to "foreman" as in foreman of a jury. But why call it "Molecule Man" where there are four figures?

No doubt the word "man" is to be taken in its broadest meaning, as in "a giant leap for mankind," which includes the world's population of women. But then why the word "Molecule?" I remember reading that Borofsky said he called the figure "Molecule Man" because our bodies are mostly composed of water molecules. That we are not as substantial as we perceive ourselves to be, may explain the holes in the figures.

Borofsky sees his work as representing people engaged in the act of coming together. To do so, however, requires effort as seen by the forward thrust of the figures. Indeed it is a struggle to overcome prejudice and bias, to understand other points of view, and to appreciate how similar we all are to one another despite superficial differences. Our basic water composition should remind us that we are all essentially at the same level despite our differences.

"Molecule Man" is a fitting subject for the justice system. It reminds us that in many cases compromise and understanding may help us avoid the struggle entailed in a lawsuit. It also speaks to the responsibility of judges to treat all litigants equally, with fairness and objectivity. It reminds us that we are all so fundamentally the same, that equality of treatment necessarily must follow.

The figures also represent the effort that judges must expend to resolve the issues in a lawsuit through the fair and dispassionate application of the law to the facts. But judicial decisions, which often involve controversial issues, are not always popular with all segments of the public. That is why it is so vital that judges not be subject to the ephemeral whim of evanescent public opinion.

Federal judges do not have to run for re-election. They decide cases free from political pressure. An organized group may not vote a federal judge out of office because of an unpopular decision. Unfortunately that is not the case with state judges. They also decide cases free from political pressure, but an unpopular decision can mobilize voters to oust the judge at election time.

The struggle for justice symbolized by the Molecule Man is weakened when judicial impartiality is so threatened. That is not to say that anyone may not legitimately argue about the wisdom of a particular decision. But the preservation of our great judicial system depends on our judges being able to pursue the struggle for justice free from partisan attack.

Whether subject to election or not, we must judge our judges with the same degree of fairness and objectivity that we expect of them.

To subject judges to organized attacks because of a single decision saps our judiciary of the vitality it needs to protect our democracy. That is when The Molecule Man weeps.

RUNNING IN PLACE FOR ELECTION

I wrote this column in November 1998, the day before the voters decided whether or not I should be retained in office for another 12 years. That accounts for the uncertain first sentence.

This may be my last column. Tomorrow is the election. The voters will decide whether to return me and a host of other Court of Appeal justices and four Supreme Court justices to office. All of these judges have served the state well. The remarkably high quality of their work, their competence, and their integrity speaks to why they should be returned to office.

But what if the voters, the vast majority of whom have no idea what the Court of Appeal does, decide for whatever reason, they have had enough of Gilbert. Then what? Would I still write the column? I don't think so. What would the Daily Journal put in the box at the bottom of column left-- Gilbert, an ex-Court of Appeal justice rejected and turned out of office by the voters, writes a monthly column for the paper? My nephew said it best in his generation's pithy jargon-- "Not."

Contrary to popular belief, victory is not necessarily assured in a judicial retention election. Judges no longer enjoy the respect that once accompanied their title. A justice has even less prestige. A few months ago I performed a wedding ceremony. It was an elegant affair that took place in a large solarium that looked over a garden resplendent with flowers. During the ceremony swans mated demurely in a nearby pond, doves beat themselves against the windowpanes, and a string quartet discreetly performed a baroque repertoire. After the ceremony, the groom's best man even mentioned me in the toast. "I want to thank the Justice of the Peace for his memorable ceremony."

If people do not know who we are or what we do, how are they going to know whether to vote for us? I was at a party recently. The host introduced me to one of the guests, Reb Sheldon. He urged Reb to vote for me in the upcoming election. Over his tentative handshake, Reb asked me in a tone that betrayed a trace of belligerence, "What is your philosophy?"

Drawing upon my undergraduate past, I opined that in the certain circumstances, Kirkegaard's teleological suspension of the ethical would be appropriate.

"I want to know about your judicial philosophy," he said. The Robert Bork hearings flashed through my mind. People were more concerned with his pronouncements about his judicial philosophy than with the judicial opinions he wrote on the D.C. circuit.

"You mean your vote depends on the few words I utter about judicial philosophy?" I asked.

"How else can I make a decision?"

He had a point. Although my judicial philosophy is reflected in my judicial opinions, it is not realistic to expect Reb to go to the law library and read my opinions and those of all the other justices on the ballot.

When I told him I could not adequately articulate my judicial philosophy in a few phrases, he said he would consult his lawyer. I assumed he was not suing me but, doing what many people do, asking their lawyer's views about the judges on the ballot.

But what about people who don't have lawyers to consult? Some will not vote on the theory that with no knowledge or information, abstention is the best policy. That approach, however, gives a more powerful voice to those who vote "no" for the wrong reasons, e.g., disaffection with government, suspicion about an unusual name, or anger over the result, not the reasoning in a single case.

Unfortunately, television and movies give most people their only impression of judges. Often they see the trial judge as a martinet, excoriating some poor defendant or his attorney. But what about justices? I'd like to see a legal show that realistically portrays them. "Court of Appeal," the T.V. show, would not be an Andy Wharhol piece merely showing a justice sitting at her desk thinking for an hour. It would be more like public television's famous series imported from Great Britain, "Upstairs Downstairs." Tension-filled episodes probing the intrigues and machinations that take place between justices and research attorneys would have viewers on the edge of their seats. The lobbying and negotiations to change a word here, add a comma there to achieve a subtle nuance, could be the stuff of gripping drama.

But even if the public has a favorable view of judges, a judge running for office has to be careful not to offend anyone or create a bad impression. Recently I pulled a hamstring muscle which brought a halt to my daily running regimen. The doctor prescribed a stationary bike as an alternative. I thought of joining the local Y in my neighborhood. It's a small facility with a few stationary bikes. I dropped by and the young lady behind the desk looked up from her computer and gave me an application. "Could I try the bike for a few minutes?" I asked. "Of course," was her reply. I tried the bike for about five minutes. It seemed O.K. I came by a few times during the next few weeks to see when there would be the fewest people. Each time she saw me she would smile or waive. A friend who was a member suggested I do a full workout before making the commitment to join. That way I would know whether a long workout on the bike would aggravate my hamstring. Great idea. I went back early one morning and asked her if I could do a full workout. The friendly face suddenly turned to a scowl. "You have been back here several times using the equipment free of charge. I cannot permit you to do this any longer."

332

I tried to explain that she was mistaken. Although I had been by several times, I had only used the equipment once for about 5 minutes. Her face hardened and the smiling eyes narrowed, then hardened. "You may not use the equipment unless you join," was her final reply. She was like a judge cutting off argument. A patron in her gym clothes, who had overheard the exchange, said "You heard her." The choice was to pay up or get out, but I didn't have my checkbook. In milliseconds I assessed the situation. Leave with a snide retort, or just leave, and, if possible, muster a smile. The Navajo motto "Better to understand than be understood" moved across my mind like words on a computer's screen saver. But at that moment my emotional state prevented me from grasping the profound wisdom of that apothegm. If there had not been an election looming on the horizon, I might have opted for a harangue. Instead, I smiled, weakly, and left sans riposte.

I was relieved that I had not given her my name. If she saw it on the ballot, that would surely mean a "No" vote. But what if she uses her computer to log onto the internet and she sees my picture next to my profile on one of the judicial websites? When you are not understood, it is hard to run for office, even when you have no opponent.

THE PAST IS NOT PAST

This column was written in 1997 when many of President Clinton's judicial appointees were rejected by the Senate Judiciary Committee. At that time I was my division's Acting Presiding Justice.

"If I shall be condemned upon surmises-all proofs sleeping else, but what your jealousies awake-I tell you tis rigour, and not law."

Winter's Tale III ii.

"I'll see their trial first. Bring in the evidence. Thou robed man of justice, take thy place."

King Lear III vi.

"Listen to you? No more. I must know the truth."

Oedipus The King.

I've been reciting lines from my favorite plays. Helps me stay in shape as **Acting** Presiding Justice of my division of the Court of Appeal.

My new post requires me to admonish attorneys who act out during oral argument. On occasion I may entertain a motion with a soliloquy or two.

My advancement came about as a result of recent legislation that increased the number of judges in my division from three to four. A panel of three judges sits on any case. On those panels in which our Presiding Justice Stone does not sit, I serve as the Acting Presiding Judge.

There was an attempt in some quarters to make my position subject to confirmation by the United States Senate Judiciary Committee. Apparently there were questions about a typo in a column I wrote back in 1988. I tried to explain that I was writing about harmless error, not harmless terror. I asserted state's rights and the Senate dropped the matter.

The situation is different for my colleague Judge Learned Foote. He is pursuing a nomination to the federal bench. He has strong support from attorneys who practice in the state court system and who have suffered, I mean, appeared before him. He is worried, however, about how the Senate Judiciary Committee might view the title of an article he wrote ten years ago, *"The Triple Threat of Double Jeopardy."*

I suggested he seek the advice of an old friend who has graced this column in the past with her sage advice, the quite elderly Anne Thrope. Her ability to unravel legal Gordian knots is legendary. You may recall she comes from a different era and prefers the quaint prefix, "Miss" before her name. I have chided her about this anachronism, but she responds that the appellation "Miss" refers to the Mississippi river for which she has a compelling affinity. "That old river and I, we just keep rolling along," she says glancing down at her hands.

Despite her age, failing eye sight, and bird-like frame, her mind is as keen, her judgment as acute as it was when she dined with Oliver Wendell Holmes and chastised him for stating "Three generations of imbeciles are enough." See *Buck* v. *Bell* (1927) 274 U.S. 200. Incidentally, Holmes fell madly in love with her and wrote her dozens of love letters. Miss Thrope authorized her estate to publish the letters on her death. Her physicians, having determined by majority vote that she still lives, the publication date is postponed.

Much like Lou Salomé, the German writer whose powerful intellect and sexuality drove philosopher Nietzsche and poet Rilke wild with desire, Thrope had a similar effect on the legal Titans of her day. It is reputed that the inveterate bachelor, Benjamin Cardozo, proposed to her. He reluctantly withdrew his proposal when he discovered she was not Jewish.

Foote wrote to Miss Thrope. What follows is their short correspondence. "Dear Miss Anne Thrope,

I seek an appointment to the federal district court. Should my name be placed in nomination, I fear the Senate Judiciary Committee may not recommend my confirmation because of the views I expressed in an article many years ago. What should I do? Yours, Judge L. Foote."
Miss Anne replied: "Dear Judge Foote,

For those who wish to step up the judicial ladder, a closed mouth keeps the foot out. If you do not secure a judgeship then run for Senate and get even. I need some rest now. Sincerely, Miss Anne Thrope."

A few days later, after she had sufficiently rested, I spoke with Miss Anne over the telephone about her advice. I was concerned that her approach would guarantee a mediocre judiciary. She countered that her advice had not been sought about achieving a superior judiciary, but about how best to achieve confirmation. She sounded tired. Before I could respond, she said something that sounded like "Links of pork . . . go round and round." What in fact she had said, I learned some time later, was . . . "Think of Bork" to which she added the surprisingly contemporary phrase, "what goes around comes around." She hung up.

I think Miss Anne was telling me that Robert Bork's nomination to the Supreme Court should have been confirmed. He was a professor, Solicitor General, and judge on the U.S. Court of Appeals for the District of Columbia Circuit. True, his past articles on constitutional interpretation reflect a radical departure from conventional thought at the time of his nomination. So what? They were provocative and challenging and fostered healthy debate and discussion. In his controversial article for the Indiana Law Journal in 1971, *Neutral Principles and some First Amendment Problems*, he cautioned that the article was "theoretical, tentative, and speculative." (See *The Tempting of America*, Robert H. Bork (1990) pg. 333, Simon and Shuster.)

Perhaps Miss Thrope, like me, did not agree with his view of the Constitution, nor with some of the decisions he rendered on the Court of Appeals. Nevertheless his opinions were well crafted, well reasoned and respected precedent. He and Judge Scalia voted the same way 98 percent of the time while both sat on that court. However one views Judge Bork's opinions, he is undeniably as qualified as Judge Scalia to sit on the Supreme Court.

Miss Thrope was suggesting that Bork's rejection by the Senate Judiciary Committee may have contributed to an insidious trend. For strictly political reasons, some members of the Committee are engaging in shameful and mean spirited attacks on qualified nominees to the federal judiciary. This can lead to an erosion of a competent judiciary. Ciphers, who lack either the courage or the intellect to express an opinion, have the best chance of confirmation.

Judge Bork has written that "[F]ederal judges are not appointed to decide cases according to the latest opinion polls. They are appointed to decide cases impartially according to law. But when judicial nominees are treated like political candidates the effect will be to chill the climate in which judicial deliberations take place, to erode public confidence in the impartiality of our judges, and to endanger the independence of the judiciary." (*The Tempting of America*, pp. 313-314.)

It is ironic and unfortunate that Judge Bork has ignored this wisdom of his own insight. He recently endorsed a fundraising letter for a conservative organization that seeks to block President Clinton's appointment of so-called "activist liberal judges." This organization uses the same campaign of distortion and falsehood that Bork asserted was used against him during his confirmation hearings. (Apparently activist conservative judges are acceptable.)

No doubt Bork's unfortunate experience was a profound disappointment to him and his supporters. He said of the campaign against his nomination: "The most serious and lasting injury . . . is to the dignity and integrity of law and of public service in this country." (*The Tempting of America*, pg. 314.)

I called Miss Thrope once again and asked her if she thought that Bork and others are now seeking to make that injury a lasting one. "Could be," she said, "but tell Judge Foote not to write about it."

THE ACTIVISM OF SUPREME RESTRAINT

When something comes to an end many of us look back and make an appraisal. For example, at the end of the day--did I accomplish anything? Was I nice to my secretary? If you are considering something more substantial, like a life coming to an end, and you are Tolstoy, you would write "The Death of Ivan Illyich." An appraisal about the past millennium might be a bit superficial for a short article. Even were we to lop off a more manageable chunk of time, like the past century, and limit our appraisal to the U.S. Supreme Court during this time, our findings may be sketchy. To embark upon such a task, we need perspective. Let's step back a little. How about 2500 years to ancient Greece and the pre Socratic philosophers?

Two philosophical schools had diametrically opposing views about the nature and structure of the world. These views still dominate our thoughts today. Heraclitus believed that everything is in a perpetual state of flux. He postulated that all that endures is change. Parmenides, of Elea, on the other hand, maintained that all remains the same and that change is merely an illusion. A member of the Eleatic school, Zeno, after whom I named a cat who roomed with me in college, offered an argument to disprove change. An arrow in flight, or a runner heading from point A to point B is always at any moment at a definite point, which is a point of rest. To express this mathematically, the arrow and the runner must continually traverse half the distance remaining. Because numbers are infinite, the arrow and the runner can never reach their destinations. Taken to its logical conclusion, they can never start.

Which of the two philosophical schools of thought best describe how our courts have decided cases over the past 100 years? After careful reflection, I have arrived at a definitive conclusion. Both. Consider the debate over the legitimacy of judicial activism versus judicial restraint which has dominated the judicial landscape from the time the Constitution was first ratified. It has raged over much of the twentieth century. Have things changed during the past century, or have they remained the same? One can make a plausible argument that all or nothing has changed.

Chief Justice Charles E. Hughes who sat from 1930 to 1941 was unabashed about judicial activism. He said that the United States Constitution means what the Supreme Court says it means. Certainly, nothing in the Constitution itself specifically grants the power of judicial review to the Supreme Court. It was not until John Marshall's opinion in *Marbury v. Madison* (1803) 5 U.S. 137 that our high court asserted its right to review the constitutionality of federal legislation, and in *Fletcher v. Peck* (1810) 10 U.S. 87 it decided the constitutionality of state legislation.

In the early part of the twentieth century the Supreme Court developed the "freedom of contract" doctrine which it used to invalidate state and federal legislation designed to set minimum wages and maximum working hours of employees. The high court seemed to favor legislation that benefited business, but to reject legislation that favored workers.

In *Lochner v. New York* (1905) 198 U.S. 45, the Supreme Court invalidated a New York statute that limited employment in bakeries to 60 hours a week, and 10 hours a day. The court reasoned that the statute was an arbitrary interference with freedom of contract guaranteed by the Due Process Clause of the Fourteenth Amendment. In a famous dissent, Justice Holmes chided the majority for its unwarranted activism. He accused the majority of deciding the case upon a laissez faire economic theory. The point was so obvious that he emphasized it did not take research to show that the statute did not infringe fundamental principles. Justice Harlan's dissent stressed that the duty of the courts is to enforce legislative enactments unless beyond all question they violate the fundamental law of the Constitution. He reasoned that was not the case here.

The *Lochner* decision did not have a lasting effect. Heraclitus must have been chortling when the high court made inroads on the *Lochner* decision with *Muller v. Oregon* (1908) 208 U.S. 412. In deference to the fairer sex, which today would have caused howls of protest, the court upheld an Oregon statute that prohibited certain industries such as factories and laundries from employing women for more than 10 hours in any one day. The court relied on detailed sociological statistics offered by lawyer Louis Brandies who represented the state. In language that would have given Gloria Steinem, and Strunk and White apoplexy, the all male court rationalized "[T]hat woman's physical structure and the performance of maternal functions place her at a disadvantage in the struggle for subsistence is obvious. This is especially true when the burdens of motherhood are upon her. Even when they are not, by abundant testimony of the medical fraternity, continuance for a long time on her feet at work, repeating this from day to day, tends to cause injurious effects upon the body, and, as healthy mothers are essential to vigorous offspring, the physical well-being of women becomes an object of public interest and care in order to preserve the strength and vigor of the race."

But then the court decided *Bunting v. Oregon* (1917) 243 U.S. 426. It upheld an Oregon statute establishing a 10-hour workday for men and women because of the well-known fact that custom did not recognize a longer workday, and the legislative requirement was neither unreasonable nor arbitrary.

One can imagine what recent critics of judicial activism would have said about these cases. These critics argue that judges should decide cases based on the text of the Constitution instead of their view about what the law should be. Yet, it seems doubtful they would have agreed with Holmes' dissent in *Lockner*. Today some members of Congress have held up many of President Clinton's judicial nominations on the ground that the nominees are too liberal and would not faithfully uphold the written text of the Constitution. It calls to mind Richard Nixon's promise to the voters when running for president that he would appoint "strict constructionist" judges. The term was supposed to mean he would appoint judges who would strictly construe the Constitution. By that he meant judges who would use restraint and base their decisions on the text as it is, instead of inventing a phantom text to reach a desired result.

This was an attack on the Warren Court. Through an expansive reading of the Bill of Rights, that court greatly extended civil liberties. It gave us *Brown v. Board of Education of Topeka* (1954) 347 U.S. 483 which held that racial segregation in public schools was a violation of the Fourteenth Amendment. The term "activist" became a pejorative to describe so-called liberal jurists.

But the term also describes so-called conservatives. Our current Supreme Court, in the name of original intent has used no restraint in reawakening ancient notions of federalism. In *Alden v. Maine* (1999) 527 U.S. 706, 119 S. Ct. 2240, the court held that a state's sovereign-immunity protected it from an action in which plaintiffs sought to enforce provisions of the federal Fair Labor Standards Act. The court based its decision on the Tenth and Eleventh Amendments. The Tenth Amendment states that powers not delegated to the United States are reserved to the states. The Eleventh Amendment refers to immunity of states from lawsuits by citizens of another state. The dissent pointed out that the literal text did not prohibit suits by citizens against their own state for violations of a federal statute. For just one other example of recent activism see *United States v. Lopez* (1995) 514 U.S. 549. Justices Souter and Stevens have followed Holmes' tradition.

Getting back to pre-Socratic philosophy, some would argue that despite the past century's judicial activity, nothing has really changed, that we are back where we started. Perhaps, but sweat still soaks the runner's headband. And when that arrow leaves the archer's bow, I prefer not to be in its path.

MORE THOUGHTS ABOUT JUDICIAL ACTIVISM

Please do not call me active. It is true I get up early in the morning. To be more accurate, I crawl out of bed and stumble on the way to the bathroom, but I'm up. I fumble while getting into my running togs. I mumble while feeding the cats, and then I hit the streets for an early morning jog where on occasion I may tumble. After showering, and a quick breakfast, I have no time for Bryant Gumble.

But that is not all. I teach a course at the California Judges College and often speak at various judicial and MCLE programs, where after the question and answer period I feel humble. I also speak before bar associations and various clubs as part of my community outreach effort. I have participated in an Inns of Court program for several years. I write a monthly column for this paper, although I miss a month now and then. I am prepared for oral argument where I ask many questions, maybe too many as far as my colleagues are concerned. On occasion, I have even read advance sheets.

Call me energetic, call me vital, call me Ishmael, but like I said, please do not call me "active." Why? Because it sounds too much like "activist." No stronger term of opprobrium can be hurled at a judge other than perhaps "corrupt" or "biased." As for "despotic," "opinionated," or "arrogant," well, nobody's perfect.

The odious term "judicial activist" permeated the public consciousness when President Nixon railed against "liberal" judges and promised to appoint judges who would strictly construe the Constitution so as to reflect the original intent of the founding fathers.

The Judicial Selection Monitoring Project in Washington D.C. has a few things to say about judicial activism. I know nothing about the project other than to have seen its views expressed on the Internet-click. The project does not hold activist judges in high repute. Restrained judges "take the law as it is," but activist judges "make up the law as they go along." Activist judges "rewrite statutes or the Constitution," and "ignore limits on their power in the search for desirable results"-click.

Sounds pretty disreputable to me. Most judges eschew the "activist" epithet and would swear under oath that they are not now, nor ever have been, nor ever intend to be a judicial activist. New judges, in particular, disavow an affinity with any kind of activism.

I hear that view expressed at The California Judges College, sponsored by the Center for Judicial Education and Research (CJER). The college offers a wide variety of courses for new trial judges. In a course I teach, I ask judges to decide a case based on *Riggs v. Palmer* (1889) 115 N.Y. 506, 22 N.E. 188. This is a case often

343

taught in law school and used by legal scholar, Ronald Dworkin, to illustrate how judges decide cases.

The facts derived from *Riggs* are as follows: The testator's grandson is a beneficiary in his will. The grandson poisons his grandfather. Grandson is convicted for the murder of his grandfather. Yet grandson has the chutzpah to claim his inheritance in the probate court.

The Probate Code states that the court shall distribute the property of a deceased testator in accordance with the testator's wishes as expressed in his or her will. There is no statute that says anything about a beneficiary not taking under the will if he kills the testator.

How would you decide the case? Probably the same as most of the judges in the class: scumbag grandson takes zilch. Rhetorically, one might ask: How could you decide otherwise? Some argue that a judge who decides otherwise should look for another job.

Most of the judges who would decide against the grandson profess a strong affinity for the principle of judicial restraint. But are not these judges ignoring limits on their judicial power and re-writing the probate statute to achieve a result they want? Is not their decision a flagrant example of judicial activism? Dworkin argues no. The decision to deny the grandson his claim reflects a legitimate exercise of judicial power. It takes into account ethical principles of the same society in which legal rules exist. I wonder whether the Judicial Selection Monitoring Project would accept this view.

But even worse than reckless judges who play fast and loose with statutes to get the result they want are the brazen ones who impose their remedies for society's ills by conjuring up words from the Constitution.

A judge I know decried in a speech what she called "Judge-Militants." They are those presumptuous judges who seek to solve society's problems "by constitutionalizing everything possible, citing constitutional rights which are nowhere mentioned in the Constitution." She cited *Brown v. Board of Education*, the 1954 school desegregation case as a "philosophical turning point" leading to a downward slide from judicial self-restraint to militant activism.

The judge's comments conjured up in my mind bands of guerilla judge militants, lurking in the darkness of the penumbra where the written word cannot be seen. With suddenness they spring from the shadows and strike with decisions that respect neither the text of the Constitution nor the principle of judicial restraint.

The recent United States Supreme court decision, *Alden v. Maine* (1999) 527 U.S. 706, 119 S.Ct. 2240 illustrates the alarming trend Justice Brown warned us about. The high court held that a state's sovereign immunity protected it from a lawsuit brought by probation officers seeking overtime pay under the federal Fair Labor Standards Act. The majority found support for its position in the Tenth and

Eleventh Amendments to the Constitution. The dissent pointed out, among other things, no language in either amendment nor elsewhere in the Constitution permits such a construction. The Eleventh Amendment refers to immunity of states from suits brought by citizens of another state, not the same state. The Tenth Amendment tells us that powers not delegated to the United States by the Constitution, nor prohibited to the states, are reserved to the states.

It seems as though the majority rewrote the Constitution to deprive citizens of remedies they might have against their state governments for violations of federal statutes. The decision allows states to violate, for example, The Americans with Disabilities Act. In short, the *Alden* decision has reinstated ancient notions of federalism and given the state primacy over the rights of its citizens. Could *Brown v. Board of Education* have led to this?

Maybe so. In the words of Chief Justice Charles Evan Hughes, "The Constitution is what the judges say it is." To that I would add-"even when it does not say anything."

Get ready for a true or false question. First the facts. These comments are spoken by a judge in court proceedings. "Sir, one of us is an idiot, and I know it's not me. On my dumbest day, I am smarter than you on your smartest day." To a lady who has kids from four different husbands, "Madam, on Father's Day your home is going to need a revolving door." Getting the attention of a litigant, "Madam, do you see my mouth moving?" The foregoing quotes are likely to make the judge subject to discipline by the Judicial Performance Commission. True or False? If you said "true," you are right if I or any of my colleagues said them. If you said "false," you are right if Judge Judy said them. In fact, Judge Judy makes millions of dollars for saying them.

These comments are tame in our age of uninhibited candor. Openness reigns supreme for everyone----except judges, whether they be supreme or not. Real judges, the ones that sit in real courtrooms and do their best to dispense real justice, are expected to reflect qualities that by today's standards are anomalous. These include, decorum, restraint, forbearance, circumspection, and probity, all of which seem better suited to the Victorian Age.

The judge who makes a remark, however innocent, that could be construed as an insult, a bias, or simply inappropriate, could wind up in a spotlight of derision before the Judicial Performance Commission. In short, judges should not call attention to themselves, and must be careful not to say anything controversial . . . unless they preside on television. Then the rules are quite different.

UCLA Law professor Michael Asimow, in an article in the Fall 1999 edition of the Judges' Journal, a publication of the American Bar Association, has written about the blitz of daytime television judges, led by the formidable Judge Judy who dispenses her brand of justice to nearly 10 million viewers.

She often offers litigants sage advice, but on occasion, a diatribe of degrading insults pour out of her mouth like a prolonged eructation. The consequence, however, is not discipline, but a raise. With abuse comes popularity. If she acted like a real judge, in a real court of law, she would probably be off the air.

One of her competitors, the redoubtable former mayor of New York, Ed Koch, took over the bench of People's Court once occupied by the distinguished Judge Wapner. Judge Wapner's fine judicial demeanor was once acceptable to humans. His current show, Animal Court, is reputed to have a large canine audience. His successor, however, Judge Koch, has gone to the dogs. He was summarily removed from the bench by a body that makes the Judicial Performance Commission seem like pussycats in comparison, the television viewing public. Why such a harsh rebuke? Apparently he was not nasty enough. The pugnacious Mayor Koch was Bambi compared to Judge Judy.

Judge Judy, on the other hand, is so feared, and therefore so popular, that like Catherine, Hannibal, Attila and Ivan, she needs only a first name. Having reached the pinnacle of formidability, descriptions like "The Great," "The Hun," or "The Terrible," are superfluous.

Professor Asimow opines that there are a variety of reasons that account for the popularity of Judge Judy. Some of them may be the public's fascination with our justice system, and the satisfaction of seeing a quick resolution to a matter based on a sense of right instead of legal technicalities. More fundamentally, Asimow speculates that people yearn for relationships with real people. That accounts for the remarkable interest in Jenni, for example, a young woman who opens her prosaic life, 24 hours a day, to any visitor to her website at jennicam.org.

I looked up her website. I am sure she is a nice person and all, but I was compelled to agree with Professor Asimow's assessment--Jenni is boring, but not as boring as I. That is why I decided not to put my diary of an appellate justice on the web. This is a typical entry. "Got up, fed the cats, went to work. Read some briefs. Had a cup of green tea. Damn, spilled some on the brief. Oh well, I can still read over the wrinkled pages. What is that blurred word? Is that a 'not?' Wrote up a draft of the case. Not sure if it's right. Read some cases that seem on point. No, they are off point." Zzzz. Get the point?

As to daytime TV court shows, Professor Asimow thinks viewers like to see a justice system controlled by a judge, and one "that rewards good values, personal responsibility and a strong sense of right and wrong." But he understandably disapproves of Judge Judy's combative style. His advice to us real judges is that "we should always be courteous and respectful to everyone" in our courtrooms and avoid emulating Judge Judy.

Good advice, but after all, we are human beings. One has to give us a little slack. Even the patron saint of judicial ethics, retired Judge David Rothman, recognizes this point. His book is the bible of judicial ethics, "California Judicial Conduct Handbook," second edition, West (1999). If we turn to chapter I, section 52, verse 1, it is written, "Judicial personality is important to the fabric of the judicial system and it would be dangerous to that system were the judiciary to become a group of faceless bureaucrats who attempt to fit into a mold in order to stay out of trouble."

He points out that judges should not become so absorbed with issues of judicial ethics, conduct, and discipline that they lose common sense and the reality that they are human beings. Excessive pressure to adopt perfect behavior can make imperfect judges.

I have a solution to resolve this conundrum. It allows sitting judges to make all the comments they wish with impunity. Here are just two I have made in the recent past: "Sir, I cannot rate your moral quotient on a scale of one to ten, so

I'll have to use fractions." "Counsel, you asked me to entertain your motion. In fact, the motion entertained me."

The secret is simply this; I made the comments to myself. You can do the same, only be extremely careful not to mutter them under your breath. With practice you can learn to say one thing, like "thank you counsel," and say in your mind, "under what exception to the bar exam do you fall?" But whatever you do, do not, under any circumstances, tell anyone about your comments, not even your dog, even if he appears before Judge Wapner. And under no circumstances write a column. Even Judge Judy does not do that-the pay isn't all that good.

WHY JUDGES ARE DULL

The judges who criticize Judge Judy are simply jealous because she says what's on her mind with impunity. Indeed, she is rewarded for it. It is quite the opposite for the rest of us. We are not sure what to do, what to say, with whom to associate, how to respond to questions from the press, or even an acquaintance at a dinner party. We are even concerned about what we said or did years ago. Did we do the right thing or the wrong thing? No wonder judges are so dull. They are afraid if they reveal even a hint of a personality, they might get in trouble.

Like many of my colleagues, I always thought of myself as an ethical person, yet like them I have become obsessed with ethics. How did this come about? It is because there are so many new rules governing judicial ethics. It has taken us to a point where we worry about minute gradations of behavior that have nothing to do with ethics.

At least we now have a book to conduct us through this bewildering quagmire. What better title than "California Judicial Conduct Handbook" West Group (1999) by that nationally known ethics guru, David Rothman, retired Judge of the Los Angeles Superior Court. It has over 700 pages. When not reading it, you can bench press it.

It is only fitting that Judge Rothman would author such a tome. I've known him for about 47 years. At Hollywood High School where we were students, he was our moral compass, our ethics mentor. We referred to him as the Venerable Rothman, even though he was a teenager. Of course we were just callow youths. We did not realize it at the time, but our questionable conduct which invariably provoked condemnation from Dave made us better candidates for a judicial career.

I'll never forget a track meet at Hollywood High School in 1953. We were in the stands waiting for the 660 race to begin when the marching band came by. One of the members of our group, who has become a prominent and influential member of the community and shall go nameless (we have a mutual understanding), announced that he thought he just might throw his half-eaten cheeseburger into the inviting aperture of the tuba. Dave Rothman, coining a term that would later be used by Richard Nixon, said with solemnity, "But that would be wrong."

Notwithstanding the moral pronouncement, the cheeseburger sailed through the air and as though drawn by a magnet, disappeared into the gaping orifice of the tuba. As Rothman shook his decisive head in cheerless disapproval, we opined that he would attain prominence as an ethicist.

After reading Rothman's book, crammed full of rules and hypotheticals, I, much like a drowning man, saw my judicial life pass through my mind. I had to confront the past that had lain in uneasy dormancy in my unconscious. It was 1982 and the Governor had appointed me to the Court of Appeal. Even before my confirmation hearing, I was beseeched by applications from research attorneys. One of the then current staff attorneys for the Second District sent me her resume. She wanted to have lunch. I felt awkward interviewing her before the hearing, yet I wanted a staff in place when I began my new job. I set up the interview despite the embarrassment I would suffer should I not be confirmed. Was this the right thing to do?

We had lunch at an Italian restaurant on La Brea just south of San Vicente. Luckily, it no longer exists and I have forgotten its name. I can't remember who paid for the lunch. I hope we went Dutch. It could be a terrible breach of ethics if either of us picked up the check.

She brought some of her work, drafts of an opinion signed by a justice. They were in a plain unmarked envelope which she surreptitiously slipped across the table to me. Should she have done that? Should I have accepted it? If not, how could I evaluate her work? I don't recall if I read it. If I did, then what? Did we have wine with our meal? Is that appropriate at lunch hour?

While leaving, we witnessed a drama which unfolded before our eyes wide shut. We were standing in the large vestibule at the entrance to the restaurant saying our good-byes. A young man and woman passed us as they were leaving the restaurant. The young man put on his coat and as he did so a plastic baggy dropped out of his coat and onto the floor. We glanced at it. Within the bag there appeared to be oregano. The couple were out of the restaurant before I could speak.

"Looks like that gentleman dropped a bag of oregano," I said. The ethical dilemma was excruciating. What to do? Grab the bag? Run out of the restaurant and down the street to give the gentleman his bag? But what if the gentleman stole the oregano from the table? I could not remember if there were jars of oregano on the table. If he stole the oregano, would it be proper for a judicial officer to do nothing?

And then I believe, though I am not sure, that another young couple entered the restaurant. What if I saw the young man spot the bag? What if a smile played across his face, much like the smile of my cat when he spots a lizard sunning himself on the patio? If the man bends down and snatches the bag, do I reprimand him and inform him that the bag belongs to someone else?

What if I do nothing and then the original couple come back looking for the bag? What if the man asks me if I saw a bag? Do I tell him what happened? Taking into account the problems that might cause, would it be proper to say "no," or to ignore him? Can this legitimately be rationalized on the premise that loss of the bag serves him right for being so careless? Could I have avoided all this by simply not agreeing to meet the research attorney for lunch?

What if this troubling incident is just some terrible April Fool's joke? If it is, would that depreciate the serious subject of judicial ethics and itself be a breach of judicial ethics? And if Judge Judy had witnessed the drama I have related, what would she have done? I can just imagine. She probably would have grabbed the bag when it was first dropped and said, "Sir, if you are such a nitwit to carry around a bag of oregano and drop it in public, your stupidity should not go unrewarded. You deserve everything you get." On the other hand, she might have kept her mouth shut. After all she would not have been on the bench at the time.

NOT A DROP TO DRINK

Almost daily I am asked about being a P.J. How does it feel? What does it mean? How are you bearing up under the weight of this mighty responsibility?

In the daytime it stands for Presiding Justice, as in "Where is the P.J.?" In the evening (and in my youth), it stands for pajamas, as in "Where are my P.J.'s?" In my college days there was a famous night spot in West Hollywood called P.J.'s, as in "Let's fall by P.J.'s and catch the Eddy Cano trio." (No one says "fall by") anymore. Apparently they do not use the word "go" to mean go somewhere. For my nephew and his girlfriend, and innumerable other teenagers, "go" has come to mean "says" as in "so he goes, wanna cruise with me?" "and I go, no way, so he goes . . . ." Incidentally, speaking of my nephew's girlfriend, her name is "P.J." Ask her what it means and she tells you or "goes," without a trace of self-consciousness, "Precious Jewel."

But to be frank, P.J. as in Presiding Justice, does not rank higher much higher than pajamas. Presiding Justice Mildred Lillie summed it up best when she described the power of a P.J.: "It is like being in charge of a cemetery. You have a lot of people under you, but nobody listens."

Of course, there are administrative duties that include budget and personnel matters, deciding motions, presiding over oral argument, and dealing with the bottled water company. Actually that last matter is usually handled by the Clerk of the Court, unless the P.J. foolishly intrudes in an area where he or she would do best to stay out of it.

It all happened when I went down the hall for my morning cup of green tea. Made from the plant Camellia Sinensis, green tea, according to leading health authorities, arms us with antioxidants, those brave soldiers defending the body from the scourge of enemy molecules known as free radicals. Eager to savor the warm refreshing stimulation from a fragrant cup of steaming hot green tea on the dawn of a new day, I approached the water cooler with eager anticipation. Before my hand reached the hot water spigot, I saw that the cooler lacked its 5-gallon bottle of water. On the floor, stacked around the headless water cooler, were four or five empty water bottles.

The water had not been delivered because the water company was under the misimpression that we had not paid our water bill. A call to the company from our clerk revealed that the company's "computer had made an error." "When would the water be delivered?" inquired the clerk. "Tomorrow," said the clipped voice of the water representative over the phone. "We want the water now," said the clerk. "We can't do it now," said the water representative, who offered no explanation why we did not receive a call before our water delivery was discontinued. What's a P.J. to do? The entire court was without bottled water. We could not use tap water, not with the President's decision not to reduce levels of arsenic in our drinking water.

I instructed the clerk to call the water company back and tell them if the water were not here in one-half hour, to cancel our order. The clerk spoke to the district manager, who acknowledged the company's mistake but offered what at best was a perfunctory apology and informed him that the water could not be delivered until some time tomorrow. The clerk, following my instructions, said, "We get the water in half an hour or we cancel." The district manager said, "Fine, cancel." We did.

But now we had no water, not today or tomorrow. The parched staff wandered up and down the halls with vacant stares softly murmuring "water." A research attorney shouted, "The Supreme Court cited us with approval and praised us in a written opinion!" Poor devil; it was a mirage. Someone had piped through our sound system the recording of the Sons of the Pioneers, singing "Water, Cool Clear Water."

As P.J. I had to do something. I asked the clerk to call another water company. Sure, they could get bottled water to us--within a day or two. The same story with other water companies. By now nearly all members of the staff were dehydrated. Their sad anxious eyes became accusing and said with a silent plea, "You are the P.J., do something." I became aware that leaders must take action. Here was a problem I did not create, yet as P.J. I had to provide an immediate solution.

The electrifying ring of the telephone distracted me from my desperation. It was the regional manger of the water company. He was the boss of the district manager who had, pardon the expression, "blown us out of the water." He wanted to come over and talk to me. My desperation gave way to rigidity. "Too late for talk now," I said. Staff, like a Greek chorus, chimed in, "Do not let the powerful snake pride tighten its coils around your soul. Speak to the regional manager." "Let him drown," I said from my sand dune in the desert. But the troops, distraught and near mutiny, implored me to reconsider. The clerk tactfully suggested that perhaps there was no harm in hearing what the man had to say.

I relented. As P.J. I had to consider the mood and the desires of the staff (within reason). The regional manager arrived within 15 minutes. I let him tread water in the clerk's office for a minute or two. The clerk then ushered him into my chambers. The manager and I shook hands. I complained about the district manager. The regional manager wanted to talk. I asked for a time estimate. The clerk reminded me that we were not in session. I let the regional manager speak. He was contrite. I was civil. He offered me a small bottle of drinking water. Concerned about the appearance of impropriety, I refused. Besides, it wouldn't do for hot tea.

He promised to deliver to us water within an hour. We both agreed the district manager, his brother-in-law, was a half-wit. With the promise that the district manager would not get fired, but would receive training in customer relations, we shook hands and he left.

The water arrived within an hour as he promised. That evening, in my P.J.'s, and in the company of my nephew and his girlfriend, P.J., I sipped a soothing cup of green tea, and mused on the vicissitudes that accompany the administrative responsibilities of a P.J. Should such a problem present itself again, would I handle it any differently? I savored the aroma of the tea and took another sip and concluded-- next time let the clerk handle it.

"GETTING IT"

My wife confronted me at breakfast the other morning. "Last night I had a nightmare," she said. "I dreamed I was you."

"I must have been sleeping too soundly to hear the screams," I replied.

She ignored my sarcasm. "Yes," she went on, "I was you, robes and all."

"I hardly think that is something to be upset . . . ." "Overruled," was her peremptory reply.

"Wait a second," I protested.

"Your objection is noted for the record," she said.

"What record?" I asked. "We are in the kitchen."

"Please don't argue with the court," she said.

"Argue with the court?"

"I believe I have heard sufficient argument on the matter. Thank you counsel . . . and would you please take out the garbage."

"Well, we are at least back to normal," I said. "Dreaming that you are me is not all that . . . ."

She interrupted me again. "You don't get it."

That got me. It is not easy for a judge to be overruled, but for a judge to be told "you don't get it," is devastating. While taking out the garbage I tried to "get it." I took a short walk in the hope that the fresh air would help me "get it." I ran into my favorite neighborhood dog, George, a Corgi mix, according to Marie, his unapologetically biased owner. George showed his enthusiasm by running here and there in irregular circles. I picked up a stick for George to fetch. "Don't waste your time. He won't get it," said Marie. "That makes two of us," I said throwing the stick and urging George to get it. He didn't get it. He did, however, slobber on my pants. I didn't mind. Dogs have a soothing influence. More neighborhood dogs with their people in tow came up and George turned his attention to the other dogs. Everyone, the people and the dogs, were friendly and, like George, I no longer cared whether I got it.

I came back home and asked my wife to explain what I didn't get. "Oh nothing," she said. "I was only teasing. A little chiding is good for people who wield power." "But I wield no power here," I protested, trying to think where I did wield it. "Thank goodness for that," she said, giving me a kiss. I didn't get it. But when I mulled over my sensitivity to the issue, I got it.

Everyone wants to "get it." Getting it has an existential quality to it. If you don't get it you hardly exist. When I was a kid we played a cruel joke about getting it. A group of us would be in on the joke with the exception of the unsuspecting victim. One person would tell an alleged joke. It would be a pointless story which ended with a sham punch line such as ". . . suddenly the polar bear yelled 'radio.'"

Everyone would laugh, showing they all got the "joke." If the person who was not in on the "joke" laughed, he or she was asked to explain the joke. Gulp!

I fessed up to not getting a number of jokes. The only trouble was I never knew whether I was the victim of the game or whether I was being told a real joke.

"Getting it" is crucial to the essence of judging, and that is no joke. Lawyers present their case to the judge in the hopes that the judge gets it. The judge then issues a decision or an opinion in the hope that the lawyers, litigants and the public get it. It is no wonder that judges like their decisions to be regarded as "right," or better yet "right on." That is far better than "wrong" or "wrong headed." But these latter epithets are innocuous in comparison to "not getting it." One can be wrong and still "get it." But it is hard to say what is worse, being wrong and "not getting it," or being right and "not getting it." Such an anomaly occurs when the result is right, but the reasoning questionable or even missing in action.

In either event, short of granting review, our Supreme Court has an oblique way of declaring that the author of a published opinion doesn't get it. It simply depublishes the opinion. The authors of such opinions who feel they do "get it" might take solace in the holding of *Anastasoff v. United States*, 223 F3d 898 (2000) where the Eighth Circuit Court of Appeals held that its rule that declares unpublished opinions are not precedent is unconstitutional because it expands judicial power beyond the bounds of Article III of the United States Constitution. Nevertheless, the practice of depublication is likely to continue, although it is used more sparingly than in the past.

Of course "getting it" is all a matter of opinion. Some would argue that *Bush* v. *Gore* is an example of the United States Supreme Court, or at least certain members of the court, not getting it, or truly getting it, just as others would say the same about the Florida Supreme Court. However subjective the notion of "getting it," I bristle whenever I hear a judge criticized for not "getting it."

I was with some friends and their daughter, a recent law school graduate now working for a prestigious appellate firm. She was greeted by a fellow graduate, a young man also dining at the restaurant. He came over to the table to say hello then gave us his unsolicited critique of judges, distinguishing them geographically.

"The Southern California judges get it," he said, but not those in Northern California." Although I fit into the Southern California category, I resented his aspersions on my northern colleagues. It occurred to me he must be losing all his cases in Northern California. "Getting it" is not only subjective, it can also form the basis for a way of life. The partners in a Los Angeles law firm engage in karate workouts to toughen themselves for courtroom battles. To make partner you have to jump out of a plane. I thought it was more important to have billable hours. The firm partners might respond that I just don't get it. So would retired Supreme Court

Justice Armand Arabian who as a paratrooper has jumped out of planes all over the world.

Then there are the opposing attorneys in depositions mentioned in *Tylo v. Superior Court*, 55 Cal.App.4th 1379 (1997), one telling the other that she doesn't get it. Their exchange would be out of place in a Jane Austen novel.

"Where are you going with this?"

"If you don't know your case, I am not going to give you my theory of the case."

"Don't raise your voice."

"I resent the fact you're telling me I don't know my case."

"You don't."

In fact she did because the Court of Appeal upheld her contentions.

Because our work is not a joke, we lawyers and judges should not be concerned about "getting it." Instead, we should do our work the best way we know how. We should give due respect to opposing points of view and avoid the pride of certainty. We should arrive at our conclusions with the recognition they may be colored by inborn prejudices and biases. In this way we enhance the stature of our profession and the quality of our lives. Get it?

A NEW REALITY SHOW

"A wonderful thing happened after the second episode of the reality series, *The Law Firm*, aired a few months ago---it was cancelled."

This is the opening sentence of a review written by my decrepit friend the ever ancient Anne Thrope. Miss Anne, as she likes to be called, once worked as a ghost writer, I mean staff attorney for the United States Supreme Court. Perhaps this is apocryphal, but she is reputed to have chastised Justice Taney for his infamous Dred Scott decision. From time to time I have called upon Miss Anne, when she is alert, to contribute to my column. Her decades of experience make her uniquely qualified to offer advice to troubled attorneys and judges. And that has been her primary contribution in the past.

But astute reader that you are, you have accurately perceived that today's column is not of that genre. And no doubt you are asking yourself why I simply did not write the review myself. The simple answer is that I have a near pathological aversion to "reality" shows. Most of these shows highlight the baser human characteristics: duplicity, mendacity, envy, betrayal, corruption, anger, and calumny, to name a few. Yes, these traits are not imaginary, but I think that portraying them as the salient characteristics of human nature skews reality.

My bias would surely hinder my writing a balanced review of *The Law Firm*. True, columnists are expected to express their views, but my distaste for this genre could distort my account of the show to as much a degree as I believed the show skewed its portrayal of the legal system. So I turned to my old pal Miss Anne to enlighten my readers.

This is what follows Miss Anne's unequivocal opening sentence:

"Rumor has it that subsequent shows already taped will be shown on NBC's cable channel Bravo. Hardly an apt term to characterize the series. There isn't a 'Boo' Channel is there? If watching tyro lawyers stumbling over their irrelevant questions to parties with frivolous lawsuits is what legal practice has come to, then Dickens was right. It is not just the law that is 'a ass,' but so are we for watching the degradation of a grand profession. To think my caregiver awakened me from a sound stupor to watch the entire show. This was a sacrifice for which this reviewer deserves commendation.

"Describing the show from A, 'awful and atrocious' to Y, had to stop at Y, there are no derogatory words beginning in Z, except maybe zombie, which is what I felt like after watching the show. Y gives us 'Yahoo,' 'yikes,' and 'yuck.'

"The senior partner of the firm, the famous litigator and TV analyst Roy Black is, I mean was, the senior partner of the firm. He oversees a bevy of newly admitted lawyers who divide into teams to litigate 'real' cases with 'real' clients presided over by 'real' judges, retired judges that is. A clause in their contract said,

'WARNING-APPEARANCE ON THIS SHOW MAY BE DETRIMENTAL TO PRIVATE JUDGING CAREERS.'

"It is rumored that in one episode, not aired, the legendary Judge Broadman, known for his unorthodox sentences in criminal cases, issued a unique ruling in a civil case. He ordered the CEO of a corporation who had defrauded the shareholders to wear a Norplant device for life. Broadman reasoned it would be detrimental to society should the CEO pass on to her offspring a genetic disposition for dishonesty.

"I wonder how the judges recruited for the show were conned, I mean induced to participate in this series designed to reveal how brand new lawyers prepare for cases that go to trial. That should have big audience appeal. Already I was suspicious. What law firm would allow newly born lawyers in shell shock from the bar examination to actually try a case? The malpractice premiums alone could lead to bankruptcy.

"Like other reality shows, this one caters to the audience's desire to see someone sacrificed, destroyed, humiliated or ruined, a sport the Romans carried to extremes before the fall of the empire. Are we far behind? The lawyers who screw up the most are told to turn in their Westlaw passwords and take a one-way trip in the elevator to the lobby. No lifelines on this show.

"We see young associates in a law firm preparing for two cases. Two lawyers are on one side and two on the other. One case involves a plaintiff suing his ex-friend for putting up a gag 'wanted' poster in his small convenience store where most patrons know plaintiff. The poster accuses plaintiff of belonging to a terrorist organization called 'EAT ME.' The poster is so obviously a bad joke that even George Bush wouldn't have sent this plaintiff to Guantanamo. The young associates interview witnesses and prepare for trial. They disparage their opponents and focus on weaknesses in their personalities. Mmmm, maybe it is like real life. Defendant lawyers lose the case and the trial judge, in an outburst of creativity, threatens to impose punitive damages on defendant if he doesn't immediately apologize to the plaintiff. Forget that punitive damages were not pled or prayed for. Even Judge Judy would have second thoughts about doing this.

"Another case involves arbitration. A savvy, business oriented dominatrix sues the person she hired to create her website. The distinguished and unflappable Judge Dion Morrow sensibly rules that the contract is too vague to be enforceable. The losing attorney utters a profanity and storms out of the office. Well, I guess that's real. No contempt powers for arbitrators.

"During the post-mortem back at the law firm, senior partner Black offers valid insights into trial advocacy. He excoriates the rude attorney at the arbitration and then fires the defendant's lawyers in the 'terrorist threat' lawsuit. Camera follows the out-of-work lawyers to the elevator which for them goes only one way.

"Why couldn't *The Law Firm* be uplifting like the one reality show I adore, 'Dancing with the Stars.' A television personality teams up with a professional dancer and competes with another similar team in a variety of dances that are judged by a trio of choreographers. Their votes are only advisory. Viewers call in and vote for the winner. The winner's prize goes to charity. Yes, there are winners and losers, but only in a tongue-in-cheek way. The contestants do not slander or excoriate each other. They are working to develop a skill that requires hours of commitment, practice, facility, and grace. The pithy comments from the judges give the viewer some insight into the complexity and artistry of the enterprise. With the exception of Dancing with the Stars, I say, down with reality shows. They lack authenticity. Yours truly, Miss Anne Thrope"

I don't agree with all of Miss Anne's comments, but I did watch Dancing with the Stars, and was cha cha cha-ing all through the house. Despite my aversion to reality shows, I must acknowledge they are a part of our culture, and . . . O.K. I have this idea for a reality show. I call it "*The Appointment*."

A group of seasoned lawyers (that leaves out those rejected from "*The Law Firm*) wish to be appointed to a single opening on the trial bench. They are put through a series of grueling tests. First they have to fill out an application. This is problematic for a busy practitioner who will have to block out a chunk of time to complete this task, say maybe three or four months. Imagine being such a lawyer. It can be disheartening to dredge up cases from decades past and list opposing counsel, particularly the ones you defeated who threatened revenge no matter what. Groups of evaluators, many of whom are anonymous, pour over your life as though you were an ex-union organizer applying for work at Wal-Mart.

You drum up support from people who may have to appear before you in the event you are selected. One is your opponent in a hotly contested business case. He wants a continuance, but your client is unalterably opposed to it. Hundreds of questionnaires are sent to people who like you, people who hate you, people who don't know you, and people who are your competitors also seeking to become the judge you want to be. And you receive questionnaires about your competitors. Do you cut a deal with them? A good or average review in exchange for a similar review from them? If you make such a deal, how do you know they will live up to the bargain? Whatever you say about them, do you believe it? Is this ethical behavior for anyone let alone a judge? Should you even consider such disgraceful conduct? Who will know? But that is not the point- or is it?

This show has all the ingredients of a top selling reality show. The participants are made to open up and reveal their lives with all their insecurities, ambitions, fears, weaknesses and strengths. Only one will get the appointment. Who will it be? I thought this show would be a winner, but someone told me there is already one like it—Survivor.

Be prepared to answer a question, but first here are the facts:

Stanley Williams, a.k.a. "Tookie," murdered the employee of a 7-11 store in Los Angeles. He and his friends then took $120 from the cash register. A few weeks later, Williams shot and killed the owner of a motel, his wife and their daughter. He took $50 from the cash drawer. Williams was tried, convicted and sentenced to death for these crimes. What followed were a series of appeals and writ proceedings in state and federal courts. The myriad issues raised in his latest federal habeas writ petition are discussed at length in the 9th Circuit's 60-page opinion affirming the district court's denial of his habeas corpus petition. You can read all about it in *Williams. v. Woodford* (9th Cir.2002) 306 F 3d 665. Williams sits on death row waiting execution for his crimes. He is the co-founder of the Crips, the infamous gang whose name is synonymous with brutality and violence.

Now the question: What do Tookie Williams and Mother Teresa have in common? Answer: Both were nominated for the Nobel Peace Prize, only Mother Teresa received the award. But Williams was also nominated for the Nobel Prize for Literature. Can't say that about Mother Teresa.

On a recent Sunday evening, the cable channel FX aired a movie, "Redemption," starring Jamie Foxx in a stunning portrayal of Williams and his journey from ruthless killer to reflective writer and peacemaker. Such a metamorphosis sounds like the hackneyed idea of a mediocre screenwriter, only it is the truth. At first, San Quentin did not make a change in William's life; he fomented gang wars and spread terror within the prison walls much as he did on the streets of Los Angeles. After he had spent six years in solitary, another prisoner heading for execution left Williams his dictionary.

The dictionary was William's Rosetta Stone. From it he learned to put words together to express ideas, and he soon began to understand that words carry greater power than a gun, the power to do good and to change lives. With the help of journalist Barbara Becnel, who interviewed Williams for a book she was writing on street gangs, Williams wrote a series of children's books carrying a common anti-gang theme. He also wrote his own memoir, "Blue Rage, Black Redemption," which chronicles his journey from the streets of South Central L.A. to prison and "redemption." His "Tookie Protocols for Peace," which ironically carries his gang moniker, has been successful in initiating peace between warring gangs. Williams methodically set out to achieve this goal "block by block" so that neighborhoods and cities have become safer. He also has reduced violence within the prison.

His website, "Internet Project for Street Peace," allows kids at risk from different parts of the world to achieve literacy and to talk to one another to find alternatives to violence. He has become an international sensation with two Nobel nominations to his name.

The film portrays Williams as a menacing young man filled with rage and hate, now transformed into a reflective man of letters, promoting peace and working from his cell to save lives. The main off-screen character, Death, was William's servant and now it may be his master if further petitions seeking review before the U.S. Supreme Court are denied. One wishes Williams had had his dictionary long before the senseless killings that led to his conviction.

Some may see the film's focus on Williams' redemption as a dramatic argument against the death penalty. But whatever one thinks about capital punishment, the film highlights how problematic it is and the questions it raises. Williams claims his innocence, but was convicted of the crimes for which he received a death sentence. His trial counsel, Joe Ingber, is a seasoned criminal defense attorney, well-known for his extraordinary skill and competence. Both the California Supreme Court in *People v. Williams* (1998) 44 Cal.3d 1127 and the 9th Circuit (*supra*) found him to have rendered competent counsel to Williams. Ingber, also known for his wit, is reputed to have mumbled under his breath after the trial judge sentenced Williams to death for each of the four murders, "will that be consecutive or concurrent?" But for the sake of discussion let us assume Williams is in fact guilty of the offenses for which he has been convicted and accept, as we must, that the death penalty is the law in California.

Does the clamor in some quarters for commutation of Williams' sentence reflect our fascination with celebrity? You may recall the case of Jack Abbott, the convicted killer whose prison book, "Belly of the Beast," gave him credentials as an upcoming important American writer. Abbott's correspondence with Norman Mailer ultimately led the Utah Parole Board to release him on conditional parole in the employ of Mailer.

Abbott appeared on the Today show, received a contract from Random House and was written up in leading magazines. After only a few weeks out of prison, he stabbed to death a waiter in a restaurant over a dispute about use of the restroom. At his trial the prosecutor read what Abbott had written about the incident: "You have sunk the knife to its hilt into the middle of his chest. Slowly he begins to struggle for his life. You can feel his life trembling through the knife." The prosecutor asked Abbott if he had written that. Abbott replied, "It's good, isn't it?"

But a comparison between Williams and Abbott is neither apt nor fair. Williams' books are for him acts of atonement, or redemption. His work has brought real good into the world and may be credited with saving lives. The earnings for Williams' work goes to helping youth at risk, not to enriching Williams. And his supporters are apparently seeking to avoid the death penalty, not to gain his immediate release from prison. But is he deserving of special treatment because of his talent? If he lives, he arguably saves lives. But what of the death row inmates who have changed and also seek redemption yet lack Williams' talent? Are they not entitled to a commuted sentence if he is?

And what of the victims and their families and friends who seek closure? Not surprisingly, the mother of the 7-11 employee, who Williams killed more than 25 years ago, wants the ultimate sentence imposed. Prosecutors who worked on the case said that Williams should die for what he did. Writing a few children's books doesn't erase that he is a murderer. But that raises the question of whether he is still a murderer.

DNA evidence has firmly established that a large number of people have been sentenced to die for crimes they did not commit. If a person has so changed that he or she is not the same person who originally committed a crime in the past, is that like a change in one's "psychological DNA"? Is it fanciful to conclude that the person we execute today is not the same person who committed horrendous crimes more than 25 years ago?

Williams says, "In order for me to experience redemption, I had to first develop a conscience . . . . That enabled me to gradually rectify my many faults...only then was I able to reach out to others and make amends." Psychologists tell us that conscience is learned. But if Williams is a different individual than the one who mindlessly killed his defenseless victims many years ago, should that matter? The prosecutor argues that Williams committed the murders and he should receive the punishment the law allows for those crimes.

[So does Sue Blake, public policy director for the Criminal Justice Legal Foundation in Sacramento. In a Daily Journal article dated April 21, 2004, she posits that a movie "glamorizing" Williams "trivializes the deaths of his victims," and gives "a cold blooded murderer," who gets caught, a break. In the same issue Williams wrote an indignant article laying the blame for his residency on death row to racism, and his trial and appellate lawyers. This is not the repentant Williams portrayed in the film. And as Blake points out, this calls into question Williams' professed redemption. If he is innocent, he does not need redemption. Citing the overwhelming evidence of Williams' guilt, Blake argues that ["j]ustice demands that crimes be punished, not reduced in proportion to the perpetrator's rehabilitation level."]

And this in turn poses the question whether rehabilitation is relevant here. Is it a concept that we no longer credit? Remarkably the 9th Circuit said, in the closing paragraph of its opinion, "Although Williams' good works and accomplishments since incarceration may make him a worthy candidate for the exercise of gubernatorial discretion, they are not matters that we in the federal judiciary are at liberty to take into consideration in our review of Williams' habeas corpus petition." *Williams v. Woodford*, *supra*, at 725.

Whatever your thoughts about Williams and the death penalty, you should see his website, "Tookie's Corner." Williams' story makes us confront the question whether redemption equals rehabilitation. And if it does, should that be a factor in the continuous and contentious debate about the death penalty?

Stanley "Tookie" Williams was executed by lethal injection at 12 :35 A.M. on December 13th 2005 at San Quentin.

FIRST THING WE DO,
LET'S KEEP THE JUDICIARY INDEPENDENT

"First thing we do, let's kill all the judges." That is what some politicians want to do to the judiciary. Proposed ways to dispatch the black-robed miscreants include: impeach them, abolish their office through legislation, or simply treat them as a trauma center and withhold funding. The threats are anything but parochial. They affect not just the judicial branch, but all citizens.

These threats were ostensibly engendered over dissatisfaction with "activist" judicial rulings, and in particular, the heart-wrenching decision in the Terri Schiavo case. All the courts involved in that tragic case were accused of judicial arrogance for a refusal to "follow the law." But that is precisely what those courts did. For all we know, the Florida trial judge who first ordered Ms. Schiavo's feeding tube removed may have wished to keep Terri Schiavo alive no matter what her condition. But he was compelled to reach his decision on the evidence and the law. Indeed, if the trial judge thought his personal beliefs would have hampered his ability to objectively view the evidence, he would have been required to recuse himself. It was the consequence of his following the law that produced a result that critics found so unacceptable.

Ironically, these critics were in effect excoriating the trial and appellate judges for not being "activists." They wished for a ruling that would have kept Terri Schiavo alive without regard for her wishes or the law. This, in turn, prompted Congress to enact a "Terri Schiavo law" giving federal courts the opportunity to hear once again a state law matter that had been concluded, and this time decide the case correctly. The legislative branch displayed contempt for the separation of powers principle they accused the courts of ignoring. When the federal courts refused to again hear the case, some congressional leaders spoke of a judiciary out of control and threatened to metaphorically "kill all the judges," or at least those whose decisions they disliked.

The original quote, "First thing we do, let's kill all the lawyers," I have often seen framed in lawyers' offices. Taken out of context, the words have been misinterpreted as reflecting a pervasive public mood about pesky lawyers creating havoc with baseless lawsuits. Far from it. They are taken from Shakespeare's Henry VI, Part II. Jack Cade, a revolutionary, seeks to overthrow the government and depose the King. While he is inciting a mob to overthrow the government, one of the ordinary citizens, Dick, a butcher, yells the famous quote, "The first thing we do, let's kill all the lawyers."

Far from denigrating lawyers, the quote speaks to the value, significance and importance of a government's judicial system. It is the hallmark of civilization.

Without it, we have anarchy and chaos. How to undermine the government and destroy it? "First thing we do, let's kill all the lawyers."

By upsetting the balance between the separate branches of government, Congress seeks to punish a judiciary for deciding cases the "wrong way." The irony of this crude attempt to usurp the separation of powers is obvious. Yet, several legislators concerned about the Schiavo case were motivated by genuinely felt moral principles, and not just crass political motives. But their dissatisfaction was with the law that the judge was bound to uphold. The trial judge could have ruled the other way if he disbelieved the testimony of Michael Schiavo concerning his wife's wishes, or if he had found unpersuasive the expert testimony concerning her mental condition. And if he had made such findings, he would have been bound to rule the other way.

It is not surprising that numerous courts in both the state and federal system refused to hear the matter. Whatever certain members of Congress felt about the Schiavo decision, federal courts determined that this was a state matter that had been concluded. And under both state and federal law, the standards of appellate review mandate deference to the trial court's findings. It is rare that trial court decisions are reversed because of insufficient evidence. It is seldom possible to make informed decisions about substantial evidence on a transcript.

That is not to say that we do not nor cannot make valid assessments from the written page. We can draw a multitude of impressions about Madame Bovary, or Anna Karenina. We can try to do the same with the unadorned and seemingly prosaic testimony of a witness in a marital dissolution action recorded in a transcript. The words come to us free from the gloss and refined literary filter of Flaubert or Tolstoy, but our insight is limited. It is the trial judge, observing the witness respond to questions under direct and cross-examination, who can best make an informed judgment on credibility. The judge then must render a judgment in accordance with the applicable substantive and procedural law, the rules governing evidence, and burdens of proof. The judiciary has no free reign; it operates under constraints.

Judges, like anyone else in public service, are and should be subject to legitimate criticism. Law professors make their living more often "burying" than praising judicial decisions. Even judges judge judges. Just look through the appellate reports. But the current debate on judicial philosophy has caused more confusion than enlightenment. The Schiavo case is an example of how radically different points of view interpret "activism" in radically different ways.

One can understand the desire of the appointing authority, be it the President of the United States, or a governor, to hope if not expect their judicial appointees to rule in a manner consistent with their own judicial philosophy. However subtly or directly these expectations may be expressed to the prospective nominee, predictability is seldom attainable. Exhaustive questionnaires, probing interviews, and recommendations from "kitchen" cabinets offer some insight, but not certainty as to how a judge will rule in a particular case. However disturbing this may be to a president or governor, that's how it is and must be with an independent judiciary as a co-equal branch of government.

California understands the importance of a truly independent judiciary. To assure that merit, apart from "political" considerations figure prominently in the selection process, we have an independent Judicial Nominees Evaluation Commission (JNE). Created by the Legislature in 1979, the JNE Commission is an agency of the State Bar created to evaluate candidates for judicial nomination or appointment by the Governor. The Commission is presently composed of 34 members reflecting the rich diversity of our state. Thirty members come from various segments of the legal community and four are public members. They are all selected by the State Bar Board of Governors. The nonpartisan neutral Commission complements the governor's investigative process. It receives and evaluates confidential questionnaires sent out to members of the legal community relative to a nominee's qualifications. Competence, integrity, work ethic, and temperament are areas the Commission explores in depth. The Commission's thorough evaluation may expose factors that make a candidate unsuitable for judicial office. This information, in turn, is beneficial to the appointing authority and to the public.

It is the judiciary from which we expect rigorous analysis, unwavering integrity, and genuine independence. The JNE Commission helps ensure that judges of this caliber are appointed to the bench. But to be effective, the Commission must enjoy the same degree of independence that is so vital to a fair and impartial judiciary.

At this critical time when the judiciary is under attack, a disturbing proposal has been advanced that threatens the vitality and function of the JNE Commission. The proposal seeks to have the Governor's Judicial Appointments Secretary attend the plenary meetings of the JNE Commission. I cannot imagine a better way to stifle a free and spirited exchange of views. It would be like having a party to litigation before an appellate court attend the conference where the justices discuss the merits of the case. The proposal is simply another way of saying, "First thing we do, let's kill the JNE Commission."

The Board of Governors appointed an ad hoc committee composed of past and current JNE Commissioners to study this proposal. Its report issued in February of this year concludes, "One of the principal reasons JNE has been able to perform its stated and statutory mission satisfactorily is that it has been independent of the political process. The presence of a representative of the Governor's Office during JNE deliberations of judicial candidates would be destructive of that independence, would be counterproductive to JNE'S ability to provide fair, candid, straightforward and unbiased evaluations to the Governor's Office, and would irreparably cripple JNE'S ability to perform its mission.

The JNE Commission is an enormously valuable independent resource, and should remain so. It does not make the judicial appointments, nor does it want to. It is an important tool in helping achieve excellence in the judiciary of the State of California."

I concur. The workings of the JNE Commission illustrate how one branch of government has a check but not authority over another branch. This is beneficial to our institutions and the public they serve. We should direct our energies to respecting and preserving the balance of power between our separate branches of government instead of destabilizing that balance. Steps to kill the JNE Commission or the judiciary puts our democracy at risk.

I therefore suggest the following: "First thing we do, let's keep alive an independent judiciary." Our democracy depends on it.

IN OUR MEMORY

STANLEY MOSK, A JUSTICE PAR EXCELLENCE

California Supreme Court Justice Stanley Mosk passed away on June 19, 2001 at the age of 88. He swore me in to the Municipal Court on Labor Day, 1975. That was my first judicial assignment. I wrote this column shortly after his 35th year on the California Supreme Court.

Just a little over a week ago, a record was broken. I mentioned it to an elderly uncle of mine who was a musician. I should have been more explicit. "It's shameful to break a good record," he said. He thought I was speaking of the kind we used to put on turntables. For him, one should take special care of a record, particularly, if it was made by Caruso, Horowitz, Bix Beiderbecke or Artie Shaw, for example. My uncle would never break a record, unless Guy Lombardo made it.

I explained that I was referring to the record broken by Justice Stanley Mosk. December 26, 1999, marked the date that he had become the longest-sitting justice of the California Supreme Court, a period of more than 35 years. My uncle said that the date was note-worthy and that he was extremely impressed, but no more than he had been before Justice Mosk broke the record.

I asked for an explanation. "Anyone can play 'Tea For Two,'" he said. "But no one can play it like Art Tatum."

What he meant was that had Justice Mosk served on the court for 32 years, 22 years, or even 10 years, he would still be one of the finest justices ever to sit on the California Supreme Court. Or to repeat a quote from a legal scholar that appeared in an editorial on Justice Mosk in the Los Angeles Times, "Mosk has been . . . one of the most influential members in the history of one of the most influential tribunals in the Western World." This is quite apart from setting the longevity record.

As my uncle implied, longevity records are not always something to boast about. Flagpole sitters come to mind. The records set by La Petomane best remain unmentioned. And then there's Harvey Steck. He was a classmate who received a perfect attendance certificate on graduation from grammar school. I stayed home extra days just to make sure I would not even come close to receiving the award. On the other hand, Justice Mosk's record is truly remarkable for the exceptional quality and the enormous quantity of opinions he produced during those 35 years, and which he continues to produce with frightening regularity.

Pick any year of the 35, and one can cite numerous significant Mosk opinions that profoundly affect our lives and make our world a better one. One notes the many opinions affecting rights, among them the following: *People v. Wheeler*, 22 Cal.3d 584 (1978), prohibits peremptory challenges for racially discriminatory purposes; *Sindell v. Abbott Laboratories*, 26 Cal.3d 588 (1980), gives the right of women with cancer whose mothers had taken the anti-miscarriage drug

DES the right to sue drug companies that manufactured the drug; *In re Lynch*, 8 Cal.3d 410 (1972), established test to determine cruel and unusual punishment; *Diamond v. Bland*, 3 Cal.3d 653 (1970), right to distribute pamphlets in shopping centers; and *People v. Marsden*, 2 Cal.3d 118 (1970), a defendant's right to new appointed counsel in a criminal trial.

Vigorous and energetic, at 87 he remains the leader in the number of opinions written. Moreover, they invariably reflect clarity, scholarship, wisdom and humanity. The sentences are crisp and lucid, each supporting those that follow and precede it. A Mosk opinion is a reader's paradise.

Justice Mosk has been in public service for more than 60 years. In 1939, he began as executive secretary for Governor Olson, this century's first Democratic governor. He served as a Superior Court judge from 1943 to 1959, one of the youngest Superior Court judges in history. While on that court, he struck down as unconstitutional racially restrictive covenants. The United States Supreme Court later followed suit.

He was elected attorney general in 1958 by the widest margin for any contested election in the nation for that year. As attorney general, he created innovative programs for law enforcement that included the establishment of a Consumer Fraud Section and a Constitutional Rights Section.

Despite his extraordinary achievements, Stanley Mosk is unassuming and down to earth. He is a person one can truly call a "gentleman and a scholar." He and his wife, Kaygey, are warm and engaging, with a twinkle in their eyes that reflects a playful sense of humor.

Justice Mosk swore me in as a Municipal Court judge on Labor Day in 1975. Immediately after administering the oath, he shook my hand and with a big smile said, "Congratulations, judge." That he was the first person to call me "judge" was a special significance to me because he is the judge who by example set the standard of excellence to which I and countless other judges aspire.

In a reflective and wistful mood, Justice Mosk recently commented on the dearth of leadership in our country today as compared to the early days of our nation. When our nation's population was less than that of Los Angeles today, it had leaders such as Jefferson, Madison, Franklin, May and Marshall. Quoting Archibald MacLeish, he has asked, "Where has all the grandeur gone?" My answer to this pensive question is simply to note that it has not all gone. Justice Mosk has kept a good part of it here.

WITKIN THE IMMORTAL SCHOLAR
I

I wrote Part I of this column in June of 1994 to celebrate the birthday of the "Venerable" Bernard Witkin who so masterfully chronicled the law of California.

It's hard to believe, but a few weeks ago Bernie Witkin turned 90. He's so much a part of our lives that hardly a day goes by without citing, quoting or speaking about him.

The other night I was at a dinner party. Among the guests were several imposing lawyers and judges, the Brahmins of the legal world. Outside, paralegals parked the cars. Inside, associates from all the major firms stood discreetly near clusters of people and took notes on their conversations. One heard esoteric phrases like "retraxit" and "post litem motam" uttered with insouciance.

Of course, the inevitable happened. One of the lawyers mentioned a problem she was working on. The judge had ruled in her favor, but she feared the ruling was wrong. She wondered what she should do on appeal. Should she argue the judge was right or fall back on the doctrine of harmless error?

Not surprisingly, no one was reticent about expressing an opinion or giving advice. Obviously, the answer depended upon whether the case was civil or criminal, but something in our discussion was far more noteworthy than our conclusion.

Interspersed in the conversation was the name "Witkin." It was repeated "with rhythmic regularity," to quote a phrase from an often-cited case concerning the substantial evidence rule. In fact, in every conversation "Witkin" was mentioned as often as "attorney fees" or "sanctions."

One would hear, "So what does Witkin say?"

"Witkin says this about this situation, but Witkin points out that this case holds…."

"If Witkin says this, then the best way to go…." And so on.

Not all the guests belonged to the legal profession, and one of them, a taxidermist – or was it a psychiatrist, I don't remember which – overheard our conversation and said something to the effect, "So who is Witkin, God or somebody?"

We paused for no longer than a second or two and did something quite remarkable for any group of lawyers and judges engaged in a discussion about the law – we agreed on something. With a casualness born of certainty we said, "Yes, he is," and went on with our discussion.

By making a comparison between Bernie Witkin and God, I don't mean to be disrespectful. But there are some striking parallels. For example, they both have created order out of chaos. The very mention of their names inspires reverence. Their books reveal the truth and are called "Bibles." Their powers and abilities are beyond our comprehension. Their influence is pervasive. They help us find the way.

But despite the ignorance of the taxidermist, or the psychiatrist, Witkin's work is becoming more and more known to the world at large.

A few years ago, I wanted to sell my car. To avoid the hassle of selling it myself, I went to a used car dealer and proposed he sell the car for me. His office was in a tiny, yet foreboding, bungalow at the back of the lot. We discussed the terms of the deal under which he would sell the car and earn his commission. We were separated by his cluttered desk and the battle-scarred years of experience that gave him the superior negotiating skills. Despite his eyes that didn't smile, I thought I was holding my own, until I noticed neatly shelved behind his desk, the entire set of Witkin on California law.

"You've…you've got Witkin," I stammered.

He put his cigar in the ashtray and narrowed the eyes that knew no joy. "Yeah. Why shouldn't I have Witkin?" he asked with a tone that lay just this side of contempt.

I couldn't think of an answer, but I knew in an instant he knew more about the Levering-Rees Motor Vehicle Sales and Finance Act than I did.

He sold the car a month or two later, but I'm sure if Witkin had not been on his shelf, I would have come out better.

But now that the world at large is learning about the importance of the word of Witkin, I've discovered yet another religious correlation. An organization is planning to place Witkin's books in hotel rooms across the country.

In the tradition of the great philosophers of the past, Witkin has systematized, catalogued, and chronicled the law. That one person could take every facet of the law, from procedure to probate, form opinion writing to statutory interpretation, and explicate it with such clarity makes the mind boggle. (Witkin would never say "boggles the mind.")

His books are masterpieces in exposition. They make the seemingly impenetrable comprehensible. A glance at Witkin and you know not just what the law is, but how it came to be what it is.

Remember the old radio show, "The Shadow"? The Shadow had the ability to "cloud men's minds." (Apparently women were invulnerable to the Shadow's talents.)

Many of us have had this experience. When trying to draft an opinion, a motion, a brief, or trying merely to express an idea, a multitude of competing thoughts cloud the mind. Here's a way out of the mist. Open any book by Witkin and you will see the model that can put you back on track.

Bernie's expansive intellect is matched by his generosity. It is not just lawyers that Bernie educates. Bernie's guidance and financial support have made California's judicial education program the finest in the world. That's why our judges are so good. CJER, The California Center for Judicial Education and Research, oversees the world-renowned California Judicial College and the many educational institutes for judges. Bernie sits as a permanent advisory member on the CJER governing committee. His advice and counsel have kept California the leader in judicial education.

So once again we want to say "Thanks Bernie," and "Happy Birthday." We wish you and that very special person, your wife Alba, the best.

It's hard to believe you are 90, but why count years when already you are immortal?

II

I wrote Part II shortly after Witkin passed away on December 23, 1995.

Bernie Witkin has left us. That's what the papers say. At one of Bernie's numerous 90th birthday celebrations held throughout California, I observed that for the immortal, 90 years was a drop in the bucket. There was no dispute that Bernie had already achieved immortality decades earlier. That's why I do not believe he's gone. The immortal are not so prosaic as to leave. They remain and enrich us.

Of course, when speaking of the immortal, we seldom use a first name. "The immortal Bernie" sounds less lofty than "The immortal Witkin." But if you were as lucky as I to be one of his friends, (along with several thousand other people), in his presence you called him Bernie. What you called him out of his presence was quite another thing. There was only one acceptable appellation, "Witkin," or if you were feeling particularly reverential, "Professor Witkin."

That's how it is with the immortal: "Moses," "Plato," "Blackstone," or "Holmes."

For ordinary mortals, to be referred to by one's last name is a less exalted form of address. When a master sergeant barks "Gadowski, I said front and center," Gadowski ranks below an aphid on the sergeant's scale of esteem. Most of us have experienced this less than deferential form of address in law school. I can still hear a certain professor asking me, before two hundred and seventy of my terrified but momentarily relieved fellow students, in a voice accustomed to sarcasm, "Gilbert, perhaps you can enlighten us on the Rule Against Perpetuities." Right.

With Bernie, of course, it's a different story. His last name commands veneration and respect. When you hear a gaggle of distinguished lawyers and jurists discussing a legal issue, someone will inevitably ask, "What does Witkin say?" Or even more appropriately, "What does Professor Witkin say?" It's a question we will be asking for years to come.

Remember the phrase we learned in law school, "the seamless web of the law?" In over thirty volumes that summarize California law, Bernie helped us to understand what those words really mean.

Bernie brought order out of chaos. He wrote about the law, explicating it in English not legalese, showing its direction and purpose, its form and substance. Bernie was the consummate writer who wrote about cases that were not always well written. From procedure to probate, he chronicled the law in California with a clarity the cases he wrote about seldom possessed. He penetrated the impenetrable, and made clearings through dense verbal underbrush.

And by example he showed us how to write. Just glance through any Witkin tome and you will be struck by the absence of footnotes. He had no need for those clutter boxes we create to dump extraneous ideas we are unable to fit into the body of an opinion or brief. Bernie's friend, Professor David Mellinkoff, author of "The Language of the Law," among other notable works, quipped that it was not profitable for Bernie to use footnotes. Bernie was paid by the page.

Bernie has trained a cadre of lawyers at Bancroft-Whitney to carry on the endless task of summarizing the law, but in the Witkin style, with simplicity, clarity and brevity. And the erudite Justice Norman Epstein, who has collaborated with Bernie for over fifteen years, will continue with his incisive review of criminal law.

For years, Bernie had refused to grant interviews. Undaunted, a determined Los Angeles Superior Court Judge Elizabeth Baron, who later served on the California Court of Appeal, persuaded Bernie to appear on camera and answer questions about his life and work. He ultimately said "yes," with the proviso he would pick the interviewers. Along with Judge Baron and retired Court of Appeal Justice Howard Weiner, I was privileged to be one of the three.

The result was a unique video interview entitled, "A Conversation with B.E. Witkin." It was produced by the California Judges Association. We did the show on a sunny April afternoon in 1994 in a television studio in Berkeley. Bernie talked about his life, offered revealing insights about decision making and the law, and gave his candid views about the ever changing California Supreme Court he had analyzed over the years. He was 90, but it was no surprise that his responses to our questions were thoughtful, candid, provocative, discerning and wise.

Just by viewing this historic video tape, one can feel Bernie's passion for the law. It's infectious. Every lawyer should see this tape.

Bernie has left his friends with vivid memories. I can see him hunched over his Royal # 5 typewriter looking like a muckraking journalist from the thirties. And there were his jokes, funny even on the twenty-fifth time. We will remember the Witkin laugh, that amplified cackle that could penetrate metal. And we will never forget his unique ability to balance a glass of wine on his head while arguing profound legal points.

The great jazz musician, Charlie "Bird" Parker, died in 1955. Parker's style influenced every jazz musician to follow him. That's why they say, "Bird Lives." It is not as strange as it first appears to speak of Charlie Parker and Bernie Witkin in the same paragraph. The Witkin tradition continues. He will be with us forever. "Witkin Lives."

OTTO KAUS EYES THE CROCODILE IN THE BATHTUB

In reflecting on the political pressures that bear upon a judge, Justice Otto Kaus could not forget there was a crocodile in his bathtub. But now the crocodile, who looked upon Kaus with bemusement, is alone. Justice Kaus did not compromise his principles, but regarded his crocodile with mild concern.

Can it be that within a period of a few short weeks two of the giants of our profession have left us? First there was Bernie Witkin, the great encyclopedist, the chronicler, who with a wide lens gave us a continuous and coherent picture of the law. And then Otto Kaus, who molded and shaped the law, and through reason and logic gave it direction and purpose. They have gone to a loftier place but they left us a rich legacy that does not lessen the pain of our loss.

Otto Kaus made a difference. He served on the California Supreme Court for only four years but his influence was strong and pervasive. During his fifteen years on the Court of Appeal, he crafted magnificent opinions that reflected a rigorous analysis of complex issues but were easy and refreshing to read. He combined insight and scholarship with practicality and civility. He made the law in California vital and relevant.

He was a gentleman, urbane, witty and kind, who put everyone at ease. He looked directly at you when he spoke, and you could see the twinkle in his eyes through which shined an elegant personality. He was homey, down to earth and unpretentious.

Two distinguished appellate practitioners, Ed Horowitz and Kent Richland, and my colleague and good friend, Justice Ken Yegan, were fortunate to have worked as research attorneys for Justice Kaus. They revered him.

They describe a man who took his work, but not himself seriously. Ed remembers Otto in his cardigan sweater coming down the hall looking like Mr. Rogers, friendly and eager to engage him in a discussion on a legal issue. To this day, Ed can think of no greater honor than to have been cornered for an hour or two by Otto Kaus. Otto's joy in working with the law, his humanity and intellect have made a lasting impression on all who knew him.

Kent Richland recalls how the law permeated Otto's life and how astonishing was his recall of the most arcane rules. One morning, Otto called Kent to say he would be a little late coming into chambers that day because his cat had scratched him. Otto assured Kent it wasn't anything serious but that he thought he was required to report the incident. Kent expressed his doubt, but Otto remembered reading about such a law. He insisted that Kent research the matter. To his amazement, Kent found that there was in fact a municipal ordinance that required that a cat scratch be reported to the animal control agency. Otto complied with the law, despite his concern about getting his cat in trouble. Otto's rectitude compels me to make an admission: I have violated this law. In fact, I have several priors. I would have made the required reports, but my cat threatened me. Otto would have understood.

Justice Yegan brings much of the wisdom he learned from Otto Kaus to our division. At our conferences, it is rare that Ken fails to remind us how Otto would have approached an issue. Otto remains for us the ideal judge. He set a standard to which all judges can take pride in striving to achieve.

Ken remembers the sometimes eccentric ways in which Otto would tackle a problem. Once, he and Otto were discussing an issue and suddenly, in mid sentence, Otto stopped and looked towards the floor with a furrowed brow. Ken, certain that Otto was formulating an answer to the problem, kept quiet. Finally, Otto broke the silence. "Ken, my socks are on inside out," he said with mock gravity. As he remedied the sock problem, he came up with the solution to the legal problem.

The Hastings Constitutional Law Quarterly, Winter 1988, Volume 15, Number 2 is devoted to an oral history of Justice Otto Kaus. It is delightful reading and reveals the warmth and humanity of this extraordinary jurist. Recalling his law school days, he, like Witkin, disliked learning the law by the "confusion" method. Perhaps that is why his opinions inform and enlighten, but never bewilder.

He was a strong believer in precedent. He argued that stare decisis as articulated in *Auto Equity Sales, Inc.* v. *Superior Court*, 57 Cal.2d 450, was jurisdictional, requiring Courts of Appeal to follow decisions on point of other Courts of Appeal. This is one of Otto's ideas that so far has not gained acceptance as evidenced by the proliferating volumes of opinions. Otto's view was much different if no one else had found a solution to a knotty problem. Then he reveled in the sheer joy of making law, because that, he said, was what a judge must do when charting undiscovered territory.

We usually do best at what we like to do. For Otto, it was obvious that his greatest pleasure was in writing. His opinions reflect his enormous intellect, his subtle and captivating wit. Otto said he had nothing to sell. He never tried to use his opinions to propagate a particular philosophy. An inveterate perfectionist, Otto always had regrets upon re-reading an opinion he had authored. Here and there he would invariable find a better word than the one he had used.

Otto said that he most wanted his opinions to be readable, to be interesting even if the subject were dull. Otto fulfilled his wish over and over again. His opinions stand as an enduring legacy, a guide to show generations of judges and lawyers the way. From that we gain comfort, but still, the crocodile in the bathtub sheds real tears.

GOVERNOR PAT BROWN SET SUPREME STANDARD

In the entertainment industry there is a widespread belief that when one notable show business personality passes on, two more will shortly follow. I put no stock in this superstition. For all the examples given, I am sure there are dozens more proving the contrary.

Despite my rejection of the show business myth, I did not expect this unsettling "rule of three" to occur even by coincidence as it did so recently in the legal profession.

Bernie Witkin and Otto Kaus recently left us. In my last two columns, I paid tribute to these exceptional men who had made such an enormous contribution to our profession. I never dreamed I would be writing yet a third consecutive panegyric about another extraordinary individual who has left us, Governor Edmund "Pat" Brown. In quite a different way, he had a profound effect upon our judiciary. True, his accomplishments in other areas were immense. He made education one of his priorities and gave us one of the best university systems in the country that opened its doors to all qualified applicants. Through his efforts we have an intricate water system, an engineering marvel composed of dams, canals, aqueducts and pumping stations, that bring water from northern to southern California.

But one of Pat Brown's most significant accomplishments was to give California a judiciary that was the finest in the nation. He gave us a state Supreme Court that was respected throughout the country, and to which other jurisdictions looked for guidance. His choice of justices was not based on a narrow litmus test. He did not inquire of his nominees how they felt about a particular issue. Although he was opposed to the death penalty, he did not pick nominees who were opposed to it. Neither he nor others acting on his behalf asked his nominees their views on abortion, civil rights, property rights, or the Constitution. He would have recoiled at the thought of anyone sending a nominee a questionnaire to ascertain how he or she would vote on a particular issue.

He was not so parochial as to appoint only those who belonged to his party. Nor was membership in any other group a prerequisite for consideration. Liberals, conservatives, D.A's , defense or plaintiff lawyers had no advantage. But neither did they have a disadvantage.

Pat Brown had a much broader litmus test. It rested on a more lofty premise and asked a deceptively simple but difficult question: Does the nominee possess the intellectual acumen, the firm independence, the exceptional character to sit on our high court? This same test applied to appointees to any court in California.

Brown's conscientious search for persons fitting these requirements gave us such great jurists as Stanley Mosk, Raymond Peters, and Mathew Tobriner, to name just a few. He gave us a towering intellect, Roger Traynor as Chief Justice. Indeed, he deserves credit for appointing Otto Kaus to the Court of Appeal, first as an associate and then as a presiding justice. Governor Jerry Brown carried on his father's tradition by appointing Kaus to the Supreme Court.

Many of us look back with nostalgia to the well-crafted and readable opinions of the Traynor court. In those days, we were not faced with a shrinking budget and an expanding case load. Therefore, substance was more important than statistics. Decisions of the Traynor court explicated rather than obscured legal principles. The court gave us much to consider and debate. We discussed what the court said, not what we thought the court said.

Decisions of the Traynor court broke new ground in civil law affecting negligence, contracts and products liability. Citizens were given more access to the court system. The court applied sweeping new constitutional principles to criminal procedure that anticipated United States Supreme Court decisions.

Today, however, we live in a different world with different values. Some Traynor court decisions have been overruled, the reach of others narrowed. It is true an era has passed, but Pat Brown's Traynor court has nevertheless left all judges a significant legacy. No matter what may be a judge's judicial philosophy, no matter whether that judge sits on the appellate or trial bench, he or she can do no better than to look to the Traynor court as a model for intellectual rigor and trenchant analysis.

Our present Supreme Court may draw on this legacy as it decides the issues of the day, ranging from property rights to biogenetics. Its justices have the good fortune to benefit from the wisdom of its senior member, Justice Mosk, an outstanding alumnus of the Traynor court. This relatively new court has the opportunity to carry on the tradition of excellence that characterizes the California judiciary.

Pat Brown said a governor is best remembered by the judges he appoints. I think this is true, and therefore for his contribution to our legal system alone, we will never forget him. No matter what legal or political theory is in vogue, no matter what tenets are currently in favor, no matter what the debate on social and constitutional issues, we will always have the standard of excellence that Governor Edmund "Pat" Brown set for the judiciary. It is a standard that any governor from any party would do well to follow.

ALLEN BROUSSARD WILL STILL BE THERE IN OAKLAND

I wrote this column in 1989 when Justice Allen Broussard retired from the California Supreme Court. He passed away in 1996. He was a good friend and one of California's fines jurist.

Oakland. Famous people have lived there. Gertrude Stein, for example. She is reputed to have said about Oakland, "There's no there, there." Maybe we shouldn't take it too seriously. She is also reputed to have said, "A rose is a rose, is a rose." She never said that. She said, "Rose is a rose is a rose."   Stein left Oakland and went to Paris. There, where apparently for Stein there was a there, she held court in her famous salon for the most important artists and writers of the 20ᵗʰ century. She may have returned again to Oakland for a minute or two, when she was traveling throughout the Untied States on her celebrated tour in 1934-35.

But Stein never went back to live in Oakland. No, not there, because there, you would not find Picasso, Braque, Hemingway or Anderson. It's also true that there, in Oakland, you will not find the Arc de Triomphe, but you will find Jack London Square. That's because Jack London was raised, there, in Oakland. Hence, the Square. If Stein had kept her mouth shut, there might have been a Stein Square.

Stein was strongly influenced by the Cubists. They made her and us see things differently than we had before. They gave a new direction to painting. Similarly, Stein sought to give a new direction to our language. She played fast and loose with punctuation and syntax in order to force us to see and think about things differently.

Jack London was also filled with ideas. Some were odious and puerile, but some were good. He showed us how to find the will to survive in a hostile environment. He cared about the weak and the poor and sought to end injustice.

Interesting place, Oakland. There is where Justice Allen Broussard has lived for many years. So, Oakland is something that he shares with Stein and London, but that's not all. He, too, wished to change our perception about the world. He, too, has made us see things more clearly. He, too, has raised our consciousness about injustice and intolerance.

A few weeks ago, the Beverly Hills Bar Association hosted its annual luncheon for the California Supreme Court. At these lunches, it has been the custom for the Chief Justice to introduce the members of the court, but because this session in Los Angeles would mark the last oral argument that Justice Broussard would hear as a sitting justice, Chief Justice Lucas, with characteristic grace, turned the task over to Justice Broussard. He first, however, gave Allen a touching tribute to which the guests responded with a standing ovation.

Allen's presentation was warm and human. It gave us the chance to see the genuine affection and esteem with which the justices hold one another. It is true there have been more dissents lately, but that can be a good thing. Individual voices, like Allen's, are important to express a vision, and to compel us to see other sides of an issue. When dissents do occur, they have been forceful, challenging and provocative. They may have been unsettling, and they may reflect philosophical differences, but they have not been marred by personal rancor or mean-spirited gibes that we see in other courts. Allen's opinions, whether by majority or dissent, made a significant contribution to the law in our state. He has made a mark that will endure.

Our Supreme Court loses one of its most distinguished jurists when Allen retires next month. He has given the judiciaries and the people of this state the benefit of his wisdom and insight for more than 27 years. We hate to see him go, but his presence will be still felt. He will continue to co-chair, along with Justice John Arguelles, the Judicial Council Advisory Committee on Race and Ethnic Bias. We will still hear his voice on issues of intolerance, injustice and inequality. And as for Oakland, Allen did not leave it for a snow bank in Alaska or an avant-garde salon in Paris. He stayed in Oakland. Take notice, Gertrude Stein. He's there.

MILDRED LILLY AND AN
AGREEMENT WITH A HIGHER COURT

I

So it is the end of the year- - yawn. It is not that I wish to denigrate 2002, nor speculate about what to expect or dread in 2003. But in light of my theme, immortality, a year is meaningless. Immortality connotes a life forever, an enduring and endless presence. Artists seemingly achieve it through their work. Parents believe they achieve it through their children. Most religions teach that our souls are immortal. I know that my theme sounds pretentious, but recent events lead me to conclude we should not reject this concept out of hand.

If immortality means we maintain a presence that affects lives after we have left this world, then I have become a card-carrying believer in immortality. Presiding Justice Mildred Lillie died on October 27, 2002. But along with countless others, I can attest to her powerful and awe-inspiring presence after what some have called her death. I am not disputing her death, mind you; I attended her funeral service. It just may be that death means the end in only a limited sense.

So many people in and out of the legal profession know about this remarkable judge. Her very life and accomplishments set an example of character, perseverance, and sheer grit. Yes, she achieved immortality through the thousands of well-crafted opinions she authored during her 44 years on the Court of Appeal. But recently, her presence touched me on a more personal level.

It is related to an incident which occurred a few years ago. It had to do with another one of my innumerable mistakes. No, this was not a legal error, on occasion, judges get the opportunity to undo that kind of error. Trial judges have the opportunity to grant motions for a new trial for example. They can reverse themselves on evidentiary rulings. Court of Appeal judges may reconsider the error of their ways in petitions for rehearing. That supposes they can get beyond the calumny in the petition. But there are some mistakes, errors in judgment, however slight and irreproachable that can create unforgettable havoc and affliction. How often does one have the opportunity to unscramble the eggs? It is rare that fortune will look down upon you, and grant a petition for rehearing, so that you can nullify the error.

Justice Lillie and I were speakers at a confirmation hearing for a newly-appointed justice to the Court of Appeal. We were sitting in the impressive courtroom at the Ronald Reagan Building. The commission members took the bench and the Chief Justice called the meeting to order. The Chief Justice made his opening remarks and explained to the assembled guests the confirmation procedure. He announced the order of speakers. Justice Lillie was first. She and I were sitting in the first row, two or three seats apart from each other. My right leg was crossed over my left leg which stuck out in the imaginary aisle to the podium, leaving little room for one to pass. I was mulling over what I intended to say when Justice Lillie got up to speak. She moved in front of me.

In the nether reaches of my mind there was a faint voice saying "pull in your legs." The voice was barely audible. Before I could react to it, I felt Justice Lillie brush against my legs. Her leg caught my extended leg. What took place in the next millisecond proved Einstein's theory. Time warped. World history passed before me at the speed of light while Justice Lillie appeared to be lifting like a swan breaking free of the water. I am not sure how or why the succeeding events occurred. Did I will them to happen? Or were they the consequence of my -for lack of a better term, let's call it- supplication? A rational explanation is out of the question, but somehow, from somewhere, a force greater than I granted me a... rehearing.

As time crumpled just prior to my receiving the grant of a rehearing, I concluded that : if anyone were to fall, as in fall down, or pitch forward and go down, it should be me, not Justice Lillie. From this followed a plea : please let it be me. Thus, was made a contract, albeit one of adhesion. At the time, I was not thinking of the aphorism, "There is no free lunch."

One will sooner win the lottery than be given the opportunity to annul the consequences of a wrong before it occurs. But that is what happened. On the way to the podium, Justice Lillie turned a stumble with a potentially disastrous outcome into a graceful, scarcely noticeable two step. She began her remarks by saying that she intended to speak on behalf of the nominee, despite Justice Gilbert's attempt to trip her. The room roared with laughter, and I laughed from the depths of a soul I did not know I had, with gratitude and a new found faith in a higher power.

Oh yes, I fulfilled my part of the bargain but not then, mind you. Without much warning, my time for performance came a few weeks later. but I am getting ahead of myself.

At the conclusion of the confirmation hearing, Justice Lillie and I briefly chatted. I apologized for my clumsy feet. She patted me on the arm and said to forget it. I remarked on how gracefully she handled the situation and told her that I wished that I had been tripped rather than her. She smiled and said, "Don't worry. You will get your chance."

So as I mentioned, I got my chance a few weeks later. I had the honor of swearing in a new crop of lawyers to the California Bar in Courtroom 22 of the Ventura Superior Court. I, along with the presiding judge of the superior court and a federal magistrate, gave them words of advice, cracked a few tasteful jokes, and wished them well. Other speakers which included representatives of the California Bar, the American Bar Association, and the Barristers, spoke in the well of the court from a podium to which was attached a microphone.

The ceremony was concluded and I left the bench with my colleagues. No, I did not trip, nor did they. In the judge's chambers adjacent to the courtroom, I took off my robe and put on my jacket. Unfortunately, I did not trip in the chambers where no one was present. No, I waited until I re-entered the courtroom where all the new admittees and their family and friends were socializing and taking pictures. I strolled around the courtroom shaking hands and offering congratulations.

Although the ceremony was over, the stupid podium still stood in the well of the court. Of course, now it served no purpose other than to take up space. Perhaps I unfairly disparage the podium. My displeasure is more properly directed at the microphone securely attached to the podium, or more specifically at the taut cord attached to the microphone, the dull gray cord that blended in so perfectly with the dull gray carpet of the courtroom so that carpet and cord were indistinguishable from one another.

When I tripped over the cord, time neither stopped nor warped. No intervention occurred. I went down fast. The alacrity with which I got up could not erase what had happened in real time two seconds earlier. I had to assure everyone that I was fine before I could crack a joke or two that no one, including myself, can remember. I thought of Camus' "The Fall," but it gave me little solace. I wondered how long the image of my mishap would stay imbedded in the minds of the new lawyers who, for all I know, would be relating this incident to their grandchildren.

And then the socializing resumed, smiles were in abundance, flashbulbs went off, and then I saw Mildred looking down on me with a sympathetic grin. "I told you, you would get your chance," she said. "I hope I don't get many more chances like this," I replied. " Don't complain," she admonished. "I know what it's like to pick yourself up." I felt good and waved good-bye to everyone. A short conversation with the immortal can be uplifting.

HISTORIC DAY AT THE LAW LIBRARY
II

I missed the opening of the Los Angeles County Law Library on December 14, 1953. They wouldn't let me out of Le Conte Jr. High School in Hollywood, California, where I was a victim, I mean student. Had the school removed my ankle restraints, I could have been there. I would have waited for the bus in front of the bowling alley on Sunset and Bronson. It would be a straight shot down Sunset Boulevard to "downtown." I would have had to take the bus because I didn't have a driver's license, let alone a learner's permit. It is fun to imagine what could have been, a leisurely stroll in the stacks, maybe stopping now and then to leaf through Cal.App.2d. Cal.App.3d was not even a gleam in the

Reporter of Decision's eye. It would be another five years before the Cal.App.2nd Reports would be graced by a Mildred L. Lillie opinion. But at age 14, what did I know from a law library? Had I been able to drive, I might have gone more often to the public library in my neighborhood, the one on Ivar Street, where I fit in with its habitués, a raggedy assortment of kooks and eccentrics.

December 14, 1953, fifty years ago, and I still remember the day well. My thoughts were on my upcoming birthday. Would I survive to celebrate it? Le Conte Jr. High School, you see, was "a rough school." A newspaper reporter (that's what they were called in those days), was only slightly exaggerating when she wrote that we had tear gas drills once a week. Just one year before *Brown v. Board of Education*, students, (a euphemism) were bussed in from a place quaintly named Roger Young Village. Its sister city was reputed to be Devil's Island. Despite their Neanderthal attributes, the Roger Young kids showed remarkable foresight by introducing methods and techniques of warfare used today by our armed forces -- slash and burn, being but one example. A visit to the law library would have given me a respite from practicing the canny skills I employed each day to stay alive.

How could I know at the time that Le Conte Jr. High School was preparing me for a legal career that would take me to the main building of the County Law Library fifty years later to celebrate its anniversary and its renaming in honor of my dear friend and colleague Mildred L. Lillie. Like today's lawyer aspiring to success, I marketed my skills as early as the seventh grade.

My seminars for the Roger Young kids on the value of good hygiene gave me cachet. I persuaded them that they could wear underwear without being sissies because it is hidden beneath their clothes. I soon became a kind of consigliore, advising on the intricacies of how to pass tests, at first instilling the basic tenet for a good start, spelling one's name correctly, and then introducing more radical concepts like studying.

And then it is November 6, 2003, a mere blink of the eye in Einstein's or Arthur Clarke's universe, and I am standing before the Swedish Blue Pearl Granite lower walls and the upper walls that look like white stone that make up the exterior monolith of the law library. If it were only 2001. I reach out towards it. The opening drums of Strauss's "Thus Spake Zarathustra" are pounding in my ears. I sense the irony and the drama of the moment. Let me explain.

Imagine you are a contestant on the popular television game show, Jeopardy (a condition in which I often find myself for writing this column). What! There are a few of you who have never watched Jeopardy? As I recall, the contestant picks a category. The game show host supplies the answer, and the contestant must come up with the question. Got it? Let's just try an easy one for practice. The category is "Courts." The answer is, "I can't count that high." And the obvious question is "What is the number of reversals from the 9th Circuit?"

Back to the library. I am transfixed. I can hear the opening two chords of Zarathustra which follow the drums, and I become a contestant on Jeopardy. The category is "Paradox." The voice of the moderator gives me the answer, "50 years old and just born." The question comes to me during the second entry of the timpani drums. "What is the Los Angeles County Law Library building on this evening?"

The 50th anniversary of this important repository of legal knowledge was reborn that very evening to bear the name of one of our most respected and revered jurists, Mildred L. Lillie. For an extra point, I had to guess what the middle initial "L." stands for. I take a wild stab -- "Library"?

I snap out of my hypnotic fascination and go inside. Ceremonies to commemorate the anniversary its renaming as The Mildred L. Lillie Law Library, are about to begin. I still have a few minutes to walk through the stacks and look at the books that carry the case names of so many of the kids bussed in from Roger Young Village 50 years ago.

The program begins with the ebullient president of the Board of Trustees of the Library, Susan Steinhauser. In a stirring opening, she explains how the Board and the library's then director, Richard Iamele, view the library as a bridge to justice for everyone by providing open access to legal information. What better name than Mildred L. Lillie to adorn the main building of the L.A. County Law Library. With grace and determination, she pried open the doors of access that had been closed to her and other women in the legal profession. And now the building dedicated to open access bears her name. This was a truly historic moment, quite apart from there being close to 100 judges in the law library, at the same time-another first.

A video presentation chronicled her life and career. The word that kept coming up was "first." Those solid common sense Lillie opinions came from the first woman justice appointed to the Second District Court of Appeal in 1958. During her 55 years as a judicial officer she made a stunning contribution to our justice system. Chief Justice George hailed her as a great jurist and scholar.

For those who did not know Justice Lillie personally, it is not easy to capture the essence of this remarkable individual. If you were to think of an amalgamation of important women in history such as Catherine the Great, Queen Elizabeth, Queen Victoria (who incidentally was no prude), Betty Crocker, Dolly Madison, Susan B. Anthony, and Golda Meir, you are getting close.

Adjectives that some have used to describe her include: formidable, resolute, elegant, stately, brilliant, human, intimidating, funny, titanic, unassuming, kind, and compassionate. She was Presiding Justice of Division 7 of the Second

District Court of Appeal, and had been the district's Administrative Presiding Justice for several years. Despite the importance of these positions, she modestly explained that her role was like that of the head of a cemetery: "You have a lot of people under you, but no one listens."

Justice Lillie might complain that we are making too big a fuss over her. But I know that she is pleased that the building that bears her name, as well as the numerous branches of the Los Angeles County Law Library throughout the county, provide access to legal information and consequently, access to justice. Our support of the library invigorates this principle and also pays tribute to an exceptional jurist. For me, it is a way of not having to say a final good-bye to a dear friend and colleague.

"I was nervous and upset." These were the words you coached your client to say before the no fault divorce law was enacted. In those days, there were few grounds to obtain a marital dissolution, what we still call "divorce" in lay terms. Not easy to prove incurable insanity, and unseemly to talk about impotence before the Bob Dole ads.

There were a few unlucky practitioners who lost default hearings before demanding judges when the client was not sufficiently prepped. Can you imagine losing a default hearing? I almost did once. The questions and answers leading up to the coup de grace, "nervous and upset" went something like this:

"You say your husband snored?"

"Yes, constantly."

"Did this keep you up at night?"

"Yes, it kept me up at night and was a continuing irritant during the day."

"During the day? You mean . . . . "

"Yes, he snored during the day when he was awake, or should I say semi-comatose. He snored in front of my friends."

"And how did this make you feel?"

"It made me feel . . . . "

"Yes?"

"It, . . it, . . . annoyed the hell out of me."

"And . . . what else?"

"What else? . . . Nervous. It made me nervous. Jumpy."

"And what else . . . ?"

"Nervous and jumpy?"

"Up- . . . up."

"Jumpy, nervous and down, and no I mean up . . . upset. That's what it made me feel. Nervous and jumpy and upset."

Whew! We won the default hearing.

When no fault divorces became law we simply asked: "Have irreconcilable differences arisen in the marriage that led to the irremediable breakdown of the marriage?"

"The what?"

"The irremediable . . . remember? The irremediable break . . . ." "Oh yeah, right. It sure did."

"Nothing further your Honor."

By the way, there is such a word as "irremediable." It got past spell check. Of course the answers to these questions had as much to do with reality as the arguments for and against ballot propositions. I get nervous and upset just thinking about it.

I thought the talismanic "nervous and upset" would no longer permeate my thoughts, until recently I began to feel nervous and upset, with the emphasis on "upset," an emotion here most definitely connected to reality.

Recently, I experienced a breakdown in our institutional memory. If memory is a bank, few people are making deposits and the account yields no interest. So that I don't go bankrupt with this metaphor, let me relate to you why I am nervous and upset.

Not long ago, I was talking to some bright young lawyers, and I mentioned Phil Gibson. One of the lawyers said, "Phil who?" They pulled me off him. As he straightened his tie, he asked with a surprisingly deferential tone, "What did I do?" I told him, after he signed a covenant not to sue, that Phil Gibson was one of our state's great Chief Justices who served as California's Chief Justice from 1940 to 1964. And he swore me into the California Bar in 1963.

I reminded him that we have a past.

"A what?"

See what I mean? I fear that the "past" is slipping from our grasp. Briefs cite the latest case that enunciates a legal principle. What about the first case that established the principle? Does the word "venerable" mean anything anymore?

It does to the Monterey Bar Association of California. Each year, the Bar Association holds the Phil Gibson Award Dinner at which a local attorney is recognized for her or his exceptional commitment to public service. Hard to imagine a better way to honor the memory of Phil Gibson who became a resident of Monterey after his retirement.

I was honored to be the speaker at the Gibson award dinner in May 2006 and had the misfortune to follow Chief Gibson's son, Blaine, who spoke eloquently about his father. I say misfortune because I was so moved by his comments that I wished he would continue speaking in place of me. (I declare under penalty of perjury that the preceding sentence is true and correct.) After the dinner, Blaine spoke with me about his father.

Phil Gibson was a jurist of exceptional ability, a human being of remarkable warmth and compassion. He was also self-effacing and modest. One would not see press releases trumpeting his accomplishments. Without fanfare Chief Gibson modernized the administrative offices of the courts and instituted pretrial procedures used today. California's premier legal chronicler, Bernie Witkin, served as Chief Gibson's senior research attorney for many years. Members of the Gibson Court included such luminaries as Justices Traynor, Peters, Schauer and Carter.

Gibson's son, Blaine, is an articulate soft-spoken lawyer who devotes his talents to helping establish businesses in Russia. His calling was prompted by his father receiving a call from President Truman in 1945. Truman asked the Chief to host the Soviet delegation for their stay in California during the signing of the United Nations Charter in San Francisco. Gibson demurred on the grounds that he was not an expert in foreign affairs. Truman replied, "That's exactly why I want you." While strolling through Muir Woods Park with the Soviet delegation, Stalin's attorney told Justice Gibson that our country does not need Communism and "I hope you never have it." Justice Gibson told Blaine that the cold war will not last forever, that the iron curtain will fall and people will be free. He expressed the wish that one day the Russians will be his friends, not his enemies. Indeed, Blaine fulfills this wish in his work.

Blaine recalls some of his father's significant opinions. In *Sei Fuji v. State of California* (1952) 38 Cal.2d 781, Gibson wrote the majority opinion striking down, as a violation of equal protection, the California Alien Land Law which prevented an alien Japanese from owning land.

In *Jackson v. Pasadena City School District* (1963) 59 Cal.2d 876, Gibson writing for a unanimous court held it a violation of equal protection for the school district to gerrymander school zones to achieve segregation.

After Gibson retired from the court, renowned appellate lawyer Ed Lascher conducted an extended interview with him. It covered a wide range of topics about the court, its justices, and the practice of law. Justice Gibson did not think the interview should be published. "Who," he wondered "would want to read my ramblings?" Just about everybody. The interview now resides with the California Supreme Court Historical Society, and we hope will soon be published.

Blaine patiently responded to my questions for a few hours. We got the hint that our discussion must come to an end when the staff began shutting the lights in the hotel dining room. Many lawyers do not know about the many achievements of Chief Justice Gibson. But unlike some broken marriages, this condition is remediable. It is about time we all know more about this great jurist who contributed so much to the development and administration of California law.

II

Lately I have been reoccupied with memory. Memory gives continuity and substance to our identity. Memory gives us a foundation from which to build the future. Memory is a source of vitality and growth.

But not everything preserved in recorded memory is worth remembering. At the top of my "things to forget" list is any list of the 100 best. Such lists are suspect, especially when they include my name. Magazines carry a list of the 100 best CPAs, 100 best lawyers, 100 best taxidermists, 100 best proctologists. According to whom? Clients? Patients? Other proctologists? The people on the list?

Even more irritating is a credible list that omits a name that unquestionably belongs there. I recently came across such a list on Wikipedia, the so called "People's Encyclopedia," where anyone may contribute information.

After perusing lists that ranged from the tallest buildings in London to tallying the Tampa Bay Buccaneers' first round draft picks, I decided to see what "the People's Encyclopedia, " had to say about the California Supreme Court. While the site gives a serviceable overview of the court's functions, its list of notable past justices is marked by a glaring omission: Phil Gibson. Gibson served as Chief Justice of the California court from 1940 to 1964. In part I of this column I have written about my meeting with Justice Gibson's son Blaine. The connection goes even deeper: It was Gibson himself who swore me into the law shortly before his retirement.

Blaine's anecdotes and the many e-mails that I have received about part I of this column have convinced me to continue with the Gibson project (not to be confused with the Tristan project…that one has music.)

One of our leading appellate lawyers, Ellis Horvitz, went straight from Stanford Law School into clerking for Justice Gibson from 1951 to 1953, before Blaine was born. Recently, Ellis and I had a leisurely lunch in an inviting French Restaurant in Ventura and he related what it was like clerking for one of California's greatest Chief Justice.

It is beyond dispute that Gibson brought the court into the 20th Century, cultivating a well-earned reputation as the state's leading court administrator. In 1941, he persuaded the Legislature to transfer the power to make rules of appellate procedure to the Judicial Council. This eventually led to the Council having rule-making power over all practice and procedure. He created the Judicial Performance Commission and found time to write 670 opinions. He left an indelible impression on case law in California.

"Gibson was short, but his commanding presence made him ten feet tall," Horvitz relates. He notes that Gibson was a warm, caring person, but when it came to work, "his tone was severe and compliments were hard to come by. It was well worth it, because the goal was to produce the best work possible." Horvitz credits his subsequent success to Gibson: "Under his tutelage, I became an appellate lawyer."

Horvitz continued, "It is not in fashion today, but Gibson taught by scolding." Schooling by scolding seldom works, even when in the service of a higher cause, but Gibson proved the exception to this rule. "The scoldings were colorful, salty, often laced with humor and warmth," Horvitz said, "Thirty to forty drafts were not uncommon. In those days they had the time to write short, concise opinions. The goal was to get the best opinion possible: not a job for the faint-hearted." Horvitz emphasized that Gibson generated excitement and riveted "our attention on the work at hand. He was relentless in demanding our best and resourceful in getting it." Under these circumstances, no one minded a little good-natured scolding now and then.

Horvitz relates how the Chief could take the edge off a compliment with a dash of humor. Horvitz had written a draft in a will contest. The Chief liked it and said so. Just as the glow was settling in, the Chief (in colorful language) inquired as to why Horvitz had given him a less-than-sterling draft opinion in another case the previous week.

In an article he wrote for the *California Review* (72 Cal.L.Rev. 503 (1984)), Horvitz described how "[t]he Chief was a stickler for clear and precise writing." Stilted or uncommon language was quickly scuttled. Gibson cautioned, "[i]f you don't talk that way, you can't write that way." Horvitz continued, "and we drafted, redrafted, and redrafted again until all the fat was trimmed and the written words carried the precise message intended. In short, we were given a graduate course in logic, composition and style."

Gibson also cautioned against paraphrasing the holding of a case. As the chief justice archly put it, " Some judge worked hard to write that opinion, and you're not yet ready to improve on it."

But Gibson's rough exterior was like a thin layer of shellac. He cared deeply about his staff and was concerned about their lives and aspirations. Horvitz recalls Gibson's "deep concern about their well-being." He harvested good work out of his staff, not just because of his formidable bearing, but also because no one could bear to disappoint him. He was admired and loved. "We worked hard for his smile."

Gibson commanded the respect of the three Governors who served the state while he was Chief Justice. When budget time came around, each Governor in his respective term would inquire, "What does the Chief want?" The late Justice Stanley Mosk observed that Gibson was respectfully called "The Little Giant" in the Legislature.

Gibson was close with his successor Chief Justice, the remarkable Roger Traynor. Traynor wrote his opinions in long hand and Gibson expressed his admiration for the formidable skill Traynor displayed. The expectation and demand that one do his or her best was the laudable goal that Gibson set for himself and all who worked in his chambers. His congeniality with (and respect for) other members of the court helped bring "the court together" and reduced "fractionalized opinions."

Gibson set high standards for himself, his staff, and the lawyers appearing before the court. Horvitz recalls an occasion when a lawyer arguing before the court misrepresented the law. After the oral argument, Gibson and his staff were having lunch in the Redwood Room across the street from the court. The lawyer walked by them. After he had passed, Gibson asked rhetorically, "Why would a lawyer misrepresent the law to this court? At least one judge will know the law, and usually seven."

Gibson left his mark as a great administrator but also as a passionate defender of constitutional rights. He struck down racial discrimination in *Sei Fuji v State*, 38 Cal.2d 718 (1952) and *Jackson v. Pasadena City School District*, 59 Cal.2d 876 (1963). In his dissenting opinion in *The Times-Mirror Co. v Superior Court*, 15 Cal. 2d 99 (1940), Gibson eloquently wrote of the "fundamental need of fearless comment on all activities affecting the public welfare, including the operations of the courts." Let us remember this great jurist whose contribution to the administration of justice in California has given us an enduring legacy. This we will not forget.

RICHARD ABBE

In April of 1991 I wrote a good-bye column about my dear friend and colleague, Justice Richard Abbe, who had just retired from Division Six, Second District of the Court of Appeal. Richard, then Presiding Justice, Steve Stone, and I had just returned from a study trip to Cuba. We, along with other judges, lawyers, journalists, and physicians, had met with judges, administrators and government officials for an exchange of ideas.

One evening, as our group was having a drink at La Bodeguita, the very place where Hemingway held court, and drank and swore, we affectionately toasted Richard. "Buena suerte Viejo," we shouted. And someone said to me, "And why do you call him Viejo?" and I, feeling the resolute hand of Papa Hemingway on my shoulder, said, "It is good you ask this question because it is a good question, an honest question, and I say to you that Señor Abbe, he sees the world as joven, because in his heart he is joven, and that is why we call him Viejo because he is the opposite; he is joven. And so when we see Señor Juez Abbe, we think he is joven, but we say 'Viejo' and everyone laughs."

And now it is with a heavy heart that I must write another good-bye column to Richard Abbe, a remarkable person who died quite unexpectedly on September 3, 2000, of an intracerebral hemorrhage.

"Sui generis" is a good term to describe Richard Abbe. All you lawyers and pharmacists know that it is a Latin term that we misuse now and then. It means one of a kind, unique, having no equal, unparalleled.

Richard Abbe was a walking collection of contradictions. I was never quite sure if he was a liberal conservative or a conservative liberal. In any event, he was highly respected by both groups. He was the ex-District Attorney of Shasta County, who vigorously opposed the death penalty. He was the most charitable person one could ever meet, ever ready to help the poor and the disadvantaged, extremely principled and moral, yet not fond of organized religion. He was not sentimental, but carried warm, passionate feelings for his family and friends. He was extremely congenial to his colleagues, but took pride in his license plate which bluntly stated with unabashed candor, "DISSENT." He had a gargantuan intellect and crisp, dry wit that always found its mark, yet he was unassuming, down to earth and self-effacing.

Known for uncompromising integrity, unwavering fairness, and fierce independence, his written legal opinions were direct, well-reasoned and to the point. "No need to ramble on," said Justice Abbe. "It is really quite simple. Simply state the holding in simple language, then move on to the next case and do the same thing again." Retired Presiding Justice, Steve Stone, called Richard Abbe a "hero, a fearless judge who exhibited both physical and intellectual prowess."

Through the hundreds of opinions he authored, he brought distinction to the Court of Appeal and played a major role in shaping the law in California. In *Raytheon v. Fair Employment and Housing Commission* (1989) 212 Cal.App.3d 1242, he wrote that an employer may not discriminate against an employee with AIDS. In *Hanson v. Department of Social Services* (1987) 193 Cal.App.3d 283, he wrote that the Department of Social Services is required to provide emergency child care services to homeless families. In *People v. Harbor Hut Restaurant* (1983) 147 Cal.App.3d 1151, he held that in order to protect our natural resources, the Department of Fish and Game could periodically inspect commercial fishing establishments without a warrant. Professor David Mellinkoff praised the opinion for simply stating that defendants asked the court to "suppress the fish." How refreshing.

Richard, Steve Stone and myself were the first members of Division Six, created in 1982. Richard and I first met at our confirmation hearing before the Judicial Appointments Commission in December of that year.

This is one event where everyone wears a suit. I noticed that Richard's pants and jacket did not match. The fabric and the contrasting shades of gray were, well, sui generis. "Nice outfit," I whispered in his ear. "I accidentally grabbed the pants to the wrong suit," he said sheepishly. He gave me a once over and then said, "I guess now you don't feel so bad wearing brown socks with your blue suit." Steve Stone was wearing polyester pants. And so was born the dress-down dress code of Division Six. We became known as the think tank with tank tops.

Richard, an avid sportsman, was a runner, a hiker, a tennis player and a cyclist. Richard, Steve and I often rode our bicycles from Santa Barbara to Ventura. Once, Richard and I served as crew in a sailboat race at Lake Tahoe. That we did not place is not pertinent to the story. After the race we anchored the sailboat off shore and, with other members of the crew, dejectedly rowed to the dock in a small skiff. Once on the dock, Richard remembered that he had left some provisions on the boat and asked me to row him back to retrieve them. It was cold and windy and the sun was setting. Against my better judgment, I agreed and got back into the skiff. It promptly capsized sending me sprawling, fully clothed, into the dark chilly waters of Lake Tahoe. When I reached the surface, sputtering water, I saw Richard casually looking down at me from the dock. No doubt he was thinking of his dissent in the last case we had just filed. "Arthur, you are as wet as your last opinion," he said holding out a hand to help pull me out of the water.

Judges on the same court are often called brothers or sisters. Richard, Steve and I were as close as brothers could be. We had a special relationship that, despite death, endures. You could call it sui generis. I suppose that is why this good-bye is not final. There will always be that sparkle in Viejo's eyes, like the sparkle of the sun on the sea. Viejo is forever joven.

I was walking down the street talking to Tom Crosby a few days ago. He was his usual self, railing about a case with which he disagreed. "The issue has the circumference of a medicine ball and they missed it."

"You are getting excited, Tom," I said.

"Of course I am. I love talking, thinking, shaping and writing about the law. That is something to get excited about."

"Hey, Tom," I said, "People will think I'm nuts. It looks like I'm talking to myself."

"I like that," said Tom. "But not to worry. People probably think you are talking on a cell phone."

"But I'm not holding a cell phone."

"I love it. If people don't think you are a little nuts, or highly unusual, then you are probably not doing your job."

Here I am walking down the street and talking to Tom Crosby. Newspapers say he passed away last month. Tom would be the first to say not to believe everything you read in the papers, or elsewhere for that matter. If you asked him if that included his own opinions, he would give you his signature Crosby smile, almost sardonic, but not quite, because of the twinkle in his eyes.

"There are exceptions for the exceptional," he would say.

In the case of the articles about Tom's passing, I don't believe entirely what I have read, not because Tom says so, but because here I am talking to him. I hear his voice, his inflections, his wry humor, his contempt for artifice and empty slogans, his insistence on rigorous analysis and thought. People like Tom don't merely "pass away." Tom is still there, in your face, challenging you to think and to be honest. His engaging and lovely wife Patty will bear me out on this. I had the good fortune to spend some stimulating and joyful hours with Tom and Patty.

Tom and I were appointed to the California Court of Appeal at the same time, in December of 1982, he to the Fourth District in Orange County, and I to the Second District, Division 6, the new Division in Ventura. We first met at a conference for new appellate justices in Berkeley shortly after our appointments. He often looked like a straight-laced Ivy League type, what with his bow ties, wire-rimmed glasses, sleeveless cardigan vest and reserved bearing. A recent photograph of Tom shows him with his arms folded. It might lead one to believe he is playing it close to the vest, or that his mind is made up and there will be no changing it. Wrong! Tom is indisputable proof that looks are deceiving, or that my perceptions are faulty.

Tom knew everything about any case that came before him and everyone else's cases, including my own. He lectured extensively on a case I wrote on writ practice (*Omaha Indemnity v. Superior Court of Santa Barbara Co.* (1989) 209 Cal.App.3d 1266). Tom supplied a stunning analysis, uncovering subtleties that enhanced my insight of the very case I wrote. In remarking about the infrequency with which writ petitions are granted, Crosby, with his characteristic wit, reminded judges and the bar that there is a reason our court is not called the Court of Writs. I lavished Tom with praise for his incisive comments. He blushed and changed the subject. He simply could not accept compliments, but was liberal in his praise of others, with one important proviso--you had to deserve it.

He was persuasive even when you disagreed with him. On a visit to Rome he e-mailed his staff that he felt he had convinced the Pope to accept *Roe v. Wade*. I could go on and tell you about his incandescent brilliance, his ironic humor, his passion for the law, and his healthy obsession with justice. But Tom and his staff speak with far more elegance than I can muster. On his retirement, Tom's staff, Bill Amsbary, John Gastelum, John Seckinger, and Bob Wolfe, put together numerous quotes from Tom's opinions. They titled it, appropriately, "The Portable Crosby." Tom did not think he was doing his job if he did not get under one's skin now and then. Nevertheless, it could also have been titled "The Quotable Crosby."

In the preface they write: "With Tom Crosby's retirement, it has been said (in the L.A. Times, no less) that our court may be losing its 'most gifted writer.' Words never failed Justice Crosby, but he has been equally good to them in return. More interested in clarity than cleverness, he was unmotivated by politics, hidden agendas or ideology. He ably filled the judiciary's side of the bargain in Justice Gilbert's 'match in heaven' between good writers and readers of judicial opinions. [¶] While Tom Crosby may not have been infallible, he certainly was unflappable. Whatever he dished out, he took in return. Whether his carefully crafted, deeply felt opinions were decertified, reversed or simply ignored – whether he was the lone dissenter or the target of a blistering riposte from a justice, brief writer or talk radio host—his typical reaction was the muttered: 'It'll make you crazy if you let it.' And he never did. [¶] It has been our luck to work with a clear-headed, plain-speaking *el jefe*. Over the years, we have seen Justice Crosby edit—indeed shred our writing. It is now our supreme pleasure, *finally*, to edit his."

Tom had much to say on every topic and issue known to humankind. His words reflect his character, wit, imagination, wisdom, compassion and intellect. Here are some gems from "The Portable Crosby." Some cases have not been published, but Tom's words live on.

"While a picture might be worth a thousand words, the jury heard at least that many." (*Akers v. Miller* (1998) 68 Cal.App.4th 1143, 1147.) "Vincent Van Gogh wrote to his brother in May 1889 that his madness should be viewed 'as a disease like any other.' More than a century later, health care insurers still do not share this outlook." (*Warner v. California Physicians Service* (1998) G016812, unpublished.) "Considering [the father's] own claims of poverty, we are puzzled why he has chosen to pay his attorneys (at $250 per hour) to pursue this appeal rather than to pay a much lesser sum to his own children. One hour of his attorney's time would cover ten months of additional support for each child." (*In re Marriage of Estrada* (2001) G027301, unpublished.) "After school and during vacation periods, the streets, beaches, homes and malls are crowded with unattended children. Some of them are lonely; some get hurt or killed; and many are victimized or victimize others. This is all a shame, one of the great failings of our otherwise fabulously wealthy society . . . ." (*In re Kamiya* (1998) G022140, unpublished.) "[Appellant] did not receive ineffective assistance of counsel; sadly, her son had an ineffective mother." (*In re Cody W.* (1994) 31 Cal.App.4th 221, 223-224.) "Whatever hat the contractor may have worn, it simply did not cover an insured head." (*Campobasso v. State Farm Fire & Casualty Co.* (1998) G016911, unpublished.)

"[Defendant] was 'guilty' of only one thing--constructive possession of an ice-cold 12-pack. A sin, perhaps, in some quarters, but a far cry from the FBI's 'most wanted list.'" (*Huynh v. Superior Court* (2000) unpublished.) "[A]n auto thief, like a second–story man apprehended in the victimized premises, has no standing to assert a reasonable expectation of privacy in the stolen car." (*People v. Melnyk* (1992) 4 Cal.App.4th 1532, 1533.) "Counsel in the defense of criminal cases is not held to a standard of miraculous prescience." (*People v. Fatone* (1985) 165 Cal.A.pp.3d 1164, 1174.)

"Our rivers may be murky, the air opaque, and the Pacific clouded with sewage and sludge; but Public Resources Code section 21166 is as clear as they once were." (Dissenting in *Fund for Environmental Defense v. County of Orange* (1988) 204 Cal.App.3d 1538.) "[Plaintiff's] unseemly haste . . . reminds us of the farmer who pulled up his crops each night to see how they were growing." (*Dynamic Concepts, Inc. v. Truck Ins. Exchange* (1998) 61 Cal.App.4th 999, 1001.)

"[T]he performance was in bad taste, but 'there is no law against bad taste,' which should 'be reassuring to much of the modern entertainment industry.'" (*People v. Janini* (2000) 89 Cal.Rptr. 244, ordered not published.) "The appearance of Halley's Comet is probably a more common occurrence than a refusal to dismiss a misdemeanor on the prosecution's motion." (*Mathis v. Superior Court* (1984) 203 Cal.Rptr. 65, 69, fn. 2, ordered not published.) "[H]omelessness is a national phenomenon, and it is not the first time it has appeared as an important social problem in this century. The attack must be on the cause, not the victims; for they in the main are no more content with their circumstances than anyone else is." (*Tobe v. City of Santa Ana* (1994) 27 Cal.Rptr.2d 386, review granted.) "A cautionary note—we spend too much time trying to make sense out of arbitration agreements precisely because litigants spend too little time in drafting them." (*National Union Fire Ins. Co. v. Nationwide Ins. Co.* (1999) 69 Cal.App.4th 709, 716.)

And here is one that for some odd reason was ordered depublished by the Supreme Court. "There is a [deplorable] trend in the Court of Appeal to abandon the application of judicial responsibility by taking cues from Supreme Court depublication practices." (*People v. Salgado* (1990), ordered not published. Not to worry, the case endures in 266 Cal.Rptr. 887, fn. 1.)

The foregoing is a mere sample of Justice Crosby's legacy. His passion for grammar equaled his passion for the proper application of legal principles. He railed against the "indefensible comma" and loathed the word "that." And so Tom, we will still carry on our conversations and I can take comfort in knowing that . . . whoops, I mean in knowing you will always be with us. Good-bye dear friend.

GOOD-BYE PAUL

Years ago when I was a trial judge I presided over a criminal case in which a physician had been charged with false advertising. He had promoted himself as an expert breast implant surgeon. Several victims testified in graphic detail how he had botched the job. The victims felt the doctor had made them look like women conjured from the imagination of Picasso during his cubist period. One of the victims could not hold her anger in check and answered questions put to her by her attorney with rambling diatribes against the doctor. I could appreciate her resentment but of course sustained the objections to her responses and struck her answers. I gently admonished her to answer the question directly and not offer her opinion about the defendant's character or guilt.

She then directed her anger at me and asked, "Who do you think you are—God?" That got everyone's attention. I took a moment to think about it. After some reflection I had to admit to myself I was not. I patiently explained that I was just a person with a job to ensure that the defendant and the people receive a fair trial, and that, however justifiable her anger, she would have to accept my evidentiary rulings. It is doubtful her outburst enhanced the People's case. The jury's "not guilty" verdict confirmed my belief that the case would have been best tried as a negligence rather than a criminal action.

The victim's displeasure with my ruling and my admonitions and directions to her brought home to me that, to many people, judges seem to act like gods. They sit at a higher level than others in the courtroom. Everyone stands when the court session begins. Judges are referred to as "Your Honor," and are usually spoken to with respect however contrary the speaker's inner thoughts.

But judges are just people, and the courtroom, whatever its architecture or furnishings, however grand or common place in appearance, is simply a formal meeting place where rules make possible the resolution of disputes. Judges, like everyone else, are subject to what is unexpected and uncertain in a seemingly impersonal universe. Of course, they, like everyone else, are subject to good and bad fortune, happiness, tragedy, illness and death.

The recent passing of Justice Paul Boland makes this point with brutal clarity. One day he appeared to be the picture of health, amiably conversing with his colleagues, and then a day or two later he had succumbed to a virulent cancer. Paul had a profound effect on litigants, lawyers, his colleagues, and the many students and externs he nurtured. He was a remarkable judge, who despite his imposing stature was a warm, gracious, self-effacing human being, on and off the bench. His abrupt end left so many of us in shock and compelled me and others to ask the question that reflects both impudence and impotence: "How can this be?"

The suddenness of Paul's untimely death forces us to acknowledge the fragility of life and to accept the searing unassailable fact of our mortality. Whatever our faith or our beliefs about the hereafter, or the meaning of life, the experience of a loss like this binds people together in their grief, bewilderment, and shared appreciation of a unique individual. It also fosters a concern for one another, a recognition that our days are numbered and an appreciation that life is a gift.

I first met Paul years ago when he was teaching at UCLA, before he was a judge, and before either of us were married. We lived in the same neighborhood and spent some good times together. We taught some programs together, and when he was hearing dependency cases as a referee, we took the bus from the Palisades to the courthouse downtown.

As often happens in life, after Paul married Margaret and moved to Pasadena, we did not see each other that much. But ironically, his death has brought us closer again.

In one of my past investigatory columns, I wrote an expose of myself getting speeding tickets now and then while driving up the coast to Ventura. I have finally graduated from traffic school with honors. Future offenses are doubtful. You may have noticed that posted throughout the city there are flashing radar signs that show your speed as you approach them. These ubiquitous signs have made me aware of and focused on my speed, which I keep within the limit. They now influence my driving even when they are not around. Paul, forgive me, but, in a similar fashion, your influence lives on. Your family and loved ones have their special relationship with you. But for others, whether a judge, a lawyer, or a friend, through the memory of your character, your commitment to your students and to justice, you will continue to affect our lives.

I have no choice but to say "Good-bye Paul." Your sudden passing is incomprehensible, but through your good work, and the example you set, you are still with us, to inspire us to live and be better at what we do and who we are. And that in turn gives us meaning in an incomprehensible world.

GOOD-BYE DAVID MELLINKOFF

They say he passed away. His name is David Mellinkoff. He was unpretentious and unassuming, but, if you did not know him, you might call him Professor or General instead of David. "General?" you ask. Most definitely. He was a five star who, with unflagging courage and relentless determination, led us into battle against unclear thinking and sloppy writing. I served as one of his lieutenants but suffered grievous injuries in most of the frays.

They say our grand warrior passed away. I attended a memorial service in which his family, colleagues and friends paid him a touching and moving tribute. Nevertheless, I can assure you he has not passed away. While I composed this column, David was looking over my shoulder with the customary twinkle in his eye. "You don't need all the adjectives in the preceding paragraph. 'Courage' and 'determination' are sufficient," he says. (Just in case he was being modest, I left the adjectives in.)

Through his books and teaching at UCLA Law School, Professor David Mellinkoff has shown judges, lawyers, and law students how to use their tools--words. *The Language of the Law*, in its 10th printing, and *The Conscience of a Lawyer*, *Legal Writing: Sense and Nonsense* have inspired us to think and to write with clarity and concision. If we could just follow the seven rules outlined in *Legal Writing: Sense and Nonsense*, West Publishing (1982), we would understand one another. They are simple yet profound:

"**Rule 1.** Peculiar. The language of the law is more peculiar than precise. Don't confuse peculiarity with precision.

Rule 2. Precise. Don't ignore even the limited possibilities of precision. The price of sloppy writing is misunderstanding and creative misinterpretation.

Rule 3. English. Follow the rules of English composition.

Rule 4. Clear. Usually you have a choice of how to say it. Choose clarity.

Rule 5. Law. Write law simply. Do not puff, mangle or hide.

Rule 6. Plan. Before you write, plan.

Rule 7. Cut. Cut it in half."

I had the pleasure to know David and his wife Ruth, a noted art historian and author of numerous scholarly works on medieval iconography. She is also an Epicurean cook and the author of several cookbooks written so clearly that even I could follow the recipes. If I liked to shop, I might have prepared a decent pheasant under glass. There were wonderful dinner parties at the Mellinkoffs where an array of fascinating guests engaged in lively and spirited discussions over sumptuous meals. But even when we were miles apart, David was there, just as he is now. In every opinion I write, David is present through every agonizing minute of the drafting, redrafting, and redrafting and redrafting.

"Does that mean you do only four drafts?" David asks. "Why not just leave it at 'drafting'? That includes all the redrafts."

See what I mean? But while I am drafting, David persists. "Does the reader know what you are talking about?" he mutters. "Do you know what the hell you are talking about? You have allowed a wandering afterthought to obscure your idea. Start over," he orders.

And on occasion when I reread one of my opinions, he pops up again, and we read it together, and we both shake our heads in dismay. "Next time be clear," he advises. "More clear?" I respond. "No, clear."

He hated pomp and pretension. That no doubt was why he opposed changing the law degree from an LL.B. to a J.D. Juris Doctor. That was a battle he did not win. He wondered what would happen when they ask is there a doctor in the house? Would the lawyers in the audience stand up? David mused on what J.D, could stand for: Juvenile Delinquent, Justice Department, Junior Deacon, or maybe just John Doe. To these I might add (David has this effect on me), John Dillinger, John Dean or even John Dory (followed by a Jelly Donut), junk dealer, justice delayed, judicial decision, jurisdictional dispute, and jail detainee.

Once David and I were giving a talk to appellate lawyers on how to write briefs when spontaneously we broke into a dialog peppered with solecisms and redundant phrases to illustrate what happens when one throws good usage to the winds. Unfortunately, I did not know that was what we were doing. It went something like this:

Arthur: David, I'll contact you so we can take lunch soon.

David: Are we playing touch football, and to where will we take our lunch?

Arthur: Location is unimportant. I just want to get together with you because your ideas have a tremendous impact on me.

David: Tackle football?

Arthur: Sports aside, maybe we can endeavor to establish the parameters for a range of ideas.

David: And explore the reasons why we need to address those issues.

Arthur: In that case we will need a stamp and an envelope.

David: The sum total of our experience is based on our past history.

Arthur: Good starting point for us to strive for a new record.

David: As opposed to an old record.

Arthur: In the final analysis it would seem that we should not get involved in a crisis situation.

David: I think you are on to something. I can tell by the smile on your face.

Arthur: Better it be there than somewhere else. But your remarks are well taken and for that I am bringing a bouquet of flowers to our lunch.

David: Better than a bouquet of chopped liver.

Arthur: I merely want to proceed so that we don't labor under false pretenses.

David: As opposed to true pretenses.

Arthur: The bottom line is for us to give a free gift to anyone who understands what we are talking about.

David: I hate gifts you have to pay for but I think we can wrap it up by prioritizing our alternatives.

Arthur: This whole discussion has taken us to a new dimension in communication and allowed us to have a meaningful dialogue.

The dialogue highlighted the obvious, but obscurity can be insidiously subtle. Just the other day I wrote in a draft of an opinion, "Plaintiff rented the store." It seemed so clear, yet something was wrong. What was it? I heard bugles in the distance and the faint thunder of horses' hooves. Mellinkoff was riding to the rescue once again. And suddenly there he was looking down at me from his spirited steed. He wore a brown gabardine suit, and as usual was neat and unadorned except for a colorful bow tie. He posed a question that solved the problem. "Is plaintiff the lessor or the lessee?" He rode off into the sunset.

Thanks for saving me once again David. I'll say good-bye with this couplet which reflects my appreciation and gives me and countless others comfort.

I miss you, but I do not grieve,
You are here; you did not leave.

A CLOSING ARGUMENT FOR JOHNNY COCHRAN

Q: When? A: The fall of 1964. Q: Where? A: Division 20, the Misdemeanor Master Calendar Court of the Los Angeles Municipal Court. Q: Who? A: Johnny Cochran and I. Q: You mention your names and not the judge presiding? A: What do you expect from two cocky Deputy City Attorneys barely past puberty? Q: But you are telling us about this today. A: Good point. The judge was Richard Schauer who eventually became Presiding Judge of the Los Angeles Superior Court and a Presiding Justice on the Court of Appeal.

Q: Impressive, but specifically what did you and Johnny Cochran do? A: We were prosecutors, seeking to put behind bars, (county jail bars that is) dangerous criminal misdemeanants who prey upon an unsuspecting public. Q: How would you characterize the two of you, first Johnny? A: Chairman of the board. Q: And you? A: Me? Q: Yes, you. Tell the truth. A: Senior vice president. Q: Who else is there? A: Lawyers, clerks, witnesses, defendants appearing with and without counsel to enter pleas of guilty or nolo contendre or to be assigned out to a courtroom for trial. Q: Do the defendants know they have a right to counsel? A: No, Miranda hadn't been decided yet. Neither had *People v. Dorado* (1965) 62 Cal. 2nd 338 (defendant must be advised of right to counsel).

Q: What are you and Johnny doing? A: We are "running" the master calendar court. Q: Why are you not trying cases in a trial court? A: We have tried hundreds of cases, but because we are preparing for special cases that have been assigned to us, the chief deputy has given us a respite in the master calendar court. A: What case is Johnny working on? A: He is preparing for a fraud case that will be defended by Melvin Belli. Q: What does Johnny say about his chances for success against such a formidable opponent? A: He is confident. Q: I didn't ask for your conclusion, I asked what did he say? A: Say exactly? Q: Yes, that would be preferable. A: "I'll kick his ass all over the courtroom." Q: Hmmm. A: Well, you asked for an exact quote.

Q: What case were you preparing for? A: The kosher chicken case. You see these chickens . . . . Q: (Interrupting) Would you mind saving that for a future column? A: I could do that. Q: We can hardly wait to read it. Isn't this column about Johnny Cochran? A: Yes, Good point.

Q: So getting back to 1964 in Division 20 of the Master Calendar Court. While you and Johnny Cochran were "running" the master calendar criminal court, did anything of significance happen? A: No, not particularly. Q: So why bring it up? A: I didn't bring it up, you are the one asking questions. Q: But you are writing this column. A: True, but enough arguing. I remember a typical Johnny Cochran exchange with the judge. Q: So tell us about it. A: Judge Schauer called the name of a defendant, "Thomas Edison Jackson." Johnny couldn't find the file. In a louder voice, Judge Schauer said, "Thomas Edison Jackson." Johnny grabbed a file in front of him and said, "Your Honor, I see the light." "Now you've done it," I whispered to Johnny. There was a stunned silence in the courtroom as Judge Schauer glared at us for what seemed an eternity. Finally he spoke. "A most illuminating remark, Mr. Cochran."

That was quintessential Johnny. He shot me a glance. "Schauer's cool," he said.

Q: So tell us more about Johnny.

A: We met in 1964, newly hired deputies at the City Attorney's Office, an ideal place for young lawyers just out of law school to get trial experience. We tried a potpourri of misdemeanors, but drunk driving cases were our staple. Have times changed. Today, a reading of .10 on the breathalyzer guarantees jail time. Back in the 60's a reading of .15 could often be negotiated down to a reckless driving.

Many in our class of '64 became successful. Irv Sepkowitz, besides being one of the funniest and nicest human beings alive, became vice president of business affairs for Universal Studios. Ira Reiner became District Attorney; John Karns, a partner in Karns and Karabian. Charlie Lloyd went on to represent professional football players and became a successful entrepreneur. Also part of the group was then bailiff Julian Dixon, who during tedious trials studied tedious case books in contracts and torts for his night law school classes at Southwestern Law School. He became a highly respected member of congress.

Johnny was not just a mentor to me, he was an inspiration and a model. His life had been a struggle from poverty in the South to opportunity in Los Angeles. Yet, he was always positive and cheerful. He exuded enthusiasm and confidence. Everyone liked him. If I was feeling down, his very presence was uplifting. You can imagine how juries responded to him. He would flash a smile, begin talking, and another drunk driver or other misdemeanant would bite the dust.

I remember only one case Johnny lost while in the City Attorney's Office. The defendant was comedian Lenny Bruce charged with obscenity for uttering words we hear on television sitcoms today. There was the possibility I might have to try a similar case against the playwright and poet then known as Leroi Jones. He later changed his name to Amiri Baraka and became New Jersey's third and most controversial poet laureate. His two one-act plays, "Dutchman" and "The Toilet," were being performed at the Coronet theater on La Cienega. I attended a performance. Sprinkled throughout the audience were plain clothes police officers furiously scribbling notes. The tough and raw language, the themes of violence and the belligerent protest against racial injustice roiled the establishment. The City Attorney's Office under the leadership of Roger Arnebergh was contemplating action. At the conclusion of the performance, actress Shirley Knight came onto the stage to rally support for freedom of artistic expression.

During the next few days, Johnny and I met with investigating officers and staff of the City Attorney's Office to discuss whether an action should be filed. I argued, with support from Johnny, that our obligation was to prosecute criminals, not artists, whose words and language were disturbing to some. I predicted we would and should lose the case should anyone in charge be dimwitted enough to file one.

"Not a bad argument," Johnny said. "Do the same in court, and you will be one hell of a trial attorney." We didn't mention Lenny Bruce.

Johnny was always strongly supportive of law enforcement, this even before his son the Highway Patrol officer was born. His thesis was simply this. Everyone has a responsibility to do their job right, and to do it with integrity and professionalism. He approached his cases with a commitment to attain the highest level of skill and competence of which he was capable. He strived for excellence. He expected others to do the same in their professions, and that included, indeed was a fundamental obligation of, law enforcement officers. "Not to much to ask," he would say, "when people's freedom and their lives are at stake."

I recall a case in which a personable police officer, who Johnny liked and admired, testified in a preliminary hearing in Judge Marion Obera's court. The officer testified that he knocked on the front door, the defendant answered and invited him into the house where he "observed large quantities of drugs." Then came the defense, something unusual for a preliminary hearing. Shortly before the officer had arrived, the defendant and his rock group had been rehearsing for an upcoming gig. They had also been recording the session. When the officer knocked, the band was taking a break, only they had forgotten to turn off the tape recorder. Need I say more? There on the tape recorder, for everyone to hear, was the pounding on the door, the rush of the officers into the room accompanied by threats and obscenities.

Johnny's disappointment was profound. He had lost a friend, and was furious that this misconduct could reflect poorly on the vast majority of police officers who are skilled professionals dedicated to fulfilling the motto of the department, "to protect and to serve." Johnny, a champion of civil rights, was particularly chagrined because here the officer was black and the defendant white. Johnny, who was ecstatic over passage of the 1964 Civil Rights Act said that at least this unfortunate incident proves we are all equal.

Johnny will always be remembered for the O.J. Simpson case. Many people are angry at him for "winning" the case. But however one may feel about O.J. Simpson, Johnny was not hired to lose the case. He pointed out flaws in the prosecution's case and the Simpson jury had a reasonable doubt. One could debate for years whether, in fact, the case was won because of Johnny's unique skill in connecting with that jury. One of the most astute commentators on the case, Ira

Reiner, predicted a "not guilty" verdict shortly after Johnny had made his opening statement. You did not have to see the jurors to know they were hanging on to every word and gesture.

Whether as a prosecutor or defense attorney, Johnny Cochran was devoted to the cause of his clients. He was a consummate trial lawyer and a warm and engaging human being. Professor Gerald Uelman is reputed to have authored the famous quote: "If it doesn't fit, you must acquit." I would add the less pithy, "Johnny's the lawyer with passion and fire. Johnny's the lawyer I most admire."

MAX SOLOMON IS GONE
THE OLD SCHOOL OF CRIMINAL DEFENSE IS CLOSED

Back in the good old days, criminal defense attorneys could ask questions of the jurors on voir dire. Under *People v. Williams* 29 Cal.3d 392 (1981), many judges allowed attorneys to ask jurors a wide range of questions to determine whether to exercise peremptory challenges. I remember one defense attorney who would ask a particularly insightful question: "What person living or dead do you most admire?"

The question recognized that there are certain people we all admire, people who influence us and who made a difference in our lives. The answer to the question often revealed something about the character of that juror. Better to have a juror who answered "Martin Luther King" or "Albert Schweitzer" than one who answered "Adolf Hitler" or "Charles Manson."

Life is interesting because of other people and the impression they make on us. They may be public figures like John F. Kennedy, or someone we have actually known, someone who has touched us in one way or another. It could be a school teacher, a spouse or even a waitress at the local coffee shop. You may have read in the papers recently that one such waitress befriended an elderly man who came into the shop each morning for coffee. She obviously added something to his life, because on his death he left her a sizable estate.

The Reader's Digest has a feature called something like "The Most Unforgettable Character I Ever Met." It has endured over the years, I suspect, because what really matter in our lives is not material things, but other people. Other people can make the impressions that affect how we think about things and how we ultimately act.

Max Solomon was a person who made a lasting impression on everyone he met. He was a criminal defense attorney of the "old school." I use the term "old school" wistfully. In the old school, the rules were different and judges exercised them with more flexibility then they do today. There was more room for a defense attorney to maneuver, to be creative. Max was a foot soldier fighting in the trenches, representing an assortment of defendants from the mob, Bugsy Siegel and Mickey Cohen, and the run-of-the-mill bookies, pimps and prostitutes.

Max was a fixture in the criminal courts building. He was known for his competence, integrity and good humor, but also because he was "colorful." If Max had not existed, Damon Runyon would have created him.

Max was diminutive, but his spirit and love for the law was gargantuan. He bore a slight resemblance to a leprechaun or a gnome. But there the similarity ended. He wasn't mischievous and he was Jewish. He wore suspenders when they weren't fashionable, and pinstriped suits with wide lapels. His face, partially obscured by large horn-rimmed glasses, looked like a Picasso creation from the cubist period.

Max had a way of getting a judge's or jury's attention. When he walked into the courtroom, everything stopped, even the clock on the wall. Max, with self-effacing humor, would attribute this effect to his looks. In fact, it was his singular presence that shone through his rumpled appearance. He was our Rumpole of the Bailey.

Max had a unique way of arguing. At a probation and sentencing hearing, his voice could sound like Louis Armstrong with a cold. At the right time that voice could move the hardest heart to feel empathy and even pity. Max would defend a bookie with a 20-page rap sheet as though he were proposing his candidacy for sainthood.

Max could effectively cross-examine without saying a word. I remember a case in which he asked an officer a question on cross-examination. After the officer gave his answer, Max took off his gigantic glasses, and just looked at the officer in disbelief. His expression of incredulity said it all. "You don't expect us to swallow that B.S., Officer."

You don't see many like Max anymore. It's a different world today. There are fewer plea bargains, and less opportunities to work out a deal for a hard working bookie or a gambler. When dealing with felonies, determinate sentences give judges less discretion. More violence has justifiably caused us to focus our attention on the rights of the victims as well as defendants. Frustrated with what we perceive to be our past failure with rehabilitation, we now concentrate on punishment. Some people even think the criminal justice system should be used as an instrument of retribution instead of rehabilitation.

I guess that's why practicing criminal law is just not as much fun as it was when Max was around. Maybe I am getting jaded, but I have a sense that there are fewer lawyers and judges who derive great joy from their work.

The Criminal Courts Bar recognized Max in the 1970's for his contribution to the profession. Max accepted the honor with grace and humility.

If we are allowed to argue our case before St. Peter, then Max did real well. Those gates opened wide. When the time comes, I hope Max will argue for me. He'll no doubt have to use the Louis Armstrong voice, and maybe take off the horn-rimmed glasses at the proper moment. Until then, so long, Max. We won't forget you.

ARTIE SHAW
HE WAS MORE THAN "GOOD ENOUGH"

I recently had a birthday. It wasn't a good one. It came at the same time of the year as all the others. I guess it wasn't all that realistic to expect this year to be different. My age makes me eligible for curmudgeon status. But I was a precocious child and became a curmudgeon at four. Well you would too, if your birthday comes, as mine does, smack dab in the middle of the holiday season, a few days before the New Year. I suppose that is why so many things other than poorly written briefs irritate me during the holiday season.

Take holiday cards for example. Every law firm in town sends its expensive custom card with a snow scene from some vague year in the nostalgic past. There is a sleigh pulled by a frisky horse with cheerful ice skaters in the background. No matter that this is Los Angeles and it's 82 degrees outside. Or maybe they send a "witty "card showing Santa being served with a complaint for flying without a permit. And for that personal touch the card bears the name of the law firm in colorful red print. Sometimes two or three different law firms send the same card. They should have a central registry like a wedding registry to avoid duplication. No matter, they all go in the basket along with the third draft of an opinion I am working on.

Holiday form letters are even more irritating. These letters often come from persons I hardly know and are filled with information about dozens of people I don't know, and never want to know or meet, ever. The assembly line letters illustrate our addiction to efficiency and our yearning to be personal. In fact, these letters are the product of lazy writers who will not take the time to craft a letter to a specific individual. Instead they assume their addressees are fungible, bound together by an enduring interest in prosaic stories about unremarkable people living tedious lives. "Dear (name of the addressee written in the blank), Mort and I painted the bathroom last March-only we ran out of paint. Since we bought the paint a long time before we started painting, we couldn't get exactly the same color, so we painted the ceiling a different color than the walls. We thought it looked kind of funny at first, but I think it's OK for a bathroom; well, at least the guest bathroom. Ronald, our dog, caught a muskrat last July, brought it into Sparky's room and dropped it in his bed. It caused quite a ruckus."

And then it occurred to me that the judicial opinions I write are similar to the form letters I detest and may be just as boring. So who am I to criticize well-meaning people who send me an insipid form letter? I needed a straight answer, and so I decided to call a friend who was not shy about voicing his opinions on any subject under the sun. From him I would not receive solace, but uncompromising honesty. What else could I expect from one who had authored a trilogy of short novels entitled, "I Love You, I Hate You, Drop Dead."

But the day after my birthday, I, and the rest of the world, suffered a devastating loss. The friend I was about to call, the legendary Artie Shaw, had passed away. I was fortunate to have known Artie for the past 15 years and his insistence on perfection strongly influenced me. But Artie was a genius to whom perfection was no stranger. To me, genius and perfection are aliens, more mystifying than the Bush twins. But to him, who no doubt was the finest clarinetist of all time, perfection was a constant yet nagging companion. This was one marriage that lasted to the end.

He was an expert in just about everything. The upstairs of his home in Newbury Park was a scaled down version of the New York Public Library. You could divide the library up into departments: the sciences, including quantum mechanics, and astrophysics, history, philosophy from pre-Socratics to the 20th Century, painting and sculpture, and literature. Yes, he read every damn one of those books at least a couple of times and remembered everything he read. He once asked me who, not what, I was reading. I said, "Proust." He then launched into an exegesis on "Swann's Way." He refused to take credit for his ability to recall everything he read. "I was born with a photographic memory," he said. "Therefore I don't get the credit." "Do you get credit for understanding all that you have read?" I asked. That question elicited a smile.

So I have been forced to ponder the dilemma of judicial opinions and form letters alone, yet I can imagine Artie's analysis. He would point out their similarities. They are written for a large audience, not just the litigants. They seek to elucidate points that are presumably of interest to a wide, albeit limited, audience. Judicial opinions that are poorly organized and dwell on facts that do not define the legal principle at issue are more like the form letters that ramble, and at best have limited interest.

I can hear Artie pointing out to me that this is entirely avoidable. One merely has to take the time and commit to writing an opinion that is clear and readable, something of interest to the reader. And the same advice can be given to the writer of an appellant's or respondent's brief, or the writer of a form letter. No one cares about the muskrat dropped in Sparky's bed, especially Sparky, a 17-year-old linebacker on his high school football team, who with fervor wishes his mother hadn't written about the muskrat incident. His grandmother loves the story.

No stranger to litigation, Artie said, "If you are a judge making important decisions, people ought to know what the hell you are talking about." Whether writing a form letter, a brief, an opinion, or engaging in a worthwhile endeavor (that should exclude columns), Artie's advice applies; "Good enough is not good enough." Printed in the program prepared for his memorial service was a poem dedicated to him by his friend, A.C. Greene, the poet, not the basketball player. It is titled, *The Soul of the Song*. It speaks to the mission of the artist, but, however limited may be our own talents, it offers insight for those who believe that "good enough is not good enough."   It reads:

He taught the clarinet to think
Not just to sing.
To explore the music it was making.
To let the fingers probe and find
The hidden places,
The crevices of meaning and emotion.
                    A good song has---------
But must be found and captured
By some divinity or other,
A melody that cannot just be played,
                    Can't be chartered,
The secret tempos and their keys
Can only be discovered
By a mind that is listening for the soul
The manuscript does not display.

THE STORIES

THE FRIGHTFUL ADVENTURE OF JUDGE
LEARNED FOOTE AND HOW IT TURNED OUT

As related by Presiding Justice Arthur Gilbert
Introduction

Many years ago Judge Learned Foote was a chronically poor writer. He was abducted by the elves of Grammaria and taken to an undisclosed location on the remote island of Haec Verba. His crime? Writing an unintelligible statement of decision. A random sample of the writing provides ample evidence of the offense. "In so far as plaintiff's contention that the cross complaint for equitable indemnity centers around an estoppel principle which coupled with the assertion of a retraxit etc." Enough. It serves no good purpose to expose innocent readers to more details of this dreadful crime.

But after his rescue Foote became a reasonably good writer. His statements of decision are to the point, and well understood by the lawyers and litigants. What happened on that island to effect such a change? After decades of silence Foote has agreed to this exclusive interview. He hopes that readers will gain some insight from his horrific experience. What follows is my interview with the renowned jurist over cafe lattes.

AG: No doubt it is painful to relive your experience on the Grammaria Island so long ago, but will you tell us what you remember about your captivity?

FOOTE: I was sentenced to a room.

AG: What kind of room?

FOOTE: It was bare other than for a crude wooden post in the middle of the room. Against the wall was a reading stand on the top of which was Black's Law Dictionary. The elves sat me down facing the post and tied my hands and legs around it. They pushed the reading stand away from the wall from which a valve protruded. One elf turned the valve a quarter turn to the right. The other elves pushed the reading stand back against the wall, then scurried out of the room, pressing their spindly fingers over their pointed ears . . . . I'm tired. I don't know that I can go on.

AG: Please don't stop now. [Interviewer's note: Foote remained silent for a moment, regained his composure and went on.]

FOOTE: The valve controlled a vent in the ceiling, out of which rushed a steady stream of deafening legalese and solecisms. The room filled with the noxious fumes of obfuscation. I knew that prolonged exposure could so damage me that I would likely never be a good writer. I began to give up hope as the onslaught brought me closer to my doom.

AG: What happened next?

FOOTE: Within seconds before it would have been too late, a rescuer, the great Knight of Clarity, Galloping Garner burst into the room. He unloosened the ropes that tied my hands, but could not untie my feet.

AG: Foote's feet.

FOOTE: Very cute.

AG: Sorry. Go on.

FOOTE: I yelled for him to turn off the valve, but he could not hear me above the din. I pulled a pad and pencil out of my pocket--how could I write the message that would save my chance of becoming a good writer? I began: "In this perilous situation I implore you to turn off the gas which is being emitted by a valve hidden behind the reading stand on the south wall. . . ." No, no, that would not do. Instead I quickly scribbled, "Turn off valve behind reading stand. Turn it a quarter turn to the left. Now!"

AG: And Garner ?

FOOTE: He knew exactly what to do. He raced to the reading stand, moved it away from the wall and turned the valve off an instant before it was too late.

AG: What made you so decide to write a crisp brief note instead of a long one?

FOOTE: I remembered where I was when the elves spirited me away and I knew instantaneously what to write.

AG: Fascinating. Where were you?

FOOTE: In the produce section of my neighborhood market.

AG: Your savior was produce?

FOOTE: No, my savior was a man hawking a vegetable chopper in the produce section. He taught me how to write.

AG: How so?

FOOTE: The vendor's livelihood depended on selling vegetable choppers. So, in short, clear, declarative sentences he told me everything I wanted to know about the chopper. He anticipated the questions I was asking myself. "Is it a hassle to clean?" he asked rhetorically. "Not a problem. You just turn this little screw clockwise, slip out the blade, and run it under water for a few seconds. Then you put it back in the machine by sliding it in the slot and turning it counter-clockwise."

He told me and then showed me how to adjust the chopper so that it would cut, shred or slice a variety of vegetables and fruits. He never assumed that I knew what he knew about the machine. He did not skip from one idea to the next, and back to the original idea again. He was organized and lucid. Without ambiguous phrases and jargon he told me exactly what I needed to know. Even without the demonstration, his comments would have made a first-class brief or motion. If one had mentioned Strunk and White to him, he would have asked how many choppers they wished to buy."

AG: And that helped you write your note to Galloping Garner?

428

FOOTE: Yes. I had to tell him where the valve was and how to turn it off. That was my goal. My first version of the note undermined that goal, like so many of the briefs and motions attorneys file in my court.

AG: And I suppose like the statement of decision that got you into trouble in the first place.

FOOTE: Yes-no need to rub it in.

AG: But what about composition and grammar?

FOOTE: Extremely important. But good writing usually falls into place when a writer has his or her goal firmly in mind. What is a lawyer's goal in writing a brief or motion? If it is to impress the client with a bewildering and impenetrable mélange of legalese, the client will be assuredly unimpressed when the motion is lost. If the goal is to win, not throw the fight, or at least to be a contender, the lawyer must change his or her approach.

AG: Isn't it obvious the goal is to win the motion?

FOOTE: Yes, but you wouldn't know it from some of the briefs I read. Lawyers must write to sell a point of view, convince the reader of the merits of their position with an economy of words. Judges have so much to read. Get to the point quickly and simply.

AG: What was your goal when you wrote the statement of decision that got you into trouble?

FOOTE: I think my goal was to write through the problem to help me understand it. Once I thought I understood it I stopped. But that was when my work should have begun. It was then my responsibility to make the reader understand the problem and how I resolved it. I should have been writing for the reader not myself.

AG: Is that why so many writers fail to achieve their goals?

FOOTE: Yes, because they know or think they know the subject so intimately they unconsciously assume the reader knows it as well as they do. It's a common phenomenon. Take a typical message left on your answering machine. The caller leaves his number, and recites it so quickly that you have to replay the message several times to understand it. If the caller wants you to call him back, why does the message go by in a blur of sound? I suspect it is because the caller knows his number so well he almost assumes that you also know it. Although he knows you do not know his number, he has not taken the time to focus on his goal, to tell you slowly and clearly what is so obvious to him. Without realizing it, he has risked not getting your call back.

AG: And this same thing occurs in briefs and motions?

FOOTE: Often it does. If the writer keeps in mind that the goal is to communicate and to inform, the rest usually falls into place. Writing for the reader also tests the writer's thinking and often shows flaws in the reasoning.

AG: So in summary what do you tell attorneys appearing in your court?

FOOTE: Once you have carefully researched and understood the legal principles you wish to present to the court through a motion or a brief, your task is far from over. You must carefully explain what you know to the reader, the judge. Though you and the judge are familiar with legal nomenclature, do not assume the judge is familiar with the facts and applicable law in your case. Do not assume that the judge has at her or his fingertips the resolution of the issues you are seeking. Persuade by a direct and readable recitation of the facts and law accompanied by a reasoned explanation of the issues to be resolved.

Judge Foote abruptly ended the interview. I protested that there were so many more questions to ask. He handed me a sheet of principles that I, dear reader, pass on to you. If you read Judge Foote's principles, you just might save youself from the harrowing experience he endured on the remote island of Haec Verba.

FEET FIRMLY ON THE GROUND: A brief browse on briefs

By Judge Learned Foote

1. Be wary of your opponent's briefs. Many are excellent but some are deficient. Approach them the way you would a sleeping tiger or a calm river--with caution. The gently flowing water may have treacherous undercurrents. The cases cited are not always pertinent to the issues, and the issues are not always fully developed. Therefore, you should always check your opponent's research.

2. In your brief, state the following succinctly:

A. The nature of the case. "Bay 0. Wolfe appeals the grant of a motion for summary judgment." "Grendel Schwartz appeals his conviction of mayhem."

B. The issues or questions to be decided.

C. What the ruling should be; you are not writing a mystery novel, so you should immediately tell the reader that the butler did it. In some cases you may want to state the desired ruling in the very first sentence. For example: "We urge the court to rule that a shareholder may be sued on a contract signed by a corporate officer."

D. Facts: pertinent ones only, please. To insure that you have stated them with scrupulous care and objectivity, check and recheck the record and transcript. Make sure that the facts in one section of the transcript do not contradict facts in another. Be careful not to mislead the court.

E. Argument: give reasons for the ruling you desire. Avoid repetition, and keep the issues distinct. Support your conclusion with cases, statutes, and above all, logic. Make absolutely certain that each case you cite stands for what you say it does.

F. Conclusion: tell the court what you want it to do.

3. In your rough draft, highlight your weaknesses and then try to write a response to the weak points. Sometimes weak points cannot be analyzed thoroughly unless an issue is written both ways. After reading your two versions, you will often know how to best argue a weak point.

4. Make the brief interesting and persuasive. It must be free from obscurity or ambiguity. "Plaintiff rented the store." Was plaintiff the lessor or the lessee? "They are ridiculing judges." Are the judges the victims or are they just acting naturally?

5. Write with the reader in mind. Most readers know as much about the case as you did before you began to work on it. Therefore, do not assume the reader knows anything about it. Explain to the reader what the case is about. Although rudimentary points should not be labored, they may be necessary as stepping stones to later points.

6. Write in a style that is crisp, concise, and that sparkles with clarity. Some concepts are complex, but they can be stated clearly. To simplify is not to patronize. Writers who obfuscate and complicate make it tough for both the reader and the writer. If the brief reminds you of Kant, rewrite it so that it reminds you of Plato. Avoid the abstract; embrace the concrete. Refer to the parties by name. Your brief comes alive with people, dogs, cats, tigers, chairs, doors, houses, cars, roads, and buildings.

7. Short sentences usually deliver more power than longer ones. Active verbs deliver more punch than passive ones. Do not say, "An objection was interposed by counsel." "Counsel objected," is better. Verbs should be close to their subjects and objects. What do you think of the following sentence? "The judge, looking surreptitiously to the side, and winking at the amused clerk, sustained the objection." I don't think much of it either.

8. Make the brief short, even though it takes a longer time to write. Use Ockham's razor and cut, cut, and then cut some more. If we analogize the writing of a brief to the making of a movie, the cutting room floor should be a mess.

9. Avoid such pests as:

____ "in connection with"
____ "with respect to"
____ "despite the fact that"
____ "the fact that"
____ "the former and the latter"
____ "it would appear that"
____ "in terms of"-unless we are talking about mathematics
____ "viable" - unless you are writing an abortion case
____ "contact"-unless you are writing about sports, electricity, or vintage aircraft
____ "while" as a synonym for although

431

_____ "parameter" as a synonym for perimeter or boundary

_____ "alternatives"-not a choice among more than two possibilities or things

_____ "meaningful" - adds little meaning, particularly when speaking of a "meaningful relationship"

_____ Avoid most adverbs, and in particular "clearly." It probably isn't clear if you have to say it. Also avoid the meaningless adverb "rather"-"He was a rather temperamental judge." Was he or wasn't he?

10. Do not pad. Be wary of adjectives. They are seductive, but they promise more than they give. The most dependable friends we have are nouns and verbs. Verbs should be active. They provide the muscle to carry your ideas forward.

11. Do not use nouns for verbs unless you plan to work for the Pentagon. Grammatical transvestites are unseemly. Radio traffic announcers tell us we "transition" from one freeway to the other; software people "input" or "access" information. Corporate executives tell their managers to "dialogue" with one another. We, at least, will never "prioritize" our options.

12. Keep in mind that the brief is more than a collection of examples of good grammar and syntax. It is an essay that should make sense and be logically sound. Its sentences and paragraphs should support one another. It should be pithy, but not every sentence should be short and declarative. Some will be longer and more complex, but all should be clear and easy to understand. In this way the brief will not be rigid like the third little pig's house of bricks, but open and flexible, like a geodesic dome.

13. A verb must agree with its subject in number. Use singular verbs with singular subjects, and plural verbs with plural subjects. "She works." "They work." Problems sometimes develop when words are placed between the subject and the verb. "The _behavior_ of those criminals who are raping and pillaging _is_ disgusting" "_One_ of the lessons the judge learned _is_ to be compassionate." "Each of the resumes has some merit." "He is one of those attorneys who _write_ (not writes) unintelligible briefs."

14. Use parallel construction: neither/nor, either/or, not only/but (also), both/and, rather/than.

Sentence elements joined by a coordinating conjunction must be parallel. "We should be concerned with good writing and with clear thinking." Gerunds should be compared with gerunds to achieve a parallel construction. "I like playing more than working."

15. After writing the masterpiece, put it away for a day or two. Then come back to it. Then revise it. Then put it away. Then revise it again. At this point you will realize that a good brief is not written, but only rewritten. If you are truly critical of your own writing, there is a good chance you will know whether it is honest and has integrity.

16. Use these rules as a reminder. I violate these rules with agonizing regularity. I would violate them many more times if they were not there as a reminder. I hope they help you too.

Even if you forget the rules, please try not to forget this general principle: Unlike the poet who writes to understand, we write to be understood.

Interviewer's post script:

Several people have asked me if Judge Foote ever went back to the produce department of his local market to purchase the vegetable chopper. I don't have the nerve to ask him.

"Your honor, Buffy wouldn't hurt a fly. Like all Pugs she is sweet, tame and friendly." The defendant gave a photo to the bailiff who handed it up to Judge Judy.

Judge Judy examined the photo. "'Pugnacious' is a better word. Looks like she's part pit bull. She bit your daughter and then you sold her to an unsuspecting buyer."

"It was only a nip."

"Maybe it's time to take a nip, . . . no, a bite out of your wallet."

Judge Judy decided the case in favor of the plaintiff who had purchased an allegedly tame Pug only to be bitten when he tried to intervene in an altercation between his new dog and a ferocious Pomeranian. "From then on," complained the plaintiff, Pit Bull Pug would bite me at every opportunity. I returned the dog, but the buyer would not return my money or pay for my doctor bills." The dog was a pussy cat compared to the ferocity of Judge Judy's verbal assault on the seller.

Judge Judy was angry, but her anger had nothing to do with the case. In fact the tongue lashing viewed by hundreds of millions throughout the world gave her a sense of calm. At the end of the show she walked swiftly to a conference room where her staff, her lawyer, and a few others from the network were gathered.

She stood at the head of the table, greeted everyone warmly and then said in a voice much softer than her television voice, "I don't care what the so-called critics say about me," she paused, "although I didn't relish Judge Wapner's comments posted all over the internet. But this Peel bastard-that's another story. He went over the line." Her tone was wistful. "See if you can do something about it." She walked out of the room. Those assembled sat quietly thinking.

Judge Judy's lawyer looked through his new file labeled *PEEL*. The file contained numerous biographical articles, but for the moment the lawyer concentrated on an article that Supreme Court Justice Peel had written a few months earlier for a local Bar Journal. Recently, the article had been posted on the internet, and had caught the attention of Judge Judy's staff. It was entitled: *Punch Judy*. The second heading read: Judy Degrades Litigants, Herself and the Judiciary."

The article attributed the decline of civility in the legal profession in large part to the "egregious antics of a harridan billed as Judge Judy. She sullies the judicial robes of her office. She mocks justice by mocking the litigants and witnesses who appear before her." Peel went on to write that Judge Judy "cannot utter a word without violating the judicial canons of ethics." He praised Judge Wapner "whose rulings in even the most bizarre small claims cases reflected the judiciary at its finest. Judge Wapner was stern when necessary, but unfailingly treated the litigants with dignity and respect. His rulings were consistently fair and well reasoned. He reflected well on the judiciary and showed the world a first-rate jurist at work." Peel repeated a quote from Judge Wapner that had appeared on the internet: "'Judge Judy is a disgrace to the judiciary.'"

Peel ridiculed Judge Judy for being divorced three times and then re-marrying one of her former husbands. "She has trouble deciding who to marry. How can she decide cases?" he mused.

These comments were inconsequential to Judge Judy, less annoying than a courteous litigant. It was the following sentences that caught the attention of her lawyers and prompted the meeting in which she implored them to do something: "It is no wonder that Judge Sheindlin, (her real name) resigned from the trial court in New York. She had no choice. It is believed by many in New York City's legal circles that Judge Sheindlin was under investigation by New York's State Commission on Judicial Conduct for the type of misconduct she engages in on television everyday. What have we come to? A television personality acquires a net worth of $100 million for pretending to be a judge that New York might not allow to sit as a judge."

After a few minutes the lawyer said, "I know what we should not do about it." Everyone in the room knew what he meant. A libel action was out of the question. It would prove to some the truth of the allegations, however false they in fact were, and the sponsors would balk. Everyone began thinking again. Several minutes passed.

The lawyer again went through the file and then said, "Just maybe there is something we can do about it . . . it's a long shot." He related his plan. Some people laughed, a few others acknowledged it was imaginative, but would yield nothing. The lawyer was determined to give it a try. He ran it by his investigator who was glad to get the work, but questioned whether the long shot would pay off. The investigator outlined a procedure that he and a colleague scrupulously followed. A month later, to his surprise and joy, the long shot paid off.

The payoff is related in investigator Peter R. Young's report. The report states that since 5 A.M. he and his assistant have been sitting in their vehicle across the street from Axel Peel's house. This is what he and his assistant have been doing for the past several weeks. But on this particular day at approximately 8:12 A.M. he "observes subject Axel Peel pull out of his driveway in a grey 2006 Infiniti M-35." Following his usual procedure, Young activates his video recorder. His camera captures the house, its driveway and the car pulling out into the street. Young's assistant follows the car at a respectful distance. Young has his camera trained on the Infiniti.

Young has been through this drill many times before, but this morning is different. The report details "subject Peel's route." The twenty minute journey comes to an end when Axel Peel drives into the driveway that leads to the underground garage of one of the state buildings. Peel drives by the security guard's window and waves. The guard waves back with a smile. Peel inserts a special card into the slit of a metal box that sits on the top of the post near the driver's window of his car. A large metal gate rises and "subject Peel" drives slowly down the ramp.

It is here that Young's report ends. But no matter, because he has successfully completed his mission. He is ecstatic and has nothing but admiration for the lawyer for whom he works. Had he been able to follow Peel into the garage as an unseen wraith, his report would have described Peel driving down an aisle and easing the car into parking space # 5, the one reserved for State Supreme Court Justice Peel.

The report would go on to say that Peel gets out of his car and walks to the private elevator reserved for the justices. He takes the elevator to the floor where his chambers are located. He walks down the hall that leads to his office. A law clerk walking by says "Hello Judge," and he returns the greeting. He walks through the door that leads to his chambers and greets his secretary who informs him that a "hot" habeas writ petition is on his desk. Peel walks into his office and peruses the writ petition.

One could well conclude there is nothing remarkable about the ordinary sequence of events just related-- except for one thing: Axel Peel is not a Supreme Court Justice. But Aston Peel, his identical twin, is.

Young would like to have followed Peel around for the rest of the day, but he had sufficient information for his purposes. He and his colleagues had been tailing the Peel brothers for the past three weeks and now the hunch of the lawyer he worked for had born fruit. Young titled his report "Peels Slip Up." He stated his conclusion in the opening line of his report: "On February 9, 2007, Axel Peel, a successful litigation attorney, temporarily traded identities with his brother Aston Peel, an occurrence that had likely occurred frequently throughout their lives."

The investigator handed his report to Judge Judy's lawyer who read it with a smile and then placed it in the Peel file. Other papers in the file recited what many in the legal profession knew about the Peel twins. They went to law school and did moderately well. They might have done better scholastically but for their active social life in which they are reputed to have traded dates-without informing their dates. Though never proven, this presumed practice was well known on campus. Nevertheless, many women went out with them. In fact, a group of those who had dated one or the other or both the Peel twins formed a club. During the three times the club met, they compared notes, and tried to determine if and when switches were made.

The twins accepted an invitation to attend the last meeting. They good naturedly agreed to answer questions in a format much like a press conference.

They used the presidential press conference as a model: they never directly answered any question and did not admit that they had ever swapped dates. The "press conference" was carried off in good humor, written up in the college newspaper and parodied in the law school's third year graduation play.

Upon graduation from law school they both passed the Bar and went into practice together under the prosaic firm name, *Peel and Peel*. Some had compared the Peel brothers to the gynecologist twins portrayed in David Cronenberg's movie, *Dead Ringers*. The comparison was not apt. The Peel twins were both strong personalities and not psychologically unbalanced as were the twins portrayed in *Dead Ringers*. This, thought Judy's lawyer, made their habit of changing identities all the more easy.

Their friends argued that the Peel twins never traded identities, but got a kick out of making people think they did. And even had they done so in college, it was all in fun and never to anyone's detriment. But one woman who claims to have dated the twins in college tried to sue. She alleged that she had a date with Aston, but that Axel took her out instead, pretending to be Aston. This, she hypothesized was done to humiliate her. No lawyer would take the case, but an article about her allegation did appear in a local newspaper.

The twins' law practice did not thrive. Aston thought it was because clients were not sure which of the twins was representing them at any particular time. They disbanded their practice and went their separate ways, each ultimately becoming litigators in large firms. They became well known and even opposed one another in a law and motion matter which received a front page story in the leading legal periodical. Neither had filed a motion to recuse the other and the trial judge just scratched his head and ruled. There was speculation that they had changed sides when arguing the motions. The senior partners from each of their respective firms questioned them about it. They both gave their usual evasive answers and before the firms could come to any resolution about how to deal with the situation, they quit.

Throughout the years, notions and speculation about the Peels trading identities ceased. They both achieved stellar reputations as canny, well prepared litigators whose ethics were beyond reproach. They were both deeply involved in local and state bar activities. Aston became a judge and was eventually appointed to the Supreme Court. Axel formed his own successful litigation firm. They both were trim and stayed in shape. Just as they looked and sounded alike, so too they aged alike, although a trained eye could see differences in the crevices on their craggy faces.

After reading investigator Young's report, Judge Judy's lawyer then read investigator Sid P. Yardley's report detailing Aston Peel's activities on February 9, 2007. He had left his house at 9 A.M. and drove north to Camarillo, California where he played in a golf tournament, posing as Axel Peel. Later in the day the twins met for dinner at Axel's house. The investigators followed the Peel twins the next morning, February 10, 2007, and this time Aston Peel left his house to go to court and Axel Peel went to his office. Young and Yardley were beaming. "We got them," said Yardley.

"Would they take such a risk over a lousy game of golf?" asked the lawyer.

"Maybe it's not such a risk," said Young. "The Supreme Court was not in session this past week. Maybe Axel Peel just went to the court and sat in his brother's chambers. He is known to drop by and have lunch with his brother. Even if they did nothing illegal, this act would embarrass the hell out of them and would lend support to the rumors about their past activities."

"That it would," said the lawyer softly. He was pleased but he was also uneasy. He wondered why the twins had even switched places. And now that his plan had produced fascinating information, what should he do with it? He decided that making it public to discredit the twins just might backfire. Would it not be better to let sleeping dogs lie? On the other hand, redacting the names of the investigators from the report and anonymously turning it over to Axel Peel just might inhibit his brother from further diatribes and unsubstantiated charges against Judge Judy. Moreover, it would avoid an allegation of extortion.

A few days later, Peter R. Young's assistant delivered an envelope to Axel Peel's law firm and left it with the receptionist at the front desk. In the envelope was a summary of the Peels' activities on the morning of February 9, 2007. Axel Peel read through the contents of the envelope and had a messenger deliver it to his brother. Immediately after reading the summary in the envelope, Aston feverishly set to work on his next Judge Judy article. Later that day when the bailiff escorted Axel into his chambers, Aston handed him a draft of the article. "Take a look at this," he said.

The article explained that in late January the Peel brothers thought they were being followed. When Axel's investigators "tailed" Young and Yardley "tailing" them, they were convinced. This led the brothers to hatch their own plan which they executed on February 8, and 9, of 2007.

They exchanged clothes and car keys in Aston Peel's chambers on the afternoon of February 8, 2007. They then went for drinks after which they went to the parking lot and drove away, Aston in Axel's Aston Martin, and Axel in Aston's Infiniti M 35. They each drove to their respective sister-in-law's houses where they spent a restful night. Aston jokes that they did not swap wives. Aston slept in a guest house, and Axel slept in a spare bedroom. The following morning, Aston left Axel's home and drove to the court. Axel left Aston's condominium and headed for the golf course. The article then quotes verbatim the unsigned report left in Axel's office.

The article concludes with a reference to Peel's earlier article and asks in mock disbelief "Could it be possible that Judge Judy was behind this scheme to silence my criticism of her? No, I am sure that Judge Judy is too busy investing her millions to bother with such a prank."

After reading the draft Axel threw it back on his brother's desk. "Do yourself a favor" he said to his brother. "Do not publish this stupid article."

"Stupid, is it?"

"You bet. It takes an unfair shot at Judge Judy. Have you watched her show. "

"Of course I have."

"So have I. You know what? I agreed with every one of her decisions."

"That's not the point," said Aston. The manner in which they are rendered, sickens me. It reflects badly on our system of justice."

"You think our changing clothes and pretending to be one another reflects well on us?"

"Doesn't hurt either of us. This article exposes a veiled threat to uncover a deceit that did not happen."

"Which we accomplished through deceit," said Axel.

"You sound like a lawyer," said his brother. They laughed.

"What really bothers me," said Axel, "was your allegations about Judge Sheindlin when she sat as a family law judge in New York."

"That was reasonable speculation based on what I read on the internet and what a prominent family law lawyer in New York said he heard was about to happen."

"Please, you are a judge. You of all people should know…."

"I didn't say it was true, and I am not broaching that subject in this article."

"You and I dislike Judge Judy's style. She calls the boyfriend who victimizes and steals from his girlfriend a deadbeat. Isn't that what most of us are thinking to ourselves? Maybe he deserves to be demeaned. Whatever Judy is, and however crude her form of justice, she sets things right for more than a hundred million people, and she does it in a courtroom."

"That's what drives me nuts," said Aston.

"Think twice before you attempt to tarnish her. Making public our little deception could make you look petty, self righteous, and even envious. And that could undermine your judicial decisions. Set the standard for excellence by example rather than a smug attack."

Axel turned his head slightly to the left, and raised his eyebrows, a gesture he made to juries after his closing argument, a way of saying, "think about it." He got up from his chair. "Do not publish this article. I can get your draft to Judge

Judy's lawyer. That way you and she can drop this issue. She will go on administering justice in her way and you will administer it in your way."

Aston got up from his desk and the smiling brothers hugged each other.

Aston held the manuscript in his hands and could not help but think about how the deception that was not a deception had deceived, how it would put Judge Judy in her place and how much fun it would be to publish. He put the manuscript down and re-read the writ petition that had been left on his desk a few days earlier.

Around the same time Judge Judy and her staff were considering what cases to air for future shows. The criteria was different than that used by Justice Peel. But was her decision making process any different? Aston was not sure how to decide the writ petition. He went to his restroom and looked at himself in the mirror. "How carefully we look at cases and issues," he thought to himself, "but how clearly do we see the distinguishing and similar factors?" He looked at the lines in his face and said aloud, "My brother and I . . . we sure look alike."

THE LADY ON THE ELLIPTICAL MACHINE

Judge Aston Peel, newly appointed to the Los Angeles Superior Court, was exercising one early morning on the elliptical machine at the gym. He was reading a syllabus for new judges on jury selection which he placed on the plastic book holder attached to the machine. The syllabus stressed the importance of putting jurors at ease, explaining to them the reason for bench conferences and other trial interruptions that can be so exasperating. Peel was in awe of the responsibility he had so recently assumed. He tried to suppress another feeling that intruded into his consciousness: he was someone important.

It was just as he was succumbing to this headiness when without warning, Peel did what his elderly Aunt Sarah did so often, and which she talked about incessantly. To put it in Aunt Sarah's words, he "passed gas." He thought, "Flatulence, it can happen to anyone." As the woman on the adjoining elliptical machine began furiously fanning the air with her towel, Peel's bubble of importance burst and he blushed in a spotlight of humiliation. But this moment of embarrassment became a significant self-defining moment. As Sarah's late husband Jack said about politicians, opera singers, and movie stars, "They take a dump just like the rest of us." No doubt Jack would have included judges in his pantheon of prominent persons to take down a notch or two.

In an instant Aston had been demoted to what Jean Paul Sartre termed an "en soit," a person whose existence resembled more a thing or object than a unique individual. It was at that moment that Peel knew he would strive to be a humble instead of an arrogant judge. How, he wondered, could he be a person of importance when he was too mortified to even glance at the woman madly pumping the pedals of the machine next to him with her neck outstretched as far away from him as possible? Despite his discomfort, he smiled inwardly at the thought that a fortuitous fart could well be the determining factor in forming his judicial demeanor.

Peel drew upon this experience to indulge his proclivity to label events in his life with aphoristic phrases that he termed "personal headlines." Although glued to the machine and pumping like a robot in over-drive, a personal headline formed in Peel's brain: **F**orgo **A**rrogance, **R**ecognize **T**olerance. This headline would teach him that he was like everyone else and that he would be tolerant of attorneys' courtroom mishaps.

He stole a glance at the woman next to him. She was leaning forward, pedaling feverishly as if to get away from him. He hadn't realized it but he, too, was pedaling frantically, the two of them mice in their wheels, dripping with sweat and going nowhere. Peel hoped that she would leave first. She adjusted her pearl rimmed glasses. She was in for the long haul. He would be late for court if he stayed much longer.

He mused that this very thought was an indication of humility. Court could not start without him, but he did not want to be late. Yet, he could not stop pedaling. He was fearful that as he got off the machine she would get a good look at him. He reduced the resistance of the peddles so that he could peddle faster, but try as he may, he could not outrun the embarrassment that clung to him like a jacket lined with glue. Near exhaustion forced him to stop. He grabbed his towel and book and leapt off the machine. She was doing the Tour de France. She turned her head in his direction. He looked away and hurried downstairs to the showers where he tried to wash away his shame.

He liked to take the bench at 9 A.M. promptly, but this morning he was about 10 minutes late. He dashed into his chambers and grabbed one of the two robes hanging in his closet. Unfortunately, it was the one his law partners had given him as a gift to celebrate his appointment to the court, the one that was three sizes too big for his frame. He pushed the buzzer on his desk to signal the bailiff to call the court to order. The courtroom was filled with prospective jurors for a case that was ready to go to trial. The incident at the gym kept repeating over and over again in his mind, like a scene in a movie endlessly replayed.

As he walked into the courtroom he became dimly aware that he had picked the wrong robe. He gathered the bottom in his right hand so that it would be above his ankles, but when the bailiff, in stentorian tones commanded, "All rise! Facing the flag of our country and recognizing the principles for which it stands . . . ." Peel looked up at the flag, and automatically placed his hand over his heart, dropping the robe, the bottom of which now gathered in folds around his feet. As he mounted the three steps to the bench, he stepped on the front of the robe causing it to become taut. As he moved forward the robe acted as a pulley which with sudden swiftness pulled him down to the floor. The bench hid the fall from the view of prospective jurors and spectators who were sitting in the courtroom. They saw Peel's head go down and then heard the thump as mercifully his forehead hit the carpeted floor.

He was up in an instant and grabbing the folds of his robe like an ungraceful bride, he hobbled to his chair. "You think that's something? Wait till you see how I rule on motions," he said to the attorneys and spectators. They laughed and unlike the unfortunate incident on the elliptical machine, Peel was able to turn this misfortune into something positive. Later in the morning after the jury had been empaneled, Peel explained circumstantial evidence by referring to his earlier accident. "No one saw me fall, but my abrupt disappearance from view, and the thud which you probably heard, leads to the reasonable conclusion that I fell."

At the morning recess, his clerk said "good recovery."

"No injuries or nice save?" he asked.

"Both. You didn't sound incoherent, and using your fall as an example of circumstantial evidence was brilliant."

Buoyed by his success with the second mishap of the day, he said, "I bet I can use this as an example of negligence when giving the concluding jury instructions. I didn't intend to fall, but the fall was my fault. This is a lesson lost on so many defendants sued for negligence."

"Plaintiff's lawyers might like the instruction, but don't count on the defense bar, or the Court of Appeal. Better leave it alone."

He didn't tell his clerk about the incident on the elliptical machine but wished he would have been able to make a good save then as well. If the woman on the adjoining machine had been reading *Hamlet*, for example, he could have said, "You know, I believe there *is* something rotten in the state of Denmark." Fat chance of her or anyone reading *Hamlet* at the gym. It was all academic. He would never have had the nerve to make the remark. Oh well.

As the weeks went by Peel stuck to his resolve to use the elliptical machine incident as a reminder that judges are human and he switched to the treadmill. He strove to convey an image of civility and courtesy to the lawyers and litigants. He bent over backwards to make jurors feel comfortable and gave the attorneys every opportunity to try their cases, even when it was obvious they were pursuing a lost cause. He even went to great pains to explain his decisions with a written paragraph or two. Word of his judicial demeanor spread and he was asked to speak at a local Consumer Lawyers bar meeting. The topic was Civility from the Bench and the Bar.

His speech was favorably reviewed in the local bar journal. The article stressed that Peel did not simply lecture the attorneys on how to act before the court, but acknowledged the responsibility of the judiciary to treat lawyers and litigants with civility and respect.

Peel felt good about himself and when a writer for a popular legal website asked for an interview, he readily accepted. He scheduled the meeting to take place a few days later in his chambers at lunchtime.

The writer arrived at the court a few minutes before noon and sat in the audience until Peel called a recess until 1:30 P.M. His clerk ushered her into his chambers and she reached out her hand and gave him a strong handshake. She looked directly into his eyes from behind her pearl rimmed eye glasses and Peel froze with horror. "No, it can't be," he said to himself. The interior conversation continued. "Yes, it can and it is." It didn't matter that she was not wearing gym shorts. The woman on the elliptical machine was standing directly in front of him in his chambers. Did she recognize him? Her gaze seemed to linger a little too long. Did it matter that he wasn't wearing gym shorts? As if compelled by an external malignant force, he blurted out, "Well, at least we are not in Denmark."

Was that a puzzled look on her face? She let go of his hand and said, "To be . . ." and after an uncomfortable pause ended the phrase in a slow, measured cadence, "or not . . . ." She didn't finish the phrase. He offered her a seat and hung up his robe. He hoped she would not notice the sweat dampening his shirt. She began the interview with an admonition. "I will ask you a wide range of questions. Our readers like to know about judges as people, not just authority figures who decide cases. I would like to ask you about your outside interests and hobbies. If a question makes you uncomfortable, just let me know and we can move onto something else. I only ask that you be straight with me. Fair enough?"

What was Peel going to say, no, that's not fair enough? He agreed and she first asked questions about his judicial philosophy. She remarked that he came to her attention through the article about him in the bar journal. After telling her of the importance of judges treating lawyers with respect, they moved on to questions about his hobbies, the books he likes best, recent vacations, and pet peeves. Things seemed to be going smoothly and he felt his innards thawing. But then she asked if he played golf, tennis, biked or hiked. He answered "yes" to all of the above but noted that his time for these activities was constrained by his judicial workload.

It was the next question that caused an Arctic wind to blow through his body.

"Do you ever go to the gym?" she asked. The moment of truth had come.

"Sure," he said nonchalantly.

"What do you do there?" As he thought back later, his answer came a little too quickly.   "I would like to take yoga classes and Pilates," he answered, but the schedules don't work all that well for me." There was a silence. She didn't ask another question. "Why should she?" he thought to himself. His answer was not responsive. He went on. "So, lately I have been doing the treadmill and weights." Still not another question. He should have waited, but instead he said. "With my new position, I haven't been there in some time." Now a shrill voice inside of him said, "You're screwed." He argued back to the shrill voice. "You seriously think this slight exaggeration is not being straight? What do you expect me to say, 'Oh by the way I was the guy who let go the biggest most foul smelling fart next to you on the elliptical machine a few weeks ago?'"

The interview came to a close after a few more perfunctory questions. And that was that, until the article came out a few weeks later.

A week or so before the interview, Peel had ruled on a zoning ordinance banning topless bars in certain parts of the city. Plaintiff bar owner challenged the ordinance arguing it was vague and incomprehensible. Peel ruled against the bar owner. In his Statement of Decision Peel hurriedly wrote that the statute was not

446

vague and for emphasis wrote a phrase that resembled a newspaper caption: Plaintiff Understands Topless Zoning. A brief paragraph quoted him in the legal newspapers.

Elliptical lady's piece came out a week after her interview. Word of her article spread and soon it appeared in the bar journal. The headline sent Peel's coveted reputation for civility down the toilet. The headline read "Superior Court Judge Aston Peel Calls Porno Plaintiff a 'PUTZ.'" The lead paragraph began: "Even even-tempered judges have limits. Judge Aston Peel veered off the straight and narrow path of judicial civility to explore the gutter. In a speech before the Consumer Lawyers, Judge Peel decried the arrogance of judges who demean and belittle lawyers and their clients. 'No matter what the nature of the case, everyone in the courtroom is entitled to dignity and respect,' said the judge in his acceptance speech. I guess that means not quite everyone, particularly plaintiff Aron Harknok, well known pornographer, who wishes to open a lap dancing establishment in the city."

"Judge Peel did not buy Harknok's defense that the statute was vague and hard to understand. The judge who believes everyone should be treated with respect, labeled Mr. Harknok a 'PUTZ.' No, the good judge did not blurt out the epithet in open court. Instead, in his written Statement of Decision, the judge chose the not so subtle device of a mnemonic. Here is what the judge wrote: 'Plaintiff Understands Topless Zoning.' Bold the first letter of each word and you get the picture. Harknok's lawyer, an officer in the Consumer Lawyers had no comment."

"Well I have a comment," said Peel to himself. And he sat down to write a blistering letter to the bar journal, but his fingers froze on the keyboard. He certainly couldn't begin the article with something like: "This all started last month when I was exercising on the elliptical machine at the gym." Better to focus on the article itself. He wrote a brief letter that said: "A maliciously creative staff writer teased a word from a mnemonic she confabulated from a series of words that occurred in my statement of decision. I had ruled against Harknok, but it was never my intention to portray him with this offensive aspersion. That was something concocted in the mind of a writer more interested in inventing a story than reporting one." Something told him not to send the letter without running it by Alfred Luce, a veteran judge who had become his mentor.

That day at noon he sat across a luncheon table in the judge's lounge looking into blue eyes set like two small pools in the uneven terrain of Judge Luce's freckled face. Luce ran his stubby fingers through his unkempt gray hair and focused those pools directly on Peel. He and Peel had exchanged brief pleasantries before sitting down, but before Peel could say anything, Luce said, "Did you write a letter?"

"How did you know I wrote a letter?"

Without bothering to answer what he considered a naïve question, he asked, "You didn't send it did you?"

"Not yet."

"Good. May I see it?"

Peel handed his letter to Luce. Without reading it Luce tore the letter into little pieces. "I don't have to read it. In essence I know what you said. Nobody cares about your explanation, or whether it is legitimate. Your letter just keeps the issue alive." He paused. "Wonder what the Consumer Lawyers think?" He burst out laughing.

"I'm glad you're having fun with this." said Peel.

"Hey my friend. Lighten up. You don't have to explain anything to anyone, and the more you try to, the less they will believe you, and by 'they' I refer ungrammatically to the collective unsympathetic, yearning for titillation public."

"I can't worry about what the public thinks, I intend to tell the truth. I did not intend, never intended, to form a mnemonic. And if I did, I would never spell out 'PUTZ.' I'm not even Jewish."

"So what mnemonic would you have spelled out?"

"Not any-damned annoying."

"Hah! You just did it again-NADA."

"This is ridiculous. I never . . . ."

"Conscious, unconscious, however you are doing it, you are doing it."

Peel sat there dumbfounded as Luce continued. "Read *People v. Arno* (1979) 90 Cal.App.3d 505, 514, footnote 2. That's the famous Schmuck case. The author of the opinion in a stunning example of collegiality called his dissenting colleague a 'SCHMUCK' in a mnemonic. The author acknowledged that the first letter of the first word in a series of seven sentences spelled 'SCHMUCK.'" He explained that the word meant 'jewel' in German. I think I speak for most people when I tell you what I think of his explanation: **B**affling, **U**npleasant, **L**aughable, **L**apsing, **S**tartling, **H**ectoring, **I**nappropriate, **T**asteless. Guess what 'putz' means in German?"

"I don't think I want to know," said Peel

"It means a person's 'finery.' I looked it up. Of course you could always explain that is what you meant to say and join ranks with the bullshitters of this world."

"What happens when I'm up for election?" said Peel meekly.

"A judge who calls a pornographer a "putz" should get lots of votes. You've got nothing to worry about. Look at Judge Judy."

Luce extended his hand. "Son," he said. "Welcome to an exclusive club. You have become a card carrying member "

"Club?" asked Peel.

"MEEK," said Luce with a smile. "Mnemonics Establish Essential Knowledge."

"GEEK" would be a better name. Garrulous Egregiously Goofy Kooks.

"Don't knock it," said Luce.

"I'm honored, but I decline membership in MEEK."

"The meek shall inherit the earth."

"You're serious."

"Damned right I am," said Luce. "More and more people are fed up with political correctness."

"I get it," said Peel. "FUWPC."

"It's not funny," said Luce. "More and more people would like to say what they truly mean without putting their jobs or safety in jeopardy. Out of necessity we have developed a code to avoid the reproach, the scorn, and denunciation that accompanies the use of a word the censors decide is offensive. A mnemonic code enables us to speak without facing lawsuits, and hearing the cries of bigotry and insensitivity." He looked intently at Peel. "You are just one of those unfortunates who got caught. It happens from time to time. It goes with the territory."

"So I am a member of this phantom club without my even knowing it," said Peel.

"You know it," said Luce with certainty. "And you are in good company. Members of our secret club come from all the professions: lawyers, physicians, scientists, politicians, CEO's, academics, journalists, and a special branch in the judiciary."

"You use mnemonics in your decisions.?"

"Damned right. Last month a plaintiff brought an action in which the same issues had been decided against him in a previous case. I said his case was CRAP."

"You said that in a case?"

"Not directly. I said, 'Conspicuous Retraxit Abolishes Plaintiff.' I also gave his lawyer some advice on how to practice law. I simply told him, 'Controlled Rigor Advances Potential.' I just didn't get nailed like you did." Luce got up from the table. He put a hand on Peel's shoulder. "Believe me this will blow over. But just in case you get a letter from the Judicial Performance Commission, I know a good lawyer for you. He belongs to the Consumer Lawyers Bar Association."

In the weeks that followed, Peel did receive a letter from the Judicial Performance Commission informing him that an investigation was under way concerning the "alleged" epithet directed at plaintiff Harknok. The letter stressed that an investigation was prompted by a citizen's complaint and did not mean that disciplinary action would necessarily follow. The letter had Peel on edge, but within a few months, the Commission found no basis to proceed.

This was a relief, and the Consumer Lawyers did not seem to think any less of him. In fact the organization named him Trial Judge of the Year. Things were looking up, yet he could not shake a disquieting mood. He had first rejected as ridiculous Luce's claim about a secret club whose diverse members communicated with mnemonics. But it seemed that everywhere he turned, mnemonics kept popping up.

In *Jackman v. Rosenbaum Company* 260 U.S. 22 (1922), Justice Holmes wrote about a local statute that gave landowners a right to build a "party wall" incorporating an adjoining landowner's wall. Plaintiff claimed that when defendant built such a wall incorporating the plaintiff's wall, he, the plaintiff, had a right to damages under the Fourteenth Amendment. Holmes would not sanction this attack on the Constitution and pointed out that "words as 'right' are a constant solicitation to fallacy." "Words As Right"-did Holmes see this as a war" in which he was defending the Fourteenth Amendment?

Peel slapped himself in the face. He was acting like a fool. If anyone searched hard enough they could always find hidden meanings in almost anything. But then a visit to his internist for a check-up made him uneasy again. After the physical his doctor said bluntly, " I will no longer accept insurance. Can't make a penny."

Peel didn't know what prompted these words to leave his mouth, but he said sarcastically, "**C**an't **H**elp **E**mpathize, **A**bysmally **P**oor."

His doctor looked at him quizzically.

Peel asked, "So how am I?"

The doctor said, "Pulse abnormal. Yellow bile in livid liver."

What's wrong with me?" asked Peel.

"Nothing."

"But my pulse, and my liver. I don't even drink."

"Your pulse is a little high. That always happens in the doctor's office. And your liver is fine. I'm just having a little fun with a comment on your attitude. Keep exercising. Your joints are stiff. Give your knees a break. Stop running for awhile. Get off the treadmill and use the elliptical machine."

They shook hands. The doctor was friendly and asked how the judging was going. He walked Peel to the door. Peel was disconcerted. He had uttered what sounded like gibberish, "Can't Help Empathize Abysmally Poor," but he had in fact called the doctor CHEAP. And what the doctor had said to him was unnerving. "Pulse Abnormal. Yellow Bile In Livid Liver." He had said, "PAY BILL."

When Peel got home there was a note from his wife who had just left town to visit her mother. The note contained two messages reminding him how to vote at the board meeting for the condominium association that night. The first message read: "Darling, Immediately Vote On Retaining Control-Essential." Peel broke out in a sweat. "My wife belongs to the club?" he asked himself aloud. Is she threatening divorce?" He discounted the thought until he read the second message: "Darling, Important! Vote Or Receive Continuing Enmity."

The next morning he went to the gym. He followed his doctor's orders and went straight to the elliptical machine. He hadn't been there since that morning when Aunt Sarah's spirit had entered his intestines. He climbed onto the machine and stole a glance at the person on the machine next to him. It was the journalist again cycling furiously. Their eyes met and she stopped. In unison they said, "It's you."

She said, "Fortuitously, Arrangements Reunite Two."
In response Peel said, "Best, Incalculably Gigantic."
The both laughed and began the race.

ARTS AND CRAFTS

"Treat your work as a craft, then master the craft, and you will be successful." Those words my grandfather, a builder of pianos, told me when, at the impressionable age of 14, I announced at a family dinner that I would be a jazz pianist. I remember my mother saying "Please, not a musician." The type of music I would play was not relevant. To this day, the anguish of her tone lingers in my memory like a Miles Davis solo.

Through my teens and early adulthood, I considered still other unsuitable careers, which as luck or fate would have it, did not come to fruition. I did not become an English professor, a journalist, or a card carrying member of the Musician's Union. I played gigs as an avocation, and forced my views about literature on patient friends rather than hapless university students.

Throughout the years, however, my grandfather's exhortation stayed with me. He believed that his conception of a craft applied to all endeavors, artistic or otherwise. I was dimly aware of a plausible parallel between the craft of bending the wood to make the perfect curve in a grand piano and my application of harmony and theory to create a piece of music. But music also involved touch, feeling and imagination. Was it therefore something more than a craft? I wish I had discussed this issue with grandfather before he died.

But I found his axiom particularly useful in my law practice. Though I drafted complaints, agreements, and motions, I was more than a mere draftsman. I saw my work as a craft of the highest order. Then I became a judge. When I took the oath of office, it occurred to me that protecting and defending the Constitution was an undertaking too lofty for a craft. Nevertheless, my judicial work bore obvious similarities to my work as a lawyer. Therefore I did not discard the notion that judging was a craft. Nor did I dwell on it. As to the nagging thought that judging, like playing or writing music, was more than a craft, I tucked it away in a bottom drawer in my mind. But then a series of events forced me to open that drawer, wipe the dust from my vague doubt and consider it anew.

It all started when the Presiding Judge appointed me court historian. This was not a job I wanted, but I did not refuse. True, she had the absolute authority, from which there was no appeal, to assign judges to various departments and locales within our sprawling judicial district. But I accepted the job because along with most everyone else on the court, I liked her. No doubt her engaging personality, as well as her ability, got her elected P.J. And besides, I thought the role of court historian would be a cinch. Little did I know this misconception would be short lived.

It was my responsibility to oversee the publication of a history of our court in celebration of its upcoming 100th anniversary. What does one include in a court's history? Of course the most tangible embodiment of a court is the courthouse. But it occurred to me that a court cannot be judged by its building, just as a book cannot be judged by its cover. This marvelously discerning perception I planned to include in the introduction.

That is not to say I would ignore the courthouse. I would include photographs of that grandly ornate structure with its Grecian columns. Our former courthouse, built in the early 1900s, stood only four blocks from our present mundane quarters before it was razed decades ago ostensibly for "safety reasons." But I would emphasize what is far more important, the life blood of any court, its judges.

All the sitting judges had written their own brief (some not so brief) judicial autobiographies for the court's website. With minor editing, I thought my work would be a breeze. In theory, the website gave interested members of the public (that means voters) insight into their local judiciary.   A mere perusal of the biographies would lead any interested citizen to conclude that the judges of our court were without doubt the most brilliant, fair and worthy judges any concerned citizen could hope for. I didn't know whether to call it the Website of Insight or Foresight.

I thought I would include at least portions of these biographies in the publication. Editing them might create resistance from some of the judges, but with the judicious use of finesse, I thought I could accomplish the task without difficulty. But then I realized I must include in the history short biographies of retired judges and those who had passed on to the great courtroom in the sky.

This involved compiling important statistics: date of birth and death (if applicable), law school, earlier education, when appointed, and maybe a benign anecdote or plaudit recalling an accomplishment that most likely no one remembers, other than the judge –provided that he or she is still alive.

The clerk's office supplied me with a list of all the judges who had served on our court. I obtained photographs of the four judges who sat when the courthouse first opened. Any one of the portraits could have adorned a box of Smith Brothers cough drops. If one could glean from these judicial portraits even a hint of a personality trait, it would not be mirth. Their severe expressions alone were a deterrent to crime.

The project consumed more time than I had anticipated, but my labors proved beneficial. It was in my efforts to gather data about the past judicial life of one judge who had retired about 30 years ago that I considered anew my vague notions about the so-called craft of judging. His name caught my attention: Judge L. Foote.

One of the judges on our court wrote a monthly column for a legal periodical and therefore fancied himself a columnist. He had created a satirical character named Judge Learned Foote, who often appeared in his pretentious columns. I dropped in on our self-proclaimed essayist and asked him if he had based his character on retired Judge L. Foote.

"Do I look that old?" he asked. All he could tell me was that "Judge Learned Foote appears in my column as a changing composite of many judges. I have heard of Judge L. Foote, but I thought his first name was Lawrence."

I had to look to other sources. I could locate only a few of Foote's colleagues who were still alive. One preferred not to say anything, but from the others I learned a few things. He was generally regarded as bright, competent and taciturn. He did not engage much with his colleagues and was not popular with the bar. He had lived alone in an upscale condominium, and when he unexpectedly retired, he sold his condominium and moved out of state, leaving no forwarding address. There was no retirement party or even a going away luncheon. It was rumored that he had moved out of the country. His retirement check was automatically deposited in a bank account, but no one in the state or county bureaucracy could or would give me his address.

Most of the judges had called him "J.L." which I assumed stood for Judge Learned or Lawrence. His bailiff had called court into session by announcing that the Honorable Judge L. Foote was presiding. My research into state bar records showed that when Foote practiced law, he listed his first name as "Learned." When he assumed the bench, his oath of office lists his name as "Learned Foote"

I was determined to write in the court's history something about this mysterious judge called "Learned," but I had to find out more about him. I also wanted to show up our resident columnist who had used Foote's name but obviously knew nothing about him.

The court's most senior clerk suggested I call an elderly retired judge, a contemporary of Judge Foote who had taken over his courtroom when Foote retired. He was Judge Roy Fessler, a respected slightly eccentric legal scholar. I telephoned him, but his apparent hearing loss made our conversation all but impossible. To his repeated "What?" I found myself screaming into the phone. We finally agreed to meet at his house.

He lived alone in an unpretentious stucco house not far from the civic center. He was bent over but spry for a man in his late eighties. We sat at his kitchen table sharing a steaming pot of tea. I began speaking in such a loud voice that I sent the cat scurrying out of the kitchen.

"You scared O.H.," he said. "I can hear you."

The sudden restoration of his hearing I attributed to his preference for live company to a phone conversation.

"Sorry to have upset O.H. Is that Oliver...."

"Yes, Oliver Holmes. A cat with a middle name is ridiculous."

I addressed him as Judge Fessler, but he interrupted. "Don't make me feel like Methuselah, son," he said, dismissing this formal address with a wave of his hand. From then on he was "Roy." Before we talked about Judge Foote, Roy gave me a neatly typed page. "Here is my TB," he said. I thought it might be a medical report and wondered if I should be this close to him. To my relief it was what he called his "Terrific Biography," which he described as "a chronology of events in my life as a lawyer and judge which tells little about me."

"So why this interest in O.F.?" he asked with a smile.

"O.F.?"

"Old Foote."

"Well for one, his name fascinates me. It's Learned, not Larry as some people think."

"That's right. His first name is Learned. A few people called him Larry just to irritate him." Before I could ask him why, he offered yet more initials, "I.P." I didn't bother to inquire, but he explained, "Irritating Person. People like to irritate an irritating person."

At that moment I could not think of what could be more irritating than the random use of initials to express a point. I kept the thought to myself and asked, "In what way was he irritating?"

"He was aloof, a cold fish. He knew the law well, and was not shy about letting everyone know it."

"Did he have friends?" I asked.

"I was the closest thing he had to a friend, and that isn't saying much."

"What can you tell me about him?"

"His father had been a lawyer, and then the Chancellor of a small mid-western college."

"So his father named him Learned?"

"A mother would never do something like that. I think J.L. took a perverse pride in his name, but he resented his father's attempt at humor. I like a good laugh, but humor has no place in the universe when it is at the expense of a son. Once he told me without the trace of a smile that when he was a young boy his father brought him to the college and introduced him to his staff as the Chancellor's little foot. G.L. Good Lord."

"If Foote took pride in his name, why did he use the initial L.?"

"Nothing wrong with initials," said Roy.

"Did Foote have a sense of humor?"

"Not about himself. But he imagined himself a wit. He said his last name was appropriate because he liked to 'sock it' to unprepared lawyers. And he was always making literary references. He read a lot and he let everyone know that, too. He would interrupt a lawyer arguing a motion with something like '…a tale told by an idiot'…he would pause with an excruciatingly prolonged silence before finishing the quote….'signifying nothing.' I can think of better ways to endear yourself to members of the bar, but of course that's not our job."

"True enough," I answered, and then turned the tables on Roy. "But no need to go out of one's way to ….P.T.O."

There was a pause, but instead of asking what I meant, Roy continued. "Imagine telling a defendant before reading a verdict, 'what fools these mortals be.' No one in that courtroom doubted that Foote did not include himself as one of those mortals."

One thing Roy stressed was that Judge Foote was a G.L.S. (Genuine Legal Scholar). "If his name called to mind one of the finest jurists ever to live, he was damned determined to have an encyclopedic knowledge of the law, and he did. He lived and breathed the law, religiously read the advance sheets, and relished asking counsel about cases not cited in points and authorities." Roy paused, "Just occurred to me why he used the initial 'L.' A Court of Appeal opinion reversing him made reference to 'the learned trial judge.' I think he wanted to reduce the opportunities for the Court of Appeal, or anyone else for that matter, to have fun at his expense. But what can you expect from the C.A.J.--Court of Appeal Jerks."

I raised an eyebrow. But Roy said in an approving tone, "Well that's what he thought of them. O.F. often said that a statute meant what it said, not what some Court of Appeal judge wanted it to say. He had apoplexy when an appellate opinion said he had put a statute governing the treatment of mentally ill persons in a 'straight jacket.' He saw himself as a law professor in robes and railed against appellate courts for reading hidden meanings in statutes. I truly believe he thought he had mastered the C.O.J."

I waited, hoping he would explain these initials, but he did not. This time I would not give him the satisfaction of asking what they meant.

Our conversation lasted about an hour, and I thought I had learned a great deal about Judge Learned Foote. Like Cardozo he was a bachelor and a clear and concise writer who had a passion for the law. But I was puzzled by Judge Foote's sudden retirement.

"If Judge Foote loved the law so much, why did he retire?" I asked.

"Can't say for sure, but I believe it had something to do with his one other passion."

"So he did care for something other than the law?"

"I didn't say that, but what rivaled his passionate love for the law was his singular hatred of section 170.6."

Roy was referring to Code of Civil Procedure section 170.6, a peculiarity of California law which allowed a lawyer to recuse a judge from hearing a case by filing a simple motion alleging judicial prejudice. No specific declaration detailing the judge's prejudice is required. A lawyer has only to timely file the affidavit with its boilerplate language and a different judge is assigned to the case. Roy told me that the code section so infuriated Foote that he continually hounded legislators on the judiciary committee to abolish it.

Roy added, "In a moment I will show you something that leads me to believe section 170.6 had something to do with Foote's retirement. But one day he simply did not show up for court. He called the Presiding Judge and said he had sent a letter to the Governor informing him in what I am sure was a terse paragraph that effective that day he was resigning from the court. He had cleared his calendar, and that was that. He didn't say good-bye, didn't call anyone, just left. Well, when Foote retired I got his old courtroom. I have something that is immensely useful, but it will be of no use for your history book. Was it Henry Ford who said, 'History is bunk'?"

Roy left the kitchen and returned with a folder. He handed me a copy of some notes scribbled on a piece of paper. Roy told me that after he moved into Foote's old courtroom, he found a scrap of paper in Foote's desk.

It appeared to be part of the final page in a judicial diary that Foote had kept throughout most of his judicial career. It was only a fragment from the lower half of a page numbered 323. It read as follows: "An insult. Damn Stark! The statement of decision I crafted made the judgment bullet proof. And for my craft, another 170.6. 'Oh what may man within him hide, Though Angel on the outward side!' Yet I shall not 'slip so grossly, both in the heat of blood , And lack of tempered judgment afterward.' Finis."

"What the hell does it mean?" I asked.

"It means a great deal."

"And who is Stark?"

"Oh he's a lawyer who has not let age stop him. He still makes appearances now and then. He won a big case in Foote's court."

"So why does Foote damn him?"

"Can't say, but looks like Stark filed a 170.6 against him."

"Before or after the big win?"

"Good question, but who cares?"

"I do."

"Not worth the time. Look at what else he wrote."

"Quotes from Shakespeare."

"Indeed." A wave of his hand indicated he did not want to talk any more. " I'm tired," he said.

I said, "I.O."

This time Roy asked, "What's that?"

"Interview over," I answered.

Roy laughed. I thanked him for the tea and handed back to him the copy of Foote's notes. "No, keep them," he said. "I've made dozens of copies. This is very useful. Should be required reading for all judges, new and old alike."

"Why so?" I asked.

"Think about it," he said.

"Will my thinking about these enigmatic notes tell me something about Judge Foote?"

"Probably not, but they may tell you something about . . . ."

"Myself?" I asked.

"Maybe," he replied with a grin.

And then it hit me what he meant by his earlier use of the initials, C.O.J. "It will tell me something about... the craft of judging."

Roy's grin widened.

"Do I have to re-read all of Shakespeare?"

"Wouldn't hurt," he said, "but *Measure for Measure* is a good start. Think about it."

"O.K., I'm thinking," I said as I walked out the door.

"Congratulations. Keep in touch and make sure I look good in the biography."

I left Roy's house feeling unsure if in fact I truly knew anything about Judge Foote. Through perseverance I was able to find a few lawyers who had known him. They admired his mind, but detested trying cases in his court. I also confirmed that Foote was no stranger to disqualification motions under section 170.6.

I found attorney Elgin Stark's name in the lawyer's directory. He is in his nineties, but still practices law. He had appeared numerous times before Judge Foote, and in the last case he tried before him, a partnership dissolution dispute, he had obtained a large judgment. Some time later, shortly before Foote's sudden retirement, Stark was again assigned to Judge Foote, but he filed an affidavit of prejudice under section 170.6.

I called attorney Stark numerous times before he would return my call. I told him my mission, and he offered a few platitudes about Judge Foote. Indeed he and Foote were classmates at Duke Law School, although they were not and never had been socially friendly. He spoke of Foote's integrity and knowledge of the law, but would say no more. He was respectful, but his tone betrayed an absence of affection. Or did his labored breath rob his voice of emotion?

I asked him if he had ever filed motions under 170.6 against Judge Foote. Stark owned up that it was possible. I then asked whether he had filed such a motion after winning a large money judgment before Foote in an earlier case. There was silence at the other end of the line. Then Stark said that he thought it

459

inappropriate to discuss the matter and had to leave for a deposition. I asked him what he thought prompted Foote to retire. "That is a question more properly addressed to Judge Foote," he replied. Before I could press him a little more, he said "It's been nice talking to you," and then I heard the dial tone.

The quotes within the diary, I discovered, were indeed from Shakespeare's "Measure for Measure," a play whose themes remarkably apply to the judiciary today. The Duke of Vienna has been lax in enforcing the laws. Under his rule the law has become a toothless tiger. He appoints Angelo to rule in his place while he takes an ostensible leave of absence from the city. In fact the duke remains in the city disguised as a friar so that he may observe how Angelo does the job. Unlike the Duke, Angelo is a strict constructionist in the extreme. The play teaches us that justice is elusive and that under either system the law earns no respect and falls into disrepute.

The quotes in the scrap from Foote's diary were from various characters in the play, who, it seemed to me, spoke self-evident truths. I wasn't sure, however, what they told me about Judge Foote or the craft of judging.

The deadline for the court's history was drawing near and the biography I had written of Judge Foote was like all the others, bland, seemingly informative, but unrevealing.

I had to go back to Judge Roy Fessler. After all, he did say to keep in touch. The first thing he said when he greeted me at the door a week later was, "I knew you would be back within the week. I'm glad to see you." He extended his hand.

Again we sat at the kitchen table over a cup of tea.

"So you have been thinking?"

"I don't understand Judge Foote," I said.

"Of course you don't," he said. "I don't know that you can, or that it matters that you do. I could have given you even more information about him. For example, I could have told you more about the 170.6 motions. Many judges accept these affidavits with a shrug of the shoulders. Not so with Foote. He would find out all he could about the attorney who filed one against him. He would comb through Dun and Bradstreet, and inquire of all the other judges about what they knew of the lawyer. He even kept an alphabetical list of all the attorneys who had filed affidavits of prejudice against him, the date filed, and a description of the case involved. I saw it. That list grew longer and longer, but in fits and starts, not at a steady rate. Months would go by and not one affidavit would be filed, but then suddenly three or four in succession would be filed."

"I wonder why?" I mused. "Do you think it was his stern demeanor, or his insults?"

"Possibly, but who cares?"

"Somehow I think this has something to do with the craft of judging. In his diary, Foote expresses distress over the lack of appreciation for his craftsmanship."

"Maybe he crafted a good judgment or perfect statement of decision. But any judge who continually draws motions to disqualify has not mastered his profession." He paused. "There," he continued, obviously pleased with himself. "You learned something about Judge Foote."

"I don't know what to write about him. This is all I have." I handed Roy the short prosaic biography I had written.

Roy said, "It is like all the others, B.S. It nominally serves the public by providing some vital statistics. But your biography is like the opening newsreel in the movie "*Citizen Kane*." You see a short superficial history of Kane. And then the reporter probes to find out who the man really is, and what does he come up with? Nada. He never learns what 'Rosebud' means. You will never know anything of substance about Judge Foote."

"There are some things I know about him," I protested weakly. "I know he was well read. He probably crafted great statements of decision. He knew the law well, yet received an undue number of affidavits of prejudice. He read Shakespeare."

"But did he understand Shakespeare?"

"He loved being a judge, yet suddenly he rushes into retirement." "G.F.," said Roy.

"Golden Future?" I asked.

"Go figure," said Roy.

"So you kept this scrap from Foote's diary because of the quotes?"

"Not just the quotes. I could get those from the play. That the quotes come from Foote is what is significant for me. 'Oh what may man within him hide, Though Angel on the outward side!' This is what the Duke has to say about Angelo when he discovers that the seemingly proper Angelo is a scoundrel. Maybe that is how Foote sees attorney Stark after receiving the affidavit of prejudice."

"Or maybe he is contemplating how Stark sees him." I said.

"Possibly. But these words are a good reminder of how not to practice the craft of judging. Remember, the word 'crafty' comes from craft."

"What about the other quote?" I asked. "Yet I shall not slip so grossly, both in the heat of blood , And lack of tempered judgment afterward."

"Also good advice to all judges."

"Maybe this is Foote's acknowledgement that despite his anger, he will keep a cool head and rule fairly and dispassionately."

"Could be. Could also be a recognition that he cannot temper his impatience, and therefore has no choice but to retire."

461

"That would make him honorable," I said. I altered Isabella's quote and said, "We do not know what man within him hide, though *devil* on the outward side."

Roy gave me a nod of approval. I told him about another useful quote I had found in the play. It is from Isabella's observation about "proud man" (woman too) being judges. "Dress'd in a little brief authority, Most ignorant of what he's most assured, His glassy essence, - like an angry ape, Plays such fantastic tricks before high heaven As makes the angels weep; who, with our spleens, Would all themselves laugh mortal."

"Ah, perfect," said Roy. "If Foote had taken this to heart, we probably would not be here discussing his abrupt retirement."

We had finished our tea. I got up to leave.

"Before you leave, I want you to read something else." He left the room and soon returned with a book of poems by Edwin Arlington Robinson. He turned to the one entitled "Richard Corey." I remembered reading it in college. The short poem tells us that Richard Corey appears to everyone to have an enviable life. He is well spoken and refined. But the last two lines read, "And Richard Corey, one calm summer night,

> Went home and put a bullet through his head."

"That's a P.P.," said Roy.

"Powerful Poem," I said.

"I knew you would appreciate it. After all you were a literature major."

We said our good-byes, and I promised to drop in on him again. He stood in the doorway as I walked down the steps and turned to wave to him.   "How did you know I was a literature major?" I shouted.

"I read it in your biography," he yelled back.

A few weeks later I submitted my work on the court's history to the P.J. I told her about my fascination with Judge Foote, the fragment from his diary, and my conversations with Judge Roy Fessler. I handed her my entry on Foote's biography:

"Judge Learned Foote. Graduated Duke University Law School 1947. Law Review. Partner in law firm Babcock, Casares and Foote, 1948 to 1959. Superior Court Judge 1959 to 1970. *A Poem*, with apologies to Edwin Arlington Robinson

> Whenever Learned Foote took the bench,
> Nervous counsel peered up at him.
> He applied the law without a wrench.
> He ruled with care, not with whim.
>
> Mostly civil, he also glowered.

His rulings flavored with a quote,
Literati joined his ivory tower.
He lifted the law's heavy cloak.

His name, a source of fun and rumor,
But he declined a pseudonym.
Biting wit, his stab at humor.
He was proper, even prim.

Though quiet, someone heard him say,
He loved his work, he never tired.
And Judge Learned Foote, one fine summer day,
Signed a paper, and retired."

The P.J. studied it. Finally she said, "You know what? I'm going to go with this."

She then asked if she could have a copy of the notes from Foote's diary.

"Of course," I said. "It provides insight into the craft of judging."

"Yes, ….and," the sparkle in her eyes enhanced her smile, "and……..
there's a world of difference between the craft and the art of judging."